1968

ENGLISH VERSE

VOICE AND MOVEMENT FROM
WYATT TO YEATS

T. R. BARNES

ENGLISH VERSE

VOICE AND MOVEMENT FROM
WYATT TO YEATS

CAMBRIDGE
AT THE UNIVERSITY PRESS
1967

Published by the Syndics of the Cambridge University Press
Bentley House, 200 Euston Road, London, N.W.1
American Branch: 32 East 57th Street, New York, N.Y. 10022

Printed in Great Britain in the City of Oxford
at the Alden Press

CONTENTS

ACKNOWLEDGEMENTS

Thanks are due to the following for permission to quote copyright matter:

Mr. Harold Owen, Chatto & Windus, and New Directions Inc. (*Futility, Hospital Barge at Cerisy* and *The Send-Off* by Wilfred Owen); the late Mrs. Helen Thomas and Faber & Faber (*The Owl, Gone, gone again* and *The Path* by Edward Thomas); Faber & Faber and Harcourt, Brace and World Inc. (*The Boston Evening Transcript, The Love Song of J. Alfred Prufrock, Sweeney Erect*, extracts from *The Waste Land, Ash Wednesday* Part II and *East Coker* Part IV from *Collected Poems 1909–1962* by T. S. Eliot); Laurence Pollinger Limited, the Estate of the late Mrs. Frieda Lawrence and The Viking Press of New York (*Sorrow, Humming-Bird* and *Mystic* by D. H. Lawrence); The Oxford University Press (*The Habit of Perfection, Inversnaid, Thou art indeed just, Lord, Ribblesdale* and *Henry Purcell* by Gerard Manley Hopkins); The Trustees of the Hardy Estate, Macmillan & Co. Ltd., the Macmillan Company of Canada Ltd., and Crowell-Collier and Macmillan Inc. (*A Man, The Levelled Churchyard, The New Toy, The Self Unseeing, At Castle Boterel, An Unkindly May, We are getting to the End, A Young Man's exhortation, He never expected much*, and *The Farm-Woman's Winter* from *Collected Poems* by Thomas Hardy); Mr. M. B. Yeats, A. P. Watt & Son, Macmillan & Co. Ltd., and Crowell-Collier and Macmillan Inc. (*A Coat, An Appointment, The Scholars, The Balloon of the Mind, Sailing to Byzantium, Byzantium, The Circus Animals' Desertion. Under Ben Bulben, Among school children, Coole Park and Ballylee 1931* from the *Collected Poems of W. B. Yeats*); Mrs. George Bambridge, Methuen & Co. Ltd., Macmillan & Co. Ltd. and Doubleday & Co. Ltd. (*Dedication* from *Barrack Room Ballads* by Rudyard Kipling); The Literary Trustees of Walter de la Mare and the Society of Authors as their representative (*Arabia* by Walter de la Mare); The Society of Authors as the literary representative of the Estate of the late A. E. Housman, Jonathan Cape Ltd. and Holt, Rinehart & Winston Inc. (*'Tis Time I Think* and *The Vane on Hughley Steeple* by A. E. Housman).

INTRODUCTION

This book is intended to encourage the student, and, I hope, the general
reader, to listen to poetry, to help him hear some of the different
tunes that English poets make, and to give him some idea of the way
these tunes established themselves and how they changed as time went
on. It would be absurd to pretend that it 'represents', or gives a complete account of, the course of English poetry, and the student who
should regard it as a substitute for wide reading, would mistake the
book's purpose. What might be claimed is that most of the verse quoted
is interesting and worth reading in itself; that it does illustrate some
of the more important characteristics of English verse; and that the
reader who studies the poems attentively, and gets to hear their varying
rhythms, will be better equipped to tackle major works on his own
than he would be if he lacked any general experience of contrasts
between different periods and different modes of writing. The passages
of description and comment are intended as guides, as aids to hearing
and understanding: they are not to be regarded as substitutes for
experience of the texts, but as a possible means of helping to create that
experience where it doesn't exist—where a first reading yields
blankness or boredom or distaste. I take it that no one is likely to read
a book like this unless he is interested in poetry, or wants to acquire
some information about it, or is under some kind of educational
compulsion. To all readers I would say: the arts give us pleasure.
Critics may—indeed they do—disagree about the other purposes of
art, but they all agree on this. Now the statement that the arts give
us pleasure is more complicated than it sounds, for pleasure is not a
simple concept and can mean many things. But the word implies
something natural, instinctive, irrational, involving a solid impulsive
movement of the whole being. There are different degrees of intensity
in these impulses, and to them we attach varying degrees of importance. Nevertheless, behind every feeling of 'I like that', some such
movement exists.

If we are casual readers listeners or spectators and if we have the
courage of our convictions and are not to be jostled out of our likes our
dislikes or our indifference by any kind of social or educational
pressure or snobbism or consideration of what we 'ought' to feel,
we may enjoy ourselves a lot and accumulate a pile of pleasurable,

and renewable, sensations. But there may come a time when, for one reason or another, we want to, or are obliged to, think about these sensations, put them in some sort of order, and see them in some sort of relationship. We may, moreover, come to wonder why we feel as we do; why we like the work, say, of one celebrated painter, dislike that of another and remain untouched by that of a third. This is the point where, no longer satisfied simply with sensation, we begin to compare poems, examine the nature of our feelings, and the reasons for our preferences, and this is where criticism comes in. We try to see the sources of our pleasures in perspective, and have, therefore, good reasons for studying authors whose work has previously left us cold; and this is where the historical approach will aid us. We then begin to find additional pleasure in getting knowledge, and this knowledge reacts on our original pleasures and increases them. We see art as a continuous human activity, of which contemporary works are a living part. But we should always come back to our own experiences, our own taste, because it is there that the value of art lies. History and influences and schools and movements and styles and techniques and all the rest of the apparatus are ancillaries. They may be interesting in themselves, but their true use lies in the way they may deepen our feelings for, and understanding of, the poems that give us pleasure.

We must not, however, when we begin to think historically— and we are here examining poems in chronological order—be misled into thinking of poetry in terms of 'development'. There is no overall progress in art, though there are constant changes and refinements of technique; and there are periods in all cultures that have produced works which everyone is agreed are of universal importance. Our study of development in verse, of the perfecting of rhythms, of the discovery of what best suits the language, may be valuable if it helps us to tune our ears more finely, but can only be stultifying if it leads us to believe that there is somewhere some perfect measuring rod that we can apply to verse, so that we can judge it mechanically without experiencing it. We are trying to hear the poet's characteristic sounds which have their individual vibrations, but which also tend to resemble the sounds his contemporaries were making.

So each poem, or portion of a poem, is to be enjoyed for itself alone, for its uniqueness; but it can also be related to other earlier or later poems on similar themes. Each pattern—couplet, blank verse, stanza and so on—can be compared with those that precede and follow it. Some of these cross references have been made in the commentaries; I hope the reader will find many more for himself, and may thus be led to feel how the work of the poet grows out of the language of his time and the society he lives in; how it is partly conditioned by his relationship to that society, and by his concept of his function, or lack of function, within it.

One cannot talk about poetry without discussing its sound and using words like tune and rhythm, whose musical connotations may be misleading, for there is no such thing as 'pure' sound or rhythm in language. The way we feel how a poem 'goes' is the resultant of many forces. What all poems have in common is that they are organized speech; we must say them to ourselves and hear them and allow the sound of the verbal pattern to work on us. Poems may be moving, profound, witty, subtle, complex or simple, but they are also primitive in that they impose themselves upon us by their rhythm with a peculiar shock, an immediacy of pleasure. I have tried to show in some of my analysis what this rhythm is, how it works and what it is based on.

A great deal of modern criticism is concerned with close reading, with minute examination of a single poem or passage, and this is valuable. But *Paradise Lost* and *The Dunciad* and *The Task* and *The Prelude* are all meant to be read through; and so are volumes of verse. Only thus can the poet's language, the force of his habitual imagery, the temper of his mind grow upon us. 'Too long a sacrifice', said Yeats, 'can make a stone of the heart'. Too long an inspection of too few poems can make a stone of the taste. The poet intends us to pass from *Easter 1916* to *Sixteen Dead Men*, *The Rose Tree*, *On a Political Prisoner* and *The Leaders of the Crowd*; or from *The Second Coming* to *A Prayer for my Daughter*. In sequence the poems enrich each other, as they are meant to do. I would hope that my book may persuade more readers to read more poems; to regard such reading, as it was once regarded, as a normal, a nourishing, a necessary part of their literary diet, and so to extend the range of their pleasures.

1

THE SIXTEENTH CENTURY

By the beginning of the sixteenth century the grammar and pronunciation of English (though not its spelling) had begun to become stable, standardized and recognizably similar to modern usage. The language has changed much since then, but in detail rather than essentials. It was now that the influence of the new learning of the Renaissance began to make itself felt, and poets started imitating the literary forms invented and perfected by the Italians and used by the French. They believed that these literatures excelled theirs in elegance, in melody, precision, politeness and nobility, and they began to share the feeling, common to many writers of that age, that they must make their vernacular literature the equal of those of Greece and Rome.

How this was to be done, whether by imitation of ancient models, or by the development of native traditions, was the subject of many critical disputes during the next two hundred years. The details of these arguments need not concern us, since it is our business to listen to what English poets actually did with the language they wrote in: but official and academic adulation of things ancient accounts for the innumerable 'classical allusions' which often disturb a modern reader who is used to thinking of each work he tackles as an 'original', 'fire-new from the mint', the product of a single poet's private inspiration. This is a romantic view of artistic creation. Readers in the past were more accustomed to thinking of new work as an example of a 'genre' or type of literature with whose form and intention they were familiar.

We begin with quotations from the poems of Sir Thomas Wyatt, who attempted to naturalize Italian forms—the sonnet, and terza rima—and who also wrote many lyrics in which the influence of native traditions may be felt. In his epitaph on Wyatt, his friend the Earl of Surrey said this:

> A hand that taught what may be said in rhyme;
> That reft Chaucer the glory of his wit:
> A mark the which (unperfected for time)
> Some may approach but never none shall hit.

It is the nature of this tribute that should interest us. 'A hand that taught what may be said in rhyme'. These poets felt they were creating

English verse. We may assume, from the allusion to Chaucer, that Surrey didn't think that fifteenth-century poets were of any interest to him or to those of his contemporaries who shared his tastes. Chaucer was admired for his intelligence, his 'wit', his power to create character; but language had changed too much for his verse to be heard as he meant it to be. The general feeling is that after Chaucer, we are now, thanks to Wyatt, starting again. Here are three samples of his work. First, a sonnet imitated from Petrarch:

> My galy charged with forgetfulnes,
>> Thorrough sharpe sees, in wynter nyghtes doeth pas,
>> Twene Rock and Rock: and eke myn enemy, alas,
> That is my Lorde, sterith with cruelnes.
> And every owre a thought in redines:
>> As tho that deth were light in suche a case;
>> An endles wynd doth tere the sayll a pase,
> Of forced sightes and trusty ferefulnes.
> A rayn of teris: a clowd of derk disdain,
>> Hath done the wered cordes great hinderaunce:
>> Wrethed with error and eke with ignoraunce.
> The starres be hid that led me to this pain:
>> Drowned is reson that should me comfort:
>> And I remain dispering of the port.

This is a poem on a conventional theme, written in a conventional form. All sonnets have fourteen lines; all sonnets express an emotion, and most comment on that emotion, so that they tend to fall into two parts. The break in many sonnets—some would say in all 'correct' sonnets comes after the eighth line and the two parts are known as the octave and the sestet. Rhyme schemes vary. In the form usually known as Shakespearian, there are four quatrains, whose alternate lines rhyme, and a couplet. In the Petrarchan form two rhymes are distributed among the first eight lines, usually, as here, a b b a, repeated; and the last six lines have three rhymes between them. Here they are c d d c e e. In Petrarch's original sonnet they run c d e c d e.

The poem is an allegory; the 'galy' (galleon) is the poet himself, or the poet's life, and it bears a cargo of forgetfulness because his lady has forgotten him. The Lord, who is his enemy, is love; the storm is the sorrow he endures because his love-affair is unsuccessful, the stars are his lady's eyes. This is why we have said that a conventional form is used to express a conventional situation, for we are not to suppose that all sonnetteers are really writhing in agony as they write. What would Surrey find to admire about this poem? I think, its combination of strength and melody. The opening is dramatic; note how the sense runs on to the colon after the second 'Rock' and how that harsh repetition gives a sense of danger. Petrarch, the model followed by most sixteenth-century sonnetteers, used here the standard Scylla and Charybdis, which is much less forceful. In reading line three, we must take the advice of Miss Foxwell, Wyatt's editor, and 'slur the adjacent vocal syllables' of en(emy a)las; and yet it sounds right; the hurried jumbling of sounds fits the emotion: Wyatt is master of his rhythm, making it do what he wants; he is not subserviently tapping the poem out on his fingers, 'making it scan'. The next quatrain is obscure, and so are the following three lines. Wyatt has struggled to get the Italian into neat English, and has not succeeded: 'trusty fere-fulness' needs puzzling out, and it is not clear that it is the ropes of the rigging that have been twisted by error and ignorance. But the poet's voice speaks out in the last three lines (we must stress the last syllable of 'comfort'), sense and rhythm reinforce each other, especially in the strong accent (an inverted first foot) on 'Drowned', and the fading movement of the last line, where the last accent but one, which should come on 'of' is missing, thus throwing the open vowel in 'dispering' into high relief. The poem remains strangely moving, even if we don't know that the stars are a lady's eyes, or understand the convention in which it was written. It might be a poem about ambition instead of about love. It seems to have, like much poetry, an extra dimension of sense and feeling, communicating more than any paraphrase is capable of.

Next are two quotations from the Satires. The rhyme-scheme of these poems is copied from the Italian terza rima which few English poets after Wyatt have used, for the simple reason that it is much easier to find rhymes in Italian than it is in English; the form doesn't suit the genius of the language. What we should listen for in these passages is the poet's use of the iambic beat, and the interplay between voice and verse.

> My Poynz, I cannot frame me tune to fayne,
> To cloke the trothe for praise withoute desart,
> Of them that lyst all vice for to retayne.
>
> I cannot honour them that settes their part
> With Venus and Baccus all theire lyff long;
> Nor hold my pece of them al tho I smart.
>
> I cannot crowche nor knelle to do so grete a wrong,
> To worship them, lyke Gode on erthe alone,
> That are as wolffes these sely lambes among. . . .

I cannot speke and loke lyke a saint;
  Use wiles for witt, or make deceyt a pleasure;
  And call craft counceill, for proffet styll to paint.

I cannot wrest the law to fill the coffer
  With innocent blode to fede my selff fat;
  And doo most hurt where most help I offer. . . .

I cannot I, no no it will not be!
  This is the cause that I could never yet
  Hang on their slevis that way, as thou maist see,

A chipp of chaunce more than a pound of witt.
  This maketh me at home to hounte and to hawke,
  And in fowle weder at my booke to sitt. . . .

The theme of this piece is the refusal of the honest poet to live in
the corrupt world; he cannot mingle with courtiers and be silent,
therefore he has retired from court and city to the country. Some lines
are clumsy, but we should remember that the effect aimed at is one of
rough sincerity. In the next passage he uses an old fable to express
similar feelings about corruption and wealth. This symbolic contrast
between evil city and innocent country, which stretches back to the
classics, occurs again and again in English poetry and is the moral basis
of the pastoral convention.

My mothers maydes when they did sowe and spyn
  They sang sometyme a song of the feld mowse;
  That fobicause her lyvelood[1] was but thyn

Would nedes goo seke her townyssh systers howse,
  She thought herself endured to much pain;
  The stormy blastes her cave so sore did sowse.

That when the forowse[2] swymmed with the rain,
  She must lye cold and whete in sorry plight,
  And worse then that, bare meet ther did remain

To comfort her when she her howse had dight;
  Sometime a barlycorn; sometyme a bene;
  For which she laboured hard boeth daye and nyght

In harvest tyme, whilest she myght goo and glyne;
  And when her stoore was stroyed with the flood
  Then well awaye! for she undone was clene.

---

[1] Livelihood.   [2] Furrows.

Then was she fayne to take, in stede of fode,
    Slepe if she myght her hounger to begile.
    'My syster' quod she 'hath a lyving good,

And hens from me she dwelleth not a myle,
    In cold and storme she lieth warme and dry,
    In bed of downe; the dyrt doeth not defile

Her tender fote; she laboureth not as I;
    Richely she fedeth, and at the richemans cost,
    And for her meet she nydes not crave nor cry. . . .

We can hear that this charming passage is much more successful than the previous one. It is neater, more flexible, less strained, though the occasional clumsy and functionless inversion (for she undone was clene) remains to remind us of the poet's effort to get his rhyme words at the end of the line; as we turn from the first to the second poem we can almost feel the poet learning 'what may be said in rhyme.'

Next are two epigrams. The first exhibits the sort of word-play that many later Elizabethan writers delighted in but which seems to us mere frigid ingenuity; a hackneyed classical allusion completes the poem.

The fructe of all the servise that I serve
    Dispaire doeth repe, such haples hap have I;
    But tho he have no powre to make me swarve
    Yet by the fire for colde I fele I dye;
    In paradis for hunger still I sterve:
    And in the flowde for thurste to deth I drye;
    So Tantalus am I and yn worse payne,
    Amyds my helpe, and helples doth remayne.

Compare it with the next—a tiny poem, but a perfect one: not a syllable can be changed without ruining the effect.

Through out the world if it were sought,
    Faire wordes enough a man shall finde;
    They be good chepe they cost right nought
    Their substance is but onely winde.
    But well to say, and so to mene,
    That swete accord is seldom sene.

Lastly, a famous lyric. The stanza with a refrain was one of Wyatt's favourite patterns.

My Lute awake! perfourme the last
  Labor that thou and I shall wast,
  And end that I have now begon;
  For when this song is song and past
    My lute be still, for I have done.

As to be herd where ere is none,
  As lede to grave in marbill stone,
  My song may perse her hert as sone;
  Should we then sing or sigh or mone?
    No! No! my lute, for I have done.

The Rokkes do not so cruelly
  Repulse the waves continuelly
  As she my suyte and affection;
  So that I ame past remedy,
    Whereby my lute and I have done.

Prowde of the spoyll that thou hast gott
  Of simple hertes, thorough loves shot;
  By whome, unkynd, thou hast theim wone,
  Thinck not he hath his bow forgot,
    All tho my lute and I have done.

Vengeaunce shall fall on thy disdain
  That makest but game on ernest pain;
  Thinck not alone under the sonne
  Unquyt to cause thy lovers plain,
    All tho my lute and I have done.

Perchaunce the lye wethered and old
  The wynter nyght that are so cold,
  Playning in vain unto the mone;
  Thy wisshes then dare not be told;
    Care then who lyst, for I have done.

And then may chaunce the to repent
  The tyme that thou has lost and spent
  To cause thy lovers sigh and swone;
  Then shalt thou knowe beaultie but lent,
    And wisshe and want as I have done.

Now cesse, my lute: this is the last
  Labor that thou and I shall wast,
  And ended is that we begon;
  Now is this song boeth song and past
    My lute be still, for I have done.

The poet 'sings' to his lute a song bewailing the unkindness of his mistress. Wyatt creates a dramatic tension between the conventional elements and what he makes us feel are the realities of the situation. The first three stanzas are an elegant lament, beautifully cadenced, full of traditional amatory images. In stanza four the lady is addressed directly: still the imagery is of the expected kind—she has a store of simple hearts, shot for her by Cupid—but the shock comes with the sudden stab of

> Thinck not he hath his bow forgot . . .

From then on the poem gathers intensity. The poet imagines, and calls on the lady to imagine, the tables turned, and with this is mingled the theme of beauty withering, a poetic commonplace here used with ironic power. Notice how strong the inversion of the normal stresses makes such lines as

> Vengeaunce shall fall on thy disdain

and

> Perchaunce the lye wethered and old. . . .

and we may well feel that the man who can manipulate sounds with the skill exhibited in such a line as

> Playning in vain unto the mone

had little more to learn of 'what may be said in rhyme'. What starts, apparently, as a literary exercise, has turned into a bitter comment on the lady's behaviour, but not a purely personal one The line

> Then shalt thou knowe beaultie but lent

applies not merely to the lady's treatment of the poet, but her treatment of herself as a woman; beauty is a loan, not a gift; hers to use—he means in marriage—not to keep for the gratification of private powers.

Here is a sonnet by the Earl of Surrey: another conventional piece, in which all nature rejoices except the rejected lover.

> The soote¹ season, that bud and bloom forth brings,
> With green hath clad the hill and eke the vale:
> The nightingale with feathers new she sings;
> The turtle to her make² hath told her tale:
> Summer is come, for every spray now springs;
> The hart hath hung his old head on the pale;
> The buck in brake his winter coat he flings;
> The fishes float with new repaired scale;
> The adder all her slough away she slings;

¹ Sweet. ² Mate.

The swift swallow pursueth the flies smale[1];
The busy bee her honey now she mings[2];
Winter is worn that was the flowers' bale.
And thus I see among these pleasant things
Each care decays; and yet my sorrow springs!

It is an ingenious exercise—the poet allows himself only two rhymes for the whole poem—and it is not without charm; but such dull and ugly lines as

The swift swallow pursueth the flies smale

show how uncertain was his command of his medium. He was the first writer to use blank verse in English, in his translation of two books of the Aeneid, but to this aspect of his work we will return later.

We turn next to two stanzas from an anonymous poem of 1530. The author is describing 'the hugy house of sleep'.

The wonderful habitacle that we found there,
    It passeth of my reason to declare plainly!
Except of the Poet I borrow in this manner:
    Then may I show it! Thus was it truly,
    The hugy House of Sleep that resteth full surely,
Where as no sun shone, nor beam doth appear;
    But in manner as the owl light is continually.
Cock, nor dog, to trouble may be found there!

Without blasting, or blowing, of wind troublous;
    Or any noise else, that might be thought of Man,
But of a small water, of nature marvellous,
    Lethe it is called. Out of a stone it ran,
    Purling on the gravel: and, as I saw then,
    The House without gates or door. It was also
No occasion of trouble of beast, ne of Man.
    The way was full of papy[3], in as I did go.

The tune of these stanzas is very different from any we have heard in the other quotations. That these verses have a tune and a pattern, a sympathetic and attentive reader can make out. But they sound odd at first to ears accustomed to more regular verse; and this is because their tune depends largely on a general overall balance of phrases— most of the lines, for example fall into two halves—rather than on a regular succession of accented and unaccented syllables. Now listen to these stanzas, from the Induction (Introduction) to Thomas Sackville's *Mirror for Magistrates*, an interminable and immensely popular

---

[1] Small.   [2] Mingles.   [3] Poppy.

poem written in 1563, consisting of stories of great men, kings, princes and heroes of the past, from whose example modern 'magistrates' or rulers might learn, or by whose fate they might be warned.

> And sorrowing I to see the summer flowers,
>> The lively green, the lusty leas forlorn,
> The sturdy trees so shattered with the showers,
>> The fields so fade that flourished so biforn,
>> It taught me well all earthly things be born
>> To die the death, for nought long time may last;
>> The summers beauty yields to winters blast.
>
> Then looking upwards to the heavens leams
>> With nightes stars thick powdered everywhere,
> Which erst so glittered with the golden streams
>> That cheerful Phoebus spread down from his sphere,
>> Beholding dark oppressing day so near;
>> The sudden sight reduced to my mind
>> The sundry changes that on earth we find.
>
> That musing on this worldly wealth in thought,
>> Which comes and goes more faster than we see
> The flickering flame that with the fire is wrought,
>> My busy mind presented unto me
>> Such fall of peers as in this realm had be,
>> That oft I wished some would their woes descrive[1]
>> To warn the rest whom fortune left alive.

There is here no vagueness or fluidity of form: all is regular. The accents are heavy, and to each stressed syllable there is allotted one unstressed. There is a minimum of variation; rhyme is full, and everything is bound together by constant alliteration. To us, I think, it must appear monotonous, but contemporaries had no doubt that it was a technical triumph. Here was the well-defined, five-footed line that they were to take as their staple. A further stanza will hammer the point home. It describes an allegorical figure, Sleep.

> By him lay heavy Sleep, the cousin of death,
>> Flat on the ground and still as any stone,
> A very corpse, save yielding forth a breath,
>> Small keep took he whom Fortune frowned on
> Or whom she lifted up unto the throne
>> Of high renown; but as a living death,
>> So, dead alive, of life he drew the breath.

[1] Describe.

This iambic beat now dominates English verse.

In 1579 Spenser published his *Shepheardes Calendar*, a series of twelve pastoral poems, one for each month of the year. The poet offers his 'Aeglogues' or Pastorals as a sort of humble beginning, an experiment. Spenser was a professional writer in two senses: first, he felt within himself, as Milton did, a vocation for poetry; second, he believed (rightly) that his writings would commend him to the court, gain him influential patronage, and a post in the service of the crown which would provide his livelihood. So that this book is a sample of a brilliant young man's talent, an exhibition of what he could do, offering a number of solutions to the problems of English versification. Spenser was not merely concerned with verse, but also with vocabulary. 'Our mother tongue' he believed, 'which truely of itself is both ful enough for prose and stately enough for verse, hath long time been counted bare and most barren of both, Which default whenas some endeavoured to solace and recure, they patched up the holes with pieces and rags of other languages' so that 'we speke no English but gibberish.' The words he used 'though they be something hard, and of most men unused, yet both English, and also used of most excellent authors and most famous Poets'. He instances 'the olde famous poet Chaucer' and 'his scholler Lidgate' whose sounds he had 'still ringing in his ears.' So we have a deliberate effort to recreate a native tradition, but also to combine it with the forms and methods of Humanism, for he traces the Pastoral through the work of Theocritus, Virgil and 'divers other excellent both Italian and French Poets.' His attempts at linguistic reform led to nothing, but some of his rhythms were far more influential; and his belief that poetry required a special language has also not been without its effect on some later writers. Note that for prose language should be 'full' and for verse 'stately'.

The following lines are part of the fable of the Oak and the Briar, from the February Eclogue, an allegory about controversies in religion. Its rough vigour is not ineffective, but this is not one of the rhythms that later poets have found useful.

> There grew an aged Tree on the greene,
> A goodly Oake sometime had it bene,
> With armes full strong and largely displayd,
> But of their leaves they were disarayde:
> The bodie bigge, and mightely pight,
> Thoroughly rooted, and of wonderous hight:
> Whilome had bene the King of the field
> And mochel mast to the husband did yielde,
> And with his nuts larded many swine.

But now the gray mosse marred his rine,
His bared boughes were beaten with stormes,
His toppe was bald, and wasted with wormes,
His honor decayed, his braunches sere.
   Hard by his side grew a bragging brere[1],
Which proudly thrust into Thelement[2],
And seemed to threat the Firmament.
Yt was embellisht with blossomes fayre,
And thereto aye wonned to repayre[3]
The shepheards daughters, to gather flowres,
To peinct their girlonds with his colowres
And in his small bushes used to shrowde
The sweete Nightingale singing so lowde:
Which made this foolish brere wexe so bold,
That on a time he cast him to scold,
And snebbe[4] the good Oake, for he was old.

Our next piece, from June, is very different. Here the shepherd
Hobbinol pays tributes to the songs (poems) of his friend Colin Clout,
which was Spenser's name for himself, and Colin, with due modesty,
replies.

HOBBINOL
   Colin, to heare thy rhymes and roundelayes,
   Which thou were wont on wastful hylls to singe,
   I more delight, then larke in Sommer dayes:
   Whose Echo made the neyghbour groves to ring,
   And taught the byrds, which in the lower spring
   Did shroude in shady leaves from sonny rayes,
   Frame to thy songe their cherefull cheriping,
   Or hold theyr peace, for shame of thy swete layes.

   I saw *Calliope* wyth Muses moe
   Soone as thy oaten pype began to sound,
   Theyr yvory Luyts and Tamburins forgoe,
   And from the fountaine, where they sat around,
   Renne after hastely thy silver sound.
   But when they came, where thou thy skill didst showe,
   They drew abacke, as halfe with shame confound,
   Shepheard to see, them in theyr art outgoe.

COLLIN
   Of Muses *Hobbinol*, I conne[5] no skill:
   For they bene daughters of the hyghtest *Iove*,

---

[1] Briar.   [2] The air.   [3] Used to go.   [4] Rebuke.   [5] Know.

And holden scorne of homely shepheards quill.
For sith I heard, that *Pan* with *Phoebus* strove,
Which him to much rebuke and Daunger drove:
I never lyst presume to Parnasse hyll,
But pyping lowe in shade of lowly grove,
I play to please myself, all be it ill.

Nought weigh I, who my song doth prayse or blame,
Ne strive to winne renown, or passe the rest:
With shepheard sittes not, follow[1] flying fame:
But feede his flock in fields, where falls hem best.
I wote[2] my rymes bene rough, and rudely drest:
The fytter they, my careful case to frame:
Enough is me to paynte out my unrest,
And poore my piteous plaints out in the same.

The God of shepheards *Tityrus* is dead,
Who taught me homely, as I can, to make[3].
He, whilst he lived, was the soveraigne head
Of shepheards all, that bene with love ytake:
Well couth he wayle hys Woes, and lightly slake
The flames, which love within his heart had bredde,
And tell us mery tales, to keepe us wake,
The while our sheepe about us safely fedde.

Nowe dead he is, and lyeth wrapt in lead,
(O why should death on hym such outrage showe?)
And all hys passing[4] skill with him is fledde,
The fame whereof doth dayly greater growe.
But if on me some little drops would flowe,
Of that the spring was in his learned hedde,
I soone would learne these woods, to wayle my woe,
And teach the trees, their trickling teares to shedde. . . .

But since I am not, as I wish I were
Ye gentle shepheards, which your flocks do feede,
Whether on hylls, or dales, or other where,
Beare witnesse all of this so wicked deede:
And tell the lasse, whose flowre is woxe[5] a weede,
And faultless fayth, is turned to faithless fere[6],
That she the truest shepheards hart made bleede,
That lyves on earth, and loved her most dere. . . .

---

[1] It is not fitting for a shepherd to. . . .   [2] Know.
[3] Write poetry.   [4] Surpassing.
[5] Grown.   [6] Companion, mate

That these verses resemble Sackville's, is obvious; but they run more easily and are less monotonous. To the modern reader the pastoral convention may seem stilted and artificial, but let him not be put off. If we are to understand the art of the past we must try to recreate in our own minds the past's conventions. And in defence of pastoral we might point out that it can be a device for letting the poet say several things at once, which is something poets are always trying to do. The shepherd is simple, innocent, detached from the world, takes a worm's-eye view, limited but unbiased; is concerned with the realities of life not with the artifices of civilization; lives in the country, not the town; is plain, blunt and honest, not refined and corrupt; is addicted to music; the pipes he plays on solace his solitude, and symbolize poetry; he is contemplative, is faithful; is a mask or persona for the poet to adopt when he doesn't want to speak in his own voice, is surrounded by agreeable scenery; keeps sheep, and therefore can be used to evoke the powerful New Testament symbolism of sheep and shepherds and hirelings and wolves, and so on.

The opening lines of Hobbinol's second stanza show us the charming use the humanists sometimes made of the classics. In this age an ambitious young poet would feel obliged to exhibit his learning, but it is Spenser's genius for the manipulation of sound that raises these lines from pedantry to poetry. Colin expresses much of Spenser's own feelings, and we can hear, if we listen attentively, how vitality ebbs and flows. There are stiff apophthegms:

> With shepheard sittes not, follow flying fame ...

and tediously elaborated conceits:

> I soone would learne these woods to wayle my woe,
> And teach the trees, their trickling teares to shedde.

which are as wooden as anything in Sackville. But there are also lines of pure melodic energy:

> I never list presume to Parnasse hyll,
> But pyping lowe in shade of lowly grove,
> I play to please myself, albeit ill.

or

> But since I am not, as I wish I were

which delighted his contemporaries, and from which they learned a great deal. Lines like these, from *A Midsummer Night's Dream,*

> O happy fair!
> Your eyes are lodestars and your tongue sweet air!
> More tuneable than lark to shepherd's ear,
> When wheat is green, when hawthorn buds appear . . .

owe much to Spenser.

Tityrus stands for Chaucer. Note how the two stanzas which lament him are bound together by the rhymes for 'dead', and how uneven is the texture of the verse. The first two lines are simple and moving, but then the pastoral convention, that shepherds must be in love, leads Spenser to talk nonsense about Chaucer 'wayling his woes'. But the line

> And all his passing skill with him is fledde

is a fine one. The last stanza has some specimens of the sort of word-play (faultless fayth, faithlesse fere) which we have already noted beginning in Wyatt.

Spenser's most important work is, of course, the huge allegorical poem *The Faerie Queene*, written in a stanza invented by the poet and called after him. Here are two specimens from the opening of Canto Seven of the Seventh Book. They invoke the Muse; the Titanesse is Mutabilitie, or change, who seeks to wrest power from Jove, 'heav'ns King'.

> Ah! whither doost thou now thou greater Muse
>   Me from these woods and pleasing forrests bring?
>   And my fraile spirit (that dooth oft refuse
>   This too high flight, unfit for her weake wing)
>   Lift up aloft, to tell of heavens King
>   (Thy soveraine Sire) his fortunate successe,
>   And victory, in bigger notes to sing
>   Which he obtain'd against that Titanesse,
> That him of heavens Empire sought to dispossesse.

> Yet sith I needs must follow thy behest,
>   Doe thou my weaker wit with skill inspire,
>   Fit for this turne; and in my feeble breast
>   Kindle fresh sparks of that immortal fire,
>   Which learned minds inflameth with desire
>   Of heavenly things: for, who but thou alone,
>   That art yborne of heaven and heavenly Sire,
>   Can tell things doen in heaven so long ygone;
> So farre past memory of man that may be knowne.

No fair idea of Spenser's command of rhythm, of the incantatory powers of his verse can be got from short excerpts, which is all we have room for here. In this invocation to the 'greater Muse', greater because Spenser is here proposing to handle a philosophical theme, even, in a sense, a religious one, the poet sees himself as prophet and his inspiration as divine. He is still a shepherd. The woods and forests are the landscape in which the tales of magic and chivalry of the earlier books took place; hence they symbolize or stand for that previous work. Spenser's whole manner of writing and use of language (I am not now thinking of his specialized 'antique' vocabulary) is heightened and removed from normal usage, because he believes his poem, which is noble, remote, romantic and full of moral and spiritual meaning, needs such a language. To say that this verse lacks the vitality of common speech is true, but irrelevant: because such vitality was not the poet's aim. The listening reader should start by noting Spenser's dexterous modulation of vowel sounds, and easy manipulation of the iambic measure. Perhaps the first two lines

> Ah! whither doost thou now thou greater Muse
> Me from these woods and pleasing forrests bring?

might stand as an adequate example of the kind of tune which before Spenser scarcely existed in English, and after him was gratefully used by many poets. Any reader who has got to the stage of 'liking poetry', of finding it agreeable to repeat to himself phrases, lines and fragments of verse because he enjoys them, 'though his understanding has little to do with all this'; who gets from verbal arrangements that immediate pleasure which is the raw material the poet works in, must respond to these lines. Their resemblance to some of the passages we have singled out from the *Shepheardes Calendar* is obvious, but here the melody is broader and more sweeping. The effects are all the more striking because the literary devices are more subtly used. The theme of the stanzas is the relationship of the poet to his inspiration. See how the two are linked by alliteration—Muse, me—by movement, for we run on from one line to the next; by rhythm, for we have to stress 'me'; and the fact that this is an inverted stress, a variation in the metrical pattern, makes us feel the emphasis more strongly. So, too, the distortion of the normal word order (whither dost thou bring me) has its effect of emphasis and incantation, of strangeness. The 'woods and pleasing forrests' work strongly on the imagination. The use of two words for the same thing is not just a fill-up for the line: 'forrests' enlarges the scale, and brings in the whole enormous mysterious landscape of the poem so far: trees stand for nature as opposed to civilization; and for mystery; the forest ('a free space of hunting ground') stands for liberty, as opposed to the discipline of agriculture, ('husbands life is labourous and hard'); it symbolizes a life which is 'pleasing' because not dependent on the curse of Adam. And all this fits the poet's feeling because he is about to embark, unwillingly and with a sense of his inadequacy, on a task more formidable than any he has yet attempted.

Here are more quotations from the *Faerie Queene*. The first describes

> A man of hell, that cals himselfe Despaire:

who has persuaded a knight to suicide, and whom the Red Crosse Knight is come to challenge.

> That darkesome cave they enter, where they find
> That cursed man, low sitting on the ground,
> Musing full sadly in his sullein mind;
> His griesie lockes, long growen, and unbound,
> Disordred hong about his shoulders round
> And hid his face; through which his hollow eyne
> Lookt deadly dull, and stared as astound;
> His raw-bone cheekes through penurie and pine,
> Were shronke into his jawes, as he did never dine.

Beside this character there is

> A drearie corse, whose life away did pas,
> All wallowed in his owne yet luke-warme blood . . .

but when the Red Crosse knight 'with firie zeale' accuses him of murder, he points out that the body is a suicide's, calls the Red Crosse knight 'frantic' and 'rash' and continues in these famous lines:

> Who travels by the wearie wandring way,
> To come unto his wished home in haste,
> And meets a flood, that doth his passage stay,
> Is not great grace to help him over past,
> Or free his feet, that in the mire sticke fast?
> Most envious man, that grieves at neighbours good,
> And fond[1], that joyest in the woe thou hast,
> Why wilt not let him passe, that long hath stood
> Upon the bank, yet will thyself not passe the flood?

> He there does now enjoy eternall rest
> And happie ease, which thou doest want and crave,
> And further from it daily wanderest:
> What if some little paine the passage have,
> That makes fraile flesh to fear the bitter wave?

[1] Foolish.

> Is not short paine well borne, that brings long ease,
> And lays the soule to sleepe in quiet grave?
> Sleepe after toyle, port after stormy seas,
> Ease after warre, death after life does greatly please.

Well may the knight be 'charmed' with these 'inchaunted rimes'.
He begins his answer as follows:

> The knight much wondred at his suddeine wit,
> And said, The terme of life is limited,
> Ne may a man prolong, nor shorten it;
> The souldier may not move from watchful sted,
> Nor leave his stand, untill his Captaine bed.[1]
> Who life did limit by almightie doome,[2]
> (Quoth he) knowes best the termes established;
> And he, that points[3] the Centonell his roome,
> Doth license him depart at sound of morning[4] droome.

Here we have Spenser using his stanza for description, for argument,
and for the evocation of emotion; perhaps most readers would agree
that it is his melodic gifts which are most remarkable.

In one of his minor poems, a satire called *Mother Hubbard's Tale*,
he used rhymed couplets. The tale is supposed to be told by 'a good old
woman', and Spenser says

> No Muses aide me needes heretoo to call;
> Base is the style, the matter meane withall.

This suiting of style to matter was known to Elizabethan critics as
'decorum', and we have in this poem a more direct colloquial manner
of writing than Spenser considered fitting for the *Faerie Queene*. The
poem is an animal fable; an ape and a fox propose to live by trickery,
and in the following lines the ape is advising the fox on their manner
of proceeding.

> Thus therefore I advise upon the case,
> That not to anie certaine trade or place,
> Nor anie man we should ourselves applie:
> For why should he that is at libertie
> Make himselfe bond? sith then we are free borne,
> Let us all servile base subjection scorne;
> And as we bee sonnes of the world so wide,
> Let us our fathers heritage divide,
> And challenge to ourselves our portions dew
> Of all the patrimonie, which a few
> Now hold in hugger mugger in their hand,

---

[1] Bid.   [2] Judgement.   [3] Appoints.   [4] Drum

And all the rest do rob of good and land.
For now a few have all and all have nought,
Yet all be brethren ylike dearly bought:
There is no right in this partition,
Ne was it so by institution
Ordained first, ne by the law of Nature,
But that she gave like blessing to each creature,
As well of wordly livelode as of life,
That there might be no difference nor strife,
Nor ought called mine or thine: thrice happie then
Was the condition of mortal men. . . .

This verse, like the ape himself, is supple and energetic. The poet manages to make the steady regularity of the iambic beat audible, but by allowing lines to run on, by playing off the grammatical against the metrical units, he gives the verse a kind of lively conviction, quite different from the ritual, hypnotic emphasis of the verse of the *Faerie Queene*. The play of the argument is interesting too. We all have sympathy with the plea for equality:

When Adam delved and Eve span,
Who was then the gentleman?

but the plausible ape gives himself away with

Nor ought called mine or thine.

It might be argued that this piece, in which attitudes are implicit—we observe and listen, but we are not preached at—is more effective than the formal explicit moral allegories of the *Faerie Queene*: it is certainly more entertaining. And this is also due to the fact that we have to keep our wits about us as we read it, if we are to grasp all its implications. 'All men,' says the ape, 'be brethren ylike dearly bought.' Now this allusion to the Redemption, in the mouth of a character like the ape, is shocking (the devil citing scripture to his purpose): but the Profane is not made to allude to the Sacred, merely for the sake of shocking, but to make us feel that were men really brethren, really redeemed, wealth and power would not corrupt them, and the ape and the fox would not be able to be parasites.

But Spenser could also write as clumsily as this:

They sought my troubled sense how to deceive
With talk, that might unquiet fancies reave
And sitting all in seates about me round,
With pleasant tales (fit for that idle stound)
They cast in course to waste the wearie howres . . .

We end our quotations from Spenser with a piece of fine rhetorical writing, from the same poem. Jove looks down on the wickedness wrought by the fox and the ape:

> Now when high *Jove*, in whose almightie hand
> The care of Kings, and power of Empires stand,
> Sitting one day within his turret hye,
> From whence he vewes with his blacklidded eye,
> Whatso the heaven in his wide vawte containes,
> And all that in the deepest earth remaines,
> The troubled kingdome of wilde beasts behelde,
> Whom not their kindly Sovereign did welde,
> But an usurping Ape with guile suborn'd ...

When the poets of the second half of the seventeenth century 're-formed', as they thought, English versification, they prided themselves on cleaning up what they considered the incompetence of the first passage. But the tune of the second, its combination of neatness and oratorical force, they used and developed.

We have quoted sonnets by Wyatt and by Surrey; here are two more from the last quarter of the sixteenth century. The first is from Sir Philip Sidney's sequence *Astrophel and Stella*, written about 1581. Astrophel praises his lady Stella, and protests his love for her. It is the use made of this conventional material which makes the poem interesting.

> You that do search for every purling spring
> Which from the ribs of old Parnassus flows,
> And every flower, not sweet perhaps, which grows
> Near thereabouts, into your poesie wring;
> You that do dictionary's method bring
> Into your rhymes, running in rattling rows;
> You that poor Petrarch's long deceasèd woes
> With new-born sighs and denizen'd wit do sing:
> You take wrong ways; those far-fet[1] helps be such
> As do bewray a want of inward touch,
> And sure, at length stolen goods do come to light;
> But if, both for your love and skill, your name
> You seek to nurse at fullest breasts of Fame,
> Stella behold, and then begin to indite.

Obviously, an ingenious poem: equally obviously a poem which could not have been written except at a time when there was clearly defined

---

[1] Fetched.

agreement about what certain types of poem should be. Sidney makes his point by ridiculing these conventions but he could not do this unless everyone understood what he was talking about. So that this sonnet, which tells the literary artificers that they are wrong, makes its witty paradoxical point by being itself a piece of artifice. Of course, part of the pleasure we get from all good sonnets comes, whether we we are aware of it or not, from the skill with which form and content are fitted to each other, so that we are convinced the poem must be so and not otherwise, though the form is a communal, traditional one not invented by the poet. Sidney's technique is assured, as it must be if the poem is to be a success, for you cannot ridicule other people's technique unless you are at least their technical equal. Note the conventional 'purling', the mocking allusion to Parnassus, and the perhaps not sweet flowers—implying not only that the sonneteer's material is hackneyed, but that even in such a hackneyed field he is uncritical. The verb 'wring' implies awkward strain; the line about the rhymes is excellent burlesque, and again implies form for form's sake, since rows are rigid mathematical lifeless arrangements. 'Long-deceased' again brings in the idea of deadness; 'denizen'd' implies the absurd and tasteless decoration of someone not speaking his native tongue. The conclusion of the address to the foolish poets—'you take wrong ways'—is demonstratively plain and colloquial, as is the mocking line about the stolen goods. It is as if the poet is saying 'Look, I am writing a sonnet, but I can write plain English'. The thirteenth line is Spenserian in the style of its melody, and the last is magnificently emphatic. Though this poem is really more about how to write poetry than it is about Stella it nevertheless achieves a superbly elegant compliment to the lady: if it owes much to classical and Renaissance sources, it also asserts a sturdy national independence.

Elegance, assurance, and a complete command of rhythm are also the marks of the next sonnet, by Shakespeare.

> How oft, when thou, my music, music play'st,
> Upon that blessed wood whose motion sounds
> With thy sweet fingers, when thou gently sway'st
> The wiry concord that mine ear confounds,
> Do I envy those jacks that nimble leap
> To kiss the tender inward of thy hand,
> Whilst my poor lips, which should that harvest reap,
> At the woods boldness by thee blushing stand!
> To be so tickled, they would change their state
> And situation with those dancing chips,
> O'er whom thy fingers walk with gentle gait,

Making dead wood more blest than living lips.
Since saucy jacks so happy are in this
Give them thy fingers, me thy lips to kiss.

The poet gazes at the lady who is playing the virginals; the jacks are the instrument's keys, and also impertinent fellows, the poet's rivals. Melody, ingenuity, wit, are all present here, and all these elements are kept in play and balanced against each other; in this style, as in all others, Shakespeare is the master. He was often called 'sweet' by his contemporaries, and 'sugred' was an epithet applied to his sonnets, but what keeps this particular comfit from being sickly is the delicately ironic tone which makes us realize that the poet is aware of the game he is playing. Ingenious conceits—the bold wood and the blushing lips—are used with a full sense of their fashionable absurdity.

To trace all the metrical variations which sustain the poem's movement would be tedious; they are apparent to any reader who will, with his ears open, compare this sonnet with Surrey's, or with the verses quoted from *The Mirror of Magistrates*. Two lines, however, are worth detailed attention, since they conveniently illustrate the increasingly complex rhythmic effects that English verse is now capable of:

O'er whom thy fingers walk with gentle gait,
Making dead wood more blest than living lips.

We walk with a natural regular rhythm; the fingers walk because they move over the keyboard; their movement is regular because of the pulse of the music; and to say that they walk seems to give them a life of their own. The exactly regular emphasis of this line exactly echoes the sense—the line itself seems to walk: the disposition of the syllables and the meaning of the words force us to read it with a metronome beat.

The next line makes a completely different effect. It balances 'dead wood' against 'living lips' and as we read it we feel its three sections.

Making dead wood/more blest/than living lips.

—the two halves of the antithesis separated by the term of comparison. 'Making' is emphasised because its natural stress inverts the normal first foot; the d's in 'dead wood', and the modulation from the short e in dead to the short oo in wood falls with a dull thud. If we are to pronounce our consonants distinctly—and since we are reading verse we must surely do so—we cannot hurry from 'blest' to 'than' the transition from the final t to the initial th must make a slight hiatus.

This has the effect first, of focusing attention on 'blest'—the key word in the line, and one of the themes of the sonnet, since the lady is a blessing—and secondly, of bringing into relief the climactic 'living lips' which closes the comparison.

The element of wit, the play of intelligence, the critical attitude to poetic conventions which these two poems exhibit should be noted, for it is something which becomes very important in the work of Donne and the poets who are grouped with him as 'Metaphysicals'.

The charms of the Elizabethan lyric are justly famous and have been much anthologized. It is important to remember that these were true lyrics—words intended to be set to music, and in them musical and verbal form are intimately related. My first two examples show how, in the Elizabethan popular song, literary themes were handled with a neat simplicity that owes as much to folk song as to learned poetry; and they will serve to remind us that the gap between learned and popular culture was not in this age unbridgeable. The first celebrates pastoral innocence:

What pleasure have great princes
More dainty to their choice,
Than herdmen wild, who careless
In quiet life rejoice,
And Fortune's fate not fearing
Sing sweet in summer morning?
Their dealings plain and rightful
Are void of all deceit;
They never knew how spiteful
It is to kneel and wait
On favourite presumptuous
Whose pride is vain and sumptuous.
All day their flocks each tendeth;
At night they take their rest,
More quiet than who sendeth
His ship into the East,
Where gold and pearl are plenty,
But getting very dainty.
For lawyers and their pleading
They esteem it not a straw
They think that honest meaning
Is of itself a law;
Where conscience judgeth plainly,
They spend no money vainly.
O happy who thus liveth,
Not caring much for gold,

With clothing that sufficeth
To keep him from the cold.
Though poor and plain his diet,
Yet merry it is and quiet.

The second, with pleasant tune and appealing similes, cheerfully states a lover's sad case.

I serve a mistress whiter than the snow
Straighter than cedar, brighter than the glass,
Finer in trip and swifter than the roe,
More pleasant than the field of flowering grass;
More gladsome to my withering joys that fade,
Than winter's sun or summer's cooling shade.

Sweeter than swelling grape of ripest wine,
Softer than feathers of the fairest swan,
Smoother than jet, more stately than the pine,
Fresher than poplar, smaller than my span,
Clearer than beauty's fiery pointed beam,
Or icy crust of crystal's frozen stream.

Yet is she curster than the bear by kind,
And harder hearted than the aged oak,
More glib than oil, more fickle than the wind,
Stiffer than steel, no sooner bent than broke.
Lo! thus my service is a lasting sore;
Yet will I serve, although I die therefore.

Our third example is famous: it must not only be read, but listened to in Dowland's beautiful setting for lute and voice.

Weep you no more, sad fountains;
What need you flow so fast?
Look how the snowy mountains
Heaven's sun doth gently waste.
But my sun's heavenly eyes
View not your weeping,
That now lies sleeping,
Softly, now softly lies
Sleeping.

Sleep is a reconciling,
A rest that peace begets.
Doth not the sun rise smiling
When fair at even he sets?

> Rest you, then, rest, sad eyes,
> Melt not in weeping,
> While she lies sleeping,
> Softly, now softly lies
> Sleeping.

The next poem is by Thomas Campion, another lutenist composer who wrote his own lyrics, and it is really a neater, more sophisticated version of our second example. The poet plays with folk-lore and country magic:

> Thrice toss these oaken ashes in the air;
> Thrice sit thou mute in this enchanted chair;
> Then thrice three times tie up this true love's knot,
> And murmur soft: 'She will, or she will not.'
>
> Go burn these poisonous weeds in yon blue fire,
> These screech-owl's feathers and this prickling briar,
> This cypress gather'd at a dead man's grave,
> That all thy fears and cares an end may have.
>
> Then come, you fairies, dance with me a round;
> Melt her hard heart with your melodious sound.
> In vain are all the charms I can devise;
> She hath an art to break them with her eyes.

The next poem, by Raleigh, has a tough, grim wit, and packs a great deal of meaning into ten lines. We can see, in a poem like this, how Elizabethan taste admitted all sorts of verbal ingenuity and punning in serious verse, and all sorts of attitudes and feelings which post-romantic taste finds 'unpoetical':

> What is our life? A play of passion,
> Our mirth the music of division.
> Our mother's wombs the tiring houses be,
> Where we are dressed for this short comedy.
> Heaven the judicious sharp spectator is,
> That sits and marks still who doth act amiss.
> Our graves that hide us from the searching sun
> Are like drawn curtains when the play is done.
> Thus march we, playing, to our latest rest,
> Only we die in earnest, that's no jest.

A few notes on the puns may be useful. Division was a technical term in music, meaning a scale passage or run: our laughter is mocking, we laugh at other men from whom we are divided. The 'tiring house' is the theatre dressing room: the soul is clothed in the body in order to play out the brief comedy of life. Heaven is the spectator—thou,

O God, seest me: the spectator is judicious or critical like the judicious spectators who grieve at bad acting in Hamlet's speech to the players; but the word also carries the heavier meaning of judgement, and this judgement is sharp, that is, at once acute and painful. What is judged is acting, or what we do in our lives. We play, or divert ourselves, or pretend to be other than we really are, or take this world's values seriously instead of being guided by eternal ones, as we march through life. The turn from 'play' and 'jest' to 'earnest' conveys the inescapable reality of death. The imagery would be still more solid to a contemporary reader who would remember that the canopy over the stage was known as the Heavens, that in the stage itself there were traps to act as graves and descents into hell, and who had seen much marching and countermarching of stage armies.

We have now arrived at the end of the sixteenth century; and have got some slight idea of the extraordinary development in accomplishment, in varied metrical, rhetorical and melodic structure, in wit and intelligence, that Elizabethan verse exhibits. We may say that the technical problems of writing English verse have been solved. Later poets modify the tunes and refine the techniques: but they all derive from the work of the poets of this age.

2

BLANK VERSE

This chapter attempts to outline the development of blank verse from its beginnings in the sixteenth century to the end of the Jacobean age. Such a survey is bound to be inadequate and incomplete; but if the reader will get to know the chosen passages really well; above all if he will listen carefully, taking any clues he may find useful in the commentary, he will become familiar with some typical tunes, and I hope that this will help him in his general reading of Shakespeare and his contemporaries.

We cannot pretend that Surrey's blank verse (from his translation of the *Aeneid*) is anything but dull and clumsy, but historically it was of considerable importance. Here was a heroic measure (heroic in this context meaning suitable for epic or serious poems) which had two things to recommend it. First, it was unrhymed, and therefore likely to appear, to classicizing Renaissance men, to resemble the unrhymed verse of Greece and Rome: second, it employed the five-foot

ten-syllabled line already discovered by Chaucer to be suited to the
nature of the English language. Surrey is obviously labouring to get
his lines to scan, and has little general command over his rhythms.
One can't imagine reading much of him for pleasure.

> But to the hills and wild holts when they came,
> From the rocks top the wild savage roës
> Avail the hill, and on the other side,
> Over the launds, they gan take their course.
> The harts likewise, in troops taking their flight,
> Raising the dust, the mountains fast forsook.
> The child Iulus, blithe of his swift steed,
> Amids the plain now pricks by them, now these,
> And to encounter wisheth oft in mind
> The foaming boar, instead of fearful beasts
> Or lion brown might from the hill descend.
> In the meantime the heavens 'gan rumble sore;
> In tail whereof a mingled shower with hail.
> The Tyrian folk and scattered Trojan youth
> And Venus nephew the cottages for fear
> Sought round about; the floods fell from the hills.
> Queen Dido, with the Trojan prince alone,
> Chanced on a den. Our mother then, the earth,
> And Juno that hath charge of marriage,
> First tokens gave with burning gledes of flame,
> And, privy to the wedlock, lightning skies;
> And the nymphs wailed from the mountain tops.

Our next samples come from *Gorboduc*, a learned, or academic, rather
than a popular play. It appeared in 1562, and was written by Thomas
Sackville and Thomas Norton.

PHILANDER

> Tyndar, O king, came lately from the court
> Of Ferrex, to my lord your younger son,
> And made report of great prepared store
> For war, and saith that it is wholly meant
> Against Porrex, for high disdain that he
> Lives now a king, and equal in degree
> With him that claimeth to succeed the whole,
> As by due title of descending right.
> Porrex is now so set on flaming fire,
> Partly with kindled rage of cruel wrath,
> Partly with hope to gain a realm thereby,
> That he in haste prepareth to invade
> His brother's land, and with unkindly war

Threatens the murder of your elder son;
Ne could I him persuade, that first he should
Send to his brother to demand the cause;
Nor yet to you to stay this hateful strife.

Act III, Sc. i

AGROSTUS

Your Grace should now, in these grave years of yours,
Have found ere this the price of mortal joys;
How short they be, how fading here in earth,
How full of change, how brittle our estate,
Of nothing sure, save only of the death,
To whom both man, and all the world doth owe
Their end at last; neither shall nature's power
In other sort against your heart prevail,
Than as the naked hand whose stroke assays
The armed breast where force doth light in vain.

GORBODUC

Many can yield right sage and grave advice
Of patient spirit to others wrapped in woe,
And can in speech both rule and conquer kind[1];
Who, if by proof they might feel nature's force,
Would show themselves men as they are indeed,
Which now will needs be gods.

Act IV, Sc. ii

The verse is still somewhat wooden, but the beat is clear, and we see
the author beginning to play off rhetorical figures and syntactical
groupings against the steady five beat repetition. For example in the
lines

> How short they be, how fading here on earth,
> How full of change, how brittle our estate . . .

we can see that the sense is carried through several lines to finish at

> Their end at last;

making a break within the line. But the whole effect is still ponderous
and undramatic. The reader should compare Philander's speech with
the passage in *Hamlet* about the lawless resolutes sharked up by Fortin-
bras; Gorboduc's reply to Agrostus should be set beside Leonato's
speech to his brother in *Much Ado About Nothing*, where a similar
theme is handled:

[1] Natural feeling.

> ... for, brother, men
> Can counsel and speak comfort to that grief
> Which they themselves not feel; but, tasting it,
> Their counsel turns to passion, which before
> Would give preceptial medicine to rage,
> Fetter strong madness in a silken thread,
> Charm ache with air and agony with words:
> No, no; 'tis all men's office to speak patience
> To those that wring under a load of sorrow;
> But no man's virtue or sufficiency
> To be so moral when he shall endure
> The like himself ...

The next passage comes from one of the most popular of all Elizabethan plays, *The Spanish Tragedy* by Thomas Kyd (1558–1594).

VICEROY
> Infortunate condition of kings,
> Seated amidst so many helpless doubts!
> First we are plac'd upon extremest height
> And oft supplanted with exceeding hate,
> But ever subject to the wheel of chance;
> And at our highest never joy we so,
> As we both doubt and dread our overthrow.
> So striveth not the waves with sundry winds,
> As fortune toileth in the affairs of kings,
> That would be fear'd, yet fear to be belov'd,
> Sith fear or love to kings is flattery.
> For instance, lordings, look upon your king,
> By hate deprived of his dearest son,
> The only hope of our successive line.

In the Viceroy's speech we see the influence of the sententious rhetoric of Seneca, as we do in Gorboduc, but Kyd's verse has more energy; it is obviously designed for declamation, and we know it delighted contemporary audiences. The dramatic situation—the contrast between supreme power and the fears which it entails—is echoed by the antithetical pattern of the verse; and the symmetry of the structure in such lines as

> That would be fear'd yet fear to be belov'd ...

makes the meaning obvious at the first hearing. Yet there is a lack of flexibility: we can take the thumping energy while a serious theme is being discussed, but such feeble lines as

> For instance, lordings, look upon your king ...

let us down badly. For transitional passages, for normal conversation, the poet has no suitable rhythm, so that we are conscious of a ludicrous discrepancy between the heavy iambic beat, and the banality of the sense. We might compare the great speech on ceremony in *Henry V*, Act IV, Sc. i.

HIERONIMO

> O eyes! no eyes, but fountains fraught with tears;
> O life! no life, but lively form of death;
> O world! no world, but mass of public wrongs,
> Confused and filled with murder and misdeeds!
> O sacred heavens! if this unhallowed deed,
> If this inhuman and barbarous attempt,
> In this incomparable murder thus
> Of mine, but now no more my son,
> Shall unreveal'd and unrevenged pass,
> How should we term your dealings to be just,
> If you unjustly deal with those that in your justice trust?
> The night, sad secretary to my moans,
> With direful visions wakes my vexed soul,
> And with the wounds of my distressful son
> Solicits me for notice of his death.
> The ugly fiends do sally forth of hell,
> And frame my steps to unfrequented paths,
> And fear[1] my heart with fierce inflamed thoughts.
> The cloudy day my discontents records,
> Early begins to register my dreams,
> And drives me forth to seek the murderer.
> Eyes, life, world, heav'ns, hell, night, and day,
> See, search, shew, send some man, some mean, that may . . .

(a letter falleth)

> What's here? a letter? tush! it is not so!—
> A letter written to Hieronimo!

Act III, Sc. i

Hieronimo was a part extremely popular with both audience and actors ('a part to tear a cat in, to make all split') and his famous tirade is worth close study. Renaissance drama cannot be understood unless we realise the pleasure the audience took in oratory: all the great dramatic moments are occasions for set speeches, and the form of the Elizabethan theatre made it easy for the actor to make his rhetoric work. No doubt the groundlings liked the violence in Kyd's plays, but they also enjoyed the words, and in his work we can hear him constructing rhythms that shall beat them into submission. A sympathetic reader who tries to imagine himself at the *Rose* theatre or the

---

[1] Frighten.

Fortune can still feel the crude power of this piece, however its effect may be ruined by the last couplet. We should note the way the speaker's tragic predicament is related to the world, to the whole of society; and the sweeping deployment of murder, justice, revenge, the night, dreams, fiends and horror, all summed up in the hammering monosyllables at the end.

Such line as

> The cloudy day my discontent records . . .

melodious and vigorous, knitted by alliteration, may stand as a fair sample of the type of rhythmic unit on which the great speeches of the early popular Elizabethan theatre were based. *Gorboduc* is inescapably dull. We might sometimes laugh in the wrong places at *The Spanish Tragedy* but we wouldn't be bored, and one reason for this would be Kyd's skill in manipulating his blank verse.

It was our next poet, Marlowe (1564–1593), who produced the most thundering rhetoric of all. We have only to compare this passage from *Dido*, a play based on the same book of the *Aeneid* as that translated by Surrey, to see how he has transformed blank verse.

VENUS

Now is the time for me to play my part.
Ho, young men! saw you, as you came,
Any of my sisters wandering here,
Having a quiver girded to her side,
And clothed in a spotted leopard's skin?

AENEAS

I neither saw nor heard of any such.
But what may I, fair virgin, call your name,
Whose looks set forth no mortal frame to view,
Nor speech bewrays aught human in thy birth?
Thou art a goddess that delud'st our eyes
And shroud'st thy beauty in this borrowed shape;
But whether thou the sun's bright sister be,
Or one of chaste Diana's fellow nymphs,
Live happy in the height of all content,
And lighten our extremes with this one boon,
As to instruct us under what good heaven
We breathe as now, and what this world is call'd
On which by tempests' fury we are cast:
Tell us, O, tell us, that are ignorant!
And this right hand shall make thy altars crack
With mountain heaps of milk-white sacrifice.

Act I

The rhythm is still uncertain, and in places feeble: one can say nothing of a line like

> Any of my sisters wandering here

except that it is possible to count ten syllables in it; but Aeneas' reply to the goddess works up to a splendid climax:

> Tell us, O tell us, that are ignorant!
> And this right hand shall make thy altars crack
> With mountain heaps of milk-white sacrifice.

The verb 'crack' is characteristic: its vigour, unexpectedness and solid reality makes the hyperbole convincing. The speech of Callapine, from the second part of *Tamburlane* with its florid Renaissance decoration, its noise and energy, is a good sample of the most famous aspect of Marlowe's style.

CALLAPINE
> By Cairo runs to Alexandria-bay
> Darotes' stream, wherein at anchor lies
> A Turkish galley of my royal fleet,
> Waiting my coming to the river-side,
> Hoping by some means I shall be released;
> Which, when I come aboard, will hoist up sail,
> And soon put forth into the Terrene sea,
> Where twixt the isles of Cyprus and of Crete,
> We quickly may in Turkish seas arrive.
> Then shalt thou see an hundred kings and more,
> Upon their knees, all bid me welcome home.
> Amongst so many crowns of burnish'd gold,
> Choose which thou wilt, all are at thy command:
> A thousand galleys, mann'd with Christian slaves,
> I freely give thee, which shall cut the Straits,
> And bring armadoes, from the coasts of Spain,
> Fraughted with gold of rich America:
> The Grecian virgins shall attend on thee,
> Skilful in music and in amorous lays,
> As fair as was Pygmalion's ivory girl
> Or lovely Iö metamorphosed:
> With naked negroes shall thy coach be drawn,
> And, as thou rid'st in triumph through the streets,
> The pavement underneath thy chariot wheels
> With Turkey carpets will be covered,
> And cloth of arras hung about the walls,
> Fit objects for thy princely eye to pierce:
> A hundred bassoes, cloth'd in crimson silk,

Shall ride before thee on Barbarian steeds;
And, when thou goest, a golden canopy
Enchas'd with precious stones, which shine as bright
As that fair veil that covers all the world,
When Phoebus, leaping from his hemisphere,
Descendeth downward to the Antipodes:—
And more than this, for all I cannot tell.

Act II, Sc. i

However, in this sort of writing there can be no progression, and
after a time it becomes deafeningly monotonous. Either it is superb:

> A hundred bassoes, cloth'd in crimson silk,
> Shall ride before thee on Barbarian steeds . . .

or silly:

> And more than this, for all I cannot tell . . .

and we might note in passing that if Phoebus is descending, there is
no need to say he is going downwards.

What is more interesting for our purpose is the way that Marlowe
was beginning to achieve subtler effects. This speech is from *The Jew of
Malta*, 1589.

BARABAS

Thus, like the sad presaging raven, that tolls
The sick man's passport in her hollow beak,
And in the shadow of the silent night
Doth shake contagion from her sable wings,
Vex'd and tormented runs poor Barabas
With fatal curses towards these Christians.
The incertain pleasures of swift-footed time
Have ta'en their flight, and left me in despair;
And of my former riches rests no more
But bare remembrance; like a soldier's scar,
That has no further comfort for his maim.—
O Thou, that with a fiery pillar led'st
The sons of Israel through the dismal shades,
Light Abraham's offspring; and direct the hand
Of Abigail this night! or let the day
Turn to eternal darkness after this!—
No sleep can fasten on my watchful eyes,
Nor quiet enter my distemper'd thoughts,
Till I have answer of my Abigail.

Act II, Sc. i

If we listen to these lines

> The incertain pleasures of swift-footed time
> Have ta'en their flight, and left me in despair;
> And of my former riches rests no more
> But bare remembrance . . .

we shall hear not merely a resounding rhetoric invented by the poet and put indifferently into the mouths of all his characters, but a rhythm suited to the mood of a particular scene, and the emotions of a particular speaker; Barabas's self-pity is audible in the cadence which runs down to 'bare remembrance'. The poet is no longer bound by the limits of the five heavy beats; his alliteration—the r's and m's and b's—is no longer mechanically thumping—

> Mountain heaps of milk-white sacrifice—

but delicate and imperceptible.

This flexibility is even more marked in the dialogue between Faustus and Mephistophilis, from *Dr. Faustus*, 1588.

Re-enter Mephistophilis like a Franciscan friar

MEPH
> Now, Faustus, what would thou have me do?

FAUST
> I charge thee wait upon me whilst I live,
> To do whatever Faustus shall command,
> Be it to make the moon drop from her sphere,
> Or the ocean to overwhelm the world.

MEPH
> I am a servant to great Lucifer,
> And may not follow thee without his leave:
> No more than he commands must we perform.

FAUST
> Did not he charge thee to appear to me?

MEPH
> No, I came hither of my own accord.

FAUST
> Did not my conjuring speeches raise thee? speak.

MEPH
> That was the cause, but yet *per accidens*;
> For, when we hear one rack the name of God,
> Abjure the Scriptures and his Saviour Christ,
> We fly, in hope, to get his glorious soul;
> Nor will we come, unless he use such means
> Whereby he is in danger to be damn'd.

Therefore the shortest cut for conjuring
Is stoutly to abjure the Trinity,
And pray devoutly to the prince of hell.

FAUST
              So Faustus hath
Already done; and holds this principle,
There is no chief but only Belzebub;
To whom Faustus doth dedicate himself.
This word 'damnation' terrifies not him,
For he confounds hell in Elysium:
His ghost be with the old philosophers!
But, leaving these vain trifles of men's souls
Tell me what is that Lucifer they lord?

MEPH
Arch-regent and commander of all spirits.

FAUST
Was not that Lucifer an angel once?

MEPH
Yes, Faustus, and most dearly lov'd of God.

FAUST
How comes it, then, that he is prince of devils?

MEPH
O, by aspiring pride and insolence;
For which God threw him from the face of heaven.

FAUST
And what are you that live with Lucifer?

MEPH
Unhappy spirits that fell with Lucifer,
Conspir'd against our God with Lucifer,
And are for ever damn'd with Lucifer.

FAUST
Where are you damn'd?

MEPH
In hell.

FAUST
How comes it, then, that thou art out of hell?

MEPH
Why, this is hell, nor am I out of it.
Think'st thou that I, who saw the face of God
And tasted the eternal joys of heaven,
Am not tormented with ten thousand hells,
In being depriv'd of everlasting bliss?
O, Faustus, leave these frivolous demands,
Which strike a terror to my fainting soul!

FAUST
   What, is great Mephistophilis so passionate
   For being deprived of the joys of heaven?
   Learn thou of Faustus manly fortitude,
   And scorn those joys thou never shall possess. ...

Sc. iii

The magician's hyperbole is contrasted with the demon's dry staccato
answers. Lines are broken—

So Faustus hath
Already done. ...

question and answer rattle together; the torments of Mephistopholis are
echoed in

Unhappy spirits that fell with Lucifer.

Notice how the structure of these lines, with their falling repetition
of 'with Lucifer', forces us to stress the key words 'fell', 'God' and
'damned'; how this formal cadence is broken by the abrupt

Where are you damned?
In hell

leading to the horrifying climax

Why, this is hell, nor am I out of it.

These arid monosyllables carry more power than the 'mighty line'
which first made Marlowe famous: they carry the power of the
speaking voice. The poet's range has been extended.
   In the passage from *David and Bethsabe* by George Peele (1558–1598)
we can hear a softer, lyric eloquence; an elegant and charming flesh
clothes the bones of the formal rhetorical scheme. This formality,
the skeleton of the rhetoric, is an important part of the rhythmic
pattern: in organizing different sorts of sense units, it organizes the
whole sound effect and movement of the verse.

DAVID
   What tunes, what words, what looks, what wonders pierce
   My soul, incensed with a sudden fire?
   What tree, what shade, what spring, what paradise,
   Enjoys the beauty of so fair a dame?
   Fair Eva, plac'd in perfect happiness,
   Lending her praise-notes to the liberal heavens
   Struck with the accents of arch-angels' tunes,
   Wrought not more pleasure to her husband's thoughts
   Than this fair woman's words and notes to mine.
   May that sweet plain that bears her pleasant weight

Be still enamell'd with discoloured[1] flowers;
That precious fount bear sand of purest gold;
And, for the pebble, let the silver streams
That pierce earth's bowels to maintain the source,
Play upon rubies, sapphires, chrysolites;
The brims let be embrac'd with golden curls
Of moss that sleeps with sound the waters make
For joy to feed the fount with their recourse;
Let all the grass that beautifies her bower
Bear manna every morn instead of dew,
Or let the dew be sweeter far than that
That hangs, like chains of pearl, on Hermon's hill,
Or balm which trickled from old Aaron's beard. . . .

                                                    Act I, Sc. i

Here the first two pairs of lines are symmetrically arranged rhetorical
questions; in each a series of subjects precedes a single verb; in each
the first three sense-units are single feet but 'wonders' and 'paradise',
the last terms in each series, have two and three syllables respectively.
In the first line the last syllable is the verb 'pierce', and we read straight
on to the comma after the verb's object, 'my soul'; but the verb in
the second question, 'enjoys', begins a line.

                                        . . . what wonders pierce
        My soul . . .

balances, but is different from

                                            . . . what paradise
        Enjoys the beauty

Piercing the soul is a more energetic business than enjoying beauty.
Not only are there delicate variations within the symmetry, but those
variations are part of the way in which the sense is communicated.
The poet is no longer content to make his lines scan, and pace on with
sonorous regularity, he is ingeniously varying their form and tune.
He is becoming something of a virtuoso, and this metrical and linguistic
virtuosity was much to the taste—especially the court taste—of this
period. The next section of the speech consists of a comparison between
Eve and Bathsheba, in which we may note the studied disposition of
the phrases between the subject, Eva, and the verb 'wrought'. After the
comparison comes a long exquisitely managed piece of decoration,
a dazzling and delightful series of images, pinned together by alliteration, and supported by the steady iambic beat:

                            [1] Many coloured.

> The brims let be embrac'd with golden curls
> Bear manna every morn instead of dew

and so on.

The reader should compare these lines with those quoted from *Cymbeline*. Shakespeare's 'furred moss' is an image of very different quality from Peele's 'golden curls', and altogether he seems to have added an extra dimension to language. But we should realize that, supreme as Shakespeare's genius was, the scope of his achievement owes much to the labours of his predecessors, to the amount and quality of work already done.

Young Clifford's speech, from *Henry VI* Part 2, resembles in many ways poetry we have already studied.

YOUNG CLIFFORD

> Shame and confusion! all is on the rout;
> Fear frames disorder, and disorder wounds
> Where it should guard. O war, thou son of hell,
> Whom angry heavens do make their minister,
> Throw in the frozen bosoms of our part
> Hot coals of vengeance! Let no soldier fly.
> He that is truly dedicate to war
> Hath no self-love, nor he that loves himself
> Hath not essentially but by circumstance
> The name of valour. (*Seeing his dead father*)
>   O, let the vile world end,
> And the premised flames of the last day
> Knit earth and heaven together!
> Now let the general trumpet blow his blast,
> Particularities and petty sounds
> To cease! Wast thou ordained, dear father,
> To lose thy youth in peace, and to achieve
> The silver livery of advised age,
> And, in thy reverence and thy chair-days, thus
> To die in ruffian battle? Even at this sight
> My heart is turn'd to stone: and while 'tis mine,
> It shall be stony. York not our old men spares;
> No more will I their babes: tears virginal
> Shall be to me even as the dew to fire,
> And beauty that the tyrant oft reclaims
> Shall to my flaming wrath be oil and flax.
> Henceforth I will not have to do with pity:
> Meet I an infant of the house of York,
> Into as many gobbets will I cut it
> As wild Medea young Absyrtus did:
> In cruelty will I seek out my fame.

As did Aeneas old Anchises bear,
So bear I thee upon my manly shoulders;
But then Aeneas bare a living load,
Nothing so heavy as these woes of mine.

                                                                    Act v, Sc. ii

The vigour, the simple rhythm, the horror at the end, the classical allusions, the resonance remind us of Marlowe; the generalities about war echo similar moralizings in *Gorboduc*; and the invocation of the last day, when Clifford finds his father's body, recalls some of Hieronymo's lines. But we are aware also of three things. First, that this writer is very intelligent:

> He that is truly dedicate to war
> Hath no self-love, nor he that loves himself
> Hath not essentially but by circumstance
> The name of valour. . . .

The symmetry of the movement—in towards 'self-love' and then out again towards 'valour'—is not just a conventional text-book pattern, like the rhetorical questions in David's speech, but an essential part of the total meaning of the lines. Second, the majestic sounds have an ease of movement which Marlowe rarely compassed.

> Now let the general trumpet blow his blast
> Particularities and petty sounds
> To cease!

really sounds like the end of the world; but there is no straining after effect. Thirdly, this poet, who can achieve exquisite effects of lyric pathos, as in

> The silvery livery of advised age,

stiffens his feelings with images—'thy chair-days', for example—drawn not from literature but from everyday reality. He is writing in the mode of his time, and all the rhythmic effects his contemporaries and predecessors had perfected are at his command. For example

> Henceforth I will not have to do with pity . . .

exploits the same sort of simplicity that we have noted Marlowe using in Dr. Faustus; yet to all this he adds an indefinable tune of his own. We may feel that the characteristic play on 'stone' and 'stony', and the allusions to Medea and Absyrtus, Aeneas and Anchises are period furniture, and that as far as the last eight lines are concerned Kyd or Marlowe could do as well or better: but other passages are far beyond them.

The second speech, from *Henry VI* Part 3, shows Shakespeare pushing to its limit the effect of rhetorical repetition.

KING
   ... O God! methinks it were a happy life,
   To be no better than a homely swain;
   To sit upon a hill, as I do now,
   To carve out dials quaintly, point by point,
   Thereby to see the minutes how they run,
   How many make the hour full complete;
   How many hours bring about the day;
   How many days will finish up the year;
   How many years a mortal man may live.
   When this is known, then to divide the times,
   So many hours must I tend my flock;
   So many hours must I take my rest;
   So many hours must I contemplate;
   So many hours must I sport myself;
   So many days my ewes have been with young;
   So many weeks ere the poor fools will ean;
   So many years ere I shall shear the fleece:
   So minutes, hours, days, months and years,
   Pass'd over to the end they were created,
   Would bring white hairs unto a quiet grave.
   Ah, what a life were this! how sweet! how lovely!
   Gives not the hawthorn-bush a sweeter shade
   To shepherds looking on their silly sheep
   Than doth a rich embroider'd canopy
   To kings that fear their subjects' treachery?
   O, yes, it doth; a thousand-fold it doth
   And to conclude, the shepherd's homely curds,
   His cold thin drink out of his leather bottle,
   His wonted sleep under a fresh tree's shade,
   All which secure and sweetly he enjoys,
   Is far beyond a prince's delicates,
   His viands sparkling in a golden cup,
   His body couched in a curious bed,
   When care, mistrust, and treason wait on him.
                               Act II, Sc. v

This is certainly an exhibition of the sort of literary virtuosity the age delighted in, and the homely swain is a standard ingredient in the pastoral poetry of the time. (In *Henry IV* Part 2 he is domesticated:

        He whose brow with homely biggin bound
        Snores out the watch of night. ...)

But though Shakespeare is doing here the sort of thing his contemporaries had done, he does it much better than they. He commands, as always, a wide sweep of rhythm, and his 'How many . . .' 'So many . . .' units are all made to move steadily and sweetly to the conclusion

> Would bring white hairs unto a quiet grave.

But we also see the characteristically Shakespearian 'homely curds' and 'cold thin drink'—the solidly observed reality. And how sinister are the abstractions 'care, mistrust and treason', how real they are made to seem. They follow up the curds, the bottle, the tree, the delicates, the cup and the bed, so that we instinctively apprehend them as persons and we don't often feel so about personifications. They 'wait' in two senses—as servants, and as assassins.

Henry VI is an abstract, almost allegorical, figure. The Bastard in *King John* is a credible individual. Here he speaks as the body of Prince Arthur is being carried away.

BASTARD
> I am amazed, methinks, and lose my way
> Among the thorns and dangers of this world.
> How easy dost thou take all England up!
> From forth this morsel of dead royalty,
> The life, the right and truth of all this realm
> Is fled to heaven; and England now is left
> To tug and scamble and to part by the teeth
> The unowed interest of proud-swelling state.
> Now for the bare-picked bone of majesty
> Doth dogged war bristle his angry crest
> And snarleth in the gentle eyes of peace:
> Now powers from home and discontents at home
> Meet in one line; and vast confusion waits,
> As doth a raven on a sick-fallen beast,
> The imminent decay of wrested pomp.
> Now happy he whose cloak and cincture can
> Hold out this tempest. . . .

Act IV, Sc. iii

This speech begins and ends with his own reflections on his own predicament. He is stumbling into a knowledge of a world more complex and more unpleasant and more dangerous than he had imagined it to be. The middle section of the speech beginning with

> From forth this morsel of dead royalty. . . .

does more than express the Bastard's feelings; it contains the theme of the play. Yet it is not the sort of abstract moralizing we have had in *Gorboduc*. The splendidly simple line

> How easy dost thou take all England up!

(we may compare the cadence of

> Why, this is hell, nor am I out of it ...)

leads directly to a consideration of the consequences of the young prince's death. The first sentence balances 'life', 'right' and 'truth' against 'tug', 'scamble' 'part by the teeth' and its first element ends with the semi-colon after heaven, breaking the line; the second finishes with a full stop after 'state', at the end of a line. Grammatical structure is played off against the metrical pattern; whereas in the previous speech metre has tended to dictate the grammatical and rhetorical form. Now the theme has been stated, we have two symmetrical passages both pegged on the form 'Now ... and', concluding with the simile of the raven waiting for the dying beast to become carrion. We cannot, it is obvious, discuss Shakespeare's rhythm, his tune, without discussing what he is saying; the two things are inextricably mixed up. The situation is horrible, it is ugly, and harsh ugly words are used to express it. The rhythm of such lines as

> To tug and scamble and to part by the teeth

depends in part on the energy we have to put into pronouncing them. We open our mouths on 'part' and shut them on 'teeth', as the dogs get a grip on their prey; saying the line makes us, as it were, enact its meaning; and the full-vowelled Marlovian majesty of the next line,

> The unowed interest of proud-swelling state ...

is in ironic contrast. In the very sound of the verse we hear the difference between appearance—the proud-swelling state—and reality—the dog-fight. From thoughts about the state of England we are brought back to the character, to the person who is saying all this, who shivers and pulls his cloak around him, and wonders about his own safety. The flight of rhetoric does not tamely stop as Callapine's does, it dies away naturally into the action of the drama and its people. Shakespeare's verse is becoming supple enough to change its tone and intention without our being aware of the harsh shifting of gears.

Lord Bardolph's speech, from *Henry IV* Part 2, is another sample of Shakespeare's middle-period verse, and its formally worked out symmetrical similes are characteristic of much of his writing at this time.

LORD BARDOLPH
                    . . . a cause on foot
Lives so in hope, as in an early spring
We see the appearing buds; which to prove fruit,
Hope gives not so much warrant as despair
That frosts will bite them. When we mean to build,
We first survey the plot, then draw the model;
And when we see the figure of the house,
Then must we rate the cost of the erection;
Which if we find outweighs ability,
What do we then but draw anew the model
In fewer offices, or at least desist
To build at all? Much more, in this great work,
Which is almost to pluck a kingdom down
And set another up, should we survey
The plot of situation and the model,
Consent upon a sure foundation,
Question surveyors, know our own estate,
How able such a work to undergo,
To weigh against his opposite; or else
We fortify in paper and in figures,
Using the names of men instead of men;
Like one that draws the model of a house
Beyond his power to build it; who, half through,
Gives o'er and leaves his part-created cost
A naked subject for the weeping clouds,
And waste for winter's churlish tyranny.

                                    Act i, Sc. iii

The central image is of 'work', of building—to pluck a kingdom down
and set another up. This is a rhythm of a typical human activity—
perhaps *the* typical human activity, since it is characteristic of humans
to be civilized and civilization means cities and cities have to be built
and they are not built in a day, and they are always being pulled down
and reconstructed and they may bear (possibly) some relation to the
Civitas Dei, the City of God. We are led up to this climax and down
from it, by means of a series of images drawn from the workings of
human reason and intelligence, from specifically human, rational,
forseeing activities—plots, models, figures, costs, foundations,
surveyors, estates, fortifications, papers; and all this is sandwiched
between two blocks of images drawn from nature, from spring and
winter, life and death, the rhythms of universal existence. So we are
led outwards, from the particular political struggle which is the theme
of the play, to a more general consideration of man struggling by his
use of reason to extend and maintain and modify his civilization and

outwards again to think of man in relation to the world, to the natural laws to which inescapably he is bound. Shakespeare's rhetoric is not a mere decoration: the drama is in the poetry and the poetry is in the drama; we cannot separate them.

Rosalind's speech from *As You Like It* combines energy, strength and lightness; the verse moves with, and reinforces, her ironic intonations. She is speaking to Phebe, a foolish girl who has refused an honest suitor.

ROSALIND

And why, I pray you? Who might be your mother,
That you insult, exult, and all at once
Over the wretched? What though you have no beauty,—
As, by my faith, I see no more in you
Than without candle may go dark to bed,—
Must you be therefore proud and pitiless?
Why, what means this? Why do you look on me?
I see no more in you than in the ordinary
Of nature's sale-work. 'Od's my little life,
I think she means to tangle my eyes too!
No, faith, proud mistress, hope not after it:
'Tis not your inky brows, your black silk hair,
Your bugle eyeballs, nor your cheek of cream,
That can entame my spirits to your worship.
You foolish shepherd, wherefore do you follow her,
Like foggy south, puffing with wind and rain?
You are a thousand times a properer man
Than she a woman: 'tis such fools as you
That makes the world full of ill-favour'd children;
'Tis not her glass, but you, that flatters her;
And out of you she sees herself more proper
Than any of her lineaments can show her.
But, mistress, know yourself: down on your knees,
And thank heaven, fasting, for a good man's love:
For I must tell you friendly in your ear,
You are not for all markets. . . .

Act III, Sc. v

We are still aware of the five-stressed line as the basic rhythmic unit, but into it proverbial phrases and colloquialisms fit easily. Shakespeare makes us hear Rosalind's feelings, and her ironic awareness of the situation; he parodies the conventional literary vocabulary of sentiment, and also, in

. . . down on your knees
And thank heaven, fasting, for a good man's love. . . .

expresses a deep and serious emotion. His verse is becoming still more flexible, capable of registering rapidly, but without disorganizing the overall structure of the speech, the most minute variations of tone.

This development is easily seen if we compare this passage from *The Two Gentlemen of Verona* with the opening of Ophelia's lament over Hamlet.

VALENTINE
> I know him as myself; for from our infancy
> We have conversed and spent our hours together:
> And though myself have been an idle truant,
> Omitting the sweet benefit of time
> To clothe mine age with angel-like perfection,
> Yet hath Sir Proteus, for that's his name,
> Made use and fair advantage of his days;
> His years but young, but his experience old;
> His head unmellow'd, but his judgement ripe;
> And, in a word, for far behind his worth
> Come all the praises that I now bestow,
> He is complete in feature and in mind
> With all good grace to grace a gentleman.

Act II, Sc. iv

OPHELIA
> O, what a noble mind is here o'erthrown!
> The courtier's, soldier's, scholar's eye, tongue, sword:
> The expectancy and rose of the fair state,
> The glass of fashion and the mould of form,
> The observ'd of all observers, quite, quite down!
> And I, of ladies most deject and wretched,
> That suck'd the honey of his music vows,
> Now see that noble and most sovereign reason,
> Like sweet bells jangled, out of tune and harsh;
> That unmatch'd form and feature of blown youth
> Blasted with ecstasy. . . .

Act III, Sc. i

Both define a gentleman: the first uses formal antitheses, neat and ingenious—the meaning, we feel, is being put into a predetermined form; and the concluding jingle on 'grace' is the sort of thing that pleased the 'habituated ear' of an audience accustomed to admire verbal ingenuity for its own sake. When Ophelia speaks we are aware not of form but of feeling. The rhetorical scheme is there if we look for it: indeed it is quite easy to see how one speech grows, so to speak, out of the other. But the verse movement swings with Ophelia's feelings, carries the sense into us, convinces us of the uniqueness of this experience. It is interesting to note how the break between Ophelia's description of Hamlet's state, and her expression of her feelings about it is emphasized by the triple repetition of the long i sound: 'quite, quite down' leads to 'and I' and forces our attention on to the pronoun and on to Ophelia's predicament. The lines which follow are what everyone recognizes as 'poetry' because of the pathos they so exquisitely express. They are indeed beautiful, but we must remember that any definition of poetry which restricts its use to this manner of writing must give us a distorted view of Shakespeare's work, and of the nature of poetry in general.

The King's speech from *Hamlet* is a piece of oratory. Claudius, newly crowned and newly married, holds his first court.

KING
    Though yet of Hamlet our dear brother's death
    The memory be green, and that it us befitted
    To bear our hearts in grief and our whole kingdom
    To be contracted in one brow of woe,
    Yet so far hath discretion fought with nature
    That we with wisest sorrow think on him,
    Together with remembrance of ourselves.
    Therefore our sometime sister, now our queen,
    The imperial jointress of this warlike state,
    Have we, as 'twere with a defeated joy,—
    With an auspicious and a dropping eye,
    With mirth in funeral and with dirge in marriage,
    In equal scale weighing delight and dole,—
    Taken to wife: nor have we herein barred
    Your better wisdoms, which have freely gone
    With this affair along. For all, our thanks.

                            Act i, Sc. ii

Under the orotund pomp of the King's words, his smooth Machiavellian command of the situation, we sense his uneasy guiltiness as he explains his 'o'er-hasty marriage'. Note, to begin with, how supple the verse is. No longer is the line felt to be the basic unit; and the piled-up over-running clauses not only contribute to the oratorical effect, they hint at Claudius' underlying feelings. He gets to his point through a forest of excuses. The linguistic ingenuity of 'wisest sorrow', 'defeated joy', 'an auspicious and a dropping eye', and the elaborate antitheses all here combine to present a character and a situation. So with the syntax. See how long it takes him to get from the auxiliary verb and the subject 'have we', to the crucial past participle and its complement 'taken to wife'. Note, too, the ambiguity of 'your better wisdoms' which may be flattering (Polonius and Co. are wiser than I) or, if we take it to imply 'those who agree with me', a warning to dissentients. 'Freely' implicates the whole court, who are therefore part of the rottenness of Denmark. Once again we can trace many of the formal elements of this speech back to earlier work. But they here convey a greater density of meaning: above all they are not used for their own sake, as demonstrations of virtuosity, but to convey a specific and unique experience. 'They contain within themselves the reason why they are so and not otherwise.'

Increasing density of meaning may also be remarked in this scene from *All's Well that Ends Well*.

KING
   What's he comes here?
                  (*Enter Bertram, Lafeu, and Parolles*)
FIRST LORD
   It is the Count Rousillon, my good lord,
   Young Bertram.
KING
   Youth, thou bear'st thy father's face;
   Frank nature, rather curious than in haste,
   Hath well compos'd thee. Thy father's moral parts
   May'st thou inherit too! Welcome to Paris.
BERTRAM
   My thanks and duty are your majesty's.
KING
   I would I had that corporal soundness now,
   As when thy father and myself in friendship
   First tried our soldiership! He did look far
   Into the service of the time, and was
   Discipled of the bravest: he lasted long;
   But on us both did haggish age steal on,
   And wore us out of act. It much repairs me
   To talk of your good father. In his youth
   He had the wit, which I can well observe
   To-day in our young lords; but they may jest
   Till their own scorn return to them unnoted
   Ere they can hide their levity in honour:
   So like a courtier, contempt nor bitterness
   Were in his pride or sharpness; if they were,
   His equal had awaked them; and his honour,
   Clock to itself, knew the true minute when
   Exception bid him speak, and at this time

His tongue obey'd his hand: who were below him
He used as creatures of another place;
And bow'd his eminent top to their low ranks,
Making them proud of his humility,
In their poor praise he humbled. Such a man
Might be a copy to these younger times;
Which follow'd well, would demonstrate them now
But goers backward.

BERTRAM
His good remembrance, sir,
Lies richer in your thoughts than on his tomb,
So in approof lives not his epitaph
As in your royal speech.

KING
Would I were with him! He would always say—
Methinks I hear him now; his plausive words
He scatter'd not in ears, but grafted them,
To grow there and to bear,—'Let me not live,'—
Thus his good melancholy oft began
On the catastrophe and heel of pastime,
When it was out,—'Let me not live,' quoth he,
'After my flame lacks oil, to be the snuff
Of younger spirits, whose apprehensive senses
All but new things disdain; whose judgements are
Mere fathers of their garments; whose constancies
Expire before their fashions.' This he wish'd:
I after him do after him wish too,
Since I nor wax nor honey can bring home,
I quickly were dissolved from my hive,
To give some labourers room.

SECOND LORD
You are lov'd sir;
They that least lend it you shall lack you first.

KING
I fill a place, I know't . . .

Act I, Sc. ii

The King's speeches really form a discourse on the nature of the
'moral parts' he admired in Bertram's father, and which go to form
the ideal Renaissance courtier, soldier gentleman: just as Lord Bardolph's speech is a discourse about political revolt. Neither is dull;
but we can see that the King sounds more like an individual—his
age, his weakness, his sense of his own infirmities are all to be felt.
We seem to hear a man talking, not a character making a speech;
his voice rises and falls across the metrical pattern, now enunciating

maxims, now giving a dying cadence to the old man's pathos. The parentheses in the passage beginning

> Would I were with him ...

echo the tone of reminiscing age: they help to create a person, but they do not only do this, for their content—the words that 'grow' and 'bear', the 'good melancholy' that reflects the inevitable progress of life from youth to age—leads us to compare what Bertram really is, with what he ought to be, which is one of the themes of the play. The moral qualities discussed are all made solid and real; the whole speech is a tissue of actions; we are unaware of its formal arrangement, of the transitions from 'bravery' to 'wit' to 'pride', 'honour', 'humility'. In this it differs from earlier work—King Henry VI's lament, for example, where part of the effect is precisely due to the fact that the rhetorical form is so brilliantly, so triumphantly displayed. But when such a speech was over there was often a clumsy anti-climactic shift to meaner matters. Here the verse can move surely from the complex to the simple in such lines as

> This he wish'd
> I after him do after him wish too ...

through to the pathetic conclusion

> I fill a place, I know't

no uneasy gap separates the rhetorical flight from the 'necessary business of the play'.

The misogynist Timon has broken all human ties, but the natural necessity of hunger still binds him.

TIMON
> That nature, being sick of man's unkindness,
> Should yet be hungry! Common mother, thou,
> Whose womb unmeasurable and infinite breast
> Teems, and feeds all; whose self-same mettle,
> Whereof thy proud child, arrogant man, is puff'd,
> Engenders the black toad and adder blue,
> The gilded newt and eyeless venom'd worm,
> With all the abhorred births below crisp heaven
> Whereon Hyperion's quickening fire doth shine;
> Yield him, who all thy human sons doth hate,
> From forth thy plenteous bosom one poor root!
> Ensear thy fertile and conceptious womb,
> Let it no more bring out ingrateful man!
> Go great with tigers, dragons, wolves and bears;
> Teem with new monsters, whom thy upward face

Hath to the marbled mansion all above
Never presented! O, a root! dear thanks!—
Dry up thy marrows, vines, and plough-torn leas;
Whereof ingrateful man, with liqorish draughts
And morsels unctuous, greases his pure mind,
That from it all consideration slips! . . .

Timon of Athens IV, iii

He prays to nature the 'common mother' of all life for 'one poor root', and adjures her to bring forth no more men. The rhythmic virtuosity of the passage, its vigour and noble sonority—

With all the abhorred births below crisp heaven
Whereon Hyperion's quickening fire doth shine . . .

—mighty lines indeed—need no comment. But it is worth paying close attention to the use of language, typical of the mature Shakespeare, and trying to find out some of the ways in which the extraordinary density of meaning, already remarked on and particularly noteworthy in this passage, is achieved. Perhaps it will be a useful guide if we examine four points: the words puff'd, crisp, and marbled, and the image chain unctuous—greases—slips. First, puff'd: Man, we know has breathed into him the breath of life. Timon says man shares this life-principle, this 'mettle' with the lowest and most repulsive creatures, and yet he is proud and arrogant. 'Puff'd' summarizes and reinforces his meaning with its associations: man is puffed up; puffing is breathing, but breathing in an incompetent, ludicrous manner, like the 'seld-shown flamens' in *Coriolanus* who 'puff to gain a vulgar station'; puffing implies shortness of breath, in itself an image of the insignificant span of life; to pronounce 'puff' is to make a noise expressive of contempt. In a similar way the striking epithet 'crisp' calls up a whole collection of feelings and sensations the very opposite of those associated with the poisonous and slimy 'abhorred births'. 'Marbled' conjures up ideas of remote cold pitiless splendour; and 'greases' forces on us a feeling of physical repulsion for the slippery customer whom Timon hates so much. Man is not content with roots; he must by all means, including violence ('plough-torn') have luxury, feed grossly; and in his selfishness (ingratitude) he ceases to consider, to think about, to ponder on, the true nature of his relation to the world and to other men.

The speech from *Coriolanus* is spare and bony; it states a situation, analyses a character, and draws a conclusion.

AUFIDIUS
All places yield to him ere he sits down;
And the nobility of Rome are his:

The senators and patricians love him too:
The tribunes are no soldiers; and their people
Will be as rash in the repeal, as hasty
To expel him thence. I think he'll be to Rome
As is the osprey to the fish, who takes it
By sovereignty of nature. First he was
A noble servant to them; but he could not
Carry his honours even: whether 'twas pride,
Which out of daily fortune ever taints
The happy man; whether defect of judgement,
To fail in the disposing of those chances
Which he was lord of; or whether nature,
Not to be other than one thing, not moving
From the casque to the cushion, but commanding peace
Even with the same austerity and garb
As he controll'd the war; but one of these—
As he hath spices of them all, not all,
For I dare so far free him—made him fear'd,
So hated, and so banish'd: but he has a merit,
To choke it in the utterance. So our virtues
Lie in the interpretation of the time;
And power, unto itself most commendable,
Hath not a tomb so evident as a chair
To extol what it hath done.

                                        Act IV, Sc. vii

The facts at the beginning are nakedly and curtly set down—the
first three have a line apiece. This is a soldier speaking. The allusion to
the osprey is important. There was believed to be a hierarchy in the
natural order (we still speak of the lion as the king of beasts) so the
osprey taking the fish was acting his right and necessary part in this
order, and the simile expresses Aufidius' belief that Coriolanus is a
sort of force of nature, so the fall of Rome is inevitable. The long
sentence which analyses the hero's weaknesses is brilliantly managed.
Note how the clauses, the sense units, overrun the line endings, and
stop at different points within the line: how pride, judgement, nature
stand out at the end of lines: how emphatic are the three climactic
verbs—feared, hated, banished; how at this point, the conclusion
of the long analytical period, the rhythm runs away from the metrical
norm. The lines

> As he hath spices of them all, not all,
> For I dare so far free him—made him fear'd ...

are regular. The next line,

> So hated, and so banish'd: but he has a merit,

has no less than thirteen syllables. The climax is, of course, 'banish'd';
the conclusion 'but etc.' is Aufidius' wry envious comment on this
man, still a successful rival, though nominally now Aufidius' second
in command, who appears to have some special quality that makes
rational analysis useless. He will succeed, and men will follow him,
whatever defects he may exhibit. The broken rhythm well conveys
the envy Aufidius feels. Extra syllables are frequent in the whole
passage: many lines have weak endings and many sense units conclude
within the line on unaccented syllables:—'honours even', 'which he
was lord of', 'casque to the cushion', 'so hated and so banish'd'.
'Peace' and 'war', important dramatic themes, stick out, on the other
hand, because they fall on the strong beat. The conclusion, about virtue
and power (two other important themes) is nobly elegiac. Up to
now the speech has been in character; we have heard the clipped dry
accents of the soldier summing up a situation. The concluding lines
are choric comment on the nature of power and virtue.

The passage from *Cymbeline* has been chosen as an example of the
strange and complex music of Shakespeare's later blank verse. Its
melody, its exquisite cadences

> ... The bird is dead
> That we have made so much on ...

or

> With fairest flowers,
> Whilst summer lasts, and I live here, Fidele,
> I'll sweeten thy sad grave. ...

must make an immediate effect on any sympathetic reader; what is
not so obvious is its compressed energy.

Re-enter ARVIRAGUS *with* IMOGEN, *as dead, bearing her in his arms.*

BELARIUS
> Look, here he comes,
> And brings the dire occasion in his arms
> Of what we blame him for!

ARVIRAGUS
> The bird is dead
> That we have made so much on. I had rather
> Have skipp'd from sixteen years of age to sixty,
> To have turn'd my leaping-time into a crutch,
> Than have seen this.

GUIDERIUS
> O sweetest, fairest lily!
> My brother wears thee not the one half so well
> As when thou grew'st thyself.

BELARIUS

    O melancholy!
Who ever yet could sound thy bottom? find
The ooze, to show what coast thy sluggish crare
Might easiliest harbour in? Thou blessed thing!
Jove knows what man thou mightst have made; but I
Thou died'st, a most rare boy, of melancholy.
How found you him?

ARVIRAGUS

      Stark, as you see:
Thus smiling, as some fly had tickled slumber,
Not as death's dart, being laugh'd at; his right cheek
Reposing on a cushion.

GUIDERIUS

      Where?

ARVIRAGUS

      O' the floor;
His arms thus leagued: I thought he slept, and put
My clouted brogues from off my feet, whose rudeness
Answer'd my steps too loud.

GUIDERIUS

      Why, he but sleeps:
If he be gone, he'll make his grave a bed;
With female fairies will his tomb be haunted,
And worms will not come to thee.

ARVIRAGUS

      With fairest flowers,
While summer lasts, and I live here, Fidele,
I'll sweeten thy sad grave: thou shalt not lack
The flower that's like thy face, pale primrose, nor
The azured harebell, like thy veins; no, nor
The leaf of eglantine, whom not to slander,
Out-sweeten'd not thy breath: the ruddock would
With charitable bill—O bill, sore shaming
Those rich-left heirs that let their fathers lie
Without a monument!—bring thee all this;
Yea, and furr'd moss besides, when flowers are none,
To winter-ground thy corse.

GUIDERIUS

      Prithee, have done;
And do not play in wench-like words with that
Which is so serious. Let us bury him,
And not protract with admiration what
Is now due debt. To the grave. . . .

              Act IV, Sc. ii

Note that 'skipped' in its normal well-worn sense of leaving something out, brings in 'leaping time' and 'crutch'. If we feel Guiderius' conceit about the lily might perhaps deserve to be called 'wench-like', old Belarius' speech is solid enough. He has known sadness; that Imogen should die is an additional sadness, made more poignant by her grace and youth. The first image is from plumbing the depth; in the depths there is ooze; the crare is a flat bottomed boat used for coastal traffic, that can sail up a creek at high tide and comfortably settle on the mud when the tide recedes. We cannot say when melancholy will come into our lives, or that we have suffered as intensely as it is possible for man to suffer—'Who is it that can say I am at the worst?' The idea is a commonplace, but the images make us feel it anew. How inexplicably right is 'crare';—substitute any other monosyllabic vessel, and the effect is gone. 'Craft' would be the best, because it resembles most closely the sound of 'crare'. Obviously, part of the effect of these lines, and hence part of their total meaning, depends on their sound. This after all is one of the universally accepted character-istics of poetry. But usually when the word 'sound' is used in such a context, it is implied that the sound is 'beautiful', and that it fits the sense as 'echo', and the Tennysonian doves in the immemorial elms are invoked. Relevant considerations here, I would suggest, should include the sort of effort we have to make when we pronounce 'sluggish crare', and 'easiliest', words which convey the sensation of sliding over and settling into the ooze. Equally vividly we are made to feel the simple act of Arviragus taking off his shoes because they are too noisy. The language is not only melodious—'pure poetry' as some call it—it is also alive. The images are not static, they live and proliferate and cause our thoughts and feelings to proliferate too. The pun on bill and the allusion to the rich-left heirs may be regarded as characteristic Renaissance enrichment, an elaborate piece of moralizing ornament; but it has its dramatic point here, for the three persons in this scene live a life of pastoral simplicity, and stand for innocence, and may therefore appropriately compare nature and virtue (the robin) with man's corruption (the rich-left heir). Yet the world of nature has its laws that must be obeyed, and the boys are old enough, and have learned enough from Belisarius to know what those laws are: nothing, perhaps, is more remarkable in this fragment than its stern conclusion, in which feeling is subjugated to duty. Once again we hear how Shakespeare changes his tune to suit his purpose.

We include three samples of Jacobean blank verse. In the first, from *The Alchemist*, Ben Jonson uses it for comedy. The rhythmic line is free and sinuous, closely following the inflections of the dialogue;

yet the basic beat is audible, giving a discipline that prose would lack.

Subtle is the bogus alchemist, 'Captain' Face his agent, the tobacco-seller Drugger one of his gulls. The character they are discussing—the foolish gentleman up from the country—is one of the stock figures in comedy, and his interest in duelling, as we know from *Twelfth Night* and *As You Like It*, was another standard theme for ridicule. It is Subtle's part to seem loath to accept gifts, Face's to screw them out of the customers. Drugger is in love with the foolish gentleman's sister.

FACE
                    What's her brother, a knight?
DRUGGER
    No, sir, a gentleman, newly warm in's land, sir,
    Scarce cold in his one-and-twenty, that does govern
    His sister here; and is a man himself
    Of some three thousand a year, and is come up
    To learn to quarrel and to live by his wits,
    And will go down again, and die i' the country.
FACE
    How! to quarrel?
DRUGGER
                    Yes, sir, to carry quarrels
    As gallants do, and manage 'em by line.
FACE
    'Slid, Nab, the Doctor is the only man
    In Christendom for him! He has made a table,
    With mathematical demonstrations,
    Touching the art of quarrels. He will give him
    An instrument to quarrel by. Go, bring 'em both,
    Him and his sister. And, for thee, with her
    The Doctor haply may persuade. Go to.
    Shalt give his worship a new damask suit
    Upon the premises.
SUBTLE
    O, good Captain!
FACE
                    He shall,
    He is the honestest fellow, Doctor.—Stay not,
    No offers; bring the damask, and the parties.
DRUGGER
    I'll try my power, sir.
FACE
    And thy will too, Nab!

SUBTLE
  'Tis good tobacco, this! What is't an ounce?
FACE
  He'll send you a pound, Doctor.
SUBTLE
  O, no.
FACE
                 He will do't.
  It is the goodest soul.—Abel, about it.
  Thou shalt know more anon. Away, be gone.

                                    Exit DRUGGER

  A miserable rogue, and lives with cheese,
  And has the worms. That was the cause, indeed,
  Why he came now. He dealt with me in private,
  To get a med'cine for 'em.

                                    Act II

We can note how brilliantly Jonson has compressed a complete
biography into six lines in Drugger's first speech, and how much this
compression owes to the images—'newly warm', 'Scarce cold'. Three
things are going on here. First we are given information essential to
the plot; second, Drugger's uncritical factual reporting conveys his
peculiarly silly simple-mindedness; third, the speech creates the character of the gentleman. We seem to see him, his only aim in life to be
a 'roaring boy' for a few years, and then to vegetate on his estates,
like Justice Shallow, telling boring stories of 'the chimes at midnight'.
Jonson's skill is evident in the way he manages Face's short eager
sentences. The eleven-syllabled line is becoming a standard variation;
indeed some writers tend to make it their staple metrical unit. Ending
lines, and sense units within lines, on unaccented syllables ('art of
quarrels', 'and his sister', 'the premises', 'honestest fellow', 'Doctor')
here makes for lightness and speed, the two main characteristics of this
verse. The change when Drugger is gone, and the crooks are alone, is
amusing.

If we compare Lady Allworth's speech from Massinger's *A New
Way to Pay Old Debts* with the King's from *All's Well That Ends Well*,
we can see what a competent practitioner made of blank verse in the
closing years of our great dramatic period. Lines with weak or feminine
endings are frequent; the bombast of earlier verse is thus avoided,
but instead we have a rather limp monotony.

LADY ALLWORTH
  These were your father's words: 'If e'er my son
  Follow the war, tell him it is a school

C

Where all the principles tending to honour
Are taught, if truly followed: but for such
As repair thither, as a place to which
They do presume they may with license practise
Their lusts and riots, they shall never merit
The noble name of soldiers. To dare boldly,
In a fair cause, and for their country's safety,
To run upon the cannon's mouth undaunted;
To obey their leaders, and shun mutinies;
To bear with patience the winter's cold
And summer's scorching heat, and not to faint,
When plenty of provision fails, with hunger;
Are the essential parts make up a soldier,
Not swearing, dice, or drinking.'

                                                      Act I, Sc. ii

The language is clear, but in detail uninteresting. We need only compare

> To run upon the cannon's mouth undaunted . . .

with

> Seeking the bubble reputation
> Even in the cannon's mouth. . . .

or

> To bear with patience the winter's cold
> And summer's scorching heat

with

> Yea, like the stag when snow the pasture sheets,
> The barks of trees thou browsedst . . .

to see the difference. But clarity, dignity and precision Massinger has, and these were to be virtues much prized by later poets.

Here are some line from *Philaster* by Beaumont and Fletcher, produced about 1610. The Princess Arethusa has declared her love for the dispossessed Philaster, and she wonders how, amid the dangers of the court, they may 'devise to hold intelligence'.

Philaster replies that he has a page whom he will send to serve the princess, and carry letters between them. In the following speech he describes how he found him.

> I have a boy,
> Sent by the gods, I hope, to this intent,
> Not yet seen in the court. Hunting the buck,
> I found him sitting by a fountain's side,
> Of which he borrowed some to quench his thirst
> And paid the nymph again as much in tears.

A garland lay him by, made by himself
Of many several flowers bred in the vale,
Stuck in that mystic order that the rareness
Delighted me: but ever when he turned
His tender eyes upon 'em, he would weep,
As if he meant to make 'em grow again.
Seeing such pretty helpless innocence
Dwell in his face, I asked him all his story:
He told me that his parents gentle died,
Leaving him to the mercy of the fields,
Which gave him roots; and of the crystal springs,
Which did not stop their courses; and the sun,
Which still, he thanked him, yielded him his light.
Then took he up his garland, and did show
What every flower, as country people hold,
Did signify, and how all ordered thus,
Expressed his grief; and, to my thoughts, did read
The prettiest lecture of his country-art
That could be wished: so that methought I could
Have studied it. I glady entertained
Him, who was glad to follow; and have got
The trustiest, loving'st, and the gentlest boy
That ever master kept. . . .

Act I, Sc. ii

This is a pretty, pastoral set-piece, self-consciously poetical; the verse is fluent, melodious and lucid. The reader should compare it with Titania's speech in *A Midsummer Night's Dream* Act II, Sc. ii beginning

Set your heart at rest;
The fairy-land buys not the child of me. . . .

with the passage quoted above from *Cymbeline*, beside which it looks pale indeed, and with the Attendant Spirit's lines about the shepherd lad, from *Comus*.

There is much Jacobean dramatic blank verse which is more complex and vital than these passages from Massinger and Beaumont and Fletcher; but the kind of clarity and ease that they command appealed to those writers who later in the century were to make of verse a vehicle for discourse. Dryden admired the verse of Beaumont and Fletcher more than that of any of their contemporaries, because it was courtly and gentlemanlike. We do not have to agree with this judgement, but we should remember it and try to understand why it was made.

3

THE SEVENTEENTH CENTURY

It is customary to refer to one group of poets in the first half of the seventeenth century as Metaphysical. The connotations of this term, which is perhaps more meaningful than some other literary labels, have been neatly summarized by Professor Grierson. 'It lays stress,' he says, 'on the right things ... the more intellectual, less verbal character of their wit compared with the conceits of the Elizabethans; the finer psychology of which their conceits are often the expression; their learned imagery; the argumentative, subtle evolution of their lyrics; above all the peculiar blend of passion and thought, feeling and ratiocination which is their greatest achievement.'

The most important of these poets was John Donne (1573–1631), and I begin by quoting some lines from Thomas Carew's elegy on him, published in the 1633 edition of Donne's poems.

> The Muses garden with Pedantique weedes
> O'rspred, was purg'd by thee; The lazie seeds
> Of servile imitation throwne away,
> And fresh invention planted; Thou didst pay
> The debts of our penurious bankrupt age;
> Licentious thefts, that make poetique rage
> A Mimique fury, when our soules must bee
> Possest, or with Anacreons Extasie,
> Or Pindars, not their owne; The subtle cheat
> Of slie Exchanges, and the jugling feat
> Of two-edged words, or whatsoever wrong
> By ours was done the Greeke, or Latine tongue,
> Thou hast redeem'd, and open'd Us a Mine
> Of rich and pregnant phansie, drawne a line
> Of masculine expression, which had good
> Old Orpheus seene, Or all the ancient Brood
> Our superstitious fooles admire, and hold
> Their lead more precious, then thy burnish't Gold,
> Thou hadst beene their Exchequer, and no more
> They each in others dust had rak'd for Ore.
> Thou shalt yield no precedence, but of time,
> And the blinde fate of language, whose tun'd chime
> More charmes the outward sense; Yet thou maist claime
> From so great disadvantage greater fame,

> Since to the awe of thy imperious wit
> Our stubborne language bends, made only fit
> With her tough-thick-rib'd hoopes to gird about
> Thy Giant phansie, which had prov'd too stout
> For their soft melting Phrases.

This is what an intelligent contemporary thought of Donne's achievement. He sees him as a clearer of litter, a sweeper away of classical allusions, classical conventions, all the more slavish borrowings with which the Renaissance poets decorated their works. The lines about the two-edged words refer to the Elizabethan delight in puns and jingles; next, clumsy neologisms are attacked; Donne is praised for writing English, and his English is praised for being greater than Greek or Latin. Carew is here expressing the kind of literary patriotism which Jonson vaunted in his lines, quoted below, on Shakespeare. Greek and Latin may be more melodious, but melody charms the 'outward sense'; and moreover only English, tough, harsh and stubborn, is a fitting medium for such genius as Donne's. The very qualities of the language which humanists might condemn, turn out to be its chiefest virtues.

These lines are themselves 'metaphysical' in their combination of thought and feeling expressed through conceits. Carew is arguing, discussing, thinking; his poem is at once a work of criticism, of appraisal, of eulogy. Indeed, so well has he expounded his subject's virtues that later comment can do little but explain, expand and illustrate his points. His deep feeling informs the verse with its vigour, for this is no conventional elegy: the poet's admiration for his master burns in the poem.

Before we go on to examine some of Donne's poems, we might look at the structure of these couplets, and compare them with Jonson's, with Donne's own, with Spenser's earlier and Dryden's later ones. They lack a 'tun'd chime', and they are not always easy to follow. It is an alert and practised reader who wholly grasps, first time, the full significance of the sentence which begins

> The subtle cheat
> Of slie Exchanges. . . .

and ends

> They each in others dust had rak'd for Ore.

Dryden would have tidied this up; but the Metaphysical poets expected vigilance: they open a mine, and leave the reader to do his own digging.

The first of Donne's poems I want to examine is the fifth of the

Elegies, *His Picture*, probably written in the last decade of the sixteenth century.

ELEGIE V—HIS PICTURE

Here, take my Picture; though I bid farewell,
Thine, in my heart, where my soule dwels, shall dwell.
'Tis like me now, but I dead, 'twill be more
When wee are shadowes both, than 'twas before.
When weather-beaten I come backe; my hand,
Perhaps with rude oares torne, or Sun beams tann'd,
My face and brest of hairecloth, and my head
With cares rash sodaine stormes, being o'rspread,
My body'a sack of bones, broken within,
And powders blew staines scatter'd on my skinne;
If rivall fooles taxe thee to'have lov'd a man,
So foule, and course, as, Oh, I may seeme than,
This shall say what I was: and thou shalt say,
Doe his hurts reach mee? doth my worth decay?
Or doe they reach his judging minde, that hee
Should now love lesse, what hee did love to see?
That which in him was faire and delicate,
Was but the milke, which in loves childish state
Did nurse it: who now is growne strong enough
To feed on that, which to disus'd tasts seemes tough.

Note, to begin with, the 'real-life' situation. The poet is going away—perhaps to join the Cadiz expedition of 1596–1597—an overseas posting, we might say, and he gives his beloved a picture to remember him by. Nevertheless, this is not a simple poem, but one which holds and balances many conflicting emotions and attitudes. It begins abruptly—

Here, take my Picture. . . .

The poet's feelings burst forth; he cannot stay for formality, or even for common politeness. In both the literary and the social sense this is an 'unconventional' poem. Then the poet implies that though the lady needs a picture to remind her of her lover, he (because the male is worthier than the female?) doesn't need a picture of her, because her image is engraved in his heart 'where his soul dwells', and his love is not dependent on anything physical. Next comes a wry and harsh allusion to death, to the fact that he may not return. The picture resembles him. It is a good 'likeness'; yet is not reality, but a 'shadow'; therefore, if he is dead, and becomes a 'shade' it will resemble him still more. A poem of sentiment does not exclude wit—and macabre wit at that.

Then he compares what he may be when he returns with what the picture represents him to be now. The grammar of the next sentence is:

'When . . . I come back'—the worse for wear, and other girls ask what you can see in me—'this'—the picture—'shall say what I was'. The vivid evocation of perils and suffering—note the energy of

> My body'a sack of bones, broken within,
> And powders blew staines scatter'd on my skinne;

is horrifyingly real, but we also feel that the poet is ironically asking for sympathy, and we are pulled up short by the 'rival fooles'. They are his sweetheart's girl friends, imagined tittering at the strange, batterd bearded figure that he 'may be then', and wondering what she finds attractive in him. He tells her what to say in reply. She can point to the picture and prove by its means that she fell in love with 'as proper a man as ever went on neat's leather'. She is untouched by the damage time and danger have done to him; her worth remains the same. Moreover—and here is the keystone of the poem—his mind is unchanged, though his body may be, and his love for her is in his judging mind, not his body. A child is fed first on milk, then weaned and given solids. So love, in its childish state, feeds on beauty. But the love of the poet and the lady is no longer childish, no longer needs to nourish itself on beauty, though the returned poet may now seem too tough a morsel for the immature tastes of the 'rival fooles', who are 'disus'd' (unaccustomed) to such a diet. The wit does not exclude seriousness. The hurried harsh energy of the verse echoes and enforces the feeling of the poem, and the last line, so difficult to pronounce, embodies in its awkwardness the difficulty the 'rival fooles' have in chewing the tough sailor.

Our next example is another love poem; we might call it a love lyric, but it is far removed from the warbling simplicity of most Elizabethan words for music.

A VALEDICTION: FORBIDDING MOURNING

> As virtuous men passe mildly away,
>   And whisper to their souls to go,
> While some of their sad friends do say
>   The breath goes now, and some say, no:
>
> So let us melt, and make no noise,
>   No teare-floods, nor sigh-tempests move;
> 'Twere profanation of our joyes
>   To tell the layetie our love.

Moving of th'earth brings harmes and feares;
   Men reckon what it did and meant,
But trepidation of the spheares,
   Though greater farre, is innocent.

Dull sublunary lovers love
   (Whose soule is sense) cannot admit
Absence, because it doth remove
   Those things which elemented it.

But we by a love, so much refin'd,
   That ourselves know not what it is,
Inter-assured of the mind,
   Care lesse eyes, lips, and hands to misse.

Our two soules therefore, which are one,
   Though I must goe, endure not yet
A breach, but an expansion,
   Like gold to ayery thinnesse beate.

If they be two, they are two so
   As stiffe twin compasses are two;
Thy soule the fixt foot, makes no show
   To move, but doth, if the'other doe.

And though it in the center sit,
   Yet when the other far doth rome,
It leanes, and hearkens after it,
   And growes erect, as that comes home.

Such wilt thou be to mee, who must
   Like th'other foot, obliquely runne;
Thy firmnes makes my circle just,
   And makes me end where I begunne.

Once more the poet bids his love farewell, but his tone here is
gentler, and there is no hint of mockery. He uses a four-line stanza,
the lines rhyming alternately, with commanding expertise. We feel,
when we read Donne, that the basic rhythms of English verse, its
main metrical patterns, are now known and established and present
no difficulty, so that the poet is free to vary them, to experiment,
to speak through them. Verse has other pleasures besides those of
incantation.

The best way into this poem is probably to examine its imagery.
First, an image of death, for parting is a kind of death. The virtuous

man is calm, he has the confidence of faith, no agonizing struggles, he whispers to his soul, and so peaceful is his parting that friends cannot tell the moment of death. Notice how Donne dramatizes this scene, in the speeches of the friends. As the virtuous man's soul parts from his body, so should the lovers part from each other. There must be no cataclysm of grief—no floods or tempests. The laity—those who do not know what true love is—must not be made aware of what is happening, for this would profane the lovers' relationship, which is, as the sequence of images implies, sacred.

The next stanza illustrates what Dr. Johnson meant when he spoke of images being 'yoked violently together'. What have earthquakes and the movement of the spheres to do with parting lovers? The former are, like floods and tempests, disturbances in the natural order, and they were thought to be evidences of God's wrath, which is why men inquire into their meaning, as well as calculate the damage done. The spheres, in which, according to the old astronomy, the sun, planets and stars were fixed, are heavenly. (The moon's sphere was nearest the earth and the fall of man corrupted only 'sublunary' things.) These concentric spheres were first supposed to rotate on a single axis, an imaginary extension of the poles; then, to account for the movements of the planets and the precession of the equinoxes, deviations from concentric motion, or 'trepidations', were imagined. Such 'trepidations' are, of course, immensely more powerful than any mere disturbance of the earth's surface, but since they are part of the heavenly order, they are 'innocent'. The poet's love, greater than that of ordinary mortals, is both celestial and innocent, and, as the next stanza, which is figuratively tied to the preceding one by the epithet 'sublunary', makes quite clear, the love that the poem celebrates is not dependent on the body; it is not made of earthly 'elements'. So mysterious is its power 'that we ourselves know not what it is'; yet the mystery is secure—the lovers are assured of it.

Now come two stanzas in which two more 'unpoetic' images are yoked to reinforce this conclusion, the first from the craft of the gold-beater, the second from the use of compasses, an instrument indispensable to the mathematician, the astronomer, the navigator, a symbol of the new learning, and one capable of constructing the perfect figure, the circle, emblem of eternity.

Gold is the most precious of metals, and therefore apt to represent the poet's most precious love: it is also the most ductile, and therefore can be beaten thinner without disintegrating (to make gold leaf) than any other metal. So though the lovers are separated in space, their love is unbroken, and never can be broken, since it is, so to speak, infinitely ductile. The simile of the compasses is easy to follow. We speak of a pair of compasses, yet the pair is one thing, and so the two lovers are really one. The poet must travel, his beloved must stay at home. She controls him, however distant he may be, she is his centre, and is the cause of that perfection in his life which is symbolized by the circle.

It is customary to call such ingeniously worked out analogies 'conceits'. They form the substance of much metaphysical poetry, and the instructed reader got pleasure from working them out. Dr. Johnson's famous remark about these poets is relevant here: 'If their conceits were far-fetched, they were often worth the carriage'; and the reader must decide for himself their value.

They are apparent in another poem,

A VALEDICTION: OF WEEPING

Let me powre forth
My teares before thy face, whil'st I stay here,
For thy face coines them, and thy stampe they beare,
And by this Mintage they are something worth,
For thus they bee
Pregnant of thee;
Fruits of much griefe they are, emblemes of more,
When a tear falls, that thou falls which it bore,
So thou and I are nothing then, when on a divers shore.

On a round ball
A workeman that hath copies by, can lay
An Europe, Afrique, and an Asia,
And quickly make that, which was nothing, *All*,
So doth each teare,
Which thee doth weare,
A globe, yea world by that impression grow,
Till thy teares mixt with mine doe overflow
This world, by waters sent from thee, my heaven dissolved so.

O more then Moone,
Draw not up seas to drowne me in thy spheare,
Weepe me not dead, in thine armes, but forbeare
To teach the sea, what it may doe too soone;
Let not the winde
Example finde,
To doe me more harme, then it purposeth;
Since thou and I sigh one anothers breath,
Who e'r sighes most, is cruellest, and hasts the others death.

The poem is remarkable for its rhythmic subtlety, and much of its effect depends upon the tension between the formal stanza pattern and the emotion which struggles within it. The poet begs to be allowed to give way to tears while he is still in his mistress' presence and offers 'witty' reasons for a display which might be considered unmanly, but which he is powerless to resist. 'Powre forth' is no mere hyperbole; it is an image of relentless power. As he gazes, weeping, at his mistress, each tear that he sheds bears her reflection, her image, and this it is that gives the tears their value, as the king's head makes the genuine coin. Her image makes the tears 'pregnant'—gives them life and meaning. They are the results of the grief of parting, and they symbolize the greater grief of separation. When they splash on the ground the image is destroyed; so the lovers, who together make up a world, become nothing when they are separated. The stanza moves from the uninhibited passionate opening, through the ingenuity of the conceits to the bleak bareness of the last line.

The tears are spherical. The geometrical figure is in itself nothing, like the figure nought. Cover it with maps, and it becomes a terrestrial globe, an image of the world, or of everything. So the tear bearing the beloved's reflection becomes an emblem of their love, which is the world they live in. When she weeps too, the tears become a flood to destroy that world. He begs her, who has more power over the sea, for their love is a supernatural power, not subject to the corruptions that infect all sublunary things, to cease weeping and sighing. He recalls to himself and to her the real waves and winds which may threaten him on his travels. Do not, he says, remind Nature of her destructive powers. And sighs were believed to exhale a part of the animal spirits, and thus shorten life:

> When thou sigh'st thou sigh'st not winde,
> But sigh'st my soule away. . . .

So the lovers must contain their grief, be stoical.

That the poem is brilliantly ingenious is evident; but its true force lies in its unity, in the ordering of incantation, dramatic urgency, wit, fantasy, passion and reality within its chosen form.

In 1610, Elizabeth, the daughter of Donne's kind patron Sir Robert Drury, died at the age of fourteen. The poet composed a *Funerall Elegie* and then in 1611 wrote another poem in her praise, entitled *An Anatomie of The World, The First Anniversary*; in 1612 there followed *Of the Progress of the Soule, The Second Anniversary*. 'Verse' wrote the poet in the concluding couplet of the first of these tributes, 'hath a middle nature: Heaven keepes Soules, the grave keepes bodies, Verse

the Fame enroules'; lines which express one of the functions of the
Renaissance poet. But no single 'fame', still less that of a child of fourteen, could justify a series of annual lamentations. We do not know
whether Donne intended such a series; we do know that his contemporaries found the poems out of proportion, and that Ben Jonson said
'if it had been write of the Virgin Mary it had been something' to
which Donne's reply was 'that he described the Idea of a Woman,
and not as she was.' The poems interest us because in them we see
Donne's acute, tortured mind pondering and puzzling over the state of
the world around him, and his own relation to it and to its Creator.
The term 'anatomy' means a dissection, and also a skeleton: so the
poem dissects the world to show the bony truth beneath fleshly
appearances. The tributes to the dead girl form a kind of standard of
virtue and harmony against which the corruptions of society are
measured.

If we compare the passages I quote with those from Dryden's
Religio Laici and *The Hind and the Panther* we can see that Dryden's
poems are really directions for social and political action; or directions
for obtaining that state of mind from which rational political and
social actions may flow. Donne, on the other hand, exhorts individual
readers to seek the truth, that they may be saved; he turns from the
new philosophy to religion. Dryden sees no incompatibility between
them—he accepts a compromise. The contrast in views can be heard in
the very tone and tune of the verse the two men write. I go into this
detail because I want the reader to feel that style is not an ornament,
but the product of a complex of social and personal relationships.

First some lines from the *Funerall Elegie*

> The world containes
> Princes for armes, and Counsellors for braines,
> Lawyers for tongues, Divines for hearts, and more,
> The Rich for stomackes, and for backes, the Poore;
> The Officers for hands, Merchants for feet,
> By which, remote and distant Countries meet.
> But those fine spirits which do tune, and set
> This Organ, are those peeces which beget
> Wonder and love . . .

Here is the social order, the body politic, of which all classes are
members—an everyday figure, but in Donne a vital one. (We may
compare the fable of the body and its members told by Menenius
at the beginning of *Coriolanus*.) Notice how packed is the complex
of thought and feeling; how we are made to regard the rich with

contempt and the poor with pity; how the increasing importance of
trade in this age is implied. Notice, too, the characteristic pun on
'organ', and how this pun drives home the point of the passage, that
it is the quality of the soul that gives value to the body. The ambiguous
term 'peeces' obviously refers to more than the 'piece of virtue' who
was the ostensible theme of the poem. Such 'peeces' are of course saints;
but also, surely, any admirable production of man's spirit, including,
perhaps, this poem. So 'wonder and love' are the values Donne would
have govern the world. Dryden's views are more lucid, certainly more
practical, but they are workaday beside Donne's.

The next passage shows Donne persuading his reader to turn from
the new Baconian science, with its emphasis on the evidence of the
senses, to the revelations of religion.

> Poore soule, in this thy flesh what does thou know?
> Thou know'st thy selfe so little, as thou know'st not,
> How thou didst die, nor how thou wast begot.
> Thou neither know'st, how thou at first cam'st in,
> Nor how thou took'st the poyson of mans sinne.
> Nor dost thou (though thou know'st, that thou art so)
> By what way thou art made immortall, know.
> Thou are too narrow, wretch, to comprehend
> Even thy selfe: yea though thou wouldst but bend
> To know thy body. Have not all soules thought
> For many ages, that our body'is wrought
> Of Ayre, and Fire, and other Elements?
> And now they thinke of new ingredients,
> And one Soule thinkes one, and another way
> Another thinkes, and 'tis an even lay.
> Knowst thou but how the stone doth enter in
> The bladders cave, and never break the skinne?
> Knowst thou how blood, which to the heart doth flow,
> Doth from one ventricle to th'other goe?
> And for the putrid stuffe, which thou dost spit,
> Knowst thou how thy lungs have attracted it?
> There are no passages, so that there is
> (For ought thou know'st) piercing of substances.
> And of those many opinions which men raise
> Of Nailes and Haires, doest thou know which to praise?
> What hope have we to know ourselves, when wee
> Know not the least things, which for our use be?
> Wee see in Authors, too stiffe to recant
> A hundred controversies of an Ant;
> And yet one watches, starves, freeses, and sweats,
> To know but Catechismes and Alphabets

Of unconcerning things, matters of fact;
How others on our stage their parts did Act;
What *Caesar* did, yea, and what *Cicero* said.
Why grasse is greene, or why our blood is red,
Are mysteries which none have reached unto.
In this low forme, poore soule, what wilt thou do?
When wilt thou shake off this Pedantery,
Of being taught by sense, and Fantasie?
Thou look'st through spectacles; small things seeme great
Below; but up into the watch-towre get,
And see all things despoyl'd of fallacies:
Thou shalt not peepe through lattices of eyes,
Nor heare through Labyrinths of eares, nor learne
By circuit, or collections to discerne.
In heaven thou straight know'st all, concerning it,
And what concerns it not, shalt straight forget.

From *The Second Anniversary*

The poet exhorts us to realize our ignorance of ourselves and of the world around us. Again, a philosophical platitude, but one which Donne quickens; he 'proves' in Keats' phrase 'philosophy upon our pulses'. The 'poyson of mans sin' is Adam's, the theologian's 'original sin'. We move on from the soul, sin and immortality, to the physical structure of the body. Old ideas are compared with new, and the confusion of the new is mocked by such phrases as ' 'tis an even lay'. The whole of this passage illustrates Donne's command of colloquial idiom, and the ease with which he moves from intense formal rhetoric to common speech reminds us of Shakespeare. In his youth Donne was a great frequenter of plays and the influence of dramatic verse is strong in his poetry. It is characteristic of him that he spares us none of the horrors of physical existence; equally characteristic both of the poet and his period is the *mélange* of medieval and modern scientific ideas. Problems about the piercing of substances, and nails and hair (they are inanimate and yet they grow) jostle with queries about the circulation of the blood. Next, the fact-finding scientist, and the pedantic humanist historian are both ridiculed; and, in conclusion, the soul is told to reject the teaching of the senses, and of 'Fantasie', which here means imaginative speculation—the word carries as well overtones of nonsense, deception and falsehood. We must try and perceive things not through eyes and ears (compare Marvell's *Dialogue between the Soul and Body*) but get up into the watch tower—take, as far as we can, God's eye view of things: the truth is to be found in revelation.

We may term all this reactionary. History, we may say, was on the

side of science. But such objections are of doubtful relevance. Donne
states what he believes to be a truth about man. We may put the poet
neatly in his historical pigeon-hole; we may 'place' his theology and
his science, and share neither: but the truth remains, and the truth is
uncomfortable.

We have discussed the 'heroic couplet' and recommended the reader
to observe the different tunes which different periods produce in this
pattern. A more detailed analysis of some of these lines may be helpful.
Start at

> Wee see in Authors, too stiffe to recant,

(too pig-headed to admit they are wrong)

> An hundred controversies of an Ant;

(man's reason is incompetent to reveal the truth of even the most
insignificant of beings).

Here the couplet is complete in itself; but the next sentence spreads
over five lines. In the first,

> And yet one watches[1], starves, freeses and sweats

the vigour comes from the way the main stresses are made to fall on
the verbs; 'freezes' hits us with especial force because the stress is
inverted. The metre leads us to expect ti pom, and instead we get pom
ti. Donne is here doing what Jonson accused him of—'not keeping
of accent'—but the distortion justifies itself: to make the line scan would
destroy its power. The light rhyme sweats/Alphabets, and the syntax
hurry us on to the point of the passage, that all these are 'unconcerning
things, matters of fact', and we should feel here the poet's contempt
for fact—the full conclusive rhyme underlines it. We may note in
passing the implication of Catechisms and Alphabets, both elementary
systems, beginnings—letters, for example, are of no importance in
themselves—and the general feeling is of childishness and incompetence. Then follow—the sentence has not finished yet—examples
of matters of fact, and with some shock the reader finds history, in
particular the history of antiquity, so much beloved by the Renaissance,
derided. Caesar and Cicero are classed with the ant.

All writers of verse, at any rate all writers of long discursive poems,
rearrange the syntax sometimes, in the interests of scansion or rhyme.
It was one of the aims of later poets to avoid such lines as

> How others on our stage their parts did act

[1] Keeps awake

(instead of did act their parts); but the simplicity and directness of

> What *Caesar* did, yea, and what *Cicero* said.
> Why grasse is greene, or why our blood is red. . . .

is precisely the sort of thing that Dryden exploited. What he would never have done is to split the two rhyming lines, allowing the first to end one argument and the second to begin another. The urgency of Donne's verse in part depends on this play of sense unit against the couplet; Dryden makes sense and couplet work together. We can compare these couplets with those by Spenser and Ben Jonson.

Paradox, wit, the animated and passionate play of intelligence are equally apparent in Donne's religious poetry. Here is *Good Friday, 1613. Riding Westward*. The poem is constructed upon a conceit: The Crucifixion took place in the East. I am riding westward, and so have turned my back on my Redeemer. But I am too great a sinner to face Him. I turn my back that I may be scourged ('whom He loveth He chasteneth') and made fit to 'turne my face'.

> Let mans Soule be a Spheare, and then, in this,
> The intelligence that moves, devotion is,
> And as the other Spheares, by being growne
> Subject to forraigne motions, lose their owne,
> And being by others hurried every day,
> Scarce in a yeare their naturall forme obey:
> Pleasure or business, so, our Soules admit
> For their first mover, and are whirld by it.
> Hence is't, that I am carryed towards the West
> This day, when my Soules forme bends toward the East.
> There I should see a Sunne, by rising set,
> And by that setting endlesse day beget;
> But that Christ on this Crosse, did rise and fall
> Sinne had eternally benighted all.
> Yet dare I'almost be glad, I do not see
> That spectacle of too much weight for mee.
> Who sees Gods face, that is selfe life, must dye;
> What a death were it then to see God Dye?
> It made his owne Lieutenant Nature shrinke,
> It made his footstoole crack, and the Sunne winke.
> Could I behold those hands which span the Poles,
> And turne all spheares at once, peirc'd with those holes?
> Could I behold that endlesse height which is
> Zenith to us, and our Antipodes
> Humbled below us? or that blood which is
> The seat of all our Soules, if not of his,
> Made durt of dust, or that flesh which was worne

By God, for his apparell, rag'd, and torne?
If on these things I durst not looke, durst I
Upon his miserable mother cast mine eye,
Who was Gods partner here, and furnish'd thus
Halfe of that Sacrifice, which ransom'd us?
Though these things, as I ride, be from mine eye,
They'are present yet unto my memory,
For that looks towards them; and thou look'st towards mee,
O Saviour, as thou hang'st upon the tree;
I turne my backe to thee, but to receive
Corrections, till thy mercies bid thee leave.
O thinke mee worth thine anger, punish mee,
Burne off my rusts, and my deformity,
Restore thine Image, so much, by thy grace,
That thou may'st know mee, and I'll turne my face.

The poem's bare Euclidean beginning is intended, as so often in
Donne, to puzzle us into attention. What can be the connection
between Good Friday and geometry? In the old cosmology the
spheres were supposed to be moved by intelligences or angels. Each
sphere, in moving, affected others, so their motions were occasionally
eccentric, and this accounted for the movements of the planets, or
wandering stars. So our souls are driven by pleasure or business to
irregular paths: truly perfect motion would be directed by God. On
this day the poet's 'natural motion' should turn him towards the East,
but business takes him in the opposite direction. Note the speed and
clarity of these opening couplets. We are 'hurried' and 'whirl'd'
through the argument in a sentence of eight lines; the ninth and tenth
sum up. The imperfect West/East rhyme echoes the imperfection of
the universe, and its inhabitants, and the poet; the placing of 'This
day' at the beginning of the tenth line brings us back to the theme of
the poem—Good Friday.

There follows a meditation on this theme, a string of paradoxes, puns,
conceits, informed by intense feeling. The Sunne/Son rises in the East—
Christ is 'lifted up' on the cross. His rising is His setting, because He dies,
but His death or setting begets endless day because it destroys death in
whose darkness mankind would otherwise have been benighted. Note
how many ideas and feelings are 'yoked together' by the rise—set, rise
—fall, day—night paradoxes; how much is said in how small a space.

The poet next reflects on his own state of sin which unfits him to
contemplate the Crucifixion. No man (not even Moses) can see the
living God and live; to see God die must therefore be an unimaginably
intense kind of death. These lines are monosyllabic, as are many others
in the poem, and the simple, beating words contrast dramatically with

the elaboration of the conceits. In the next two lines we must remember that wink means to blink, to shut both eyes. Donne is recalling the Gospel story: 'There was darkness over all the land . . . the earth did quake and the rocks rent'. Nature is called God's lieutenant because the powers of Nature carry out God's will; the earth is His footstool.

Then comes a contrast between the infinite powers of God, and His Humanity. God's hands span the poles—He created the universe and moves it; God's greatness makes meaningless our petty measurements of Zenith and Antipodes; yet this Being is tortured and dies. The blood is the seat of the soul because the soul dwells in the body. God was man and therefore could shed blood; but as He is God, that blood was not the seat of His soul. Yet His blood is the seat of all our souls since by it we are redeemed. The presence of the Virgin brings in again the theme of humanity, and helps to make of this whole passage a picture. Donne is creating a verbal counterpart to the painted and carved Crucifixions which play so large a part in Christian art and iconography.

Now the poem moves towards its conclusion. The poet's bodily eyes face westwards, but his mind's eye turns towards the East; and then comes the thought, implicit in the basic conceit of 'riding westward', that the Redeemer's face is towards the poet, who begs for correction, in the double meaning of putting to rights and punishing. In him the image of God is deformed and corrupt. God's grace only can make him worthy to be acknowledged by God, worthy to turn his face.

Next, one of the sixteen *Holy Sonnets*.

> Death, be not proud, though some have called thee
> Mighty and dreadfull, for, thou art not so;
> For, those, whom thou thinkst, thou dost overthrow,
> Die not, poore Death, nor yet canst thou kill me.
> From rest and sleepe, which but thy picture bee,
> Much pleasure, then from thee, much more must flow,
> And soonest our best men with thee do go,
> Rest of their bones, and soul's deliverie.
> Thou'rt slave to Fate, Chance, kings, and desperate men,
> And dost with poyson, warre, and sicknesse dwell,
> And poppie, or charmes can make us sleepe as well,
> And better than thy stroake; why swell'st thou then?
> One short sleep past, we wake eternally,
> And death shall be no more; death, thou shalt die.

The theme is simple—'O Death, where is thy sting?' The language is plain, the tone assured and full of energy. This is a lively poem about death, and a simple, calm denial 'for thou art not so' establishes its feeling. We meet again the theme of death and sleep, of the picture and reality. As sleep refreshes us, and delivers us from life, so does death. Death has no power in himself; we die when it is our fate to do so, or by accident, or through the exercise of arbitrary power, or we are murdered. Death, so to speak, 'lives' in bad and miserable company. Drugs, or what, I suppose, we should now call hypnosis, are more efficient than he. The whole trend of these images is to cut death down to size; 'why swellst thou then?' repeats the theme of the first lines of the sonnet. In the concluding couplet only one word— eternally—is not a monosyllable; the meaning is hammered into us, an effect at least partly due to the effort we must make if we are to enunciate the words with their awkward combinations of consonants. 'One short sleep past' is not easy to say, and neither are the two th's in De*th, *thou. . . . As we have seen, this sacrifice of mellifluousness to energy caused some readers to condemn Donne's verse as harsh; yet were it not for this crude colloquial force the latinate 'eternally' would not soar as serenely as it does; nor would the elegiac cadence of

> Rest of their bones and soul's delivery

resound so nobly. It is this dramatic control over movement and tone, here exhibited within 'the sonnet's narrow plot of ground', which gives Donne's verse its range and power.

Next another religious poem, George Herbert's *The Windows*. Herbert (1593–1633) rejected a court career to become (not without a struggle) a country parson. His poetry is a kind of diary of his religious life.

> Lord, how can man preach thy eternall word?
>   He is a brittle crazy glasse:
> Yet in thy temple thou dost him afford
>   This glorious and transcendent place,
>   To be a window, through thy grace.
>
> But when thou dost anneal in glasse thy storie,
>   Making thy life to shine within
> The holy Preacher's; then the light and glorie
>   More rev'rend grows, and more doth win;
>   Which else shows watrish, bleak and thin.
>
> Doctrine and life, colours and light, in one
>   When they combine and mingle, bring
> A strong regard and aw: but speech alone
>   Doth vanish like a flaring thing,
>   And in the eare, not conscience ring.

Here again is the metaphysical conceit ingeniously worked out. Man is imperfect—as fragile and easily broken as glass. Yet, by the grace of God he can become a window through which the glory of

God shines, as the window transmits the sunlight. We feel here, as we do in the Donne elegy, the dramatic reality of the scene. The priest is in the church, meditating on his own unworthiness. The windows which give him his metaphor are real windows, and these windows may tell in stained glass the story of Christ: so may the preacher's life be an imitation of Christ. Note that the colour gets into the glass by the process of annealing—through intense heat, symbolizing the suffering of Christ, and of the preacher, his servant. The transmission of God's teaching may, like sunlight through plain glass, be 'watrish, bleak and thin'; but if practice accords with precept (we remember Chaucer's parson—'first he wrought and afterwards he taught'), if the preacher's life is as it were an image of his doctrine, his living words will move the consciences of his congregation, not merely go in at one ear and out at the other.

As with Donne, there is an extraordinary concentration of meaning in a small space, and, within the formal metrical scheme, an easy telling movement of colloquial freedom. We hear the poet's voice. The first line is particularly interesting. Plain, simple, dramatic, it is, to use Herbert's own phrase, a 'pious ejaculation'. It exploits one of the commonest characteristics of spoken English—the way in which meaning varies with emphasis or intonation. For example, such a sentence as 'I saw him' can imply three different shades of meaning according to which word we stress. So

> Lord, how can man preach thy eternall word . . .

can carry three meanings according to whether we stress how, can, or man. In fact this complexity (whether it is explicit or not in our consciousness) makes us give equal stresses to the first four words. By the simplest, yet subtlest, means, the poet varies the basic iambic rhythm.

Herbert's verse exhibits not only metaphysical ingenuity, but vivid drama and a limpid music. In the next poem, *Jordan*, he rejects the conventions of pastoral, and the elaboration of much late sixteenth-century writing. We can compare the sonnet by Sydney, and the Shakespeare sonnet which begins 'My mistress eyes are nothing like the sun,' but Herbert's poem is more serious than these, and his themes are more than literary.

JORDAN

> Who says that fictions only and false hair
> Become a verse? Is there in truth no beautie?
> Is all good structure in a winding stair?
> May no lines passe, except they do their dutie
>   Not to a true, but painted chair?

Is it no verse, except enchanted groves
And sudden arbours shadow course-spunne lines?
Must purling streams refresh a lovers loves?
Must all be vail'd, while he that reades, divines,
    Catching the sense at two removes?

Shepherds are honest people; let them sing:
Riddle who list, for me, and pull for Prime:
I envie no mans nightingale or spring;
Nor let them punish me with losse of ryme,
    Who plainly say, *My God, My King.*

The title refers to Naaman, who when told he could be cured of his leprosy by washing in the Jordan, replied haughtily, 'Are not Abbana and Pharpar, rivers of Assyria, better than all the waters of Israel?' To wash in Jordan is therefore to accept the true God and reject the false; to find redemption through the humble and local rather than the exotic; in Herbert's case, to become a parish priest and reject a worldly career.

The poem begins with a series of blunt commonsensical questions. Fictions are not true; false hair creates false beauty, and truth needs no such adornments. The second question, so plain in appearance, reverberates with problems going back to Plato, who excluded poets from his Republic. It is more difficult to construct a spiral staircase than a straight one, but the straight one may be Jacob's ladder. The 'painted chair' is a throne, symbol of kingship, and bowed to even when the king is not sitting on it. 'Wee here obey', wrote Donne, 'The statecloth where the Prince sate yesterday'. But this is a false, not a true chair, whose worshippers are making obeisance to a worldly, not a heavenly, king. 'My God, My King' in the last line of the poem looks back to this 'painted chair' and clinches with finality the poet's expression of his faith. The second stanza, still in question form, ridicules the clichés of fashionable verse, hinting that the poetasters seek to conceal defective technique (course-spunne lines) by using the accepted terms, and its last two lines attack the deliberate obscurity of minor metaphysical practitioners. All this gives force to 'Shepherds are honest people; let them sing. . . .' Singing is a spontaneous simple expression of feeling; the shepherd is both poet and priest; the poet 'sings' as the shepherd King David sang, to the Lord. 'Sing' is here opposed to 'riddling', and Herbert is here using for his own purpose, which is devotional, Jonsonian critical ideas. Shepherds are honest, and honesty tells plain truth; they are people—'men speaking to men', in Wordsworth's phrase. The simply 'honest' statement about shepherds carries therefore a great weight of meaning, partly because it is in the very convention—the pastoral convention—against whose decadence the poem is a protest. Other people can be modishly obscure, other people can compete for fame. The nightingale and the spring are two common poetic properties the poet proposes to do without; they also imply that he rejects the world and accepts his vocation.

So this is a dexterous and complicated poem in praise of simplicity; yet it communicates a profound and plain conviction of the truth of the poet's feelings, and it does this through his control of tone and melody. The poem creates the beauty in which there is truth.

The last poem of Herbert's which we shall quote exhibits the same drama, poignancy, melody and control characteristic of this great poet's work.

THE COLLAR

I struck the board, and cry'd, No more.
    I will abroad.
What? shall I ever sigh and pine?
My lines and life are free; free as the rode,
Loose as the winde, as large as store.
     Shall I be still in suit?
Have I no harvest but a thorn
To let me bloud, and not restore
What I have lost with cordiall fruit?
     Sure there was wine
Before my sighs did drie it: there was corn
  Before my tears did drown it.
Is the yeare onely lost to me?
  Have I no bayes to crown it?
No flowers, no garlands gay? all blasted?
    All wasted?
Not so, my heart: but there is fruit,
    And thou hast hands.
Recover all thy sigh-blown age
On double pleasures: leave thy cold dispute
Of what is fit, and not; forsake thy cage,
    Thy rope of sands,
Which pettie thoughts have made, and make to thee
  Good cable, to enforce and draw,
    And be thy law,
While thou didst wink and wouldst not see.
    Away; take heed:
    I will abroad.

> Call in thy death's head there: tie up thy fears.
> He that forbears
> To suit and serve his need,
> Deserves his load.
> But as I rav'd and grew more fierce and wilde
> At every word,
> Me thoughts I heard one calling, *Childe:*
> And I reply'd, *My Lord.*

There was another influence at work in English verse during this period, besides that of the metaphysical school. Ben Jonson (1573?–1637) the greatest dramatist of his time after Shakespeare, was a convivial, learned and belligerent neo-classic critic. In his practice he illustrated, and in his theory proclaimed, the classic virtues of proportion, clarity and elegance, virtues which he rarely found in his predecessors. 'Spenser,' he grumbled, 'writ no language'.

The next quotation, from his poem on Shakespeare, gives some idea of the quality of his mind, his critical principles, and the way he insisted that 'art' must be thought about and 'sweated' for. Such ideas, often at the service of a much narrower conception of poetry, were very important later in the century. We can also see the sturdy English Jonson, nourished on the classics, claim equality with them for his native literature. This is a constant and growing theme in Renaissance writing—we find it also in Milton. Men felt antiquity bestride them like a colossus; and sometimes they felt themselves 'petty men', 'peeping about'; yet they also came to believe they were the equals of the men of the past. They quarried the classics, but as time went on felt satisfied with the edifices they had constructed, partly from the past and partly from native materials. Here are the lines:

> My Shakespeare rise; I will not lodge thee by
> Chaucer or Spenser, or bid Beaumont lie
> A little further, to make thee a room.
> Thou art a monument, without a tomb,
> And art alive still, while thy book doth live,
> And we have wits to read and praise to give.
> That I not mix thee so, my brain excuses—
> I mean with great, but disproportioned Muses—
> For if I thought my judgement were of years,
> I should commit thee surely with thy peers,
> And tell how far thou didst our Lyly outshine,
> Or sporting Kyd, or Marlowe's mighty line.
> And though thou hadst small Latin and less Greek,
> From thence to honour thee I would not seek
> For names, but call forth thund'ring Aeschylus,

> Euripides, and Sophocles to us,
> Pacuvius, Accius, him of Cordova dead,
> To life again, to hear thy buskin tread
> And shake a stage; or, when thy socks were on,
> Leave thee alone for the comparison
> Of all that insolent Greece or haughty Rome
> Sent forth, or since did from their ashes come.
> Triumph, my Britain, thou hast one to show,
> To whom all scenes of Europe homage owe.
> He was not for an age, but for all time!
> And all the Muses still were in their prime,
> When like Apollo he came forth to warm
> Our ears, or like a Mercury to charm.
> Nature herself was proud of his designs,
> And joyed to wear the dressing of his lines,
> Which were so richly spun, and woven so fit,
> As since, she will vouchsafe no other wit.
> The merry Greek, tart Aristophanes,
> Neat Terence, witty Plautus now not please,
> But antiquated and deserted lie,
> As they were not of Nature's family.
> Yet must I not give Nature all: thy art,
> My gentle Shakespeare, must enjoy a part;
> For though the poet's matter nature be,
> His art doth give the fashion; and that he
> Who casts to write a living line, must sweat—
> Such as thine are—and strike the second heat
> Upon the Muses' anvil; turn the same,
> And himself with it, that he thinks to frame;
> Or, for the laurel, he may gain a scorn,
> For a good poet's made, as well as born;
> And such wert thou. . . .

Note Jonson's desire to classify, to rank authors; and note especially the line about 'great, but disproportioned Muses'. Proportion was one of Jonson's ideals. He is not above using the conceit:

> Thou art a monument, without a tomb,

He expects his readers to be as familiar with the classics as he is, and to know that 'buskin' and 'sock' stand for tragedy and comedy. So did Milton when in his turn he spoke of the 'buskin'd stage' and 'Jonson's learned sock'. This sort of thing can harden, and in many cases did harden, into a conventional poetic diction, a kind of language divorcing poetry from reality, from what Jonson would have called 'Nature'. To him it is a kind of useful shorthand, a quick reference to a whole

world of ideas, and feelings. See how he believes European culture to
have sprung from the ashes of Greece and Rome; but this metaphor
makes poetry a phoenix, and one phoenix is as good as another—in
this case better. Two phrases in this poem—'Marlowe's mighty line'—
and—'He was not for an age but for all time'—have become proverbial.
This line, and some others, notably

> Nature herself was proud of his designs,
> And joyed to wear the dressing of his lines . . .

and

> For a good poet's made, as well as born . . .

have an easy grace, an unforced plainness, which was to become the
staple of verse after the Restoration. They seem to be the voice of
'nature', but they are the result of art. They may not be 'great' but
they are not 'disproportioned'.

Here are two lyrics by Jonson, showing the polished strength,
the compression and neatness, which the 'sons of Ben'—those poets
who were his admiring followers—tried to emulate. We may be sure
that these poems, for all their apparent slightness, have been turned
many times on the anvil of the Muses.

EPITAPH ON ELIZABETH, LADY H—

> Wouldst thou hear what man can say
> In a little? Reader, stay.
> Underneath this stone doth lie
> As much beauty as could die,
> Which in life did harbour give
> To more virtue than doth live.
> If at all she had a fault,
> Leave it buried in this vault.
> One name was Elizabeth;
> Th'other let it sleep with death,
> Fitter where it died to tell,
> Than that it lived at all. Farewell.

HYMN TO CYNTHIA

> Queen and huntress, chaste and fair,
> Now the sun is laid to sleep,
> Seated in thy silver chair,
> State in wonted manner keep.
>   Hesperus entreats thy light,
>   Goddess excellently bright.

> Earth, let not thy envious shade
> Dare itself to interpose;
> Cynthia's shining orb was made
> Heaven to clear, when day did close.
>   Bless us then with wishèd sight,
>   Goddess excellently bright.
>
> Lay thy bow of pearl apart
> And thy crystal-shining quiver;
> Give unto the flying hart
> Space to breathe, how short soever;
>   Thou that mak'st a day of night,
>   Goddess excellently bright.

Next, these lines from *To Penshurst*, a poem celebrating the life of a great country house, the seat of the Sidney family. The poet praises the residence of a patron, and this is the sort of 'official' verse which many Renaissance poets produced. It was part of their recognized function to 'illustrate', to render illustrious by the exercise of their art, the leaders of the society in which they lived, but this poem is more than a personal panegyric.

> Thou art not, Penshurst, built to envious show
> Of touch or marble, nor canst boast a row
> Of polished pillars, or a roof of gold;
> Thou hast no lantern whereof tales are told,
> Or stair, or courts; but stand'st an ancient pile,
> And these grudged at, art reverenced the while. . . .
>
> Then hath thy orchard fruit, thy garden flowers,
> Fresh as the air, and new as are the hours.
> The early cherry, with the later plum,
> Fig, grape, and quince, each in his time doth come;
> The blushing apricot and woolly peach
> Hang on thy walls, that every child may reach.
> And though thy walls be of the country stone,
> They're reared with no man's ruin, no man's groan;
> There's none that dwell about them wish them down,
> But all come in, the farmer and the clown,
> And no one empty handed, to salute
> Thy Lord and Lady, though they have no suit.
> Some bring a capon, some a rural cake,
> Some nuts, some apples. Some that think they make
> The better cheeses, bring 'em; or else send
> By their ripe daughters, whom they would commend
> This way to husbands, and whose baskets bear
> An emblem of themselves in plum or pear.

But what can this, more than express their love,
Add to thy free provisions, far above
The need of such; whose liberal board doth flow
With all that hospitality doth know?
Where comes no guest but is allowed to eat,
Without his fear, and of thy Lord's own meat;
Where the same beer and bread, and self-same wine
That is his Lordship's shall be also mine. . . .

These, Penshurst, are thy praise, and yet not all.
Thy Lady's noble, fruitful, chaste withal;
His children thy great Lord may call his own,
A fortune in this age but rarely known.
They are, and have been taught religion; thence
Their gentle spirits have sucked innocence.
Each morn and even, they are taught to pray
With the whole household, and may every day
Read in their virtuous parents' noble parts
The mysteries of manners, arms, and arts.
Now, Penshurst, they that will proportion thee
With other edifices, when they see
Those proud ambitious heaps, and nothing else,
May say their lords have built, but thy Lord dwells.

These lines admirably represent Jonson's ordered sinewy, masculine
strength. The couplets are freely handled—a sort of rustic harshness
would, according to contemporary ideas of literary decorum, fit
the style to the theme—but among them we can hear, as in

> The blushing apricot and woolly peach
> Hang on thy walls, that every child may reach

with its precise, exact, balanced epithets, and the way its grammatical
and metrical units are fitted together, a forerunner of the standard
'Heroic couplet' of a later age. The poem celebrates a way of life
(idealized perhaps?) whose sturdy moral values are by implication
contrasted with those of the new race of profit seekers at court, in
commerce, and in industry who were satirized in *The Alchemist* and
Volpone. It may well be compared with Chaucer's account of the
Franklin, in the *Prologue* to the *Canterbury Tales*, to which Jonson is
obviously indebted, with the description of Timon's villa in Pope's
third *Moral Essay*, with Cobbett's views on the gentry of his day, and
even with Fanny Price's regrets about the proposed improvements at
Sotherton.

In the following lines from the speech by the ghost of Sylla which
starts the tragedy of *Catiline* Jonson is using the couplet for truly
'heroic' purposes.

> Dost thou not feel me, Rome? not yet! is night
> So heavy on thee, and my weight so light?
> Can Sylla's ghost arise within thy walls,
> Less threatening than an earthquake, the quick falls
> Of thee and thine? Shake not the frighted heads
> Of thy steep towers, or shrink to their first beds?
> Or, as their ruin the large Tyber fills,
> Make that swell up, and drown thy seven proud hills?
> What sleep is this doth seize thee so like death,
> And is not it? wake, feel her in my breath:
> Behold, I come, sent from the Stygian sound,
> As a dire vapour that had cleft the ground,
> To engender with the night, and blast the day;
> Or like a pestilence that should display
> Infection through the world. . . .

The strength and driving harshness of the lines fit their rhetorical intention, and the fact that they are intended for declamation on a public stage controls their structure and movement. The elaboration of the metaphysical conceit would here be out of place. The kind of tune Dryden later exploited for his kind of public verse we can hear in the couplet

> Behold, I come, sent from the Stygian sound,
> As a dire vapour that had cleft the ground . . .

and we can hear, too, how monosyllables are exploited,

> What sleep is this doth seize thee so like death . . .

a device we have noted in other poets.

Here is a fragment of another Prologue, to *The Staple of News*, where the movement of the verse is adjusted to the needs of colloquial intimacy. The player is telling the audience what the poet bade him say, and the passage expresses Jonson's seriousness of purpose, his insistent appeal to the intelligence, and gives an entertaining picture of the behaviour of the groundlings. It is worth comparing tone matter and structure with those of Pope's satires. 'Medley's' was an 'ordinary' or eating house; and 'Dunstan' and the 'Phoenix', taverns.

> For your own sakes, not his, he bade me say,
> Would you were come to hear, not see a play.
> Though we his actors, must provide for those
> Who are our guests here, in the way of shows,
> The maker hath not so; he'd have you wise,
> Much rather by your ears, than by your eyes;
> And prays you'll not prejudge his play for ill,

Because you mark it not, and sit not still;
But have a longing to salute, or talk
With such a female, and from her to walk
With your discourse, to what is done, and where,
How, and by whom, in all the town, but here.
Alas! what is it to his scene, to know
How many coaches in Hyde-park did shew
Last spring, what fare to-day at Medley's was
If Dunstan or the Phoenix best wine has?
They are things—but yet the stage might stand as well,
If it did neither hear these things, nor tell. . . .

Lastly the first, second and fifth stanzas from the *Ode to Himself*, occasioned by the 'vulgar censure' 'by some malicious spectators' of his play *The New Inn*. Here the rhetoric is deployed in a stately elaborate stanza, which aims at an effect of nobility and dignity; and this kind of writing came to be known as Pindaric from its supposed resemblance to the *Odes* of Pindar. The reader may compare these lines with those quoted from the *Ode on the Morning of Christ's Nativity*, and from Dryden's *Mistress Anne Killigrew*. The mode continues through the eighteenth century (Gray and Collins); the most famous Romantic example is Wordsworth's *Immortality* ode; and contemporary exercises are Auden's elegiac tributes to Yeats and Freud. The word 'fastidious' carries here a sense of *arrogant* dislike.

Come leave the loathèd stage,
And the more loathsome age;
Where pride and impudence, in faction knit,
Usurp the chair of wit,
Indicting and arraigning every day,
Something they call a play.
Let their fastidious, vain
Commission of the brain
Run on, and rage, sweat, censure, and condemn;
They were not made for thee, less thou for them.

Say that thou pour'st them wheat,
And they will acorns eat;
'Twere simple fury still thyself to waste
On such as have no taste;
To offer them a surfeit of pure bread,
Whose appetites are dead.
No, give them grains their fill,
Husks, draff to drink and swill.
If they love lees, and leave the lusty wine,
Envy them not; their palate's with the swine. . . .

> Leave things so prostitute,
>   And take th' Alcaic lute;
> Or thine own Horace, or Anacreon's lyre;
>   Warm thee by Pindar's fire:
> And though thy nerves be shrunk, and blood be cold
>   Ere years have made thee old,
>   Strike that disdainful heat
>   Throughout, to their defeat,
> As curious fools, and envious of thy strain,
> May, blushing, swear no palsy's in thy brain. ....

To end with, another lyric, exemplifying what Jonson wrote, when he turned from the 'loathed stage' to his loved classics. This song, *To Celia*, is imitated from Catullus, and its tone and movement are audible in Herrick, the cavalier lyrists, and those of the Restoration. It is interesting to compare these octosyllabic couplets with Milton's and Marvell's.

> Come, my Celia, let us prove,
> While we may, the sports of love;
> Time will not be ours for ever:
> He at length our good will sever.
> Spend not then his gifts in vain:
> Suns that set, may rise again;
> But if once we lose this light,
> 'Tis with us perpetual night.
> Why should we defer our joys?
> Fame and rumour are but toys.
> Cannot we delude the eyes
> Of a few poor household spies?
> Or his easier ears beguile,
> So removèd by our wile?
> 'Tis no sin love's fruit to steal,
> But the sweet thefts to reveal:
> To be taken, to be seen,
> These have crimes accounted been.

We have already quoted Carew's *Elegy* on Donne, in which the style itself is a tribute to the dead master. The style of Carew's other works, especially that of his lyrics, owes much to the Jonsonian ideals of clarity and discipline. He could at times exploit the metaphysical conceit in a way that seems to modern ears absurd, but which contemporary taste so much admired, as in these lines from the poem on the death of Maria Wentworth:

So though a Virgin, yet a Bride
To every Grace, she justifi'd
A chaste Polygamie, and dy'd.

but in this poem, *To my inconstant Mistris*, we hear the kind of clear sonorous yet sinewy melody, the perfect control of tone and feeling common to the best poems of 'the sons of Ben'.

When thou, poore excommunicate
From all the joyes of love, shalt see
The full reward, and glorious fate,
Which my strong faith shall purchase me,
Then curse thine owne inconstancy.

A fayrer hand than thine, shall cure
That heart, which thy false oathes did wound;
And to my soul, a soul more pure
Than thine, shall by Loves hand be bound,
And both with equall glory crown'd.

Then shalt thou weepe, entreat, complain
To Love, as I did once to thee;
When all thy teares shall be as vain
As mine were then, for thou shalt bee
Damn'd for thy false Apostasie.

It is interesting and useful to compare this poem with Wyatt's 'My lute, awake...'. Last, Carew's most famous lyric:

A SONG

Ask me no more where *Jove* bestowes,
When *June* is past, the fading rose:
For in your beauties orient deep,
These Flowers as in their causes sleep.

Ask me no more whither doe stray
The golden Atomes of the day:
For in pure love heaven did prepare
Those powders to enrich your hair.

Ask me no more wither doth hast
The Nightingale, when *May* is past:
For in your sweet dividing throat
She winters, and keeps warm her note.

Ask me no more where those starres light,
That downwards fall in dead of night:
For in your eyes they sit, and there,
Fixèd, become as in their sphere.

Ask me no more if East or West,
The Phenix builds her spicy nest:
For unto you at last she flyes,
And in your fragrant bosom dies.

In the poems of Marvell (1621–1678) metaphysical wit is combined
with Jonsonian neatness. There is, in Mr. Eliot's admirable phrase,
'a toughness beneath the slight lyric grace'. Here is *A Dialogue Between
the Soul and Body*.

SOUL

O Who shall, from this Dungeon, raise
A Soul inslav'd so many wayes?
With bolts of Bones, that fetter'd stands
In Feet; and manacled in Hands.
Here blinded with an Eye; and there
Deaf with the drumming of an Ear.
A Soul hung up, as 'twere, in Chains
Of Nerves, and Arteries, and Veins.
Tortur'd, besides each other part,
In a vain Head, and double Heart.

BODY

O who shall me deliver whole,
From bonds of this Tyrannic Soul?
Which, stretcht upright, impales me so,
That mine own Precipice I go;
And warms and moves this needless Frame:
(A fever could but do the same.)
And, wanting where its spight to try,
Has made me live to let me dye.
A Body that could never rest,
Since this ill Spirit it possest.

SOUL

What Magick could me thus confine
Within anothers Grief to pine?
Where whatsoever it complain,
I feel, that cannot feel, the pain.
And all my Care its self employes,
That to preserve, which me destroys:
Constrain'd not only to indure
Diseases, but, whats worse, the Cure:

And ready oft the Port to gain,
Am Shipwrackt into Health again.

BODY

But Physick yet could never reach
The Maladies Thou me dost teach;
Whom first the Cramp of Hope does Tear:
And then the Palsie Shakes of Fear.
The Pestilence of Love does heat:
Or Hatred's hidden Ulcer eat.
Joy's cheerful Madness does perplex:
Or sorrow's other Madness vex.
Which Knowledge forces me to know;
And Memory will not foregoe.
What but a Soul could have the wit
To build me up for Sin so fit?
So Architects do square and hew
Green Trees that in the Forest grew.

Verbal dexterity is not divorced, in verse such as this, from feeling. The horror of the situation is vividly present; the wit and irony, the skilful play, allow us to contemplate the horror, to think about it as well as suffer it; perhaps irony is the only defence against despair. The senses deceive us, for they can only communicate perceptions of the illusory, mortal, physical world. The body, that dungeon, is full of instruments of torture. Again, correspondences are precisely worked out. The nerves, arteries and veins are chains that connect the body's activities and keep it in motion. The head is vain because it considers itself the chief, the ruler, of the body, though this is not so: the prisoner soul is the true king. The pun on 'double' shows us Marvell using the 'new Philosophy'—in this case Harvey's discovery of the circulation of the blood; the heart is literally 'double' but also false.

But the body sees the soul as a tyrant, and a torturer too. It is impaled, skewered, by the soul and forced (alone among animals) to walk upright, in danger of falling; and the fall can be fatal, for it is the fall of man, which could never have happened if man had not had a soul. The term 'frame' means something constructed, a machine, and 'needless' means unnecessary; the body has no need of the soul—it is of no more use than a fever—indeed it is a fever, or disease. The body sees itself possessed by this 'ill spirit', which is seeking somewhere to exercise its malignancy, and has made the body live only in order to let it die, for the fall of man 'brought death into the world and all our woe'.

The soul, which cannot 'feel' in the body's sense, because it is an incorporeal essence, is compelled to suffer the body's diseases. The

D

body uses the soul, the seat of reason, to preserve itself, yet death of the body means freedom for the soul; diseases are painful in themselves, but the cure is still more painful. (Seventeenth-century medicine did indeed torture its patients, but the remark is at the same time one of the stock jokes about doctors.) The 'port' is death, and the concluding couplet a paradox. Restored health, which is safety for the body, is shipwreck for the soul. Perhaps the lines also imply that the ill are likely to be more virtuous, readier to listen to the soul, than the healthy. 'The devil was sick—the devil a monk would be. . . .'

But the body replies that agonizing as physical ills may be they are nothing compared with the maladies of the soul; for the passions of hope, fear, love, hatred are worse than any disease, however painful. And only man, the upright animal, suffers from them, because only he has a soul. And thanks to the soul, man has the capacity for know-ledge and therefore understands what ails him. His memory, due again to the soul, keeps his miseries ever before him. The soul builds him up—constructs his personality, his character—and it is precisely the soul's passions which make him fit for sin. The image of building leads on to the architect, and the beautiful final couplet. Architects cut down and shape (note the brutal energy of 'square and hew') the wild trees of the forest. First, perhaps, we feel the pathos of green trees in the forest, of innocent natural beauty. But then we may consider that the architect builds houses, homes, palaces, towns, temples, with them. He stands for civilization, and you cannot have civilization and the forest. Man, is, inescapably, an architect. He cannot return, on all fours, to the wild.

The Fair Singer is a slight and charming love lyric in which the metaphysical conceit is used with playful ingenuity; indeed it was in the skill with which the game was played, the convention exploited, that the seventeenth-century reader of verse such as this found much of his pleasure. The lady's beauty is dazzling, her voice enchanting: she has made a conquest of the poet who is her prisoner. The war—captivity conceit is resolved in the last stanza, where the lady's beauty and voice become the wind and sun, natural powers against which the poet is helpless, as a ship might be against an enemy bearing down with the sun behind him.

> To make a final conquest of all me,
> Love did compose so sweet an Enemy,
> In whom both Beauties to my death agree,
> Joyning themselves in fatall harmony;
> That while she with her Eyes my Heart does bind,
> She with her Voice might captivate my Mind.

I could have fled from One but singly fair:
My dis-intangled Soul it self might save,
Breaking the curled trammels of her hair.
But how should I avoid to be her Slave,
Whose subtile Art invisibly can wreath
My Fetters of the very Air I breath?

It had been easie fighting in some plain,
Where Victory might hang in equal choice.
But all resistance against her is vain,
Who has the advantage both of Eyes and Voice.
And all my Forces needs must be undone,
She having gained both the Wind and Sun.

Our last poem is the famous *To His Coy Mistress*. We will not attempt a detailed commentary on it, but only ask the reader to ponder the way in which a poetic convention, usually handled with deftness charm and pathos, as in Jonson's *To Celia*, Herrick's *Gather Ye Rosebuds*, or Waller's *Go Lovely Rose*, is suddenly charged with wry grimness. Marvell makes his favourite measure follow every change of mood and turn of thought; the poem laments the remorseless grinding of Time's jaws (chaps) and then defies him, in the name of a power greater than he.

Had we but World enough, and Time,
This coyness Lady were no crime.
We would sit down, and think which way
To walk, and pass our long Loves Day.
Thou by the *Indian Ganges* side
Should'st Rubies find: I by the Tide
Of *Humber* would complain. I would
Love you ten years before the Flood:
And you should if you please refuse
Till the Conversion of the *Jews*.
My vegetable Love should grow
Vaster than Empires, and more slow.
An hundred years should go to praise
Thine eyes, and on thy Forehead Gaze;
Two hundred to adore each Breast:
But thirty thousand to the rest.
An Age at least to every part,
And the last Age should show your Heart.
For Lady you deserve this State;
Nor would I love at lower rate.

But at my back I alwaies hear
Times winged Charriot hurrying near:
And yonder all before us lye
Desarts of vast Eternity.
Thy beauty shall no more be found;
Nor, in thy marble Vault, shall sound
My ecchoing Song: then Worms shall try
That long preserv'd Virginity:
And your quaint Honour turn to dust;
And into ashes all my Lust.
The Grave's a fine and private place,
But none I think do there embrace.

Now, therefore, while the youthful hew
Sits on thy skin like morning dew,
And while thy willing Soul transpires
At every pore with instant Fires,
Now let us sport us while we may;
And now, like am'rous birds of prey,
Rather at once our Time devour,
Than languish in his slow-chapt pow'r.
Let us roll all our Strength, and all
Our sweetness, up into one Ball:
And tear our Pleasures with rough strife,
Thorough the Iron gates of Life.
Thus, though we cannot make our Sun
Stand still, yet we will make him run.

John Milton (1608–1674) was above all a dedicated writer, who saw himself as *vates*, the poet as prophet. *Paradise Lost* is intended to 'justify the ways of God to man', and moral and religious purposes inform almost all his poetry. To express them he forged a style which is noble, magniloquent and resonant, though sometimes stiff and unyielding. But he was also a man of an intense sensibility which seems sometimes to be at odds with his conscious purposes, and this can give a strange evocative resonance to his verse, and make it speak directly to readers who no longer share his theological views, or regard him as a teacher.

First, two short quotations from the famous *L'Allegro* and *Il Penseroso*. Thse are really 'exercise' poems, demonstrations of skill, a pair of 'characters', literary portraits, to hang, so to speak, one on either side of the mantelpiece. They are charming, neat, accomplished and harmless; it is this last quality, perhaps, which accounts for their persistence in anthologies, especially in schools, where their many classical allusions must have put a lot of beginners off poetry for good.

We should be concerned as we read them with Milton's rhythm and the special qualities of his language.

> Streit mine eye hath caught new pleasures
> Whilst the Lantskip round it measures,
> Russet Lawns and Fallows Gray,
> Where the nibling flocks do stray,
> Mountains on whose barren breast
> The labouring clouds do often rest:
> Meadows trim with Daisies pide,
> Shallow Brooks, and Rivers wide.
> Towers and Battlements it sees
> Boosom'd high in tufted Trees,
> Where perhaps som beauty lies,
> The Cynosure of neighbouring eyes.
> Hard by, a Cottage chimney smokes,
> From betwixt two aged Okes,
> Where Corydon and Thyrsis met,
> Are at their savory dinner set
> Of Hearbs, and other country messes
> Which the neat-handed Phyllis dresses;
> And then in haste her Bowre she leaves
> With Thestylis to bind the Sheaves;
> Or if the earlier season lead
> To the tann'd Haycock in the Mead. . . .
>
> (*L'Allegro*)

> Thus night oft see me in thy pale career,
> Till civil-suited Morn appeer,
> Not trickt and frounc't as she was wont,
> With the Attick Boy to hunt,
> But Cherchef't in a comly Cloud,
> While rocking Winds are piping loud,
> Or usher'd with a shower still,
> When the gust hath blown his fill,
> Ending on the russling Leaves,
> With minute drops from off the Eaves.
> And when the Sun begins to fling
> His flaring beams, me Goddes bring
> To arched walks of twilight groves,
> And shadows brown that *Sylvan* loves
> Of Pine, or monumental Oake,
> Where the rude Ax with heaved stroke,
> Was never heard the Nymphs to daunt,
> Or fright them from their hallow'd haunt. . . .
>
> (*Il Penseroso*)

This is surely a special language, a style deliberately detached from the rhythms of common speech, learned, allusive and elegant. How different are these couplets from Marvell's! It is interesting to see what varying uses two poets—contemporaries at that—can make of the same language, and what dissimilar tunes they can make out of the same basic metrical pattern. We must, however, beware of criticizing Milton for not achieving what he did not attempt. These verses are delightful incantations; they exhibit the young poet's learning, taste and skill, but the fact remains that this is a kind of *appliqué* work, in which stylistic formulae are stuck on to the subject matter, the raw material.

> While Cynthia checks her dragon yoke
> Gently o'er th'accustomed Oke.

is a studied, elaborate way of saying that the moon is over the top of the oak tree where the poet likes to see it—the scene is, to use a word of later coinage, picturesque. We may note, too, the apt (monotonously apt?) epithets—'russet lawns', 'fallows grey', 'nibling flocks', 'labouring clouds' and so on. This sort of thing had a great, some would say distastrous, influence on later work. The pastoral convention lacks the freshness of Spenser; the personifications make lifeless processions. Yet a real voice is speaking here, for even the slightest of Milton's verses are stamped with his personality.

A stately music, ordering the young Milton's varied interests and feelings, exhibiting his technical resources, and echoing the rhythms and images of his masters binds together the stanzas of the *Ode on the Morning of Christ's Nativity*. Here he is saying that Christ's birth cannot herald the return of Paradise, for God's ways must be justified by the crucifixion, and the Providential working out of man's redemption, before the end of the world can come.

> But wisest Fate says no,
> This must not yet be so,
>   The Babe lies yet in smiling Infancy,
> That on the bitter cross
> Must redeem our loss:
>   So both himself and us to glorifie:
> Yet first to those ychain'd in sleep,
> The wakefull trump of doom must thunder through the deep,
>
> With such a horrid clang
> As on mount *Sinai* rang
>   While the red fire, and smouldring clouds out brake:
> The aged Earth agast

With terror of that blast,
Shall from the surface to the center shake,
When at the worlds last session,
The dreadfull Judge in middle Air shall spread his throne.

In the next stanzas the poet imagines the defeated pagan Gods fleeing
from their temples, and his ambivalent feelings about the classics—
they are false, but they are beautiful—permeate these lines, in which
the poetry seems to run counter to the argument.

> The Oracles are dumm,
> No voice or hideous humm
>   Runs through the archèd roof in words deceiving.
> *Apollo* from his shrine.
> Can no more divine,
>   With hollow shreik the steep of *Delphos* leaving.
> No nightly trance, or breathed spell,
> Inspire's the pale-ey'd Priest from the prophetic cell.
>
> The lonely mountains o're,
> And the resounding shore,
>   A voice of weeping heard, and loud lament;
> From haunted spring, and dale
> Edg'd with poplar pale,
>   The parting Genius is with sighing sent,
> With flowre-inwov'n tresses torn
> The Nimphs in twilight shade of tangled thickets mourn.

Spenserian rhythms can be heard in the alexandrines which close
each stanza. In the last quotation we see Milton using the fashionable
conceit, in the image of the sun getting up in the morning, which has
a quaintly domestic effect, scarcely in keeping with the magnificence
of the rest of the poem. The next part of this verse shows his familiarity
with the faery poetry of Spenser and Shakespeare.

> So when the Sun in bed,
> Curtain'd with cloudy red,
> Pillows his chin upon an Orient wave,
> The flocking shadows pale,
> Troop to th'infernall jail,
> Each fetter'd Ghost slips to his severall grave,
> And the yellow-skirted *Fayes*,
> Fly after the Night-steeds, leaving their Moon-lov'd maze.

Arcades formed 'part of an entertainment presented to the Countess
Dowager of Derby at Harefield, by some noble Persons of her Family'.
I quote from the words of the Genius, or presiding spirit, of the woods.

The speech celebrates the virtues of the countess, and at the end the 'noble persons' 'who appear on the scene in Pastoral Habit'

> Approach, and kiss her sacred vesture's hem.

Before this the Genius has announced that the music of the spheres

> worthiest were to blaze
> The peerless height of her immortal praise.

Eulogizing a possible patron seems a strange task for a Puritan poet, but Milton in his early days, as we see from *Lycidas* and *Comus*, was not averse from devoting his talents to the public uses of poetry, at the same time making the temporal social form a vehicle for his noblest sentiments. To him may be applied the words he used of Edward King:

> he knew
> Himself to sing, and *build* the *lofty* rhyme.

Notice the words I have italicized. To 'build' implies that poetry is a deliberate construction, an artefact, curiously wrought; and it must be 'lofty'. Indeed this line is a brief compendium of Milton's aims and methods. Loftiness is achieved not by idiomatic, but by latinized English—'he knew... to sing'. The generalized, literary-conventional 'to sing' stands for 'writing poetry'. And all is arranged in clear regular sonority, with the 'sense variously drawn out' from line to line. Here is the quotation from *Arcades*:

> When Eev'ning gray doth rise, I fetch my round
> Over the mount, and all this hallow'd ground,
> And early ere the odorous breath of morn
> Awakes the slumbring leaves, or tasseld horn
> Shakes the high thicket, haste I all about,
> Number my ranks, and visit every sprout
> With puissant words, and murmurs made to bless,
> But els in deep of night when drowsiness
> Hath lockt up mortal sense, then listen I
> To the celestial *Sirens* harmony,
> That sit upon the nine enfolded Sphears,
> And sing to those that hold the vital shears,
> And turn the Adamantine spindle round,
> On which the fate of gods and men is wound.
> Such sweet compulsion doth in musick ly,
> To lull the daughters of *Necessity*,
> And keep unsteddy Nature to her law,
> And the low world in measured motion draw
> After the heavenly tune, which none can hear
> Of human mould with grosse unpurged ear. . . .

These are 'heroic couplets' which the reader should compare with those of Spenser, Donne, Jonson and Dryden. They are freely handled, but not rough or vigorous, and the influence of the *Faerie Queene* and of early Shakespeare, especially of *A Midsummer Night's Dream*, is audible. The resounding nobility is Milton's own. The daughters of Necessity are the three fates Lachesis, Clotho and Atropos, who turn the axis of the concentric spheres which form the universe, and spin and cut the thread of Man's life. According to Plato—Milton is here making a version of a passage in *The Republic*—as the spheres turned they gave forth musical notes which together made up their harmony. We may compare Lorenzo's speech in *The Merchant of Venice:*

> Look how the floor of heaven
> Is thick inlaid with patines of bright gold;
> There's not the smallest orb which thou beholdest,
> But in his motion like an angel sings,
> Still quiring to the young-eyed cherubim:
> Such harmony is in immortal souls;
> But, whilst this muddy vesture of decay
> Doth grossly close us in, we cannot hear it.
>
> Act v, Sc. i

Milton does not offer the energy of 'muddy vesture of decay' or 'grossly close us in'; but 'the young-eyed cherubim' is just the sort of language-pattern he could adopt. His own peculiar music is here best heard in the couplet

> And turn the Adamantine spindle round,
> On which the fate of gods and men is wound.

a sort of relentless, marching rhythm which was later adapted by Dryden. The whole passage is imbued with Milton's intense moral feeling—that preoccupation with the nature of the universe, and its relation to God which forms the subject of *Paradise Lost* and *Paradise Regained*.

Next are two passages from *Comus*. This masque, like *Arcades*, is a social piece, presented at Ludlow Castle in 1634 in honour of the Earl of Bridgewater's appointment as Lord President of Wales, when the parts of the brothers and the sister were played by his children. The theme of the masque is the triumph of chastity, but it is more than this. It is, in parts, a kind a dramatization of the two sides of Milton's character; of the choices before him—the world and his vocation; the society he is celebrating, and the revolutionary forces that were to overthrow it; the church, and the private conscience. The tensions between all these opposing forces inform the rhythms of the verse.

Our first quotation is from the speech Comus makes to the lady when he has her in his power. He offers her his enchanted cup, which she refuses, telling him that

> ... none
> But such as are good men can give good things,
> And that which is not good is not delicious
> To a well-govern'd and wise appetite.

Comus replies:

> O foolishnes of men! that lend their ears
> To those budge doctors of the *Stoick* Furr,
> And fetch their precepts from the *Cynick* Tub,
> Praising the lean and sallow Abstinence.
> Wherefore did Nature powre her bounties forth
> With such a full and unwithdrawing hand,
> Covering the earth with odours, fruits, and flocks,
> Thronging the Seas with spawn innumerable,
> But all to please, and sate the curious taste?
> And set to work millions of spinning Worms,
> That in their green shops weave the smooth-hair'd silk,
> To deck her sons, and that no corner might
> Be vacant of her plenty, in her own loyns
> She hutch't th'all-worship't ore, and precious gems
> To store her children with; if all the world
> Should in a pet of temperance feed on Pulse,
> Drink the clear stream, and nothing wear but Frieze,
> Th'all-giver would be unthank't, would be unprais'd
> Not half his riches known, and yet despis'd,
> And we should serve him as a grudging master,
> As a penurious niggard of his wealth,
> And live like Nature's bastards, not her sons,
> Who would be quite surcharged with her own weight,
> And strangled with her waste fertility;
> Th'earth cumber'd, and the winged air dark't with plumes. . . .

The first thing to note about this passage is its energy. The extraordinary, rash, proliferating abundance of nature is embodied in verse which we can truly call dramatic; it not only conveys the fullness of the earth, but also the ingenuity, the cunning, the dangerous intelligence of the speaker. How powerfully his contempt for the Puritan virtues is expressed, through the scorn-charged image of the 'lean and sallow Abstinence'—a personification that works, that is not a mere stylistic ornament—through the 'budge doctors' (does it matter whether we know what budge means?) the 'pet of temperance', 'nature's bastards', 'grudging', 'penurious'. And at the end, in characteristically Miltonic fashion, the period overflows, like nature's bounty. We might take

> And live like Nature's bastards, not her sons,

as a climax; but irresistibly the verse drives on, repeating and summing up the argument, the previous ideas, primed by harsh verbs— 'surcharged,' 'strangled', 'cumbered', 'dark't'—to finish with the thunderous and sinister

> Th'earth cumber'd, and the winged air dark't with plumes. . . .

where the open-vowelled 'dark't' seems to cast a shadow over the earth.

One more passage from *Comus*, exhibiting a different kind of melody. Sir Henry Wotton, in a letter to Milton about this work, said: 'I should much commend the Tragical part, if the Lyrical did not ravish me with a certain Dorique delicacy in your Songs and Odes, whereunto I must plainly confess to have seen yet nothing parallel in our language . . . .' Our quotation is blank verse, not a song or ode, but it exemplifies, I think, the sort of quality Wotton meant by 'Dorique delicacy'. Note that to Wotton this is 'modern' poetry—he has not heard anything quite like it before. The Attendant Spirit tells how 'a certain shepherd lad' has given him a precious herb, 'of sovran use'. By its powers, he says,

> I knew the foul enchanter though disguised,
> Enter'd the very lime-twigs of his spells,
> And yet came off. . . .

Here is his description of the shepherd.

> He lov'd me well, and oft would beg me sing,
> Which when I did, he on the tender grass
> Would sit, and hearken even to extasie,
> And in requital ope his leather'n scrip,
> And shew me simples of a thousand names
> Telling their strange and vigorous faculties;
> Amongst the rest a small unsightly root,
> But of divine effect, he cull'd me out;
> The leaf was darkish, and had prickles on it,
> But in another Countrey, as he said,
> Bore a bright golden flowre, but not in this soyl:
> Unknown, and like esteem'd, and the dull swayn
> Treads on it daily with his clouted shoon
> And yet more med'cinal is it then that *Moly*
> That *Hermes* once to wise Ulysses gave;
> He call'd it *Haemony*. . . .

One cannot, I think, read these lines without feeling 'that more is meant than meets the ear', or rather that what meets the ear is charged with a degree of feeling far beyond the needs of the dramatic situation. When Milton uses a dramatic form it seems sometimes that much of what he has to communicate, much that is personally important to him, is mediated, not overtly through character and action and rhetoric, as it is in Shakespeare or Ben Jonson, but through passages which may seem mere graceful flourishes, unrelated to the pattern of the drama or its theme, but which yet are strangely impressive, which contain a meaning of their own, a profound and personal intensity.

Suppose we try to account for the power of this passage by paraphrasing it something like this:

The attendant spirit was played by Henry Lawes, who composed the music for the masque; so we can perhaps think of Milton as the Shepherd Lad. This fits the pastoral convention of the poet as shepherd: Spenser referred to himself in the same way—'A shepherd boy, no better do him call'. That Milton was passionately fond of music, 'even to extasie', we know. We may therefore assume an autobiographical content for these lines, a kind of private intimacy within the public framework. Might not the simples stand for Milton's poems, the product of 'that one talent which is death to kide' and might not the small unsightly root symbolize *Comus* itself, Milton's own work in general, and that work seen as modern, north European? The 'bright golden flower' will then stand for classical Mediterranean culture, for the great works of Greece and Rome. So here we have Milton saying that his verse is dull and insignificant compared with his friend's music; that neither he nor perhaps any of his countrymen will ever write as well as the ancients; that such talents as his are ignored by society— the 'dull swain'—but that nevertheless such talents are 'divine'.

Whatever conflicts of opinion there may be over *Paradise Lost* we must agree that it is Milton's loftiest building, raised to the 'highth' of his great argument. A great argument—'unattempted yet in prose or rhyme'—demands a great style. The poet chooses blank verse, rejecting the 'troublesom and modern bondage of Rimeing' because 'true musical delight' 'consists only in apt Numbers, fit quantity of Syllables, and the sense variously drawn out from one Verse into another.'

Our first quotation describes the palace built in Hell for Satan and his angels.

> Anon out of the earth a Fabrick huge
> Rose like an Exhalation, with the sound
> Of Dulcet Symphonies and voices sweet,

Built like a Temple, where *Pilasters* round
Were set, and Doric pillars overlaid
With Golden Architrave; nor did there want
Cornice or Freeze, with bossy Sculptures grav'n,
The Roof was Fretted Gold. Not *Babilon*,
Nor great *Alcairo* such magnificence
Equal'd in all their glories, to inshrine
Belus or *Serapis* their Gods, or seat
Thir Kings, when *Aegypt* with *Assyria* strove
In wealth and luxurie. Th'ascending pile
Stook fixt her stately highth, and strait the dores
Op'ning thir brazen foulds discover wide
Within, her ample spaces, o're the smooth
And level pavement: from the arched roof
Pendant by suttle Magic many a row
Of Starry Lamps and blazing Cressets fed
With *Naphtha* and *Asphaltus* yielded light
As from a sky. The hasty multitude
Admiring enter'd, and the work some praise
And some the Architect: his hand was known
In Heav'n by many a Towred structure high,
Where Scepter'd Angels held their residence,
And sat as Princes, whom the supreme King
Exalted to such power, and gave to rule,
Each in his Herarchie, the Orders bright.
Nor was his name unheard or unador'd
In Ancient *Greece*; and in *Ausonian* land
Men called him *Mulciber*; and how he fell
From Heav'n, they fabl'd, thrown by angry *Jove*
Sheer o're the Chrystal Battlements: from Morn
To Noon he fell, from Noon to dewy Eve,
A Summers day; and with the setting Sun
Dropt from the Zenith like a falling Star,
On *Lemnos* th'*Aegean* Ile: thus they relate,
Erring; for he with this rebellious rout
Fell long before; nor aught avail'd him now
To have built in Heav'n high Towrs; not did he scape
By all his Engins, but was headlong sent
With his industrious crew to build in hell.

It is easy to see how the sense is variously drawn out. At the beginning
the subject of this passage, the 'fabric huge' comes at the end of one
line, and the verb 'rose' starts the next, so the reader's voice is compelled to carry on the movement, which embodies the sense. The
first word, 'anon', alerts us; something is happening at once, now;

'out of the earth' has a quick triple rhythm; and then we have to say 'a fabric huge rose' and the energy needed to pronounce this, to say the hard c of fabric, aspirate the following h, roll the initial r just after coping with the ge on the end of huge, forces us to attend to and to feel the prodigy. 'Like an exhalation' has an easy dying fall—the whole thing was as simple as breathing out. Similarly we can note how the passage about Babylon and Cairo gets much of its force from the fact that the last three lines all end in verbs. The flowing cadences of the famous lines about Mulciber surely need no comment. Note how in this noble style, nouns are usually clothed in epithets—'Fabric huge', 'dulcet symphonies', 'Doric pillars', 'Golden Architrave', 'bossy Sculptures', 'stately highth', 'brazen foulds' etc. But the most important thing is to see that the rhythmic unit in this verse is the sentence, which may end at almost any point in the line. Feel the cadence of each sentence, and then its relationship with the cadences which precede and follow it. Milton has a number of favourite tunes which you will soon get to recognize, and he never allows the ear to get too bewildered; he comes back every now and then to lines of stately and sonorous regularity:

> Of Dulcet Symphonies and voices sweet . . .
> Where Scepter'd Angels held their residence . . .
> Each in his Herarchie, the Orders bright . . .

and the malignantly contemptuous final

> With his industrious crew to build in hell.

If we compare the whole poem to a temple, 'a fabrick huge', we can consider the fable, the argument, the theology, the characters to be the pillars, or main structure; and this structure is decorated with cornice, frieze and bossy sculptures. We admiring enter—we follow the movement of story, dispute, analysis and (for the temple contains shrines and altars) prayer. We also examine the details, the carvings which adorn it. Some seem to exist in their own right, some we can at once see refer to the meaning of the whole building.

The reference to Babylon, Alcairo, Belus and Serapis is such a carving. These are symbols of power, of luxury, of false religion. Milton must write his (literally) prehistoric epic in terms of history; the divine and the diabolic must be expressed in human imagery; he must express eternal beings in terms of temporal ones. He needs to make us feel the scale of this infernal temple, so he compares it to what we know of the great remote past. (He can rely on his readers knowing their Bible.) History is the result of the Fall—his theme—and Satan brought about the fall, and his angels became false gods, Belus and Serapis, and when they corrupted men they corrupted power, for it should not be the purpose of states to strive or compete 'in wealth and luxury'; puritans don't approve of affluence. We can hear the scorn in the repeated 'thir glories' 'thir Gods', 'thir Kings'. The rolling remoteness of the proper names makes its effect, whether we think like this or no—we have Mr. Eliot's authority for saying that you have to read Milton twice, once for the sound and once for the sense. This 'bossy sculpture' is striking at first glance, but further inspection shows its close relation to the whole building.

What about Mulciber? He had been in charge of developments in Heaven. He has fallen. So far is apt—another symbol of the theme, but it's a classical, not a biblical story, though one, of course, which Milton's 'fit' audience would be familiar with; yet Jove is not Jehovah. He is in fact as much a devil as Belus or Serapis; yet Mulciber did no harm to men—he taught them building. From morn to noon to dewy eve on a long summer's day gives us the scale, but there's nothing ponderous, vast or noble about it—the lines are lyrically beautiful. In theory the shooting star is a portent of evil: yet who can feel it so? But we are pulled up with a harsh jerk at

> thus they relate,
> Erring . . .

the very placing of that word at the beginning of a line gives it tremendous force. It is almost as if Milton is pulling himself up, as well as his reader, catching himself out in nostalgia for the classics which were a part of his mind and sensibility, and part of his inspiration, for his very poetic form, the epic, is classical. 'Men' who named him Mulciber are wrong; the reader is a man and is involved in this error. Mulciber is a devil again. He is jeered at—naught availed him now to have built in Heaven high towers—Renaissance architects, we must remember, were expected to be, and were, experts in fortification and war machines: so he and his contractors, his industrious crew, are firmly damned. Yet we can't forget him falling, for the charm and cadence of the lines stay with us; it was surely no ignoble vision that the men of Lemnos saw. The effect, to return to our temple simile, is a bit like seeing a Green Man in a Christian church. One way of accounting for such passages, which are sometimes, as in our third quotation, formal similes, is to think of them as resting places along the route, or as some would say, oases in the desert. As a glance at the commentators will convince you, it takes all sorts to read Milton. Perhaps the best advice is to take your pleasure where you find it.

More prolonged and deeper reading may relate the nature of that pleasure to the architecture of the whole poem.

The description of the creation, which follows next, should be compared with the speech of Comus and also with the passage in the beginning of the masque which contains the lines

> The Sounds, and Seas with all their finny drove
> Now to the Moon in wavering Morrice move. . . .

The dignity is there, but some of the vitality has gone. Milton's object is of course different; we see him here striving (too hard?) to raise his subject matter to the 'highth' of his great argument, to be lofty.

> And God said, let the Waters generate
> Reptil with Spawn abundant, living Soule:
> And let Fowle flie above the Earth, with wings
> Display'd on the op'n Firmament of Heav'n.
> And God created the great Whales, and each
> Soul living, each that crept, which plenteously
> The waters generated by thir kindes,
> And every Bird of wing after his kinde;
> And saw that it was good, and bless'd them, saying
> Be fruitful, multiply, and in the Seas
> And Lakes and running Streams the waters fill;
> And let the Fowle be multiply'd on the Earth.
> Forthwith the sounds and Seas, each Creek and Bay
> With Frie innumerable swarme, and Shoales
> Of Fish that with thir Finns and shining Scales
> Glide under the green Wave, in Sculles[1] that oft
> Bank the mid Sea: part single or with mate
> Graze the Sea weed thir pasture, and through Groves
> Of Coral stray, or sporting with quick glance
> Show to the Sun thir wav'd coats dropt with Gold,
> Or in thir Pearlie shells at ease, attend
> Moist nutriment, or under Rocks thir food
> In jointed Armour watch: on smooth the Seale,
> And bended Dolphins play: part huge of bulk
> Wallowing unweildie, enormous in thir Gate
> Tempest the Ocean: there Leviathan
> Hugest of living Creatures, on the Deep
> Stretcht like a Promontorie sleeps or swimmes,
> And seems a moving Land, and at his Gilles
> Draws in, and at his Trunck spouts out a Sea.

[1] Shoals.

The opening lines closely follow the first chapter of Genesis.

> And God said, let the waters bring forth abundantly the moving creature
> that hath life, and fowl that may fly above the earth in the open firmament
> of heaven.
> And God created great whales, and every living creature that moveth,
> which the waters brought forth abundantly, after their kind: and God
> saw that it was good.
> And God blessed them, saying, Be fruitful, and multiply, and fill the
> waters in the seas, and let fowl multiply in the earth.
>
> Chapter 1, verses 20–22

We can see the Miltonic machine turning this into blank verse—
inverting 'fill the waters', expanding 'the water in the seas', and adapting
'let fowle multiply in the earth'. But the lines are clearly intended to
recall the Bible; their cadences are close to those of the original;
the poet wants us to feel that this is God's word. His own characteristic
movement takes over again at 'Forthwith the Sounds and Seas...',
and certainly the noise is noble. The fish are charming; the poet who
wrote about the sounds and seas in Comus clearly wrote

> Show to the sun thir wav'd coats dropt with Gold ...

'on smooth' is Miltonic, not English, diction; the 'bended' dolphins
are curiously stiff—they are heraldic rather than living creatures.
Leviathan has, indeed, a laborious strength:

> and at his Gilles
> Draws in, and at his Trunck spouts out a Sea. ...

The monosyllables, the placing of 'draws in' and 'spouts out', the
way 'a sea' is delayed till the end of the line convey a suitably gigantic
and clumsy force. It is the work of a master technician, but the poet
does not seem so deeply involved as he does in Comus, nor does
Leviathan himself seem so impressive as he does when he makes his
appearance with his 'scaly rind' in Book I.

Our third quotation is—not to crack the wind of our poor analogy—
a bit of one of the pillars of Milton's temple. Satan has defied Death
and Sin, emerged from the gates of Hell and braved the realms of
Chaos and Old Night. Milton the technician is here at his most
ingenious in such lines as

> So eagerly the fiend
> Ore bog or steep, through strait, rough, dense or rare,
> With head, hands, wings, or feet pursues his way,
> And swims or sinks, or wades, or creeps, or flyes ...

where the sinister zest of the devil ('eagerly') and his hound-like persistence ('pursues his way') are embedded in difficulty and danger and nightmare effort. The formlessness of chaos is conveyed by the use of adjectives as abstract nouns—'rough, dense or rare'; it is no good asking rough what? because this is chaos. The vagueness contrasts with the precision of the nouns and verbs which deal with Satan's struggle.

The devil alights on the outermost of the concentric spheres enclosing the newly created earth.

> Meanwhile upon the firm opacous Globe
> Of this round World, whose first convex divides
> The luminous inferior Orbs, enclos'd
> From *Chaos* and th'inroad of Darkness old,
> *Satan* alighted walks: a Globe farr off
> It seem'd, now seems a boundless Continent
> Dark, waste, and wild, under the frown of Night
> Starless expos'd, and ever-threatning storms
> Of *Chaos*, blustring round, inclement skie;
> Save on that side which from the wall of Heav'n
> Though distant farr som small reflection gaines
> Of glimmering air less vext with tempest loud:
> Here walk'd the Fiend at large in spacious field.
> As when a Vultur on *Imaus* bred,
> Whose snowie ridge the roving *Tartar* bounds,
> Dislodging from a region scarce of prey
> To gorge the flesh of Lambs or yeanling Kids
> On Hills where Flocks are fed, flies towards the Springs
> Of *Ganges* or *Hydaspes*, *Indian* streams;
> But in his way lights on the barren plaines
> Of *Sericana*, where *Chineses* drive
> With Sails and Wind thir canie Waggons light:
> So on this windie Sea of Land, the Fiend
> Walk'd up and down alone bent on his prey . . .

This is a dramatic moment. Notice how sinister is the repetition of the innocent verb 'walks'.

> *Satan* alighted walkes . . .
> Here walk'd the Fiend at large in spacious field . . .
> Walk'd up and down alone bent on his prey . . .

Milton is here making his effect with the simplest possible language. To walk in the fields is the most harmless of pleasures—God walked in the garden in the cool of the evening—but here it is the Fiend who walks, seeking whom he may devour. Note how 'at large' both reinforces the scale of 'spacious', and conveys the sense of range and freedom—but the freedom of an escaped wild beast or dangerous prisoner. See too, how the pacing regularity of

> Here walk'd the Fiend at large in spacious field

contrasts with the malignant triple rhythms of

> Walk'd up and down alone bent on his prey ...

The scale is here forcefully realized: the 'globe farr off' becomes a 'boundless continent'. Milton's imagination is working on the material offered by 'the new philosophy', the vastly enlarged concept of the universe, though he keeps the old Ptolemaic system of spheres. There is pathos in the glimpse of heavenly light, and Satan still retains traces of his past glory; he knows what he has lost; we feel his desperation as well as his menace, and this feeling runs through the whole passage, to be echoed in 'alone' in the last line. We are shown the isolation of this new world, precarious between the storms of chaos and the distant light of heaven; it, too, is exposed and alone.

In the simile Satan is likened to a solitary bird of prey. See how all the details of this 'sculpture' are relevant to the theme. The vulture 'dislodges'—he falls like a stone, he moves house—from inhospitable mountains where there is little to eat. The mountains 'bound' or confine the 'roving Tartar' symbol of cruelty, power and barbarous disorder, as the gates of hell confined Satan. The vulture will 'gorge', not merely feed, on the weak and innocent, as Satan has promised Death he will on earth. The springs, symbols of life, of Ganges and Hydaspes stand for Eden. (It is of interest that Milton here repeats a rhythm and form he has already used in the passage about Dagon in Book I:

> Of Abbana and Pharpar, lucid streams ...

You will find many such repetitions in the course of the poem.) Sericana (China) stands for the firm opacous globe on which Satan has just alighted. What are the Chineses doing? The obsolete plural inevitably gives them, to a modern ear, a quaint willow-pattern quality which can't have been in the original, and cannot therefore have anything to do with Milton's meaning. There are two things, I think, to be said about them. First, they add to the strangeness, the remoteness, of the whole thing; the Vulture travels distances so vast that even he must alight. Second, they interest us in themselves; they are a decoration, something that has caught Milton's fancy in the course of his reading, and that he offers to us. The fact that the whole poem is a celebration of God's purposes, doesn't mean that it is not also a work of art, in which the artist's imagination is, in parts, at play. In spite of its pillars, pilasters and architraves, Milton's temple has something Gothic about it, 'richly dight'. And so at last we come back to Satan, and to the story.

In some such way as this, it seems to me, should *Paradise Lost* be read, at any rate for a start.

Our next major author is John Dryden (1631–1700). It will be useful for us to think of him as a public poet: a man who discussed in verse the problems of his time, who talked to his readers on terms of easy equality, and who sought to base his work on reason and tolerance. The wounds left by revolution and civil war had to be healed, a new synthesis arrived at, and common sense might be a better guide than fanaticism. Men must agree to differ; they must accept new knowledge, new social and economic patterns, and make them work.

In the *Secular Masque* written at the end of his life in 1700, he makes Momus say to Mars, who has just been celebrating war,

> Thy sword within the scabbard keep,
>   And let mankind agree;
> Better the world were fast asleep
>   Than kept awake by thee.
> The fools are only thinner,
>   With all our cost and care;
> But neither side a winner
>   For things are as they were.

Janus and Chronos conclude

> 'Tis well an old age is out
> And time to begin a new.

In this tough, jaunty, sceptical way he asserts the values he admired. We shall note that the tone of *Religio Laici*, a poem celebrating the Church of England, differs little from that of *The Hind and the Panther* written after his conversion to Roman Catholicism. And it is this tone of voice, this manner—these manners, if you like—that we must listen for and respond to.

Here he is, at the age of eighteen, still at school, manipulating the metaphysical conceit in the *Elegy on the Death of the Lord Hastings*. The elegy, we must remember, is a public form, and it is a part of the poet's function to produce such tributes. The reader should know that the young Lord died of the smallpox.

Blisters with pride swelled, which through his flesh did sprout
Like rosebuds, stuck in the lily-skin about.
Each little pimple had a tear in it,
To wail the fault his rising did commit;
Which, rebel-like, with its own lord at strife,
Thus made an insurrection 'gainst his life.
Or were these gems sent to adorn his skin,
The cabinet of a richer soul within?
No comet need foretell his change drew on,
Whose corps might seem a constellation. ...

The shell of the conceit is there, but we have only to turn back to Donne or Herbert or Marvell to see that the shell is empty. Absurd these lines may be, but they show remarkable technical accomplishment for a boy of eighteen. Turn from this to the mature Dryden. The next quotation comes from *Religio Laici* (1682), a defence of the Church of England, which is seen as a rational compromise between the authoritarian dogmatism of Rome and the ignorant fanaticism of the proliferating sects which were the result of the Reformation.

In times O'ergrown with rust and ignorance
A gainful trade their clergy did advance;
When want of learning kept the layman low
And none but priests were authorised to know;
When what small knowledge was in them did dwell
And he a God who could but read or spell;
Then Mother Church did mightily prevail;
She parcelled out the Bible by retail,
But still expounded what she sold or gave,
To keep it in her power to damn and save.
Scripture was scarce, and as the market went,
Poor laymen took salvation on content,
As needy men take money, good or bad;
God's word they had not, but the priest's they had.
Yet, whate'er false conveyances they made,
The lawyer still was certain to be paid.
In these dark times they learned their knack so well,
That by long use they grew infallible.
At last a knowing age began to inquire
If they the Book or that did them inspire;
And making narrower search they found, though late,
That what they thought the priest's was their estate,
Taught by the will produced, the written word,
How long they had been cheated on record.
Then every man, who saw the title fair,
Claimed a child's part and put in for a share,

Consulted soberly his private good,
And saved himself as cheap as e'er he could.
   'Tis true my friend (and far be flattery hence),
This good had full as bad a consequence;
The Book thus put in every vulgar hand,
Which each presumed he best could understand,
The common rule was made the common prey,
And at the mercy of the rabble lay.
The tender page with horny fists was galled,
And he was gifted most that loudest bawled;
The spirit gave the doctoral degree,
And every member of a Company
Was of his trade and of the Bible free.
Plain truths enough for needful use they found,
But men would still be itching to expound;
Each was ambitious of the obscurest place,
No measure ta'en from Knowledge, all from Grace.
Study and pains were now no more their care,
Texts were explained by fasting and by prayer:
This was the fruit the private spirit brought,
Occasioned by great zeal and little thought.
While crowds unlearned, with rude devotion warm,
About the sacred viands buzz and swarm;
The fly-blown text creates a crawling brook
And turns to maggots what was meant for food.
A thousand daily sects rise up and die,
A thousand more the perished race supply:
So all we make of Heaven's discovered will
Is not to have it or to use it ill.
The danger's much the same, on several shelves
If others wreck us or we wreck ourselves. . . .

We might begin by comparing these couplets with others we have quoted. Their clarity and precision is achieved by fitting the syntactical unit into the metrical pattern, while keeping as far as possible the normal word order, and a general tone of easy and vigorous conversation. As Dr. Johnson said, the 'metre has neither weakened the force nor clouded the perspicuity of argument'. Dryden carelessly dismisses the past—a time 'o'ergrown with rust and ignorance'. The moderns know more; they are therefore better. The poet has confidence in his own age, in the values he is recommending, and in his own place in his age as the mediator of those values. Then comes the significant word 'trade': the vocabulary of commerce—retail, market, on account, money—or of the law—conveyances, estate, will, title—dominates the first paragraph. Religion discussed in these terms hardly seems man's chief end, and we are in a mental climate very different from that of Donne or Herbert. Yet the book is the Bible and the Will is God's Will. Dryden's tone implies that whatever religion may be, it is certainly not worth cutting anyone's throat about, or, we may add, burning them at the stake. The indictment against Catholicism is made by such phrases as 'kept the layman low' and 'they learned their knack so well' (consider the implications of the word 'knack') 'that by long use' (the 'new' 'knowing' age suspects 'use' or custom) 'they grew infallible' (there is something contemptuous in the weak rhyme.) The faults of the reformed churches are implied by such lines as

> And saved himself as cheap as e'er he could,

where 'private good' and 'cheap' recall the close association between the City and the Puritan party; though they at the same time imply a gibe at the secular wealth of the Roman church. But the word 'child' reminds us that we are all the children of one Father, and we can speak direct to him. Then comes a more detailed analysis of the defects of the reformed churches, through which we are led to see that what is needed is a balance between two extremes: between an infallible church, using Christian truth for its own ends, and the anarchy of the unsocial, dangerous, disorderly fruits of the 'private spirit'. Such a balance, the poem goes on to say, is to be found in the Anglican compromise. We can note the distinction between the layman— it is a bad thing to 'keep him low'—and the 'rabble' who lay 'vulgar hands' on the Bible, who 'presume' to understand it, but are not fit to do so. If the medieval church 'parcelled out the Bible by retail' the sixteenth- and seventeenth-century sectarians made it their 'prey'; between corporate and private selfishness there is nothing to choose. We shall be able to see, I think, that the layman, to whom this poem is addressed, is Dryden's public, and that the qualities he can be deduced to possess are those the poet believed to be necessary if the new age was to produce a stable society. Dryden is still a court poet (however different his court may have been from those of 'Eliza and our James'), and his layman has aristocratic affiliations. He despises 'horny fists', tradesmen, and those who claim private spiritual inspiration; persons whom Dryden described elsewhere as the 'dregs of a democracy'. Gentlemen don't 'bawl'. Then comes the key line:

> Plain truths enough for needful use they found. . . .

All that is 'needful' is in the Bible, and is 'plain' or obvious to common sense, that sense which is common to all men. In the eyes of the rational layman the theological disputes of the 'past age' stand by implication condemned. The line

> No measure ta'en from Knowledge, all from Grace ...

glances at the controversy about justification by faith, and stresses the necessity of knowledge, the use of intelligence and reason. The 'layman' is capable of such knowledge, the 'rabble' not. The sectarian attitudes are branded not only as socially inferior, unworthy a gentleman's attention, but as reactionary, out of the mainstream of reason and progress. Neither texts nor anything else can be explained by 'fasting and by prayer'; 'great zeal' is a mere nuisance. All this is summed up, and the main point of the passage driven home, by the splendid conceit about the flies on the sacred viands, with its fierce antithetical climax:

> And turns to maggots what was meant for food,

a line which admirably exemplifies Dryden's technique. It is metrically regular, natural plain English—a 'plain truth'; it has the virtues of good expository prose. Yet the metrical exactitude, the alliteration, the placing of the twin stresses of 'maggots' and 'food', the terms of the antithesis, the way we are forced to enunciate the d and the two t's in 'And turns to' and the two f's in 'meant for food'—all these details help to organize our feelings, and this sort of concentrated effect is possible only in verse. The apparent ease, the simplicity of the lines is the result of a keen ear, a clear mind, self-confidence, and hard labour.

The reader is invited to make a similar detailed commentary for himself on the next passage, from the *The Hind and the Panther*, written in 1687, in defence of Roman Catholicism after the poet's conversion in 1686, a year after James II's accession to the throne. 'Such proselytes' said Evelyn tartly, 'were no great loss to the church', but our modern reader must be more concerned with the attitudes Dryden is recommending than with the question of his sincerity. The poem is an allegory, or extended fable, in which the 'milk-white Hind' represents Catholicism, and the Panther,

> Sure the noblest next the Hind
> And fairest creature of the spotted kind,

the Church of England. Other beasts represent the sects and among them the 'wolfish race' stands for the Presbyterians and Calvinists. I have cut a long passage which purports to give the history of these sects because it is sufficient for our purpose to feel the parallel implied

between the extermination of the real wolf in Britain and the necessity
of controlling the Calvinist, who is politically dangerous. The 'rule
of the saints' means the destruction of society, which will by them be
'Drawn to the dregs of a democracy'.

> More haughty than the rest, the wolfish race ⎫
> Appear with belly gaunt and famished face; ⎬
> Never was so deformed a beast of grace. ⎭
> His ragged tail between his legs he wears ⎫
> Close clapped for shame; but his rough crest he rears, ⎬
> And pricks up his predestinating ears. ⎭
> His wild disordered walk, his haggered eyes,
> Did all the bestial citizens surprise;
> Though feared and hated, yet he ruled a while,
> As captain or companion of the spoil.
> Full many a year his hateful head had been
> For tribute paid, nor since in Cambria seen;
> The last of all the litter scaped by chance
> And from Geneva first infected France. . . .
> As, where in fields the fairy rounds are seen,
> A rank sour herbage rises on the green;
> So springing where these midnight elves advance
> Rebellion prints the footsteps of the dance.
> Such are their doctrines, such contempt they show
> To heaven above and to their Prince below
> As none but traitors and blasphemers know.
> God like the tyrant of the skies is placed,
> And kings, like slaves, beneath the crowd debased.
> So fulsome is their food that flocks refuse
> To bite, and only dogs for physic use;
> As, where the lightning runs along the ground,
> No husbandry can heal the blasting wound;
> Nor bladed grass nor bearded corn succeeds,
> But scales of scurf, and putrefaction breeds:
> Such wars, such waste, such fiery tracks of dearth
> Their zeal has left, and such a teemless earth.
> But as the poisons of the deadliest kind
> Are to their own unhappy coasts confined,
> As only Indian shades of sight deprive,
> And magic plants will but in Colchos thrive,
> So presbytery and pestilential zeal
> Can only flourish in a common weal.
>   From Celtic woods is chased the wolfish crew;
> But ah! some pity e'en to beasts is due:
> Their native walks, methinks, they might enjoy,
> Curbed of their native malice to destroy.

> Of all the tyrannies on human kind
> The worst is that which persecutes the mind.
> Let us but weigh at what offence we strike;
> 'Tis but because we cannot think alike.
> In punishing of this, we overthrow
> The laws of nations and of nature too.
> Beasts are the subjects of tyrannic sway,
> Where still the stronger on the weaker prey;
> Man only of a softer mould is made,
> Not for his fellows' ruin, but their aid:
> Created kind, beneficent and free,
> The noble image of the Deity. . . .

The interest of this passage lies in the way the description of the wolf, and the social effects of his bestial doctrines, are contrasted with the way the poet thinks he should be treated. The beast is 'very proud revengeful and ambitious'; he is also ridiculous—he wears his tail, his Geneva cloak, close clapped for shame. He pricks up his predestinating ears—the Puritan fashion of close-cropped hair made their ears seem to stick out, while long-haired gentlemanly cavaliers concealed theirs. Note how the alliteration heightens the ridicule, and how 'predestinating' enforces the doctrinal point. We may compare Marvell's lines from the *Horatian Ode*:

> The Pict no shelter now can find
> Within his parti-coloured mind . . .

The final indictment is that

> Presbytery and pestilential zeal
> Can only flourish in a commonweal . . .

Allegiance to the monarchy is the true bond of society.

> Take but degree away, untune that string,
> And, hark, what discord follows!

If there is a stable monarchy, if we do not live in Colchos or amid Indian shades, zeal holds no danger for us, it is no longer pestilential, or plague-bearing. Therefore, we can afford to be tolerant and if we are tolerant we shall have no more wars of religion, a conclusion which is introduced by two similes. The effect of Calvinism is likened first to the allegedly poisonous fairy rings ('whose footsteps do the green sour ringlets make') destroying the virtues of good pasture; and second, to the lightning-blasted ground, where nothing will grow, where the earth is 'teemless'. These are images of disorder, such as we can find in Shakespeare, but they lack the intensity, the felt belief, of similar passages in Shakespeare and Donne.

The wolfish crew being driven from the Celtic woods is an allusion to the Revocation of the Edict of Nantes, but the force of the passage is not dependent on our being able to identify exactly historical allusions, for if Dryden were nothing more than a polemical writer we should not still be reading him. The important theme is given in the next line:

> But ah! some pity e'en to beasts is due . . .

a dramatic turn, after the bitter invective of what has gone before. The wolf must have no political power—his 'native malice to destroy' must be curbed, yet there is no need to exterminate him. Then comes the noble couplet:

> Of all the tyrannies on human kind
> The worst is that which persecutes the mind.

Dryden can here salute the author of *Areopagitica*. Beasts prey on beasts, for 'tis their nature to; man is made to aid his fellows, but the beast, the sect, is less than human. We may, perhaps, see 'man' here as an equivalent to 'layman' in the previous passage, and his qualities—kind, beneficent and free—those that Dryden is trying to establish. The theme of the two poems differs but the author's temper of mind, his tone, remains the same. Worth remarking is the easy movement of

> 'Tis but because we cannot think alike . . .

How elegantly and how imperceptibly are the accents of everyday speech fitted to the stresses of the metre!

Next come two stanzas from another of Dryden's elegies, the *Ode on the Death of Mrs. Anne Killigrew* who died of smallpox at the age of twenty-four. He is here again called on to perform a public function, and it is interesting to compare these lines with those on Lord Hastings, and see how the poet's mature work differs from his prentice efforts. He has now perfected a plain resonant sonorous marching verse. If we think, as we read it, of Donne's *Anniversaries*, or of *Lycidas*, the comparison will show great losses: but we must take Dryden's poem for what it is, a grand piece of baroque decoration.

> Thou youngest virgin-daughter of the skies,
>   Made in the last promotion of the blest;
> Whose palms, new plucked from Paradise,
> In spreading branches more sublimely rise,
>   Rich with immortal green above the rest:

Whether adopted to some neighbouring star,
Thou roll'st above us in thy wandering race,
  Or in procession fixed and regular
Moved with the heaven's majestic pace,
  Or called to more superior bliss,
Thou treadst with seraphims the vast abyss:
Whatever happy region be thy place,
Cease thy celestial song a little space;
Thou wilt have time enough for hymns divine,
Since Heaven's eternal year is thine.
Hear then a mortal Muse thy praise rehearse
  In no ignoble verse,
But such as thy own voice did practise here,
When thy first fruits of poesy were given,
To make thyself a welcome inmate there;
  While yet a young probationer
  And candidate of Heaven.

There isn't a single original idea: only a very adroit handling of conventional materials, allied in feeling and intention to the huge allegorical paintings of the period, those ceilings

Where sprawl the saints of Verrio or Laguerre.

We may smile at the use of the term 'promotion', and the idea of the young lady's palms being greener than green; but we must surely agree that Dryden is quite right—the verse is *not* ignoble, and we enjoy his obvious pleasure in his own virtuosity, and his sublime confidence in the power of his 'mortal Muse'.

The second stanza can be put beside Donne's sonnet which begins

At the round earth's imagined corners blow
Your trumpets angels. . . .

The material is similar, but in Dryden's stanza there is little of Donne's deep religious feeling. Yet Dryden is serious about the 'sacred poets' and their 'heavenly gift of poesy'. Such assurance—note the invincible progress of the piled clauses—when—when—when—and the un-arguable finality of the two sets of triple rhymes—can only come from a deep-rooted belief in the poet's calling, and a solid conviction of his place in society.

When in mid air the golden trump shall sound,
  To raise the nations underground;
When in the Valley of Jehosophat
The judging God shall close the book of Fate,

And there the last assizes keep
For those who wake and those who sleep;
When rattling bones together fly
From the four corners of the sky;
When sinews o'er the skeletons are spread,
Those clothed with flesh, and life inspires the dead;
The sacred poets first shall hear the sound,
And foremost from the tomb shall bound,
For they are covered with the lightest ground;
And straight, with inborn vigour, on the wing,
Like mounting larks to the new morning sing.
There thou, sweet saint, before the quire shall go,
As harbinger of Heaven, the way to show,
The way which thou so well hast learned below.

The following song shows Dryden's lyric writing in the Jonsonian-Cavalier tradition. Poise and polite elegance he can command, but not the charm of Carew, or the hidden fire of Marvell.

A Song to a Fair Young Lady
Going out of Town in the Spring.

Ask not the cause, why sullen Spring
   So long delays her flowers to bear;
Why warbling birds forget to sing,
   And winter storms invert the year;
Chloris is gone, and Fate provides
To make it spring, where she resides.

Chloris is gone, the cruel fair;
   She cast not back a pitying eye;
But left her lover in despair,
   To sigh, to languish, and to die.
Ah, how can those fair eyes endure,
To give the wounds they will not cure!

Great god of love, why hast thou made
   A face that can all hearts command,
That all religions can invade,
   And change the laws of every land?
Where thou hadst placed such power before
Thou shouldst have made her mercy more.

When Chloris to the temple comes,
   Adoring crowds before her fall;

> She can restore the dead from tombs,
>   And every life but mine recall.
> I only am by love designed
>   To be the victim for mankind.

To end with, the lines *To the Memory of Mr. Oldham*, who became famous in 1679 for his Satires on the Jesuits, and who died at the early age of twenty-nine. Dryden admired his work, and this poem is a moving tribute. Note the neo-classic implication that only time and practice can produce the 'correct' poet; but note, too, the feeling, very real in Dryden, that genius is above the 'dull sweets' of correctitude.

> Farewell, too little and too lately known,
> Whom I began to think and call my own:
> For sure our souls were near allied, and thine
> Cast in the same poetic mould as mine.
> One common note on either lyre did strike,
> And knaves and fools we both abhorred alike.
> To the same goal did both our studies drive:
> The last set out the soonest did arrive.
> Thus Nisus fell upon the slippery place,
> Whilst his young friend performed and won the race.
> O early ripe! to thy abundant store
> What could advancing age have added more?
> It might (what nature never gives the young)
> Have taught the numbers of thy native tongue.
> But satire needs not those, and wit will shine
> Through the harsh cadence of a rugged line.
> A noble error, and but seldom made,
> When poets are by too much force betrayed.
> Thy generous fruits, though gathered ere their prime,
> Still showed a quickness; and maturing time
> But mellows what we write to the dull sweets of rhyme.
> Once more, hail and farewell! farewell, thou young,
> But ah! too short, Marcellus of our tongue!
> Thy brows with ivy and with laurels bound;
> But fate and gloomy night encompass thee around.

4

THE EIGHTEENTH CENTURY

The great poet of the first half of the eighteenth century was Alexander Pope (1688–1744), who inherited from Dryden the perfected, formal heroic couplet: here is his own account of the matter.

> We conquer'd France, but felt our captive's charms:
> Her arts victorious triumphed o'er our arms;
> Britain to soft refinements less a foe
> Wit grew polite, and numbers learn'd to flow.
> Waller was smooth; but Dryden taught to join ⎫
> The varying verse, the full resounding line, ⎬
> The long majestic march, and energy divine. ⎭
> Though still some traces of our rustic vein.
> And splay-foot verse remain'd, and will remain;
> Late, very late, correctness grew our care,
> When the tired nation breathed from civil war.

We begin with some lines from the precocious *Pastorals*; written, he says, when he was sixteen. The reader will recognize some of the lines, since they were lifted by a librettist for one of Handel's operas, and the tune Handel set them to is well known.

> This harmless grove no lurking viper hides,
> But in my breast the serpent love abides.
> Here bees from blossoms sip the rosy dew,
> But your Alexis knows no sweets but you.
> O deign to visit our forsaken seats,
> The mossy fountains and the green retreats!
> Where'er you walk, cool gales shall fan the glade,
> Trees, where you sit, shall crowd into a shade;
> Where'er you tread the blushing flowers shall rise,
> And all things flourish where you turn your eyes.

This is the sort of verse with which an ambitious young talent would seek to recommend itself to the world of letters in 1704. It is easy to mock the conventions—the serpent love lurking in the poet's breast (we have come a long way from Donne's

> The spider love which transubstantiates all,
> And can convert Manna to gall. . . .)

the muses, the rosy dew. The pat, inevitable epithets are little more
than padding: indeed, we see how bits of lines can be prefabricated.
Take a demonstrative adjective, or a definite or indefinite article,
a two-syllable adjective and a monosyllabic noun:

> This harmless grove

and two feet of your necessary five are done. So—'the rosy dew', 'no
lurking viper', 'the mossy fountains' and 'the green retreats.' These
remarks can be applied to a very great deal of eighteenth-century
verse. At worst, this is a kind of apparatus one has to put up with;
yet such verse is always clear, and can have a precision, a directness,
an exactitude that is one of the virtues of the age. What is most
immediately important is that such strictures do not apply to Pope's best
verse. We may note in passing that the four lines stolen by Handel's
librettist are strikingly melodious; the young Pope has already mastered
the technique of this sort of verse, has 'learned to dance' and is beginning
to play tunes of his own composing.

Here are more examples of melodious, picturesque, 'faery' writing,
in the tradition derived from Spenser and Milton, which seemed to
many readers, especially in the latter half of the century, to be more
truly 'poetic' than the satiric manner. The first two are from *Windsor
Forest* a poem begun in 1705 and published in 1713.

> There, interspersed in lawns and opening glades,
> Thin trees arise that shun each other's shades.
> Here in full light the russet plains extend;
> There, wrapt in clouds, the bluish hills ascend.
> Even the wild heath displays her purple dyes,
> And midst the desert fruitful fields arise,
> That crown'd with tufted trees and springing corn,
> Like verdant isles the sable wastes adorn. . . .

In the next lines the poet describes the tyranny of the Norman
conqueror who destroyed farms to make 'chases' for hunting in.

> Proud Nimrod first the bloody chase began,
> A mighty hunter, and his prey was man:
> Our haughty Norman boasts that barbarous name,
> And makes his trembling slaves the royal game.
> The fields are ravish'd from the industrious swains
> From men their cities, and from gods their fanes:
> The levelled towns with weeds lie covered o'er;
> The hollow winds through naked temples roar;
> Round broken columns clasping ivy twined;

> O'er heaps of ruin stalk'd the stately hind;
> The fox obscene to gaping tombs retires,
> And savage howlings fill the sacred quires. . . .

The enlightened poet, and his enlightened reader, enjoying the benefits of 'Fair Liberty, Britannia's Goddess' which are the gifts of 'great Anna'—

> 'Let discord cease!'
> She said,—the world obey'd, and all was peace!

can from the safe shore enjoy the 'pleasing Horror' of this potent evocation of ruin. This mode of writing is of minor interest compared to the great satires; yet they are often enriched by its echoes and 'great Anna' enlivens a famous couplet in *The Rape of the Lock*. Consider for example, the strange, remote pathos in the final lines of this account, from the fourth *Moral Essay* of Timon's villa, where nature has been forced to bow to a false and distorting taste.

> The suffering eye inverted nature sees,
> Trees cut to statues, statues thick as trees;
> With here a fountain, never to be play'd;
> And there a summer-house that knows no shade;
> Here Amphitrite sails through myrtle bowers;
> There gladiators fight, or die in flowers;
> Unwater'd see the drooping sea-horse mourn,
> And swallows roost in Nilus' dusty urn. . . .

From *Eloisa to Abelard* (1717) come these lines, which resume the imagery and feeling of what we may call the 'Gothic' element in the faery way of writing. Much of this material was used by Gray and Collins, and reappears, in very different linguistic guise, in Scott, Coleridge, Keats and the Victorians. Eloisa, in her convent, remembers her lover.

> In these lone walls, their days eternal bound,
> These moss-grown domes with spiry turrets crown'd,
> Where awful arches make a noon-day night,
> And the dim windows shed a solemn light. . . .
> The darksome pines that o'er yon rocks reclined
> Wave high, and murmur to the hollow wind,
> The wandering streams, that shine between the hills,
> The grots that echo to the tinkling rills,
> The dying gales that pant upon the trees,
> The lakes that quiver to the curling breeze;
> No more these scenes my meditation aid,
> Or lull to rest the visionary maid.

E

> But o'er the twilight groves and dusky caves,
> Long-sounding aisles, and intermingled graves,
> Black melancholy sits, and round her throws
> A death-like silence, and a dread repose:
> Her gloomy presence saddens all the scene,
> Shades every flower, and darkens every green,
> Deepens the murmur of the falling floods,
> And breathes a browner horror on the woods. . . .

In 1712, he published *The Rape of the Lock* an Heroi-Comical poem. It is an amusing, brilliant, complex work. In our first quotation the heroine is getting up (not very early) in the morning.

> And now, unveil'd, the toilet stands display'd,
> Each silver vase in mystic order laid.
> First, robed in white, the nymph intent adores,
> With head uncover'd, the cosmetic powers.
> A heavenly image in the glass appears,
> To that she bends, to that her eyes she rears;
> The inferior priestess, at her altar's side,
> Trembling begins the sacred rites of pride.
> Unnumber'd treasures ope at once, and here
> The various offerings of the world appear;
> From each she nicely culls with curious toil,
> And decks the goddess with the glittering spoil.
> This casket India's glowing gems unlocks,
> And all Arabia breathes from yonder box.
> The tortoise here and elephant unite,
> Transform'd to combs, the speckled, and the white.
> Here files of pins extend their shining rows,
> Puffs, powders, patches, bibles, billets-doux.
> Now awful beauty puts on all its arms;
> The fair each moment rises in her charms,
> Repairs her smiles, awakens every grace,
> And calls forth all the wonders of her face;
> Sees by degrees a purer blush arise,
> And keener lightnings quicken in her eyes.
> The busy sylphs surround their darling care,
> These set the head, and those divide the hair,
> Some fold the sleeve, whilst others plait the gown;
> And Betty's praised for labours not her own.

This, we must remember, is a parody epic; the fun lies in the fact that the trivial and the everyday is treated in heroic terms. The young lady at her dressing-table is a priestess at her altar. The toilet is 'unveiled', the vases are 'mystic', the lady-priestess is 'rob'd in white'. She first 'adores' 'the cosmetic powers', but then the 'heavenly image' in the glass—herself; she is the object of her own worship, and these are the 'sacred rites of pride'. The clash of meaning between 'sacred' and 'pride' is powerful. Pride 'The never failing vice of fools' is first on the list of the seven deadly sins; 'by that sin fell the angels' (ladies are frequently referred to as angels) and we can feel that the fun is serious. The whole world contributes luxurious offerings to this goddess. We believe in her beauty, but placing of 'bibles' amid these elegant trifles invites us to wonder about the values that rule her life, and the life of the social group she belongs to. This is, we may say, satirical; yet satire seems a harsh, butterfly-breaking term to use. What unifies the passage is the tone, the exquisite tact with which its elements are displayed. In the *Essay on Criticism* (1709) Pope had written

> Without good breeding truth is disapproved;
> That only makes superior sense beloved.

There is tough sense behind the account of Belinda dressing; the poem is 'about' human behaviour and human society. But Pope rarely lets harshness obtrude and the passage ends with the playful 'machinery' of the sylphs, the 'inferior priestess' becomes Betty again, and we are back in the gay, frivolous elegant world.

This complexity, and this underlying seriousness, are to be seen more clearly in our next quotation. Belinda and her friends have gone by water to Hampton Court (a royal residence, the centre of this society), where they are to take coffee, and play cards, and where the lock is to be lost.

> Close by those meads, for ever crown'd with flowers,
> Where Thames with pride surveys his rising towers,
> There stands a structure of majestic frame,
> Which from the neighbouring Hampton takes its name.
> Here Britain's statesmen oft the fall foredoom
> Of foreign tyrants, and of nymphs at home;
> Here thou, great ANNA! whom three realms obey,
> Dost sometimes counsel take—and sometimes tea.
> Hither the heroes and nymphs resort,
> To taste awhile the pleasures of a court;
> In various talk the instructive hours they pass'd,
> Who gave the ball, or paid the visit last;
> One speaks the glory of the British Queen,
> And one describes a charming Indian screen;
> A third interprets motions, looks, and eyes;
> At every word a reputation dies.

Snuff, or the fan, supplies each pause of chat,
With singing, laughing, ogling, and all that.
  Meanwhile, declining from the noon of day,
The sun obliquely shoots his burning ray:
The hungry judges soon the sentence sign,
And wretches hang that jurymen may dine;
The merchant from the Exchange returns in peace,
And the long labours of the toilet cease.

Here the seriousness is not in question. We move from great Anna to the wretch in the dock—the whole social order is in these lines; and behind them is the notion of the heroic, the epic of noble deeds making the sordid reality more sordid. It is a curious fact that the classical models were only life-giving when they were mocked. Direct, serious imitation is sterile, and yet, paradoxically, the burlesque is deadly serious. There are Olympian suggestions in the opening lines —'for ever crown'd with flowers'—and in the periphrasis for Hampton Court we can see the elegant artificiality noted in the *Pastorals* here made a vehicle for mockery. Next the anticlimax, worked by the pun on 'fall', bumping us down from 'foreign tyrants' to 'nymphs'. The monarch herself comes next, and we see that the poet's target is the life and manners of those who rule society, and set the tone of its behaviour. Once more, the ideal of nobility, 'the high Roman, fashion', which is behind all this, points the contrast with modern triviality. So with the characters in the poem, the heroes and the nymphs. What should be their pleasures? What should be the pleasures of a court? These are exalted beings; surely their pastimes are noble? The next series of neat couplets in which the second line deflates the first, answers these implied questions with the trivial facts. See the force of 'instructive'—this is precisely what these hours are not—and how the 'epic' diction

One speaks the Glory of the British Queen

alternates with the chat of daily life. The word 'motion' used to mean a puppet-show, and the puppeteer was called the 'interpreter'. These people are manipulated by malicious gossip, and fear for their reputations, or, to use the term that Pope uses so ambiguously, 'honour'. If these are the pleasures, and the manners, of a court, where, we may ask, are true values to be found? Later, in the person of Clarissa, the poet supplies an answer. This would not be a truly Augustan poem if he didn't.

'Meanwhile,' as the sun sets, business in the city (the city that the court rules and despises) is quickly despatched. The opening couplet of the new paragraph, with its formal periphrasis, again illustrates the mock epic style, but it has a sinister resonance. 'Obliquely' carries ominous overtones. Suddenly the poet presents us with the criminal in the dock. His case is quickly over. Why? Because judge and jury are hungry. The lines which have been amusingly juggling foreign tyrants against nymphs, and counsel against tea startle us with a savage antithesis, between the wretch and the juryman, hanging and dining. The baseness of this world, of everything which is done under the sun, is lit for a moment by a flash of lightning. We return via commerce (the merchant who returns in peace is no soldier, the Exchange no battlefield) to frivolity again, with the 'long labours of the toilet'.

In the *Essay on Criticism* Pope speaks of

> The generous pleasure to be charm'd with wit.

Wit is a key word in the critical vocabulary of this period, and obviously its connotations are much wider than they are today. Rather than try to define them, we might point to such a passage as this, where wit in the modern sense is present, for example in the play of meaning in such phrases as 'the long labours of the toilet', but where the grimmest of purposes are not excluded.

When the scheming baron has snipped off the lock, the hapless nymph laments her fate:

> What mov'd my mind with youthful lords to roam?
> Oh had I stay'd, and said my prayers at home!

and then, when 'the pitying audience melt in tears', Clarissa endeavours to make peace:

> Then grave Clarissa graceful waved her fan;
> Silence ensued, and thus the nymph began:—
> Say, why are beauties praised and honour'd most,
> The wise man's passion, and the vain man's toast?
> Why deck'd with all that land and sea afford,
> Why angels call'd and angel-like adored?
> Why round our coaches crowd the white-gloved beaux,
> Why bows the side-box from its inmost rows?
> How vain are all these glories, all our pains,
> Unless good sense preserve what beauty gains:
> That men may say, when we the front-box grace,
> Behold the first in virtue as in face!
> Oh! if to dance all night, and dress all day
> Charm'd the small-pox, or chased old-age away;
> Who would not scorn what housewife's cares produce,
> Or who would learn one earthly thing of use?

To patch, nay ogle, might become a saint,
Nor could it sure be such a sin to paint.
But since, alas! frail beauty must decay,
Curl'd or uncurl'd, since locks will turn to grey;
Since, painted or not painted, all shall fade,
And she who scorns a man must die a maid;
What then remains but well our power to use,
And keep good humour still whate'er we lose?
And trust me, dear! good-humour can prevail,
When airs, and flights, and screams, and scolding fail;
Beauties in vain their pretty eyes may roll;
Charms strike the sight, but merit wins the soul.
So spoke the dame, but no applause ensued. . . .

A trite moral, you may think: a platitude. But look more closely.
The lines which begin

Oh! if to dance all night. . . .

are at once a lament for the frailty of youth and beauty, and a reminder,
like the wretches and the jurymen, of the grim realities of life. The
reader of Pope must keep his intelligence alert and his ears open for
these delicate modulations of feeling. The poet would, moreover, at
this point expect the reader to pick up an Homeric echo. Here, from
his own translation, is the speech made by Sarpedon to Glaucus in the
twelfth book of the *Iliad*. The poem works if we don't catch this echo,
but its meaning is enriched if we do. Comparison of the two passages
can teach the reader much about the nature of the mock-heroic joke.

Why boast we, *Glaucus*! our extended Reign,
Where *Xanthus*' Streams enrich the *Lycian* Plain,
Our num'rous Herds that range the fruitful Field
And Hills where Vines their purple Harvest yield,
Our foaming Bowls with purer Nectar crown'd;
Our feasts enhanc'd with Music's sprightly Sound?
Why on those Shores are we with Joy survey'd,
Admir'd as Heroes, and as Gods obey'd?
Unless great Acts superior Merit prove,
And vindicate the bount'ous Pow'rs above.
'Tis ours, the Dignity they give, to grace;
The first in Valour, as the first in Place.
That when with wond'ring Eyes our martial Bands
Behold our Deeds transcending our Commands,
Such, they may cry, deserve the sov'reign State,
Whom these that envy, dare not imitate!
Could all our care elude the gloomy Grave,

> Which claims no less the fearful than the brave,
> For Lust of Fame I should not vainly dare
> In fighting Fields, nor urge thy Soul to War.
> But since, alas! ignoble Age must come,
> Disease, and Death's inexorable Doom;
> The life which others pay, let us bestow,
> And give to Fame what we to Nature owe;
> Brave tho' we fall, and honour'd if we live,
> Or let us Glory gain, or Glory give!

'Good sense' is another of the social ideals of the period; not a very exalted one, some readers may think, but still a possible line of defence against the small-pox, old age and death. No one listens, of course. There follows an epic conflict and the apotheosis of the lock, which flies skywards to become a comet. Here is the poem's splendidly rhetorical conclusion. There is one topical allusion, to Partridge, an astrologer of the time and a frequent butt of Pope's circle.

> But trust the Muse—she saw it upward rise,
> Though mark'd by none but quick, poetic eyes:
> (So Rome's great founder to the heavens withdrew,
> To Proculus alone confess'd in view:)
> A sudden star, it shot through liquid air,
> And drew behind a radiant trail of hair.
> Not Berenice's locks first rose so bright,
> The heavens bespangling with dishevell'd light.
> The sylphs behold it kindling as it flies,
> And pleased pursue its progress through the skies.
> This the beau monde shall from the Mall survey,
> And hail with music its propitious ray;
> This, the blest Lover shall for Venus take,
> And send up vows from Rosamonda's Lake.
> This Partridge soon shall view in cloudless skies,
> When next he looks through Galileo's eyes
> And hence the egregious wizard shall foredoom
> The fate of Louis, and the fall of Rome.
> Then cease, bright nymph! to mourn thy ravish'd hair,
> Which adds new glory to the shining sphere!
> Not all the tresses that fair head can boast,
> Shall draw such envy as the Lock you lost,
> For after all the murders of your eye,
> When, after millions slain, yourself shall die;
> When those fair suns shall set, as set they must,
> And all those tresses shall be laid in dust,
> This lock the Muse shall consecrate to fame,
> And 'midst the stars inscribe Belinda's name.

Next a short passage from the second of the *Moral Essays*, '*Of the Character of Women*'.

> Pleasures the sex, as children birds, pursue,
> Still out of reach, yet never out of view;
> Sure, if they catch, to spoil the toy at most,
> To covet flying, and regret when lost:
> At last, to follies youth could scarce defend,
> It grows their age's prudence to pretend;
> Ashamed to own they gave delight before,
> Reduced to feign it, when they give no more:
> As hags hold sabbaths less for joy than spite,
> So these their merry, miserable night:
> Still round and round the ghosts of beauty glide
> And haunt the places where their honour died.
> See how the world its veterans rewards!
> A youth of frolics, an old age of cards;
> Fair to no purpose, artful to no end,
> Young without lovers, old without a friend;
> A fop their passion, but their prize a sot,
> Alive, ridiculous; and dead, forgot!
> Ah, friend! to dazzle let the vain design;
> To raise the thought, and touch the heart, be thine!
> That charm shall grow, while what fatigues the ring,
> Flaunts and goes down, an unregarded thing:
> So when the sun's broad beam has tired the sight,
> All mild ascends the moon's more sober light,
> Serene in virgin modesty she shines,
> And unobserved the glaring orb declines.

We begin with the 'general truth' which it was one of the objects of the neo-classic poets to inculcate: women are silly and frivolous. The simile is worked out clearly and in detail; it is not, like Donne's compasses, a startling conceit; the ideas are not 'yoked violently together', but developed reasonably out of the original picture of the children and the birds. We note how the implication: child—childish bears on the whole tone of the passage, and how charged with meaning are the verbs: catch, spoil, covet, regret. Then comes the couplet about the sex's follies. When, in Pope's writings, we get what we may call a big moral word like 'prudence', we should look carefully at its implications. Here one 'prudence', the virtue as it should be, as it is known and approved by Pope and his readers, is contrasted with another 'prudence', a label for the kind of behaviour practised by the aged ladies, and approved by the 'beau monde'. And what is their prudence? To pretend to be still capable, denying the age that everyone else can see, of actions so silly that even youth cannot excuse them. They are ashamed to admit to the love affairs of their youth (lest their 'honour' might be 'stained'); but now that they are beyond love-affairs, they still claim to have them. They are among those who did not applaud Clarissa's common sense. Their social merriment, which to the truly prudent observer is miserable, is like a dance of witches—we note the cruel emphasis on 'hags'—like witches they meet to do evil: 'at every word a reputation dies'. The paragraph concludes with an extraordinarily moving couplet, at once savage and pathetic, in which the first line echoes the rhythm of the dance, both ball and sabbath, whose circular movement is 'artful to no end'.

> Still round and round the ghosts of beauty glide
> And haunt the places where their honour died.

The exquisitely modulated vowels are an image of the music. The alliteration enforces the strict rhythm; 'ghosts of beauty' makes it a *danse macabre*; and the ball-room, we see in the next line, was, in the past, when beauty was real and not a ghost, the scene of the nymph's fall. The arrangement of the second line forces us to emphasize haunt, honour and died—forces us to feel about the values of the *beau monde*, the world.

The line which begins the next paragraph:

> See how the world its veterans rewards...

implies that the world, aristocratic society, is a battlefield where all fight for pre-eminence. The old, the veterans, can no longer fight, and they are ill-used or neglected as all old soldiers tend to be, left to beg at 'the town's end for life'. Then we are back in the ball-room, where the young dance and the old play cards, and the next lines sum up the indictment—this life squanders its talents on a purposeless existence. They fall in love with a well-dressed fool, they marry a rich drunkard. The final couplet knocks the nails into the coffin.

Consider in detail Pope's ingenious manipulations. Verbs are omitted for brevity's sake. The antitheses are forced on our minds by both sound and syntax, for the second half of the line is a kind of mirror image of the first. We begin with the fop and end with the sot, and the two short o's tie the two words together. The two close neighbours 'passion' and 'prize' alliterate. This alliteration, and the close proximity of the two words, force us to think of their difference. In this world your passion is one thing and your prize another. You suppress your feelings in favour of advancement; but even so your feelings have been wasted on a worthless object, and the prize you gain at the expense of these feelings is equally worthless. The fact that verbs are omitted makes us pause at the comma: 'Alive' (they were) 'ridiculous'. The contempt is underlined by the change from the long 'i' in 'alive' to the short ones in 'ridiculous'; the last syllable of 'ridiculous' bears only the slightest stress, so the flat middle of the line makes the heavily stressed 'dead' all the more emphatic. Moreover, we have three d's to pronounce, one at the end of 'and' and two in 'dead', and the effort we have to make over them helps to isolate the word, leaving 'forgot' to crack like a pistol shot at the end of the line.

The apostrophe which follows, with its reference to the vain, to raising the thoughts and touching the heart, and the sun's broad beam and so on, exhibits the Augustan love of moralizing generalities, and of a special poetic diction. What Pope has to say is undeniably true, it is exact and has a noble sound; but this sort of formal magniloquence is what wears least well in eighteenth-century verse. It is useful here to make a comparison with Donne. Yet in the middle of this passage we are jerked to attention again by the superb

> while what fatigues the ring,
> Flaunts and goes down, an unregarded thing. . . .

You say Ooh! at the exploding rocket ('flaunts') but you take no notice of the descending stick.

Lastly, the conclusion of another moral essay, *On the Use of Riches*: the story of Sir Balaam. The reference in the first line is to 'the Monument built in memory of the Great Fire of London, with an inscription importing that city to have been burnt by the Papists. This inscription has since been erased.'

> Where London's column, pointing at the skies
> Like a tall bully, lifts the head, and lies;
> There dwelt a citizen of sober fame,
> A plain good man, and Balaam was his name;
> Religious, punctual, frugal and so forth;
> His word would pass for more than he was worth.
> One solid dish his week-day meal affords,
> An added pudding solemnised the Lord's:
> Constant at church, and 'Change; his gains were sure;
> His givings rare, save farthings to the poor.
> The devil was piqued such saintship to behold,
> And longed to tempt him like good Job of old:
> But Satan now is wiser than of yore,
> And tempts by making rich, not making poor.

Roused by the prince of air, the whirlwinds sweep
The surge, and plunge his father in the deep;
Then full against his Cornish lands they roar,
And two rich shipwrecks bless the lucky shore.
Sir Balaam now, he lives like other folks,
He takes his chirping pint, and cracks his jokes:
'Live like yourself,' was soon my lady's word;
And lo! two puddings smoked upon the board.

Asleep and naked as an Indian lay,
An honest factor stole a gem away:
He pledged it to the knight; the knight had wit,
So kept the diamond, and the rogue was bit.
Some scruple rose, but thus he eased his thought,
'I'll now give sixpence where I gave a groat;
Where once I went to church, I'll go now twice—
And am so clear too of all other vice!'

The tempter saw his time; the work he plied
Stocks and subscriptions pour on every side,
Till all the demon makes his full descent
In one abundant shower of cent. per cent.,
Sinks deep within him and possesses whole,
Then dubs director, and secures his soul.

Behold Sir Balaam, now a man of spirit,
Ascribes his gettings to his parts and merit;
What late he call'd a blessing, now was wit,
And God's good providence a lucky hit.
Things change their titles as our manners turn:
His counting-house employ'd the Sunday morn;
Seldom at church ('twas such a busy life)
But duly sent his family and wife.
There (so the devil ordain'd) one Christmas-tide
My good old lady catch'd cold and died.

A nymph of quality admires our knight;
He marries, bows at court, and grows polite:
Leaves the dull cits, and joins (to please the fair)
The well-bred cuckolds in St. James's air:
First, for his son a gay commission buys,
Who drinks, whores, fights and in a duel dies:
His daughter flaunts a viscount's tawdry wife;
She bears a coronet and pox for life.
In Britain's senate he a seat obtains,
And one more pensioner St. Stephen gains.
My lady falls to play; so bad her chance,
He must repair it; takes a bribe from France;
The House impeach him, Coningsby harangues;
The court forsake him, and Sir Balaam hangs:

> Wife, son, and daughter, Satan! are thy own,
> His wealth yet dearer, forfeit to the crown:
> The devil and the king divide the prize
> And sad Sir Balaam curses God and dies.

In 1738, the year in which Pope issued the Epilogue to his satires, Samuel Johnson (1709–1784) published his first important poem, *London*, and in 1749 came the *Vanity of Human Wishes*, from which the following lines are taken.

> Unnumbered suppliants crown Preferment's gate,
> Athirst for wealth, and burning to be great;
> Delusive Fortune hears the incessant call,
> They mount, they shine, evaporate, and fall.
> On every stage the foes of peace attend,
> Hate dogs their flight, and insult mocks their end.
> Love ends with hope, the sinking statesman's door
> Pours in the morning worshipper no more;
> For growing names the weekly scribbler lies,
> To growing wealth the dedicator flies;
> From every room descends the painted face,
> That hung the bright Palladium of the place;
> And, smoked in kitchens, or in auctions sold,
> To better features yields the frame of gold;
> For now no more we trace in every line
> Heroic worth, benevolence divine:
> The form distorted justifies the fall,
> And detestation rids the indignant wall.

The solid, confident, tread of the couplets is immediately obvious. They are the work of a man who expresses the truth—the 'general truth'—of what he knows, and who also works in an accepted mode, who uses, even while he modifies it, an accepted tradition. His theme, given in his title, is one of the great common places: all is vanity, fame is fleeting, 'emulation hath a thousand sons which one by one pursue'. The 'great' are at the mercy of envy, chance and time. Wordsworth was later to inveigh against the eighteenth-century habit of using personifications, and it can, of course, become a sterile trick; but here it is functional. Preferment, fortune, hate, insult, detestation in this passage do a great deal of work and carry a great load of meaning; they are one of the means by which Johnson crams his couplets so full. The majestic regularity of the verse movement allows of many subtle variations. In this line (with which it is interesting to compare Pope's 'flaunts and goes down. . . .') consider the effect of 'evaporate':

> They mount, they shine, evaporate, and fall. . . .

The first, second and last feet are all heavily and solidly regular, the stresses falling on the monosyllabic verbs. 'Evaporate' occupies the third and fourth feet. It has only one really strong stress; the end of the word dies away—appropriately enough, so that this part of the line is lighter and weaker, and, since the four syllables are all in one word, quicker than the rest. All this reinforces its meaning—that the great vanish 'as though they have never been'. The eager movement of the crown of flatterers is conveyed in the one example of enjambment:

> ... the sinking statesman's door
> Pours in the morning worshipper no more.

These worshippers (of 'the bitch goddess, success') get there early to attend the great man's levee; but 'morning' also implies the falsity of their worship, which only happens during the service, so to speak, and plays no part in their lives. The passage is permeated by savage but controlled irony, which condemns the venal writer as well as the power seeker, and the whole structure is filled with living details. Note how the mechanically accurate stresses of

> For growing names the weekly scribbler lies. ...

echo the mechanical nature of the scribbler's work. Then the great man's portrait is taken down and put in the smoky kitchen, while the gilded frame, 'well saved', surrounds another face, no more heroic or divine than the one it replaces, though of course the flatterers say it is. Johnson would expect his reader—and this is characteristic of the period, to catch the allusion in Palladium, 'a safeguard of liberty, from the statue of Pallas, on which the safety of Troy depended'. This is a mock-heroic touch. It is worth, perhaps, paraphrasing the last couplet:

> The form distorted justifies the fall,
> And detestation rids the indignant wall.

The portrait's removal, symbolic of the removal of its subject, is justified, by the scandalous things that are said of him now. These things are distortions; they are therefore not the truth; but a distorted face is ugly, therefore away with it. But distortions are no truer than the former attributes of heroism and divinity, since both are but the fantasies of self-seeking flatterers, who now detest what they once adored. The transferred epithet (indignant wall) conveys, in its pompous absurdity, the fundamental falsity of the whole proceeding. It is the virtue of this style, this diction, to compress such a wide range of meaning into so small a compass, and to convey, in its fierce but always measured condemnation, the moral values which the poet upholds, and which his subjects betray.

Here is Johnson's poem *On the Death of Mr. Robert Levett*. Levett was a doctor, an old friend of Johnson's, who had shown him great kindness. The reader may like to compare the poem with the entry quoted by Boswell, in 'one of his memorandum books'. 'January 20, Sunday. Robert Levett was buried in the church-yard of Bridewell, between one and two in the afternoon. He died on Thursday 17, about seven in the morning, by an instantaneous death. He was an old and faithful friend; I have known him from about '46. *Commendavi.* May God have mercy on him. May he have mercy on me.'

> Condemn'd to Hope's delusive mine,
> As on we toil from day to day,
> By sudden blasts, or slow decline,
> Our social comforts drop away.
>
> Well tried through many a varying year,
> See Levett to the grave descend;
> Officious, innocent, sincere,
> Of every friendless name the friend.
>
> Yet still he fills Affection's eye,
> Obscurely wise and coarsely kind;
> Nor, letter'd Arrogance, deny
> Thy praise to merit unrefined.
>
> When fainting Nature call'd for aid,
> And hovering Death prepared the blow,
> His vigorous remedy display'd
> The power of Art without the show.
>
> In Misery's darkest cavern known,
> His useful care was ever nigh;
> Where hopeless Anguish pour'd his groan,
> And lonely Want retired to die.
>
> No summons, mock'd by chill delay;
> No petty gain, disdain'd by pride;
> The modest wants of every day,
> The toil of every day supplied.
>
> His virtues walk'd their narrow round,
> Nor made a pause, nor left a void;
> And sure the Eternal Master found
> The single talent well employ'd.

The busy day—the peaceful night,
Unfelt, unclouded, glided by;
His frame was firm—his powers were bright,
Though now his eightieth year was nigh.

Then with no fiery, throbbing pain,
No cold gradations of decay,
Death broke at once the vital chain,
And freed his soul the nearest way.

These lines show Johnson's characteristic precision, dignity and discipline. They are deeply imbued with melancholy, but there is no easy, self-indulgent release of feeling. All is expressed through the medium of those 'large general truths' which Johnson and the other Augustan critics believed it to be the poet's task to inculcate. Consider the first stanza. In life we are like prisoners condemned to the mines. These are mines of hope because in them we seek to find reward—but they are delusive, for the ore is worthless. Our only comforts are social, the relationships we achieve with our fellow toilers, which are inevitably destroyed, by accident and sudden death (explosions, 'blasts', in the mines), or by old age and time. The verb 'drop' conveys suddenness, helplessness, fatality. It is most important, in reading the verse of the period, to realize the exactness of such phrases as 'social comforts'. We know that decorum required a noun to be decently clothed with an epithet, and we are aware that in much of the more routine verse of the time such structures tend to be hackneyed and dull; but in a poem like this they are precise and vital for Johnson is saying exactly what he means. Such terms as 'social' are, it is true, abstract and intellectual, yet here they carry an immense range of feeling. Such verses do not offer the pleasures of Donne or the pleasures of Keats, but they have their own kind of austere flavour, a taste worth acquiring, even at the cost of some effort.

Much eighteenth-century verse is discursive and moralizing, and we have chosen examples from the works of three poets, Thomson, Goldsmith and Cowper. The reader must remember that at this time verse was still read in bulk, and was still felt to be a normal way of expressing general sentiments, views on life, on social questions, even, as in Dyer's *Fleece*, on farming methods; so from this point of view Wordsworth's *Prelude* and *Excursion* may be seen as the end of a long tradition of discursive, meditative poetry. The typical Romantic and post-Romantic poem is intense, personal and short. No one now, for example, would discuss education in verse, as Cowper did in his *Tirocinium*. And it is impossible to demonstrate the virtues of an amiable and civilized poem like his *Task* for instance, by means of short excerpts. It must be read as a whole; only then will its quiet rhythms make their full effect.

James Thomson (1700–1748) is best known for *The Seasons*, published between 1726 and 1730. The poem celebrates nature's changing moods, and affords the poet opportunities to reflect on life, on society, on any topic that interests him. Thomson's work seemed to contemporaries to be full of original sentiments; especially were they impressed by his feeling for nature—meaning, by that obscure term, the beauties of landscape, sky, storm and sunshine. The post-Wordsworthian reader is likely to be less impressed. Here is a typical passage:

> The north east spends his rage; he now shut up
> Within his iron cave, th'effusive south
> Warms the wide air, and o'er the void of heaven
> Breathes the big clouds with vernal showers distent.
> At first a dusky wreath they seem to rise,
> Scarce staining ether; but by swift degrees,
> In heaps on heaps the doubling vapour sails
> Along the loaded sky, and mingling deep
> Sits on th'horizon round a settled gloom:
> Not such as wintry storms on mortals shed,
> Oppressing life; but lovely, gentle, kind,
> And full of every hope and every joy,
> The wish of Nature. Gradual sinks the breeze
> Into a perfect calm; that not a breath
> Is heard to quiver thro' the closing woods,
> Or rustling turn the many twinkling leaves
> Of aspen tall. Th'uncurling floods, diffus'd
> In glassy breadth, seem thro' delusive lapse
> Forgetful of their course. 'Tis silence all,
> And pleasing expectation. Herds and flocks
> Drop the dry sprig, and mute-imploring eye
> The falling verdure. Hush'd in short suspense,
> The plumy people streak their wings with oil,
> To throw the lucid moisture trickling off;
> And wait th'approaching sign to strike, at once,
> Into the general choir. Even mountains, vales,
> And forests seem, impatient, to demand
> The promis'd sweetness. Man superior walks
> Amid the glad creation, musing praise,
> And looking lively gratitude. At last,
> The clouds consign their treasures to the fields;
> And, softly shaking on the dimpled pool
> Prelusive drops, let all their moisture flow
> In large effusion o'er the freshened world.

To a modern reader, the verse seems to stand between him and its subject. It is eloquent, well-managed, the 'sense variously drawn out' from line to line, but its Miltonic cadences (Sits on th'horizon round a settled gloom) are too derivative; and we feel the 'heroic' diction of such lines as

> The plumy people streak their wings with oil,
> To throw the lucid moisture trickling off . . .

to be ludicrously stilted. There is, perhaps, more than a touch of smugness about man 'superior walking', and we have only to put this passage beside the great 'nature's full and unwithdrawing hand' speech in *Comus* to see that we are dealing with a minor kind of poetry. Yet there is genuine feeling here, and the verse has the eighteenth-century virtue of exactitude. A sympathetic reader who will accustom his ear to the sedate rhythms, and his mind to the neo-classic diction, will find much that is agreeable in the discursive poetry of the period, work which is in many ways a kind of verse equivalent of the moralizing element in the *Spectator* and *Tatler*. Here is Thomson exploiting this vein:

> Let others brave the flood in quest of gain,
> And beat, for joyless months, the gloomy wave.
> Let such as deem it glory to destroy,
> Rush into blood, the sack of cities seek;
> Unpierc'd, exulting in the widow's wail,
> The virgin's shriek, and infant's trembling cry.
> Let some, far distant from their native soil,
> Urg'd or by want or hardened avarice,
> Find other lands beneath another sun.
> Let *this* thro' cities work his eager way,
> By legal outrage and establish'd guile,
> The social sense extinct: and *that* ferment
> Mad into tumult the seditious herd,
> Or melt them down to slavery. Let *these*
> Insnare the wretched in the toils of law,
> Fomenting discord, and perplexing right,
> An iron race! and *those* of fairer front,
> But equal inhumanity, in courts,
> Delusive pomp, and dark cabals delight;
> Wreathe the deep bow, diffuse the lying smile,
> And tread the weary labyrinths of state.
> While he, from all the stormy passions free
> That restless men involve, hears, and but hears,
> At distance safe, the human tempest roar,
> Wrapt close in conscious peace. The fall of kings,

The rage of nations, and the crush of states,
Move not the Man, who, from the world escap'd,
In still retreats and flowery solitudes,
To Nature's voice attends. . . .

This is a theme, derived from pastoral, which we hear over and over again in this age. It finds its classic expression in these lines from that most famous of eighteenth-century poems, Gray's *Elegy*, 'to whose sentiments' Dr. Johnson remarked, and it is the highest praise that representative critic can bestow, 'every bosom returns an echo.'

Nor you, ye Proud, impute to these the fault
If Memory o'er their tomb no trophies raise,
Where through the long-drawn aisle and fretted vault
The pealing anthem swells the note of praise.

Can storied urn or animated bust
Back to its mansion call the fleeting breath?
Can Honour's voice provoke the silent dust
Or Flattery soothe the dull cold ear of Death?

Perhaps in this neglected spot is laid
Some heart once pregnant with celestial fire;
Hands that the rod of empire might have sway'd,
Or wak'd to ecstasy the living lyre:

But Knowledge to their eyes her ample page
Rich with the spoils of time, did ne'er unroll;
Chill Penury repress'd their noble rage,
And froze the genial current of their soul.

Full many a gem of purest ray serene
The dark unfathom'd caves of ocean bear:
Full many a flower is born to blush unseen,
And waste its sweetness on the desert air.

Some village-Hampden, that with dauntless breast
The little tyrant of his fields withstood,
Some mute inglorious Milton here may rest,
Some Cromwell, guiltless of his county's blood.

Th'applause of listening senates to command,
The threats of pain and ruin to despise,
To scatter plenty o'er a smiling land,
And read their history in a nation's eyes,

Their lot forbad: nor circumscribed alone
Their growing virtues, but their crimes confined;
Forbad to wade through slaughter to a throne,
And shut the gates of mercy on mankind,

The struggling pangs of conscious Truth to hide,
To quench the blushes of ingenuous Shame,
Or heap the shrine of Luxury and Pride
With incense kindled at the Muses' flame.

Far from the madding crowd's ignoble strife,
Their sober wishes never learn'd to stray;
Along the cool sequester'd vale of life
They kept the noiseless tenour of their way.

Even so unself-confident a poet as Gray here wields the commanding, assured Augustan rhythm, making of his whole poem a single stately movement to which quotation can do no justice.

He was, said Johnson, this time disapprovingly, 'more than any man curiously ornate in his diction', and we know that Wordsworth singled out one of his sonnets to illustrate the kind of linguistic usage he was rebelling against. The *Ode on the Spring* is a poem which can stand as a sample of a great deal of the period's lyrical writing.

Lo! where the rosy-bosom'd Hours,
    Fair Venus' train appear,
Disclose the long-expecting flowers
    And wake the purple year!
The Attic warbler pours her throat
Responsive to the cuckoo's note,
The untaught harmony of Spring:
    While, whispering pleasure as they fly,
    Cool Zephyrs through the clear blue sky
Their gather'd fragrance fling.

Where'er the oak's thick branches stretch
    A broader, browner shade,
Where'er the rude and moss-grown beech
    O'er-canopies the glade,
Beside some water's rushy brink
With me the Muse shall sit, and think
(At ease reclined in rustic state)
    How vain the ardour of the Crowd,
    How low, how little are the Proud,
How indigent the Great!

Still is the toiling hand of Care
The panting herds repose:
Yet hark, how through the peopled air
The busy murmur glows!
The insect youth are on the wing,
Eager to taste the honied spring
   And float amid the liquid noon:
   Some lightly o'er the current skim,
Some show their gaily-gilded trim
Quick-glancing to the sun.

To Contemplation's sober eye
   Such is the race of Man:
And they that creep, and they that fly,
   Shall end where they began.
Alike the busy and the gay
But flutter through life's little day,
In Fortune's varying colours drest:
   Brush'd by the hand of rough Mischance,
   Or chill'd by Age, their airy dance
They leave, in dust to rest.

Methinks I hear in accents low
   The sportive kind reply:
Poor Moralist! and what art thou?
   A solitary fly!
Thy joys no glittering female meets,
No hive hast thou of hoarded sweets,
No painted plumage to display:
   On hasty wings thy youth is flown;
   Thy sun is set, thy spring is gone—
We frolic while 'tis May.

Here are the Hours and the Zephyrs, and all the standard neo-classic
furniture. A nightingale must be an 'Attic Warbler'; the bird cannot
sing, but must 'pour its throat'. Note the slightly patronizing attitude
to nature implied in the 'untaught harmonies of Spring', which is
a sort of equivalent of the Miltonic patronage of Shakespeare who
'warbled his native wood-notes *wild*', and compare the beginning of
the second verse with the lines from *Windsor Forest* and *Eloisa to
Abelard*. The whole scene is veiled in literature; the epithets are trite,
the personifications frigid. Yet in

> Brush'd by the hand of rough Mischance,
> Or chill'd by Age...

there is some energy (Blake did it better) and the pathos peeps through
at the end.

But when Gray writes what might be called a mock-lyric, the
tension set up between the formal language and the trivial subject
produces an elegantly witty piece, a minuscule example of the genre
which in the hands of Pope produced some of the century's finest
poetry.

ON A FAVOURITE CAT,
DROWNED IN A TUB OF GOLDFISHES

'Twas on a lofty vase's side,
Where China's gayest art had dyed
  The azure flowers that blow,
Demurest of the tabby kind,
The pensive Selima, reclined,
  Gazed on the lake below.

Her conscious tail her joy declared:
The fair round face, the snowy beard,
  The velvet of her paws,
Her coat that with the tortoise vies,
Her ears of jet, and emerald eyes,
  She saw; and purred applause.

Still had she gazed, but 'midst the tide
Two angels forms were seen to glide,
  The genii of the stream:
Their scaly armour's Tyrian hue
Though richest purple to the view
  Betray'd a golden gleam.

The hapless Nymph with wonder saw:
A whisker first, and then a claw,
  With many an ardent wish,
She stretch'd, in vain, to reach the prize—
What female heart can gold despise?
  What Cat's averse to fish?

Presumptuous maid! with looks intent
Again she stretch'd, again she bent,
  Nor knew the gulf between—
Malignant Fate sat by and smiled—
The slippery verge her feet beguiled;
  She tumbled headlong in!

Eight times emerging from the flood
She mew'd to every watery God
    Some speedy aid to send:—
No Dolphin came, nor Nereid stirr'd
Nor cruel Tom nor Susan heard—
    A favourite has no friend!

From hence, ye Beauties, undeceived,
Know one false step is ne'er retrieved,
    And be with caution bold:
Not all that tempts your wandering eyes
And heedless hearts, is lawful prize,
    Nor all that glisters, gold!

What we may call the social terms used in this poetry—the Proud, the
Great, Ambition, Grandeur, the Poor, Penury and so on, are generalized; they make no precise reference to the way society is run. There are
rich and poor, great and small; there is an aristocratic social order,
and the aristocrats are warned to do their duty, and reminded of the
limitations of human power; the terms fit, but there is no attempt at
documentation. One of the interesting things about Oliver Goldsmith
(1728-1774) is that his two major poems, *The Traveller* (1764) and
The Deserted Village (1770) are full of such direct observation of the
realities of society and of the changes taking place within it. His
scheme of values is traditional, and he is one of the first of a long line
of critics of society whose views may be crudely summed up in
Animal Farm terms as 'agriculture good—industry bad'. (Compare
Blake's remark about the arts growing cold 'when commerce settles
on every tree'.) He is a kind of Burkean conservative, and he has many
acute and damaging comments to make. Consider the following
lines from *The Traveller*:

Fir'd at the sound, my genius spreads her wing,
And flies where Britain courts the western spring;
Where lawns extend that scorn Arcadian pride,
And brighter streams than fam'd Hydaspis glide,
There all around the gentlest breezes stray,
There gentle music melts on every spray;
Creation's mildest charms are there combin'd,
Extremes are only in the master's mind!
Stern o'er each bosom reason holds her state
With daring aims irregularly great;
Pride in their port, defiance in their eye,
I see the lords of humankind pass by;
Intent on high designs, a thoughtful band,

By forms unfashion'd, fresh from nature's hand,
Fierce in their native hardiness of soul,
True to imagin'd right, above control.
While even the peasant boasts these rights to scan,
And learns to venerate himself as man.
   Thine, freedom, thine the blessings pictur'd here,
Thine are those charms that dazzle and endear;
Too blest, indeed, were such without alloy,
But foster'd even by freedom ills annoy;
That independence Britons prize too high,
Keeps man from man, and breaks the social tie;
The self-dependent lordlings stand alone,
All claims that bind and sweeten life unknown:
Here by the bonds of nature feebly held,
Minds combat minds, repelling and repell'd.
Ferments arise, imprison'd factions roar,
Represt ambition struggles round her shore,
Till over wrought, the general system feels
Its motions stop, or frenzy fire the wheels.
   Nor this the worst. As nature's ties decay,
As duty, love, and honour fail to sway,
Fictitious bonds, and bonds of wealth and law,
Still gather strength, and force unwilling awe,
Hence all obedience bows to these alone,
And talent sinks, and merit weeps unknown;
Till time may come, when, stript of all her charms,
The land of scholars, and the nurse of arms,
Where noble stems transmit the patriot flame,
Where kings have toil'd, and poets wrote, for fame,
One sink of level avarice shall lie,
And scholars, soldiers, kings, unhonour'd die.

The poet has just been talking about the Dutch who

> to servitude conform,
> Dull as their lakes that slumber in the storm . . .

and he is celebrating British freedom. (We may remember that James Thomson is the author of *Rule Britannia*). Such self-congratulation on the result of 'the glorious revolution' is often to be heard in the period. We may smile wryly today at seeing 'the lords of human kind pass by', and at the tribute to English eccentricity, 'irregularly great'; yet we can see that Goldsmith is aware of the growth and change of the real society he lives in, aware, too, of the dangers that such growth and change entail. There is, he believes, a social tie which is 'natural', made up of 'duty, love and honour': compared to this the bonds of

wealth and law are 'fictitious'. (Compare Burns and the field-mouse—
'I'm truly sorry man's dominion/Has broken nature's social union'.)
To break this tie, to reduce everything to 'a level sink of avarice'
corrupts all values. The reader should compare this piece, its sentiments,
diction, imagery and verse movement, with the passage quoted from
Ben Jonson's *Penshurst*. It is also interesting to listen to Goldsmith
expressing similar feelings in prose. Here are two quotations from
The Citizen of the World. The first describes England:

> 'Yet from the vernal softness of the air, the verdure of the fields, the
> transparency of the streams and the beauty of the women; here love might
> sport among painted lawns, and warbling groves, and carol upon gales
> wafting at once both fragrance and harmony.'

Here we see the same sort of 'poetic' diction that vitiates Gray's *Ode
on the Spring*, and the opening lines about 'Arcadian Pride' and
'fam'd Hydaspes' at the beginning of the passage under discussion.
Our second quotation exhibits, on the other hand, the balance and
clarity of good eighteenth-century expository prose.

> 'It is extremely difficult to induce a number of free beings to co-operate
> for their mutual benefits; every possible advantage will necessarily be
> sought; and every attempt to procure it must be attended with new
> fermentation.'

This parallels the lines beginning

> Here by the bonds of nature feebly held . . .

and illustrates how the discursive poet versified ideas which he could
also adequately express in prose. The reader should try and decide what,
if anything, Goldsmith has gained or lost by dressing his thoughts in
heroic couplets. We must repeat that short passages cannot do justice
to the total rhythm; this sort of verse must be read, as it was intended
to be read, in quantity. Goldsmith's best work has a lightness and
clarity which mark him out from among his contemporaries and we
feel a genuine personal pressure behind it.

William Cowper (1731–1800) is an attractive poet. He was a
religious melancholic, gloomily Calvinistic, and convinced of his own
damnation. But in his more lucid moments he was a tender, sensitive,
humorous man, much of a recluse, but capable of sharp observation
of the world around him. Chesterton said that 'he was damned by
John Calvin—he was very nearly saved by John Gilpin.' Some of his
writing was a kind of occupational therapy, and these lines from
The Task, a poem suggested by 'a lady fond of blank verse' who

'demanded a poem of that kind from the author', show how he set
about it.

> There is a pleasure in poetic pains,
> Which only poets know. The shifts and turns,
> The expedients and inventions multiform,
> To which the mind resorts, in chase of terms
> Though apt, yet coy, and difficult to win—
> To arrest the fleeting images, that fill
> The mirror of the mind, and hold them fast,
> And force them fit, till he has pencilled off
> A faithful likeness of the forms he views;
> Then to dispose his copies with such art,
> That each may find its most propitious light,
> And shine by situation, hardly less
> Than by the labour and the skill it cost;
> Are occupations of the poet's mind
> So pleasing, and that steal away the thought
> With such address from themes of sad import,
> That, lost in his own musings, happy man!
> He feels the anxieties of life, denied
> Their wonted entertainment, all retire.
> Such joy has he that sings.

This verse is accomplished, agreeably manipulated, Miltonic in
cadence, thoroughly literary. Here is the opening of Book V, *The
Winter Morning Walk* which may be compared with the passage from
The Seasons.

> 'Tis morning; and the sun, with ruddy orb
> Ascending, fires the horizon; while the clouds
> That crowd away before the driving wind,
> More ardent as the disk emerges more,
> Resemble most some city in a blaze,
> Seen through the leafless wood. His slanting ray
> Slides ineffectual down the snowy vale,
> And, tinging all with his own rosy hue,
> From every herb and every spiry blade
> Stretches a length of shadow o'er the field.
> Mine, spindling into longitude immense,
> In spite of gravity, and sage remark
> That I myself am but a fleeting shade,
> Provokes me to a smile. With eye askance
> I view the muscular proportioned limb
> Transformed to a lean shank. The shapeless pair,
> As they designed to mock me, at my side
> Take step for step; and, as I near approach

The cottage, walk along the plastered wall,
Preposterous sight! the legs without the man.
The verdure of the plain lies buried deep
Beneath the dazzling deluge; and the bents,
And coarser grass, upspearing o'er the rest,
Of late unsightly and unseen, now shine
Conspicuous, and in bright apparel clad,
And fledged with icy feathers, nod superb.
The cattle mourn in corners where the fence
Screens them, and seem half petrified to sleep
In unrecumbent sadness. There they wait
Their wonted fodder; not like hungering man,
Fretful if unsupplied; but silent, meek,
And patient of the slow-paced swain's delay.
He from the stack carves out the accustomed load,
Deep-plunging, and again deep-plunging oft
His broad keen knife into the solid mass;
Smooth as a wall the upright remnant stands
With such undeviating and even force
He severs it away: no needless care,
Lest storms should overset the leaning pile
Deciduous, or its own unbalanced weight.

We recognize what we might term the standard diction: 'ruddy orb',
'snowy vale', 'rosy hue', 'fleeting shade'; but we also feel, as we do
with Goldsmith, that this is written by a person. The agreeable fancy
about the shadow; the gently ironic twist to the moralizing (In spite of
gravity and sage remark/That I myself am but a fleeting shade) and
above all the lovingly exact observation, are all characteristic qualities.
Some lines—for example the opening ones—might come from any
competent verse of the period, but the snow, the gloomy cows, and
above all, the passage about the haystack, have all really been seen.
Cowper intends us to smile at the pomposity of 'the muscular propor-
tioned limb', and we may smile to ourselves about the 'unrecumbent
sadness' of the cows, and note the characteristic latinisms like
'deciduous', but reality comes through the period flavour, the stilted
diction. *Paradise Lost* is working in the background, which makes the
poem, in a mild Cowperian way, mock heroic. As you read his
instructions for making a cold frame for cucumbers, and come across
the line 'The stable yields a stercoraceous heap' you may think it
ludicrous. But you will be wrong if you file it away as yet another
example of 'gaudy and inane phraseology'; the poet sees the joke too.
After all, he made it.

Here are some lines from *Tirocinium, or A Review of Schools,* a

satirical indictment of eighteenth-century education. They show
Cowper handling the heroic couplet with pungency, ease and freedom.
There is no doubt that he found neo-classic shackles irksome (he said
that poetry has become 'a mere mechanic art / and every warbler has
the tune by heart') but he was not a strong enough character to break
them and in this passage he seems happy enough to use the traditional
methods. He is condemning middle-class parents for sending their
sons to 'great schools' for the sake of possible social advancement.

> The great indeed, by titles, riches, birth
> Excused the incumbrance of more solid worth,
> Are best disposed of where with most success
> They may acquire that confident address,
> Those habits of profuse and lewd expense,
> That scorn of all delights but those of sense,
> Which, though in plain plebeians we condemn,
> With so much reason all expect from them.
> But families of less illustrious fame,
> Whose chief distinction is their spotless name,
> Whose heirs, their honours none, their income small,
> Must shine by true desert, or not at all,
> What dream they of, that with so little care
> They risk their hopes, their dearest treasure, there?
> They dream of little Charles or William graced
> With wig prolix, down flowing to his waist;
> They see the attentive crowds his talents draw,
> They hear him speak—the oracle of law.
> The father, who designs his babe a priest,
> Dreams him episcopally such at least;
> And, while the playful jockey scours the room
> Briskly, astride upon the parlour broom,
> In fancy sees him more superbly ride
> In coach with purple lined and mitres on its side.
> Events improbable and strange as these ⎫
> Which only a parental eye foresees ⎬
> A public school shall bring to pass with ease. ⎭
> But how? resides such virtue in that air,
> As must create an appetite for prayer?
> And will it breathe into him all the zeal,
> That candidates for such a prize should feel,
> To take the lead and be the foremost still
> In all true worth and literary skill?
> 'Ah, blind to bright futurity, untaught
> The knowledge of the world, and dull of thought!
> Church-ladders are not always mounted best

By learned clerks and Latinists professed.
The exalted prize demands an upward look,
Not to be found by poring on a book.
Small skill in Latin, and still less in Greek,
Is more than adequate to all I seek.
Let erudition grace him or not grace,
I give the bauble but the second place;
His wealth, fame, honours, all that I intend,
Subsist and centre in one point—a friend.
A friend, whate'er he studies or neglects,
Shall give him consequence, heal all defects.
His intercourse with peers and sons of peers—
There dawns the splendour of his future years;
In that bright quarter his propitious skies
Shall blush betimes, and there his glory rise.
Your Lordship and *Your Grace!* What school can teach
A rhetoric equal to those parts of speech?
What need of Homer's verse or Tully's prose,
Sweet interjections! if he learn but those?
Let reverend churls his ignorance rebuke,   ⎫
Who starve upon a dog's eared Pentateuch,   ⎬
The parson knows enough, who knows a duke.'   ⎭

This verse is freer than Johnson's; it is more directly, more personally didactic, more particular, less generalized. And besides the traditional variants of triple rhymes and alexandrines, Cowper allows himself more frequent enjambements, when the sense demands them:

> . . . the playful jockey scours the room
> Briskly. . . .

We hear, too, Evangelical distrust for the established church. Cowper, like Goldsmith, is alive to the new ideas and feelings of his age.

A last quotation will illustrate both his moral earnestness, his humanitarianism, and the difficulties that beset him when he tries to break away from his age's conventions.

THE NEGRO'S COMPLAINT

Forced from home and all its pleasures,
  Afric's coast I left forlorn;
To increase a stranger's treasures,
  O'er the raging billows borne.
Men from England bought and sold me,
  Paid my price in paltry gold;
But, though theirs they have enrolled me,
  Minds are never to be sold.

Still in thought as free as ever,
  What are England's rights, I ask,
Me from my delights to sever,
  Me to torture, me to task?
Fleecy locks and black complexion
  Cannot forfeit nature's claim;
Skins may differ, but affection
  Dwells in white and black the same.

There are seven stanzas in all, but it is needless to quote more. We applaud the sentiments in spite of the poem rather than because of it; the neat jigging trochees have nothing to do with the theme. The reader must compare this with Blake's handling of similar subjects, for it is in comparison with work like this that one aspect of his originality becomes most immediately apparent. We concur with, and forget, Cowper's 'Minds are never to be sold'; we never forget Blake's 'mind-forged manacles'.

The Augustan tradition supported one last good poet, and he was George Crabbe (1754–1832). He writes of the life around him— all of it; he presents English provincial society as it is, and firmly rejects poetic conventions about the necessary dignity of subject matter.

           . . . I paint the cot
  As truth will have it and as bards will not.

The couplet illustrates the nature of his verse. Linguistically and formally, he is of his age. He 'paints the cot'—this we recognize as standard diction for 'describes the cottage'. But he feels profoundly the antithesis between 'truth' and 'bards'. He rebels not only against the pastoral convention, but against the belief that poetic decorum demanded a lofty, noble, generalized theme. It is difficult for a modern reader to realize quite how original this work is. The idea of poetic decorum persisted in the critical establishment well into the nineteenth century, and even Byron, who admired his technique and thought him superior to the 'Lake school of poetry' deplored his subject matter. 'Crabbe's the man', he said, 'but he has a low subject.' 'Low', we remember, is the epithet Dr. Johnson applied to the 'blanket of the dark' passage in Macbeth. Crabbe writes about squires, parsons, parish clerks, paupers, criminals, farmers, dissenters, gipsies, all the grades of life to be found between the hall and the workhouse. His range and his humanity remind us of Chaucer, his irony of Jane Austen.

The Parish Register consists of a string of anecdotes and character sketches; as the parson turns over the pages, names catch his eye, and he muses on them. In later work, Crabbe expanded anecdotes into full-length tales. This account of the Widow Goe is an example of his early manner.

> Next died the Widow Goe, an active dame,
> Famed ten miles round, and worthy all her fame;
> She lost her husband when their loves were young,
> But kept her farm, her credit, and her tongue:
> Full thirty years she ruled, with matchless skill,
> With guiding judgment and resistless will;
> Advice she scorn'd, rebellions she suppress'd,
> And sons and servants bow'd at her behest.
> Like that great man's, who to his Saviour came,
> Were the strong words of this commanding dame;—
> 'Come', if she said, they came: if 'go', were gone;
> And if 'do this,'—that instant it was done:
> Her maidens told she was all eye and ear,
> In darkness saw and could at distance hear;—
> No parish business in the place could stir,
> Without direction or assent from her;
> In turn she took each office as it fell,
> Knew all their duties and performed them well;
> The lazy vagrants in her presence shook,
> And pregnant damsels fear'd her stern rebuke;
> She look'd on want with judgement clear and cool,
> And felt with reason and bestow'd by rule;
> She match'd both sons and daughters to her mind,
> And lent them eyes, for Love, she heard, was blind;
> Yet ceaseless still she throve, alert, alive,
> The working bee, in full or empty hive;
> Busy and careful, like that working bee,
> No time for love or tender cares had she;
> But when our farmers made their amorous vows,
> She talk'd of market-steeds and patent-ploughs.
> Not unemploy'd her evenings pass'd away,
> Amusements closed, as business waked the day;
> When to her toilet's brief concern she ran,
> And conversation with her friends began,
> Who all were welcome, what they saw, to share;
> And joyous neighbours praised her Christmas fare,
> That none around might, in their scorn, complain
> Of Gossip Goe as greedy in her gain.
>   Thus long she reigned, admired, if not approved;
> Praised, if not honour'd; fear'd, if not beloved;—
> When, as the busy days of Spring drew near,
> That call'd for all the forecast of the year;
> When lively hope the rising crops survey'd,

And April promised what September paid;
When stray'd her lambs where gorse and greenweed grow;
When rose her grass in richer vales below;
When pleas'd she look'd on all the smiling land,
And viewed the hinds, who wrought at her command;
(Poultry in groups still follow'd where she went);
Then dread o'ercame her,—that her days were spent.
'Bless me! I die and not a warning giv'n,—
With *much* to do on Earth, and ALL for Heav'n!—
No reparation for my soul's affairs,
No leave petition'd for the barn's repairs;
Accounts perplex'd, my interest yet unpaid,
My mind unsettled, and my will unmade;—
A lawyer haste, and in your way, a priest;
And let me die in one good work at least.'
She spake, and, trembling, dropp'd upon her knees,
Heaven in her eye and in her hand her keys;
And still the more she found her life decay,
With greater force she grasped those signs of sway:
Then fell and died!—In haste her sons drew near,
And dropp'd, in haste, the tributary tear;
Then from th'adhering clasp the keys unbound,
And consolation for their sorrows found.

A firm Augustan rhythm works vigorously, and it is immediately apparent that, for Crabbe, the tradition he writes in is living. But we also feel, though it is not easy to say precisely why, that we are not listening to a copy of the verse of Pope or Johnson or Goldsmith. Within its tradition it is original, owing more, one would say, to Dryden than to any immediate predecessors. Two aspects of this piece are especially worth noting. First, there is no physical description of the widow—there are, indeed, only three adjectives 'active', 'famed' and 'worthy'. Second, that the whole character is presented through action: we are told what she, her sons, her servants, her neighbours *did*. The only thing she lost was her husband, everything else she kept; and this antithesis lays the foundation of the whole piece. It may seem at first that the phrase 'when their loves were young' is a flaccid bit of conventionally elegant periphrasis; for fill-in phrases are to be found in Crabbe, as indeed, they are in Chaucer; but this is not one of them. There is a quiet irony behind it. Its very literariness, in this context, points the contrast between convention and reality. Crabbe is, in other words, using a polite literary device to emphasize that this is not polite literature; and in addition the phrase gives a splendidly full rhyming stress to 'tongue'.

She 'kept', she 'ruled', she 'scorned', she 'suppressed': she is a figure of power. The allusion to the centurion gives this power a kind of mock-heroic emphasis; and Crabbe would, I think, expect his reader to feel a further irony in the allusion. The centurion was humble: 'I am not worthy that thou shouldest enter under my roof'; and Christ said of him: 'I have not found so great faith no, not in Israel'. The widow is certainly not humble, and her faith is a faith in property. We see her power spreading over all the details of her private life and public business. In both spheres she works indefatigably, sparing no one, dispensing justice without charity. In the lines about her children's marriages, a masterpiece of compression, we see another instance of Crabbe's ironic use of convention; and this occurs again in the line about the farmer's 'amorous vows'. Notice how she 'runs' to her 'toilet's brief concern' (not for nothing is she called the Widow Goe) and the reasons why she kept a good table. The couplet

> Thus long she reigned, admired, if not approved;
> Praised, if not honour'd; fear'd, if not beloved. . . .

sums up her career. The antithetical deployment of the big moral words 'admired' 'approved' 'praised' 'honoured' 'feared' 'beloved' defines her defects and her virtues. These abstractions have effective solidity because they are not lightly or vaguely used, but grow out of and refer to, the ordered detail of Crabbe's picture of the widow, and out of the moral orientation of his whole fictional world. The lines about the spring have a running rhythmic energy; the beauty is there, in the gorse and the greenweed, the grass and the smiling land; but the eye of the beholder is implied as well in 'busy' 'forecast' 'paid' 'richer'. The one touch of rustic charm in the whole piece, the poultry, seems to make the widow's collapse the more unexpected, and she becomes for a moment a pathetic figure. But she remains unchanged to the end. Belated piety struggles with habitual prudence, and their relative importance to her is conveyed with ironic neatness in the line

> A lawyer haste, and in your way, a priest. . . .

She clutches the keys, the symbols of her power, till her sons prise them from her dead hand. Note the repetition of 'haste': the sons hurry to their mother and they hurry to get their grief over, so that they may get down to serious business. The tombstone tone of 'tributary tear' and 'consolation for their sorrows' adds the final touch of irony. The difference between what 'consolation' means to the sons and what it may mean, for example, to Crabbe in his parish ministrations, sums up the moral world of the Widow Goe and her like. Yet—and this is where it seems right to place Crabbe in the Chaucerian tradition—there is a humane sympathy in this portrait; so much energy, so much life, is admirable in itself.

William Blake (1757–1827) was an almost exact contemporary of Crabbe, but no two poets could be more unlike. We see in Crabbe the last great craftsman of the Augustan tradition: in Blake a rebel against that tradition. Crabbe was approved and appreciated by the intelligent public of his day; Scott, Jane Austen and Byron all read him with pleasure: Blake was solitary, almost unknown, deemed mad. It is no part of our business to attempt to disentangle Blake's complex, obscure and private symbolism. The reader should start with *Poetical Sketches* and *Innocence and Experience*, and then go on to the miscellaneous poems and fragments, expecially *The Everlasting Gospel* and *Auguries of Innocence*. The prose fragments and marginalia are full of excellent things. Do not waste time puzzling over obscurities, or worry over the fact that Blake switches from crack-brained eccentricity to sublimity, or to dazzling commonsense all in a few lines. Look for what your mind can feed on, and use the commentators as aids only, not as repositories of truth. With Blake we are in the modern world, and none of us can afford to neglect him.

We will begin with the famous poem from his first volume: *To the Muses*.

> Whether on Ida's shady brow,
>   Or in the chambers of the East,
> The chambers of the sun, that now
>   From antient melody have ceas'd;
>
> Whether in Heav'n ye wander fair,
>   Or the green corners of the earth,
> Or the blue regions of the air,
>   Where the melodious winds have birth;
>
> Whether on chrystal rocks ye rove,
>   Beneath the bosom of the sea
> Wand'ring in many a coral grove,
>   Fair Nine, forsaking Poetry!
>
> How have you left the antient love
>   That bards of old enjoy'd in you!
> The languid strings do scarcely move!
>   The sound is forc'd, the notes are few!

F

This is obviously an eighteenth-century poem. It has the polish, the perfection, the stately regularity of the period; it has the correct poetic furniture;—Ida's shady brow, Muses, and lyres; it is perfectly accomplished; it proves, if proof were needed, that Blake had learned his trade. If he departed from convention, it was not for lack of skill: his choice was deliberate. He said himself that 'execution is the chariot of genius', and all his best work has this remarkable technical excellence. But, of course, the poem is a protest against the very type of excellence it exhibits, and the protest gives the poem its tension and power. (He said the Greeks were wrong to call the Muses the daughters of Memory.) And the bards are not stage figures, they are seers and prophets, like the one whose voice calls upon the Earth, in the introduction to the *Songs of Experience*. Blake himself is a seer, who wants a poetry capable of expressing his vision of truth, that imagination which he believes to be divine. The last two lines, with their metronomic accuracy

> The languid strings do scarcely move!
> The sound is forc'd, the notes are few!

are a kind of parody of the sort of pattern he felt must be broken, if he were to tell the truth that was in him; they are in themselves, in their sound and imagery, the reason why poetry is impoverished.

The next poem shows Blake experimenting with a different sort of form, and making a pastiche of an Elizabethan lyric. He was not the only writer of his period to feel that 'antient melody' was sweeter than modern. Dilettantes and antiquarians were examining afresh the ballads, medieval and Elizabethan literature. Such interest had never wholly died but it now began to influence the taste of the general reader.

> My silks and fine array,
>   My smiles and languish'd air,
> By love are driv'n away;
>   And mournful lean Despair
> Brings me yew to deck my grave:
> Such end true lovers have.
>
> His face is fair as heav'n,
>   When springing buds unfold;
> O why to him was't giv'n,
>   Whose heart is wintry cold?
> His breast is love's all worship'd tomb,
> Where all love's pilgrims come.

> Bring me an axe and spade,
>   Bring me a winding sheet;
> When I my grave have made,
>   Let winds and tempests beat:
> Then down I'll lie, as cold as clay.
> True love doth pass away!

This lyric is as accomplished in its way as *To the Muses*, but it has a completely different tune, and we hear in it the combination of feeling and eloquence (note the onward movement in 'lean Despair/ Brings me yew') that the best Elizabethan lyrics have.

The next piece *To Spring*, traditional enough in theme, should be compared with Thomson, Gray and Cowper.

> O thou with dewy locks, who lookest down
> Thro' the clear windows of the morning, turn
> Thine angel eyes upon our western isle,
> Which in full choir hails thy approach, O Spring!
>
> The hills tell each other, and the list'ning
> Vallies hear; all our longing eyes are turned
> Up to thy bright pavillions: issue forth,
> And let thy holy feet visit our clime.
>
> Come o'er the eastern hills, and let our winds
> Kiss thy perfumed garments; let us taste
> Thy morn and evening breath; scatter thy pearls
> Upon our love-sick land that mourns for thee.
>
> O deck her forth with thy fair fingers; pour
> Thy soft kisses on her bosom; and put
> Thy golden crown upon her languish'd head,
> Whose modest tresses were bound up for thee!

Blake is here experimenting. The lines are blank verse, but they don't sound like it. The poem is divided into quatrains, but the quatrains don't rhyme. We feel beneath the metre the forms and rhythms of the Authorized version—the 'antient bards' here are King David and the author of the *Song of Solomon*. Note the delicate modulations of the last line; the way we have to give equal stresses to 'were bound up', and then pause—the change from p to f makes us do this—so isolating the last foot and making 'thee' sound triumphant; the world is the bride of the spring.

The preface to this volume tells us that 'The following sketches
were the production of untutored youth, commenced in his twelfth,
and occasionally resumed by the author till his twentieth year; ...
his friends have still believed that they possessed a poetic originality,
which merited some respite from oblivion. These opinions remain,
however, to be now reproved or confirmed by a less partial public.'
That public ignored the new poet, and Blake remained isolated. He
had a few intelligent patrons but no sustaining contact with intelligent
readers—a few cranks, a few devotees, but no true audience. Blake is
fearless, direct, convinced of the truth of his vision, but his art becomes
the art of solitude, the stream of inspiration loses itself in the sands of
private symbolism, and the accomplished craftsman turns into a
windy rhetorician. Even a prophet, when he comes down from the
mountains, must have someone to say 'Thus saith the Lord' *to*, and if
there's no one there it tends to affect his prophecy. Blake is the first
of a long line of poets and artists who feel themselves to be, and who
indeed are, outside the community. They have, as Eliot says, to create
the taste by which they are to be appreciated, and they are sometimes
dead before that happens.

Innocence and Experience, said Blake, are 'contrary states of the
human soul'. The two series of 'Songs' have a symmetry, though not
an exact one. First, here is the *Chimney Sweeper* from *The Songs of
Innocence*.

> When my mother died I was very young,
> And my father sold me while yet my tongue
> Could scarcely cry ' 'weep! 'weep! 'weep! 'weep!'
> So your chimneys I sweep, & in soot I sleep.

> There's little Tom Dacre, who cried when his head,
> That curl'd like a lamb's back, was shav'd: so I said
> 'Hush, Tom! never mind it, for when your head's bare
> You know that the soot cannot spoil your white hair.'

> And so he was quiet, & that very night,
> As Tom was a-sleeping, he had such a sight!
> That thousands of sweepers, Dick, Joe, Ned, & Jack,
> Were all of them lock'd up in coffins of black.

> And by came an Angel who had a bright key,
> And he open'd the coffins & set them all free;
> Then down a green plain leaping, laughing, they run,
> And wash in a river, and shine in the Sun.

Then naked & white, all their bags left behind,
They rise upon clouds and sport in the wind;
And the Angel told Tom, if he'd be a good boy,
He'd have God for his father, & never want joy.

And so Tom awoke; and we rose in the dark,
And got with our bags & our brushes to work.
Tho' the morning was cold, Tom was happy & warm;
So if all do their duty they need not fear harm.

This is a poem about injustice and cruelty which bears some resemblance in general tone and feeling to Cowper's poem about the negro. It appears to offer a trite and comforting moral, and might be taken for a kind of tract reconciling the poor to their lot—put up with injustice on earth, for you are earning your place in heaven. Yet the poem is enough tinged with Blake's peculiar vision—we have only to look attentively at the bright clear imagery—to make such an account seem crude. Blake is really celebrating the indestructibility of the state of innocence, even in the midst of misery.

Next, the chimney sweep in the world of Experience.

A little black thing among the snow,
Crying ' 'weep! 'weep!' in notes of woe!
'Where are thy father & mother? say?'
'They are both gone up to the church to pray.

'Because I was happy upon the heath,
'And smil'd among the winter's snow,
'They clothed me in the clothes of death,
'And taught me to sing the notes of woe.

'And because I am happy & dance & sing,
'They think they have done me no injury,
'And are gone to praise God & his Priest & King,
'Who make up a heaven of our misery.'

Here is a direct, dynamic indictment of the society which exploits such cruelty, and the religion which condones it. The orthodox conception of the jealous God, the legalistic, sterile, negative morality of organized religion, supporter and justifier of the state's cruel power, all combine to oppress the poor. And perhaps the worst thing about them is their insensitiveness. The child is still in the world of innocence; he can still laugh and sing; therefore they persuade themselves they have done him no injury.

Here are the two parallel poems on *Holy Thursday*. The children come from Foundling Hospitals and Blake's first poem is praising the philanthropy which is trying to better the lot of the poor. He is here sharing in and expressing a current of feeling that grew throughout the century.

> 'Twas on a Holy Thursday, their innocent faces clean,
> The children walking two & two, in red & blue & green,
> Grey-headed beadles walk'd before, with wands as white as snow,
> Till into the high dome of Paul's they like Thames' waters flow.
>
> O what a multitude they seem'd, these flowers of London town!
> Seated in companies they sit with radiance all their own.
> The hum of multitudes was there, but multitudes of lambs,
> Thousands of little boys & girls raising their innocent hands.
>
> Now like a mighty wind they raise to heaven the voice of song,
> Or like harmonious thundering the seats of Heaven among.
> Beneath them sit the aged men, wise guardians of the poor;
> Then cherish pity, lest you drive an angel from your door.

How unlike are the rhythms to those of the orthodox verse of the period! These strings are not languid, these notes not forced. The poem is simple, strong, hymn-like, child-like; deliberately kept within the compass of a child's imagination. In the world of Innocence, old age and infancy are happy together. But in the world of Experience things are different.

> Is this a holy thing to see
> In a rich and fruitful land,
> Babes reduc'd to misery,
> Fed with cold and usurous hand?
>
> Is that trembling cry a song?
> Can it be a song of joy?
> And so many children poor?
> It is a land of poverty!
>
> And their sun does never shine,
> And their fields are bleak & bare,
> And their ways are fill'd with thorns:
> It is eternal winter there.
>
> For where-e'er the sun does shine,
> And where-e'er the rain does fall,
> Babe can never hunger there,
> Nor poverty the mind appall.

Like much of Blake's best verse, this is bare, stripped of all trimmings. This is not a mere political poem. Society is at fault, truly: 'It is a land of poverty'; but this is not all. Blake sees 'poverty in the midst of plenty', but he also sees a profound cause for this. Man has denied nature. Where the sun shines and the rain falls there is no poverty. The necessary change must be religious, in man's whole outlook and behaviour. We are not invited to a pastoral or Wordsworthian retreat, but to a regeneration of the spirit. As he wrote in *The Everlasting Gospel*:

> When the rich learned Pharisee
> Came to consult him[1] secretly,
> Upon his heart with Iron pen
> He wrote, 'Ye must be born again.'

One of the finest, sternest and most naked Songs of Experience is *London*.

> I wander thro' each charter'd street,
> Near where the charter'd Thames does flow,
> And mark in every face I meet
> Marks of weakness, marks of woe.
>
> In every cry of every Man,
> In every Infant's cry of fear,
> In every voice, in every ban,
> The mind-forg'd manacles I hear.
>
> How the Chimney-sweeper's cry
> Every black'ning Church appalls;
> And the hapless Soldier's sigh
> Runs in blood down Palace walls.
>
> But most thro' midnight streets I hear
> How the youthful Harlot's curse
> Blasts the new born Infant's tear,
> And blights with plagues the Marriage hearse.

Man has bound, enslaved, hired out for gain, placed unjust legal restrictions upon, not only the city, his own creation, but upon nature too, upon the Thames, the river, symbol of natural life. Not for Blake does it 'glide at its own sweet will'. In the first version of the poem the streets and the Thames were 'dirty'; and the emendation lets us see Blake packing and concentrating his meaning, 'loading' in Keats's famous phrase, 'every rift with ore'. The characteristic expression of this city is a ban, a curse, a prohibition; and all this springs from man's mind and his reason which have constructed a false

---

[1] Jesus.

philosophy, denying the power of the imagination. 'Poetry fettered',
said Blake, using the same metaphor, 'fetters the human race'.

We can see that in the *Ode on the Spring* Gray organizes his diction
in accordance with literary conventions. Its departures from the norm
of prose are governed by agreed theories about poetic decorum,
about what is proper and suitable for serious verse. Blake's departures
from such a norm (a cry cannot appal a church, a sigh cannot run in
blood down a wall) are governed not by convention, but by the
imaginative necessities of the particular poem he is writing, and they
are also nearer to the living idiom of the language. In no other way
could he have crammed, so dramatically, so much meaning into four
lines. The Chimney-sweeper, the Soldier, and the Harlot, stand for
the victims; the Church and the Palace for the oppressors. There is no
difficulty about this symbolism. The source of life, in this society, is
tainted: marriage is death. Oppression produces the youthful harlot,
who in turn infects the oppressor.

London deals with the city, with society, with 'what man has made
of man'. In the next poem Blake's theme is a human passion, a private
feeling, and his symbolism is stranger. The poem is called *A Poison
Tree*.

> I was angry with my friend:
> I told my wrath, my wrath did end.
> I was angry with my foe:
> I told it not, my wrath did grow.
>
> And I water'd it in fears,
> Night & morning with my tears;
> And I sunnèd it with smiles
> And with soft deceitful wiles.
>
> And it grew both day and night,
> Till it bore an apple bright;
> And my foe beheld it shine,
> And he knew that it was mine.
>
> And into my garden stole
> When the night had veil'd the pole:
> In the morning glad I see
> My foe outstretch'd beneath the tree.

We recognize the same power, the same compression, that we find
in *London*, but paraphrase is not only difficult—it is irrelevant. In one
sense the the images are clear and sharp; both these poems exemplify

Blake's dictum that 'Nature has no outline, but imagination has'. Yet the fact that we cannot say what the fruit *is*, does not detract from the potency of the symbol, or the poem.

The first stanza alludes obviously to the biblical precept: 'Let not the sun go down upon thy wrath'. When this precept was disobeyed 'My wrath did grow'. In this form the metaphor is dead, but Blake brings it to life. The wrath is a living organism 'watered' and 'sunned' not by the forces of nature, but by the evil and hypocrisy of the human heart:

> The Gods of the earth and sea
> Sought thro' Nature to find this Tree;
> But their search was all in vain:
> There grows one in the Human Brain.

Tree and fruit are symbols of temptation, reminding us of the fruit that 'brought death into the world and all our woe'. How much is compressed into the next two lines:

> And my foe beheld it shine,
> And he knew that it was mine. . . .

Because he knows it is mine, he is impelled, and the poet knows that he will be impelled, to steal it. His act is horribly inevitable; it is fated and fatal, but the fate resides within the thief's own heart. In the fallen evil world of experience, men, by wiles and hypocrisy, manipulate, and are manipulated by, their fellows. Blake makes the point by leaving out all explanation. 'He beheld', 'he knew': that is sufficient. The theft takes place in deepest night; heaven does not peep through the dark; the Pole, the star we take our direction by, is veiled. Finally, a climax of evil, the joy in the death of the foe, conveyed by the placing of 'glad' in the line

> In the morning glad I see.

and in the agonized 'outstretch'd' in the final naked couplet. Perhaps these lines also throw some light on the poem:

> To be in a passion you good may do,
> But no Good if a Passion is in you.

Our next poem, *Auguries of Innocence*, consists of a series of octosyllabic couplets, for the most part complete in themselves, each encapsulating an image, each intended to shock, to startle, to puzzle the reader, to shake him into attending to what the bard has to tell him. Like all prophets Blake wanted action; he wanted to change people.

AUGURIES OF INNOCENCE

To see a World in a Grain of Sand
And a heaven in a Wild Flower,
Hold Infinity in the Palm of your hand
And Eternity in an hour.

A Robin Red breast in a Cage
Puts all Heaven in a Rage.
A dove house fill'd with doves & Pigeons
Shudders Hell thro' all its regions.
A dog starv'd at his Master's Gate
Predicts the ruin of the State.
A horse misus'd upon the road
Calls to Heaven for Human blood.
Each outcry of the hunted Hare
A fibre from the Brain does tear.
A Skylark wounded in the wing,
A Cherubim does cease to sing.
The Game Cock clip'd & arm'd for fight
Does the Rising Sun affright.
Every Wolf's & Lion's howl
Raises from Hell a Human Soul.
The wild deer, wand'ring here & there,
Keeps the Human Soul from Care.
The Lamb misus'd breeds Public strife
And yet forgives the Butcher's Knife.
The Bat that flits at close of Eve
Has left the Brain that won't Believe.
The Owl that calls upon the Night
Speaks the Unbeliever's fright.
He who shall hurt the little Wren
Shall never be belov'd by Men.
He who the Ox to wrath has mov'd
Shall never be by Woman lov'd.
The wanton Boy that kills the Fly
Shall feel the Spider's enmity.
He who torments the Chafer's sprite
Weaves a Bower in endless Night.
The Catterpiller on the Leaf
Repeats to thee thy Mother's grief.
Kill not the Moth nor Butterfly,
For the Last Judgement draweth nigh.
He who shall train the Horse to War
Shall never pass the Polar Bar.
The Begger's Dog & Widow's Cat,

Feed them & thou wilt grow fat.
The Gnat that sings his Summer's song
Poison gets from Slander's tongue.
The poison of the Snake & Newt
Is the sweat of Envy's foot.
The poison of the Honey Bee
Is the Artist's Jealousy.
The Prince's Robes & Beggar's Rags
Are Toadstools on the Miser's Bags.
A truth that's told with bad intent
Beats all the Lies you can invent.
It is right it should be so;
Man was made for Joy & Woe;
And when this we rightly know
Thro' the World we safely go.
Joy & Woe are woven fine,
A Clothing for the Soul divine;
Under every grief & pine
Runs a joy with silken twine.
The Babe is more than swadling Bands;
Throughout all these Human Lands
Tools were made, & Born were hands,
Every Farmer Understands.
Every Tear from Every Eye
Becomes a Babe in Eternity;
This is caught by Females bright
And return'd to its own delight.
The Bleat, the Bark, Bellow & Roar
Are Waves that Beat on Heaven's Shore.
The Babe that weeps the Rod beneath
Writes Revenge in realms of death.
The Beggar's Rags, fluttering in Air,
Does to Rags the Heavens tear.
The Soldier, arm'd with Sword & Gun,
Palsied strikes the Summer's Sun.
The poor Man's Farthing is worth more
Than all the Gold on Afric's Shore.
One Mite wrung from the Labrer's hands
Shall buy & sell the Miser's Lands:
Or, if protected from on high,
Does that whole Nation sell & buy.
He who mocks the Infant's Faith
Shall be mock'd in Age & Death.
He who shall teach the Child to Doubt
The rotting Grave shall ne'er get out.
He who respects the Infant's faith

Triumphs over Hell & Death.
The Child's Toys & the Old Man's Reasons
Are the Fruits of the Two seasons.
The Questioner, who sits so sly,
Shall never know how to Reply.
He who replies to words of Doubt
Doth put the Light of Knowledge out.
The Strongest Poison ever known
Came from Caesar's Laurel Crown.
Nought can deform the Human Race
Like to the Armour's iron brace.
When Gold and Gems adorn the Plow
To peaceful Arts shall Envy Bow.
A riddle or the Cricket's Cry
Is to Doubt a fit Reply.
The Emmet's Inch & Eagle's Mile
Make Lame Philosophy to smile.
He who Doubts from what he sees
Will ne'er Believe, do what you Please.
If the Sun & Moon should doubt,
They'd immediately Go out.
To be in a passion you Good may do
But no Good if a Passion is in you.
The Whore & Gambler, by the State
Licenc'd, build that Nation's Fate.
The Harlot's cry from Street to Street
Shall weave Old England's winding Sheet.
The Winner's Shout, the Loser's Curse,
Dance before dead England's Hearse.
Every night and every Morn
Some to Misery are Born.
Every Morn & every Night
Some are Born to sweet delight.
Some are born to sweet delight
Some are born to Endless Night.
We are led to Believe a Lie
When we see not Thro' the Eye
Which was Born in a Night to perish in a Night
When the Soul Slept in Beams of Light.
God appears & God is Light
To those poor Souls who dwell in Night,
But does a Human Form Display
To those who Dwell in Realms of day.

The first four lines must be read together with the title. To be able
to see the world in a grain of sand, apprehend the whole pattern of the

universe by experiencing a tiny part of it, is an augury of innocence. It means that the perceiving eye sees through appearance to reality. Such an explanation sounds vague, easily and cheaply metaphysical; but in the poem all is solid. Once we have grasped the meaning of the first four lines, the pattern of the succeeding couplets becomes clear. 'Everything that lives is holy'; so that the caged bird—a tiny, trivial injustice, which does not even appear to many respectable and humane persons to be an injustice at all—in fact affects the whole universe. Note that hell shudders at the doves (they were kept for food, not for fun, and Blake believed that 'all wholesome food is caught without the aid of a net or trap'), as Heaven rages at the caged bird. Blake looked forward to the 'Marriage of Heaven and Hell'. The cruelty that starves the dog, will bring about the ruin of the community, which, if it is to endure, must be founded on Love. The couplets illustrate many aspects of Blake's poetry. Some, like the one about the chafer's sprite, seem merely eccentric, though we must remember that for him the chafer was as potent a symbol as the redbreast. The reader is unlikely to feel the same, so this may be an example of the way Blake fails to communicate through using a private symbolism. There are, too, examples of what we have called his inspired commonsense, a shrewd insight into the workings of 'Satan's kingdom'. Such are the couplets

> A truth that's told with bad intent
> Beats all the Lies you can invent . . .

and

> The Strongest Poison ever known
> Came from Caesar's Laurel Crown.

When Blake speaks of 'doubt' he means the spirit of scientific rationalism, the way of thought that would put reason in control of society. Faith for him is faith in imagination, in the artist's vision. 'What is now known', he said, 'was once only imagined'. The classics, and Newton, Rousseau and Voltaire, were all in his mind symbols of rationalism, forgers of manacles for the mind.

'We do not', he writes, 'want either Greek or Roman models if we are but just and true to our own imagination, those Worlds of Eternity in which we shall live for ever in JESUS OUR LORD.'

The last quotation comes from one of the drafts of an unfinished poem called *The Everlasting Gospel*.

> Was Jesus Humble? or did he
> Give any proofs of Humility?
> When but a Child he ran away

And left his Parents in dismay.
When they had wander'd three days long
These were the words upon his Tongue:
'No earthly Parents I confess:
'I am doing my Father's business.'
When the rich learned Pharisee
Came to consult him secretly,
Upon his heart with Iron pen,
He wrote, 'Ye must be born again.'
He was too Proud to take a bribe;
He spoke with authority, not like a Scribe.
He says with most consummate Art,
'Follow me, I am meek & lowly of heart,'
As that is the only way to Escape
The Miser's net & the Glutton's trap.
He who loves his Enemies, hates his Friends;
This is surely not what Jesus intends;
He must mean the mere love of Civility
And so he must mean concerning Humility;
But he acts with triumphant, honest pride,
And this is the Reason Jesus died.
If he had been Antichrist, Creeping Jesus,
He'd have done anything to please us:
Gone sneaking into the Synagogues
And not used the Elders & Priests like Dogs,
But humble as a Lamb or an Ass,
Obey'd himself to Caiaphas.
God wants not Man to humble himself:
This is the Trick of the Ancient Elf.
Humble toward God, Haughty toward Man,
This is the Race that Jesus ran,
And when he humbled himself to God,
Then descended the cruel rod.
'If thou humblest thyself, thou humblest me;
'Thou also dwelst in Eternity.
'Thou art a Man, God is no more,
'Thine own Humanity learn to Adore
'And thy Revenge Abroad display
'In terrors at the Last Judgment day.
'God's Mercy & Long Suffering
'Are but the Sinner to Judgment to bring.
'Thou on the Cross for them shalt pray
'And take Revenge at the last Day.

'Do what you will, this Life's a Fiction
'And is made up of Contradiction'. . . .

> I am sure this Jesus will not do
> Either for Englishman or Jew. . . .

Wordsworth said that Blake might be mad, but that there was 'more, in his madness than in the sanity of such men as Walter Scott and Lord Byron.' In the poems of this neglected, isolated genius, stubbornly telling the truths his imagination presented to him, we hear, in spite of the obscurity, the crankiness, a modern voice speaking; we know he lives in the same world as ourselves. Let him have the last word:

> 'Therefore, dear reader, forgive what you do not approve, and love me for this energetic exertion of my talent.'

5

THE ROMANTICS

It is pointless to attempt to define 'Romanticism', but it may be useful to list a few of the ideas and feelings and attitudes that the poets of this period shared.

They reacted against the forms of the past, the canons of neo-classic criticism, and the conventions of neo-classic taste, 'Boileau's creaking lyre, The whetstone of the teeth—monotony in wire!' They turned to the past for inspiration, to an idealized middle ages, to the exotic, to the irrational, to the dark and horrifying, to revolution, to the workings of their own minds, the products of their own imaginations, to what was individual, rather than social, to the works of nature, rather than those of man Our purpose here is to exhibit and discuss a few typical examples of their verse. As sign-posts to the temper of the period perhaps these quotations may help.

First Rousseau. He justifies his *Confessions*, on the very first page of that work, in these words:

> 'Si je ne vaux pas mieux, au moins je suis autre.'
> (I may not be better than anybody else, but at least I am different.)

Next Blake. These words, from the preface to his *Milton*, precede the sentences quoted at the end of the last chapter.

> '... Shakespeare & Milton were both curb'd by the general malady & infection from the silly Greek & Latin slaves of the Sword.'
> 'Rouze up, O young Men of the New Age! set your foreheads against the ignorant Hirelings! For we have Hirelings in the Camp, the Court &

the University, who would, if they could, for ever depress Mental &
prolong Corporeal War. Painters! on you I call. Sculptors! Architects!
Suffer not the fashionable Fools to depress your powers. . . .'

Next Wordsworth. This passage comes from the preface to the
Lyrical Ballads, and in it he is saying what he believes the values of
poetry to be.

'The subject [poetry] is indeed important! For the human mind is capable
of being excited without the application of gross and violent stimulants;
and he must have a very faint perception of its beauty and dignity who does
not know this, and who does not further know, that one being is elevated
above another, in proportion as he possesses this capability. It has therefore
appeared to me, that to endeavour to produce or enlarge this capability
is one of the best services in which, at any period, a Writer can be engaged;
but this service, excellent at all times, is especially so at the present day.
For a multitude of causes, unknown to former times, are now acting with
a combined force to blunt the discriminating powers of the mind, and,
unfitting it for all voluntary exertion, to reduce it to a state of almost
savage torpor. The most effective of these causes are the great national
events which are daily taking place, and the increasing accumulation of
men in cities, where the uniformity of their occupations produces a craving
for extraordinary incident, which the rapid communication of intelligence
hourly gratifies. To this tendency the life and manners, the literature and
theatrical exhibitions of the country have conformed themselves. The
invaluable works of our elder writers, I had almost said the works of
Shakespeare and Milton, are driven into neglect by frantic novels, sickly
and stupid German Tragedies, and deluges of idle extravagant stories in
verse. . . .
The object of the Poet's thoughts are everywhere; though the eyes and
senses of man are, it is true, his favourite guides, yet he will follow where-
soever he can find an atmosphere of sensation in which to move his
wings. . . .'

The reader will have no difficulty in bringing this prescient passage
up to date. There are more men in cities than ever; 'the rapid communication of intelligence' has developed into the mass media of
press, film and television; our 'elder writers' are set books; the 'frantic
novels' are still with us; for the sickly and stupid German Tragedies we
can substitute, as a convenient symbol, Hollywood; and very rare
today are the readers of verse, however 'idle and extravagant'.

Next Coleridge. The quotation comes from the *Biographia Literaria.*

'The imagination then I consider either as primary, or secondary. The
primary imagination I hold to be the living power and prime agent of all
human perception, and as a repetition in the finite mind of the eternal act

of creation in the infinite I AM. The secondary I consider as an echo of the former, co-existing with the conscious will, yet still as identical with the primary in the kind of its agency, and differing only in degree, and in the mode of its operation. It dissolves, diffuses, dissipates, in order to re-create; or where this process is rendered impossible, yet still, at all events, it struggles to idealize and to unify. It is essentially *vital*, even as all objects (as objects) are essentially fixed and dead.

Fancy, on the contrary, has no other counters to play with, but fixities and definites. The Fancy is indeed no other than a mode of memory emancipated from the order of time and space; and blended with, and modified by that empirical phenomenon of the will, which we express by the word choice. But equally with the ordinary memory, it must receive all its materials ready made from the law of association.'

Lastly Shelley from *The Defence of Poetry*:

'The exertions of Locke, Hume, Gibbon, Voltaire, Rousseau, and their disciples, in favour of oppressed and deluded humanity, are entitled to the gratitude of mankind. Yet it is easy to calculate the degree of moral and intellectual improvement which the world would have exhibited, had they never lived. A little more nonsense would have been talked for a century or two; and perhaps a few more men, women, and children, burnt as heretics. We might not at this moment have been congratulating each other on the abolition of the Inquisition in Spain. But it exceeds all imagination to conceive what would have been the moral condition of the world if neither Dante, Petrarch, Boccaccio, Chaucer, Shakespeare, Calderon, Lord Bacon, nor Milton, had ever existed; if Raphael and Michael Angelo had never been born; if the Hebrew poetry had never been translated; if a revival of the study of Greek literature had never taken place; if no monuments of ancient sculpture had been handed down to us; and if the poetry of the religion of the ancient world had been extinguished together with its belief. The human mind could never, except by the intervention of these excitements, have been awakened to the invention of the grosser sciences, and to the application of reasoning to the aberrations of society, which it is now attempted to exalt over the direct expression of the inventive and creative faculty itself.

We have more moral, political, and historical wisdom than we know how to reduce into practice; we have more scientific and economical knowledge than can be accommodated to the just distribution of the produce which it multiplies. The poetry, in these systems of thought, is concealed by the accumulation of facts and calculating processes. . . . The cultivation of these sciences which have enlarged the limits of the empire of man over the external world, has, for want of the poetical faculty, proportionally circumscribed those of the internal world; and man, having enslaved the elements remains himself a slave. . . . From what other cause has it arisen that the discoveries which should have lightened, have added

a weight to the curse imposed upon Adam? Poetry, and the principle of
self, of which money is the visible incarnation, are the God and Mammon
of the world.'

The reader will note the immense importance which the creative
imagination has for these four writers. Blake has no doubt that it is the
voice of God, and Coleridge would appear, in his windier way, to
agree. For Wordsworth and Shelley it is a means of improving man;
indeed, the only means of civilizing a society which, in spite of technical progress, is sinking deeper into barbarism. The ideas which
imbue the passages I have quoted continue to work, in various forms,
throughout the nineteenth century and are still active today. According
to our view of our own period, we can say that we are still being
carried forward by the wave of Romanticism, or are wallowing in
its trough, or cast by it upon a desert shore, or paddling helplessly
in its backwash.

> 'Shakespearian fish' [wrote Yeats], 'swam the sea, far away from land.
> Romantic fish swam in nets coming to the hand;
> What are all those fish that lie gasping on the strand?

I want to begin by examining four short poems by Wordsworth, all
written in 1798, and published that year in the volume entitled *Lyrical
Ballads*. This was the period of his deepest intimacy with Coleridge,
and the book was planned as a joint production. Wordsworth was
'to choose incidents and situations from common life, and to relate and
describe them, as far as was possible, in a selection of language really
used by men, and at the same time to throw over them a certain
colouring of the imagination.' Coleridge tells us that his 'endeavours
were to be directed to persons and characters supernatural, or at least
romantic; yet so as to . . . procure for these shadows of imagination
that willing suspension of disbelief for the moment that constitutes
poetic faith . . . with this view I wrote my *Ancient Mariner*,' and this
poem was, together with *The Nightingale*, Coleridge's only contribu-
tion. The volume was consciously revolutionary in matter and technique, and its preface was a manifesto. It was greeted with indifference
or ridicule, and we can recognize the whole episode as characteristically
'modern'.

A work of fancy, according to Coleridge's definition, would
offer the reader a rearrangement of experiences he was already familiar
with; but the work of imagination confronts him with a new experience which he may find uncomfortable or shocking. So we get
the pattern, so often repeated since, of rejection by established taste,

a rejection which may range from ridicule or neglect (Blake, Keats, Hopkins) to prosecution (Baudelaire, Flaubert, Lawrence), followed by propaganda by a minority, and, in the end, acceptance. For a full consideration of its nature and importance the readers should turn to the preface itself, and to the account of Wordsworth's poetry in the latter part of the *Biographia Literaria*. We may note, and concur with, Coleridge's remark that 'the language of real life' is 'an equivocal expression'; but we must also note Wordsworth's conviction that new ideas cannot be expressed without a new language; that the starting point of poetic reform must be linguistic.

Here is the first of the poems, *Expostulation and Reply*.

'Why, William, on that old grey stone,
Thus for the length of half a day,
Why, William, sit you thus alone,
And dream your time away?

'Where are your books?—that light bequeathed
To Beings else forlorn and blind!
Up! Up! and drink the spirit breathed
From dead men to their kind.

'You look round on your Mother Earth,
As if she for no purpose bore you;
As if you were her first-born birth,
And none had lived before you!'

One morning thus, by Esthwaite lake,
When life was sweet, I knew not why,
To me my good friend Matthew spake,
And thus I made reply:

'The eye—it cannot choose but see;
We cannot bid the ear be still;
Our bodies feel, where'er they be,
Against or with our will.

'Nor less I deem that there are Powers
Which of themselves our minds impress;
That we can feed this mind of ours
In a wise passiveness.

'Think you, 'mid all this mighty sum
Of things for ever speaking,
That nothing of itself will come,
But we must still be seeking?

> 'Then ask not wherefore, here, alone,
> Conversing as I may,
> I sit upon this old grey stone,
> And dream my time away.'

The verse form is the simple traditional rhymed quatrain, familiar in ballad and hymn. (We must remember that the Wesleys appealed to 'men' in the 'language of men'.) There is no trace of 'poetic diction', unless we count 'where'er' and ''mid'; this language, we cannot doubt, is at any rate the real language of Wordsworth and Coleridge, subjected to a minimum of manipulation, and its form has been made as transparent as possible. The poet defends himself against a charge of idleness, of neglecting his books, the 'spirit breathed from dead men to their kind'; worse, he appears to have no 'purpose'; his activity, or rather his lack of it, is irrational. In his defence he adduces psychology, for this is a poem about the workings of the mind, and the way in which it apprehends the universe. Our senses continually offer us data about the world, and this happens whether we consciously will them to do so or not. By analogy, the poet argues that there are spiritual powers in the universe which can, without his conscious intervention, speak to his mind, and this is perhaps the characteristic Wordsworthian experience. He admits his passiveness, but terms it wise. In other words the poem opposes to the exercise of reason (the books) the exercise of a higher faculty, the imagination; truth can be known intuitively, by, if you like, revelation. The view is more emphatically expressed in the companion piece, *The Tables Turned*.

> Up! Up! my Friend, and quit your books;
> Or surely you'll grow double;
> Up! Up! my Friend, and clear your looks;
> Why all this toil and trouble?
>
> The sun, above the mountain's head,
> A freshening lustre mellow
> Through all the long green fields has spread,
> His first sweet evening yellow.
>
> Books! 'tis a dull and endless strife:
> Come, hear the woodland linnet,
> How sweet his music! on my life,
> There's more of wisdom in it.
>
> And hark! how blithe the throstle sings!
> He, too, is no mean preacher:
> Come forth into the light of things,
> Let Nature be your Teacher.

She has a world of ready wealth,
Our minds and hearts to bless—
Spontaneous wisdom breathed by health,
Truth breathed by cheeerfulness.

One impulse from a vernal wood
May teach you more of man,
Of moral evil and of good,
Than all the sages can.

Sweet is the lore which Nature brings;
Our meddling intellect
Mis-shapes the beauteous forms of things:—
We murder to dissect.

Enough of Science and of Art;
Close up those barren leaves;
Come forth, and bring with you a heart
That watches and receives.

The evening light, the linnet and the thrush are teachers; from them
comes 'spontaneous wisdom', beyond the reach of 'toiling reason'.
'Things' which have 'light' are opposed to 'books'; and the paradox,
that 'things'—the word is the simplest way of saying 'Nature', or
'the contents of the universe', which is a collection of 'things'—
are more illuminating, more instructive, more meaningful than the
works of the sages, is central to the poem. Yet there is a note of caution,
of delicate balance. The poet does not say that one impulse *will* teach
you, he says it *may*: whether it does or not presumably depends on
your capacity for *wise* passiveness. But there are no reservations about
the next stanza, with its fierce summary:

We murder to dissect. . . .

The structures of science are built on death. We must apprehend the
form of things (note the repetition of that word) for this is the course
of true wisdom. The intellect 'meddles', the heart 'receives'. We
must remember that 'science' in this contest bears its old meaning of
knowledge, and that Art does not stand for works of the imagination,
but for techniques, as in such phrases as 'the arts of civilization'. The
leaves are barren—they are at once leaves of books, and leaves of
fruitless trees—of barren fig trees, perhaps.

Now the *Lines Written in Early Spring*.

I heard a thousand blended notes,
While in a grove I sate reclined,
In that sweet mood when pleasant thoughts
Bring sad thoughts to the mind.

To her fair works did Nature link
The human soul that through me ran;
And much it grieved my heart to think
What man has made of man.

Through primrose tufts, in that green bower,
The periwinkle trailed its wreaths;
And 'tis my faith that every flower
Enjoys the air it breathes.

The birds around me hopped and played,
Their thoughts I cannot measure:—
But the least motion that they made,
It seemed a thrill of pleasure.

The budding twigs spread out their fan,
To catch the breezy air;
And I must think, do all I can,
That there was pleasure there.

If this belief from heaven be sent,
If such be Nature's holy plan,
Have I not reason to lament
What man has made of man?

The poet's theme is traditional; so is his attitude. He is not the first
bard to sit reclined in rustic state, nor, one supposes, will he be the
last. The 'mood' is interesting. It is 'sweet' because in it pleasant
thoughts evoke sad ones—an analysis of what earlier poets were content
to call 'melancholy', and an example of the Wordsworthian and
romantic interest in the workings of the mind, simply for its own sake.
The key word in the next stanza is 'link'. The poet, human, feels
himself a part of Nature, things. He contrasts the harmony of
'her fair works' with the miseries of society, 'what man has
made of man'. In the rest of the poem it is important to notice the
precarious balance of the poet's faith, for it is this which gives these
lines their tension and intensity. 'It *seemed*'—I cannot know this, but
I feel it, at the moment; 'I must think, do all I can'—in spite of all the

efforts of my reason; and then the twice repeated 'if' followed by the subjunctive of doubt:

> If this belief from heaven be sent,
> If such be Nature's holy plan. . . .

(We must emphasize the 'ifs', and the second 'be' if we are to give the lines their full force.)

'What man has made of man' includes for Wordsworth the French revolution and the terror, as well as the poverty and misery he saw in London and in his own countryside. The division between 'Nature's holy plan' and human society seems absolute, and this leaves the poet solitary. He laments for man, he hopes for consolation in his mystic, and private, vision of Nature's purposes and power. He 'constructs' as Mr. Eliot puts it 'something upon which to rejoice'. We are worlds away from the solidity of such a poem as Johnson's *On the Death of Mr. Robert Levett*. Does 'every bosom' return an echo to sentiments such as these?

The last of the four poems is entitled *To my Sister*.

> It is the first mild day of March:
> Each minute sweeter than before,
> The redbreast sings from the tall larch
> That stands beside our door.
>
> There is a blessing in the air,
> Which seems a sense of joy to yield
> To the bare trees, and mountains bare,
> And grass in the green field.
>
> My sister! ('tis a wish of mine)
> Now that our morning meal is done,
> Make haste, your morning task resign;
> Come forth and feel the sun.
>
> Edward will come with you;—and, pray,
> Put on with speed your woodland dress;
> And bring no book: for this one day
> We'll give to idleness.
>
> No joyless forms shall regulate
> Our living calendar:
> We from today, my Friend, will date
> The opening of the year.

Love, now a universal birth,
From heart to heart is stealing,
From earth to man, from man to earth:
—It is the hour of feeling.

One moment now may give us more
Than years of toiling reason:
Our minds shall drink at every pore
The spirit of the season.

Some silent laws our hearts will make,
Which they shall long obey:
We for the year to come may take
Our temper from today.

And from the blessed power that rolls
About, below, above,
We'll frame the measure of our souls:
They shall be tuned to love.

Then come, my Sister! come, I pray,
With speed put on your woodland dress;
And bring no book: for this one day
We'll give to idleness.

We can cite the first stanza as an example of Wordsworth's theory and practice successfully united; what greater stylistic contrast could there be than that between

Lo! where the rosy-bosomed hours. . . .

and

It is the first mild day of March. . . .

though we must remember that just as Milton's diction has had an unfortunate progeny, so the Wordsworthian revolution gave rise to unnumbered versified nature notes and weather reports. Indeed we tend to see the poems I have quoted through a haze of Victorian and Georgian 'nature poetry', and it is difficult for us to realize how original they are. We may note the 'blessing' which 'seems'—again the shadow of doubt—to yield a sense of joy, and the lines which are the core of this poem:

No joyless forms shall regulate
Our living calendar. . . .

We will conduct our lives, not according to the laws which man has made for man, for they are forms without joy. We will start our year, not on January the first, but today, because this is when we 'feel' the year to begin; and we do not need to articulate the laws our hearts will make, for 'it is the hour of feeling' not of reason. Note that Wordsworth is not preaching anarchy, any more than Blake did. There will be laws, there will be 'measure' for souls, but these laws and this measure will be drawn from imaginative apprehension of the love that is the 'blessed power that rolls through all things'.

It is interesting to compare these intensely personal and original poems with a sample of Wordsworth's earliest verse. These lines come from *An Evening Walk* 1793.

> I love beside the flowing lake to stray,
> Where winds the road along the secret bay;
> By rills that tumble down the woody steeps,
> And run in transport to the dimpling deeps;
> Along the 'wild meand'ring' shore to view,
> Obsequious Grace the winding swan pursue.
> He swells his lifted chest, and backward flings
> His bridling neck between his tow'ring wings;
> Stately, and burning in his pride, divides
> And glorying looks around, the silent tides;
> On as he floats, the silver'd waters glow,
> Proud of the varying arch and moveless form of snow.

Knowing the later work, we can recognize the keen Wordsworthian eye for detail, but the form, accomplished enough, is purely eighteenth century, and we can realize, too, how essential it was for him to break it. But he continued the eighteenth-century tradition of discursive, ruminative poetry. For this he used blank verse, and the following passages may stand as examples of his adaptation of this medium to his peculiar needs. The first is from *The Old Cumberland Beggar*.

> Him from my childhood have I known; and then
> He was so old, he seems not older now;
> He travels on, a solitary Man,
> So helpless in appearance, that for him
> The sauntering Horseman throws not with a slack
> And careless hand his alms upon the ground,
> But stops,—that he may safely lodge the coin
> Within the old Man's hat; nor quits him so,
> But still, when he has given his horse the rein,
> Watches the aged Beggar with a look
> Sidelong, and half-reverted. She who tends
> The toll-gate, when in summer at her door

She turns her wheel, if on the road she sees
The aged Beggar coming, quits her work,
And lifts the latch for him that he may pass.
The post-boy, when his rattling wheels o'ertake
The aged Beggar in the woody lane,
Shouts to him from behind; and, if thus warned
The old man does not change his course, the boy
Turns with less noisy wheels to the road-side,
And passes gently by, without a curse
Upon his lips or anger at his heart.

 He travels on, a solitary Man;
His age has no companion. On the ground
His eyes are turned, and, as he moves along,
They move along the ground; and, evermore,
Instead of common and habitual sight
Of fields and rural works, of hill and dale,
And the blue sky, one little span of earth
Is all his prospect. Thus, from day to day,
Bow-bent, his eyes for ever on the ground,
He plies his weary journey; seeing still,
And seldom knowing that he sees, some straw,
Some scattered leaf, or marks which, in one track,
The nails of cart or chariot-wheel have left
Impressed on the white road,—in the same line,
At distance still the same. Poor Traveller!
His staff trails with him; scarcely do his feet
Disturb the summer dust; he is so still
In look and motion, that the cottage curs,
Ere he has passed the door, will turn away,
Weary of barking at him. Boys and girls,
The vacant and the busy, maids and youths,
And urchins newly breeched—all pass him by:
Him even the slow-paced waggon leaves behind.

 But deem not this Man useless.—Statesmen! ye
Who are so restless in your wisdom, ye
Who have a broom still ready in your hands
To rid the world of nuisances; ye proud,
Heart-swoln, while in your pride ye contemplate
Your talents, power, or wisdom, deem him not
A burthen of the earth! 'Tis Nature's law
That none, the meanest of created things,
Of forms created the most vile and brute,
The dullest or most noxious, should exist
Divorced from good—a spirit and pulse of good,
A life and soul, to every mode of being

Inseparably linked. Then be assured
That least of all can aught—that ever owned
The heaven-regarding eye and front sublime
Which man is born to—sink, howe'er depressed,
So low as to be scorned without a sin;
Without offence to God cast out of view;
Like the dry remnant of a garden-flower
Whose seeds are shed, or as an implement
Worn out and worthless. While from door to door,
This old Man creeps, the villagers in him
Behold a record which together binds
Past deeds and offices of charity,
Else unremembered, and so keeps alive
The kindly mood of hearts which lapse of years,
And that half-wisdom half-experience gives,
Make slow to feel, and by sure steps resign
To selfishness and cold oblivious cares.
Among the farms and solitary huts,
Hamlets and thinly scattered villages,
Where'er the aged Beggar takes his rounds,
The mild necessity of use compels
To acts of love; and habit does the work
Of reason; yet prepares that after-joy
Which reason cherishes. And thus the soul,
By that sweet taste of pleasure unpursued,
Doth find herself insensibly disposed
To virtue and true goodness. . . .

We recognize in this sober verse, so admirably suited to Wordsworth's purposes, a reshaping of the eighteenth-century discursive mode. Suppler and more adaptable than Cowper's, it echoes the inflections of the poet's voice, and rarely calls attention to itself. The poet is not shackled by his theories about diction; he feels free to modify normal syntax to suit his meaning (Him from my childhood have I known); he does not shy away from latin-derived words (half-reverted); he has some resounding Miltonic cadences:

Him even the slow-paced waggon leaves behind. . . .
To selfishness and cold oblivious cares. . . .

But in his basic simplicity, in the freely handled sentence structure, endlessly varied yet never becoming slack, moving vitally as the sense moves; above all in the lovingly observed, unerringly relevant and dramatic detail, the pathos, the personal involvement in the old man's plight, the sense that he and his predicament have been freshly seen and deeply felt; judged not according to 'joyless forms', but by the 'silent laws' of the poet's own heart: all this goes to make up the character-istically Wordsworthian flavour. The rhetorical flourish

Yet deem not this Man useless, Statesman! ...

which introduces his reflections on the relations between the beggar and the community which supports him is a touch which relates the poem to its eighteenth-century predecessors; it is dramatically justified since it marks the transition from private vision to public discussion. We have met this sort of thing before in Goldsmith, but we feel that whereas Goldsmith presents the problems of his own age, Words-worth is probing into relationships between state and individual, into the nature of community, which still exist and are still unsolved. We note his profession of faith in 'Nature's law', with its characteristic terms 'spirit', 'pulse', 'life', 'soul', 'linked'. Perhaps in our breasts, as in Peter Bell's, 'these silent raptures find no place'; but we don't have to share the belief for the poem to work.

Wordsworth was a mystic; the feelings aroused in him by certain types of natural beauty were intensely religious, and much of his verse of this period is devoted to making these feelings explicit, as in this famous passage from the *Lines Written Above Tintern Abbey*, where he speaks of

> ... that blessed mood,
> In which the burthen of the mystery,
> In which the heavy and the weary weight
> Of all this unintelligible world,
> Is lightened:—that serene and blessed mood
> In which the affections gently lead us on,—
> Until, the breath of this corporeal frame
> And even the motion of our human blood
> Almost suspended, we are laid asleep
> In body, and become a living soul:
> While with an eye made quiet by the power
> Of harmony, and the deep power of joy,
> We see into the life of things. ...

Suppose the reader cannot share this mood; suppose, when he reads in the *Old Cumberland Beggar* that not even the dullest and most noxious of forms exist divorced from a spirit and pulse of good, he says to himself 'What about the anopheles mosquito?' These questions cannot be shirked. The poet, says, as clearly as he can, what he means, and we must try to follow him, and not vaguely approve, or coldly dismiss him, as a kindly person who was fond of daffodils. We have already pointed out the precarious balance of faith in such poems as the *Lines Written in Early Spring*, and the passage I have quoted from *Tintern Abbey* is continued thus:

> ... If this
> Be but a vain belief, yet, oh! how oft—
> In darkness and amid the many shapes
> Of joyless daylight; when the fretful stir
> Unprofitable, and the fever of the world,
> Have hung upon the beatings of my heart—
> How oft, in spirit, have I turned to thee,
> O sylvan Wye! thou wanderer through the woods,
> How often has my spirit turned to thee!

The anacoluthon (a construction lacking grammatical sequence) conveys the conflict, for which 'tragic' is perhaps not too strong a word, which lies at the heart of much of Wordsworth's best writing about nature.

But here, in the *Old Cumberland Beggar*, we can agree that man cannot sink so low as to be scorned without a sin (note the traditional theological term, from a universe of discourse other than that of 'Nature's law') without feeling our agreement depends on believing as Wordsworth does. Perhaps we may find the reflective part of the poem less securely controlled and duller than the description—say rather, the creation—of the Beggar, but it is lightened by such *aperçus* as 'that half wisdom half experience gives', concise, neat, owing much to the Augustan clarity and precision, though rhythmically so different. Such remarks, a kind of distilled commonsense, gleam (sometimes, alas, sparsely) in the dullest Wordsworthian stretches.

Here, to stand as a sample of the poet's writing about nature, is a passage from the last book of his great autobiographical poem *The Prelude*, a work begun in 1799, and finished in 1805, but not published, except for a few fragments, till 1850, the year of his death. He is walking up Snowdon, with a friend and a guide, to see the sun rise.

> It was a close, warm breezeless summer night,
> Wan, dull, and glaring, with a dripping fog
> Low-hung and thick that covered all the sky;
> But, undiscouraged, we began to climb
> The mountain-side. The mist soon girt us round,
> And, after ordinary travellers' talk
> With our conductor, pensively we sank
> Each into commerce with his private thoughts:
> Thus did we breast the ascent, and by myself

Was nothing either seen or heard that checked
Those musings or diverted, save that once
The shepherd's lurcher, who, among the crags
Had to his joy unearthed a hedgehog, teased
His coiled-up prey with barkings turbulent.
This small adventure, for even such it seemed
In that wild place and at the dead of night,
Being over and forgotten, on we wound
In silence as before. With forehead bent
Earthward, as if in opposition set
Against an enemy, I panted up
With eager pace, and no less eager thoughts.
Thus might we wear a midnight hour away,
Ascending at loose distance each from each,
And I, as chanced, the foremost of the band;
When at my feet the ground appeared to brighten,
And with a step or two seemed brighter still;
Nor was time given to ask or learn the cause,
For instantly a light upon the turf
Fell like a flash, and lo! as I looked up,
The Moon hung naked in a firmament
Of azure without cloud, and at my feet
Rested a silent sea of hoary mist.
A hundred hills their dusky backs upheaved
All over this still ocean; and beyond,
Far, far beyond, the solid vapours stretched,
In headlands, tongues, and promontory shapes,
Into the main Atlantic, that appeared
To dwindle, and give up his majesty,
Usurped upon far as the eye could reach.
Not so the ethereal vault; encroachment none
Was there, nor loss; only the inferior stars
Had disappeared, or shed a fainter light
In the clear presence of the full-orbed Moon,
Who, from her sovereign elevation, gazed
Upon the billowy ocean, as it lay
All meek and silent, save that through a rift—
Not distant from the shore whereon we stood,
A fixed, abysmal, gloomy, breathing-place—
Mounted the roar of waters, torrents, streams
Innumerable, roaring with one voice!
Heard over earth and sea, and, in that hour,
For so it seemed, felt by the starry heavens.

    When into air had partially dissolved
That vision, given to spirits of the night

And three chance human wanderers, in calm thought
Reflected, it appeared to me the type
Of a majestic intellect, its acts
And its possessions, what it has and craves,
What in itself it is, and would become.
There I beheld the emblem of a mind
That feeds upon infinity, that broods
Over the dark abyss, intent to hear
Its voices issuing forth to silent light
In one continuous stream; a mind sustained
By recognitions of transcendent power,
In sense conducting to ideal form,
In soul of more than mortal privilege.
One function, above all, of such a mind
Had Nature shadowed there, by putting forth,
'Mid circumstances awful and sublime,
That mutual domination which she loves
To exert upon the face of outward things,
So moulded, joined, abstracted, so endowed
With interchangeable supremacy,
That men, least sensitive, see, hear, perceive,
And cannot choose but feel. The power, which all
Acknowledge when thus moved, which Nature thus
To bodily sense exhibits, is the express
Resemblance of that glorious faculty
That higher minds bear with them as their own.
This is the very spirit in which they deal
With the whole compass of the universe:
They from their native selves can send abroad
Kindred mutations; for themselves create
A like existence; and whene'er it dawns
Created for them, catch it, or are caught
By its inevitable mastery,
Like angels stopped upon the wing by sound
Of harmony from Heaven's remotest spheres.
Them the enduring and the transient both
Serve to exalt; they build up greatest things
From least suggestions; ever on the watch,
Willing to work and to be wrought upon,
They need not extraordinary calls
To rouse them; in a world of life they live,
By sensible impressions not enthralled,
But by their quickening impulse made more prompt
To hold fit converse with the spiritual world,
And with the generations of mankind
Spread over time, past, present, and to come,

Age after age, till Time shall be no more.
Such minds are truly from the Deity,
For they are Powers. . . .

The passage follows a pattern familiar in Wordsworth, and which we
have already remarked on in the *Old Cumberland Beggar*: first he
recreates the experience, and then reflects on it, and the recreation tends
to be more moving, certainly more lively, than the reflections. Interesting or profound though they may sometimes be, we are not
infrequently reminded, as we peruse them, of Keats's phrase for Wordsworth—'the egotistical sublime'.

We are first made to feel the night and the fog. It is interesting to
work out how the poet handles the rhythm of these first three lines.
All the epithets are simple, unpoetic, exact—here, we feel, is the
celebrated doctrine about the language of men being put into practice.
But the precision and plainness of the epithets doesn't account for the
potency of the lines. If we listen closely we can hear how the rhythm
forces the meaning on us. The first three syllables have no stress; each
of the next three, 'close', 'warm', 'breeze', has. The rhythmic arrangement therefore, makes us hit them harder than anything else in the
line, for as we grasp its total meaning, we do not feel 'summer night'
to be as important as what sort of summer night it was. The run of the
next line is different. Its first two syllables, 'wan' and 'dull' are both
important and must both be stressed; the next two make a regular
foot, but we hurry over 'ing', 'with' and 'a' to strike the first syllable
of 'dripping', and the final syllable 'fog'. Any blank verse line invites
us to feel five stresses, and the distribution of these stresses within the
line reinforces the meaning. In the third line 'low-hung' balances
'wan, dull', but after that the line is regular and brings us back to the
norm again at the end of the description. We may note, too, the
effect of alliteration in 'warm' and 'wan'; in 'thick', 'covered' and 'sky';
and how the d, th, and k sounds in 'and thick that covered all the sky,'
clog the line as the mist clogs the atmosphere.

Such analysis takes a long time, and may sound pedantic, but
Wordsworth's best blank verse, simple as it may appear, is full of
these subtle modulations, based, in passages such as this, on the narrating
voice. The reader is invited to work out for himself the reasons why
lines which seem to him particularly striking 'are so and not otherwise'.

Pedestrian energy, and the earnest monotony of the climb (like
the poet, we are thankful for the diversion afforded by the hedgehog)
are competently conveyed. Wordsworth is very good at convincing
us that whatever he is describing really happened, and the moment
when he emerges into the moonlight is dramatic. The lines seem to

hurry—note the repetition of 'brighten', 'brighter', and the puzzle as to what the cause might be—and the movement goes straight through to 'fell like a flash'. One of the things that makes this description of the moonlight over the sea of mist so impressive is the way in which everything in it seems alive. The 'naked' moon which 'gazes' seems more of a real presence than Cynthia checking 'her dragon yoke/Gently o'er th'accustomed oake'; the hills 'heave their dusky backs' like sea monsters; the Atlantic 'dwindles', it is 'usurped upon'; the mist is 'meek and silent'; the cleft is a breathing place through which the sounds of nature mount to roar with a single voice.

We can easily relate this fine piece to the first lyrics we quoted. It even includes the characteristically Wordsworthian proviso— 'for so it *seemed*', The account of the value of the experience is more detailed, more elaborate, more closely argued, but in essence the same: in the presence of such beauty man cannot choose but feel; such beauty 'may teach'.

The passage which begins

> ... The power, which all
> Acknowledge when thus moved. ...

deals with the nature of the imagination, and should be put beside Coleridge's definition. 'Higher minds', those endowed with creative imagination, deal 'with the whole compass of the universe', and send abroad 'kindred mutations'. These are the works of art they create: 'kindred' because they are related to, and inspired by, the 'wisdom and spirit of the universe'; 'mutation' because the artist changes his experiences into works of art. The succeeding lines apply well to Wordsworth's own work. He has no doubt, of course, that he is one of the 'higher minds'; he, too, 'builds up greatest things from least suggestions'; he 'needs not extraordinary calls to rouse him'. The claims made on behalf of the imagination are enormous, and they are characteristically Romantic. We may note that they have little to do with the enchanted dream world which so many later poets seem to inhabit for so much of their time.

There follow other examples of Wordsworth's work, intended to give the reader some idea of his range. He used verse, notably in the series of *Poems Dedicated to National Independence and Liberty*, to comment on the public affairs of his age, with which he was deeply concerned; we are quite wrong if we think of him as a recluse. The first is a sonnet entitled *1801*.

> I grieved for Buonaparté, with a vain
> And an unthinking grief! The tenderest mood

Of that Man's mind—what can it be? what food
Fed his first hopes? what knowledge could *he* gain?
'Tis not in battles that from youth we train
The Governor who must be wise and good,
And temper with the sternness of the brain
Thoughts motherly, and meek as womanhood.
Wisdom doth live with children round her knees:
Books, leisure, perfect freedom, and the talk
Man holds with week-day man in the hourly walk
Of the mind's business: these are the degrees
By which true Sway doth mount; this is the stalk
True Power doth grow on; and her rights are these.

Napoleon had betrayed the principles of the revolution from which
the young Wordsworth had hoped so much, and the poet contrasts
the power of the 'intoxicated despot' with 'true Sway', defined
paradoxically through images of domesticity, quite remote from all
feelings normally associated with ruling men. This is a picture of a
natural order—power is a fruit that grows on a stalk. We can compare
it with similar images in Shakespeare. Duncan tells Banquo 'I have
begun to plant thee, and will labour/To make thee full of growing'
and Banquo replies 'The harvest is your own'. At the symbolic feast
Macbeth arranges to celebrate his kingship, there is no place for him;
the meeting breaks up 'in most admired disorder'. Behind Shakespeare's
images there lie the sanctions of tradition and theology; behind Wordsworth's his belief in man and nature.

It is often said that Wordsworth had no sense of humour, but he was
capable of irony, as this sonnet shows. It is the first of a short series
called *Personal Talk*.

I am not One who much or oft delight
To season my fireside with personal talk,—
Of friends, who live within an easy walk,
Or neighbours, daily, weekly, in my sight:
And, for my chance acquaintance, ladies bright,
Sons, mothers, maidens withering on the stalk,
These all wear out of me, like Forms with chalk
Painted on rich men's floors for one feast night.
Better than such discourse doth silence long,
Long barren silence square with my desire;
To sit without emotion, hope or aim,
In the loved presence of my cottage fire,
And listen to the flapping of the flame,
Or kettle whispering its faint undersong.

This is a 'mutation' of one of the 'sundry moods' in which, he tells us, 'it was pastime to be bound/within the sonnet's scanty plot of ground'. Part of the pleasure such verse as this gives comes from its complete assurance, its technical perfection. The mood is expressed with absolute honesty, the conclusion is a typically Wordsworthian melody.

Next, a poem with a more bitter irony, *A Poet's Epitaph*, composed in 1799.

> Art thou a Statist in the van
> Of public conflicts trained and bred?
> —First learn to love one living man;
> *Then* may'st thou think upon the dead.
>
> A Lawyer art thou?—draw not nigh!
> Go, carry to some fitter place
> The keeenness of that practised eye,
> The hardness of that sallow face.
>
> Art thou a Man of purple cheer?
> A rosy Man, right plump to see?
> Approach; yet, Doctor, not too near,
> This grave no cushion is for thee.
>
> Or art thou one of gallant pride,
> A Soldier, and no man of chaff?
> Welcome!—but lay thy sword aside,
> And lean upon a peasant's staff.
>
> Physician art thou?—one, all eyes,
> Philosopher!—a fingering slave,
> One that would peep and botanise
> Upon his mother's grave?
>
> Wrapt closely in thy sensual fleece,
> O turn aside,—and take, I pray,
> That he below may rest in peace,
> Thy ever-dwindling soul away!
>
> A Moralist perchance appears;
> Led, Heaven knows how! to this poor sod:
> And he has neither eyes nor ears;
> Himself his world, and his own God;
>
> One to whose smooth-rubbed soul can cling
> Nor form, nor feeling, great or small;
> A reasoning self-sufficing thing,
> And intellectual All-in-all!

Shut close the door; press down the latch;
Sleep in thy intellectual crust;
Nor lose ten tickings of thy watch
Near this unprofitable dust.

But who is He, with modest looks,
And clad in homely russet brown?
He murmurs near the running brooks
A music sweeter than their own.

He is retired as noontide dew,
Or fountain in a noon-day grove;
And you must love him, ere to you
He will seem worthy of your love.

The outward shows of sky and earth,
Of hill and valley, he has viewed;
And impulses of deeper birth
Have come to him in solitude.

In common things that round us lie
Some random truths he can impart—
The harvest of a quiet eye
That broods and sleeps on his own heart.

But he is weak; both Man and Boy,
Hath been an idler in the land;
Contented if he might enjoy
The things which others understand.

—Come hither in thy hour of strength;
Come, weak as is a breaking wave!
Here stretch thy body at full length;
Or build thy house upon this grave.

All men of reason, of science, who obey 'joyless forms', all men of
chaff, are dismissed with a savagery unusual in Wordsworth. The
soldier is welcome, for his bravery is unselfish, but only the poet, the
man of imagination is a truly sympathetic visitor. He seems a pastoral
figure, a literary descendant of the poet whose epitaph we read at the
end of Gray's *Elegy*, and he is a bit of an anti-climax after the harsh
denunciations of the early stanzas. He is also Wordsworth himself,
and a type of the Romantic poet. His strength is his own, 'come to

him in solitude'; but this solitude is also a weakness; the poet as
outcast, as hermit, can never command the strength of a poet involved
in the whole life of his time. The situation of which this poem gives
such an energetic, violent, deeply felt account, vitiates much romantic
and post-romantic verse. Indeed, Wordsworth failed to complete the
tasks he set himself, and after about 1805 his verse gets progressively
less interesting.

Next, for we are trying to exhibit his variety, a fine piece of Romantic
gloom, by Milton out of eighteenth-century Gothic horror.

YEW-TREES 1803

There is a Yew-tree, pride of Lorton Vale,
Which to this day stands single, in the midst
Of its own darkness, as it stood of yore:
Not loth to furnish weapons for the bands
Of Umfraville or Percy ere they marched
To Scotland's heaths; or those that crossed the sea
And drew their sounding bows at Agincourt,
Perhaps at earlier Crecy, or Poictiers.
Of vast circumference and gloom profound
This solitary Tree! a living thing
Produced too slowly ever to decay;
Of form and aspect too magnificent
To be destroyed. But worthier still of note
Are those fraternal Four of Borrowdale,
Joined in one solemn and capacious grove;
Huge trunks! and each particular trunk a growth
Of intertwisted fibres serpentine
Up-coiling, and inveterately convolved;
Nor uninformed with Phantasy, and looks
That threaten the profane; a pillared shade,
Upon whose grassless floor of red-brown hue,
By sheddings from the pining umbrage tinged
Perennially—beneath whose sable roof
Of boughs, as if for festal purpose decked
With unrejoicing berries—ghostly Shapes
May meet at noontide; Fear and trembling Hope,
Silence and Foresight; Death the Skeleton
And Time the shadow;—there to celebrate,
As in a natural temple scattered o'er
With altars undisturbed of mossy stone,
United worship; or in mute repose
To lie, and listen to the mountain flood
Murmuring from Glaramara's inmost caves.

I would like the poet's last word to be this sonnet, written when he was seventy-six. I do not claim it as a great poem; it can stand as a sample of the later verse, a dour comment by an old man on the way the world was going. It is entitled *Illustrated Books and Newspapers*.

> Discourse was deemed Man's noblest attribute,
> And written words the glory of his hand;
> Then followed Printing with enlarged command
> For thought—dominion vast and absolute
> For spreading truth, and making love expand.
> Now prose and verse sunk into disrepute
> Must lacquey a dumb Art that best can suit
> The taste of this once intellectual Land.
> A backward movement surely have we here,
> From manhood—back to childhood; for the age—
> Back towards caverned life's first rude career.
> Avaunt this vile abuse of pictured page!
> Must eyes be all in all, the tongue and ear
> Nothing? Heaven keep us from a lower stage!

The reader may make what application he will.

Coleridge (1772–1834) was one of the most important minds of his age—'a hooded eagle among blinking owls', said Shelley. His published work is fragmentary, in verse as well as prose; we can only point to one indubitable masterpiece—*The Ancient Mariner*. The unhappy, unsettled life, the opium addiction, the countless plans never carried through, make him a kind of type of the Romantic artist, in Baudelaire's phrase, 'une âme fêlée'. Before he formed his friendship, so fruitful for both men, with Wordsworth, he had already reacted against 'the ignoramuses and Pope-admirers', and begun to write a free, colloquially based blank verse which must have influenced Wordsworth's theories and his practice. Here is a passage from *This Lime Tree Bower my Prison* composed at Nether Stowey in 1797. The friends are Lamb, Wordsworth, and the latter's sister Dorothy. Mrs. Coleridge had 'accidentally emptied a skillet of boiling milk' on the poet's foot, so he had to sit at home while his friends went walking. The poem follows them in imagination.

> Well, they are gone, and here I must remain,
> This lime-tree bower my prison! I have lost
> Beauties and feelings, such as would have been
> Most sweet to my remembrance even when age
> Had dimmed my eyes to blindness! They, meanwhile
> Friends, whom I never more may meet again,
> On springy heath, along the hill-top edge,

Wander in gladness, and wind down, perchance,
To that still roaring dell, of which I told;
The roaring dell, o'erwooded, narrow, deep,
And only speckled by the midday sun;
Where its slim trunk the ash from rock to rock
Flings arching like a bridge;—that branchless ash,
Unsunned and damp, whose few poor yellow leaves
Ne'er tremble in the gale, yet tremble still,
Fann'd by the water-fall! and there my friends
Behold the dark green file of long lank weeds,
That all at once (a most fantastic sight!)
Still nod and drip beneath the dripping edge
Of the blue clay-stone.

The verse movement can encompass the agreeable easy familiar opening, as well as the potent imagery of the ash tree and the weeds. Wordsworth spoke in *The Prelude* of the 'dance of images' left in his mind by natural beauty, and images are of immense importance in Romantic poetry. They may, of course, be explanatory. For example, in Wordsworth's sonnet 'Nuns fret not in their convent's narrow room' the 'bees that soar for bloom/high as the highest point of Furness-fells', and are yet contented to 'murmur by the hour in foxglove bells' are an image of the poet's imagination, which can range over the whole universe, and yet can be satisfied to work within the restriction of the sonnet. The picture is charming in itself, but it carries a paraphrasable meaning. Such a paraphrase will be dry and inadequate, omitting the charm, the associations of natural activity, beauty, honey and so on; but what it says articulates the image. Wordsworth indeed offers such a version at the end of the octet of this sonnet when he says 'in truth the prison unto which we doom/ ourselves no prison is'.

What we may call the characteristically Romantic image, for example the ash tree in these lines, has an immediate and compelling resonance, and it works irrationally. Compare these lines which occur later in the poem.

            ... Pale beneath the blaze
Hung the transparent foliage; and I watch'd
Some broad and sunny leaf, and lov'd to see
The shadow of the leaf and stem above
Dappling its sunshine! And that walnut-tree
Was richly ting'd, and a deep radiance lay
Full on the ancient ivy, which usurps
Those fronting elms, and now, with blackest mass
Makes their dark branches gleam a lighter hue

> Through the late twilight: and though now the bat
> Wheels silent by, and not a swallow twitters,
> Yet still the solitary humble-bee
> Sings in the bean-flower!

The poet communicates his pleasure; we are happy to share it, happy to observe the elm trees through eyes keener than our own, and note how the ivy 'with blackest mass/Makes their dark branches gleam a lighter hue'; but we can be content to think that the key to the whole piece is clearly and unambiguously given in the verbs 'I watch'd', 'I lov'd to see'. On the other hand the narrow dell and the branchless ash seem to convey a meaning beyond themselves. They are contrasted with the 'springy heath' and 'hill-top edge' where his friends 'wander in gladness'. Can it be that Coleridge sees his friends living 'like a brook in the open sunshine'? Might the roaring dell only 'speckled by the mid-day sun' be the dark side of his own life, and he himself the branchless ash, 'unsunned and damp'? The accident effects a separation between them; he is for the moment cut off from their pleasures, and this is the occasion for this apparently straight-forward poetic meditation. But the passage echoes with a sense of a more sinister, more poignant, more permanent separation, which comes to us through the image. I have laboured the point because such images abound in Romantic poetry, and because they become later the stuff that poetry is made of.

The opening lines of the unfinished *Christabel*, composed 1797–1800 and published in 1816 may stand here for the Gothic, medievalizing, side of Romanticism.

> 'Tis the middle of the night by the castle clock,
> And the owls have wakened the crowing cock;
> Tu-whit! Tu-whoo!
> And hark, again! the crowing cock,
> How drowsily it crew.
>
> Sir Leoline, the Baron rich,
> Hath a toothless mastiff bitch;
> From her kennel beneath the rock
> She maketh answer to the clock,
> Four for the quarters, and twelve for the hour;
> Ever and aye, by shine and shower,
> Sixteen short howls, not over loud;
> Some say, she sees my lady's shroud.
>
> Is the night chilly and dark?
> The night is chilly, but not dark.
> The thin grey cloud is spread on high,

It covers but not hides the sky.
The moon is behind, and at the full;
And yet she looks but small and dull.
The night is chill, the cloud is gray:
'Tis a month before the month of May,
And the spring comes slowly up this way . . .

Note the speed and energy of the lines, the cunning way in which the metrical pattern is varied; how sinister is the image of the moon, the harshness of the late spring! A reader who turns from *Christabel* to Scott's *Lady of the Lake* or *Marmion* will quickly see how good in this kind of poem Coleridge is.

For the poet's masterpiece, *The Ancient Mariner*, we have no space, and it is not a poem to quote from, but here is that famous fragment *Kubla Khan*, all that remains of 'two or three hundred lines' composed while asleep in his chair after he had been treated with an 'anodyne', 'if that indeed can be called composition in which all the images rose up before him as *things*, without any sensation or consciousness of effort'. When he woke up Coleridge 'eagerly wrote down the lines that are here preserved'; was then 'called out by a person on business from Porlock and detained by him above an hour'. When he came back he had forgotten the rest of the poem. Scholars have traced every image and many turns of phrase to the poet's reading, so the poem might be classified, according to his own distinction, as a work of Fancy—'a mode of memory emancipated from the order of time and space'. It is an incantation, a kind of spell. The exotic, the past, mystery, terror, the supernatural, the irrational, all the romantic ingredients are here. The poet asleep in his chair is transmuted into a bard, a shaman, and the 'anodyne', no doubt opium, which put him to sleep becomes 'the milk of Paradise'. This is the sort of verse which for much of the nineteenth century became 'the poetic'—the poetry of magic and of dream.

In Xanadu did Kubla Khan
A stately pleasure-dome decree:
Where Alph, the sacred river, ran
Through caverns measureless to man
    Down to a sunless sea.
So twice five miles of fertile ground
With walls and towers were girdled round:
And there were gardens bright with sinuous rills,
Where blossomed many an incense-bearing tree;
And here were forests ancient as the hills,
Enfolding sunny spots of greenery.

But oh! that deep romantic chasm which slanted
Down the green hill athwart a cedarn cover!
A savage place! as holy and enchanted
As e'er beneath a waning moon was haunted
By woman wailing for her demon-lover!
And from this chasm, with ceaseless turmoil seething,
As if this earth in fast thick pants were breathing,
A mighty fountain momently was forced:
Amid whose swift half-intermitted burst
Huge fragments vaulted like rebounding hail,
Or chaffy grain beneath the thresher's flail:
And 'mid these dancing rocks at once and ever
It flung up momently the sacred river.
Five miles meandering with a mazy motion
Through wood and dale the sacred river ran,
Then reached the caverns measureless to man,
And sank in tumult to a lifeless ocean:
And 'mid this tumult Kubla heard from far
Ancestral voices prophesying war!
　　　The shadow of the dome of pleasure
　　　Floated midway on the waves;
　　　Where was heard the mingled measure
　　　From the fountain and the caves.
It was a miracle of rare device,
A sunny pleasure-dome with caves of ice!

A damsel with a dulcimer
In a vision once I saw:
It was an Abyssinian maid
And on her dulcimer she played,
Singing of Mount Abora.
Could I revive within me
Her symphony and song,
To such a deep delight 'twould win me,
　　That with music loud and long,
I would build that dome in air,
That sunny dome! those caves of ice!
And all who heard should see them there,
And all should cry, Beware! Beware!
His flashing eyes, his floating hair!
Weave a circle round him thrice,
And close your eyes with holy dread,
For he on honey-dew hath fed,
And drunk the milk of Paradise.

Lastly, two stanzas from *Dejection, an Ode*, written in 1802. The poet sits despondent, suffering from

> A grief without a pang, void, dark, and drear,
>   A stifled, drowsy, unimpassioned grief
> Which finds no natural outlet, no relief,
>   In word, or sigh, or tear—
> O Lady! in this wan and heartless mood,
> To other thoughts by yonder throstle woo'd,
>   All this long eve, so balmy and serene,
> Have I been gazing on the western sky,
>   And its peculiar tint of yellow green:
> And still I gaze—and with how blank an eye!
> And those thin clouds above, in flakes and bars,
> That give away their motion to the stars;
> Those stars, that glide behind them or between,
> Now sparkling, now bedimmed, but always seen:
> Yon crescent Moon, as fixed as if it grew
> In its own cloudless, starless lake of blue;
> I see them all so excellently fair,
> I see, not feel, how beautiful they are!

In the next stanza he denies the Wordsworthian belief in the 'powers
that of themselves our minds impress'. Note the implied distinction
between the poet, the man of sensibility, and 'the poor loveless ever-
anxious crowd'.

> O lady! we receive but what we give,
> And in our life alone does Nature live:
> Ours is her wedding garment, ours her shroud!
>   And would we aught behold, of higher worth,
> Than that inanimate cold world allowed
> To the poor loveless ever-anxious crowd
>   Ah! from the soul itself must issue forth
> A light, a glory, a fair luminous cloud
>   Enveloping the Earth—
> And from the soul itself must there be sent
>   A sweet and potent voice, of its own birth,
> Of all sweet sounds the life and element!

Coleridge is an exasperating writer, but he has so fine a mind that
everywhere in his work there are moments of insight, intelligence,
observation, sensibility, which make us feel it was worth while
tramping through the barren passages. For example, *France, an Ode*,
which is about the poet's feelings for the Revolution and the notion of
liberty contains a lot of rhetoric of this sort:

> I hear thy voice, I hear thy loud lament,
> From bleak Helvetia's icy caverns sent—
> I hear thy groans upon her blood-stained streams!

but it also contains this remark, a kind of final comment on one aspect of all revolutions:

> The Sensual and the Dark rebel in vain,
> Slaves by their own compulsion!

The most popular poet of the first few years of the nineteenth century was Scott (1771–1832) whose tales in verse appeared between 1805 and 1817. He acknowledged a debt to *Christabel* which he had heard read in 1800, but his narratives show no touch of Coleridge's genius.

We quote two poems, *Rosabelle* and *Proud Maisie*. The first is an accomplished piece of Gothic, but though the form and matter of the ballad are here, the spirit is missing. To apply Coleridge's definition the 'fixities and definites' with which in this poem, 'Fancy' is 'playing' are the standard stage properties of Romance; Scott has made a 'choice' among them, and arranged them in a pattern which is pretty enough, but scarcely convincing.

> O listen, listen, ladies gay!
> No haughty feat of arms I tell;
> Soft is the note, and sad the lay
> That mourns the lovely Rosabelle.
>
> 'Moor, moor the barge, ye gallant crew!
> And, gentle ladye, deign to stay!
> Rest thee in Castle Ravensheuch,
> Nor tempt the stormy firth to-day.
>
> 'The blackening wave is edged with white;
> To inch and rock the sea-mews fly;
> The fishers have heard the Water-Sprite,
> Whose screams forbode that wreck is nigh.
>
> 'Last night the gifted Seer did view
> A wet shroud swathed round ladye gay;
> Then stay thee, Fair, in Ravensheuch;
> Why cross the gloomy firth to-day?'
>
> ''Tis not because Lord Lindsay's heir
> To-night at Roslin leads the ball,
> But that my lady-mother there
> Sits lonely in her castle-hall.

"Tis not because the ring they ride,
And Lindsay at the ring rides well,
But that my sire the wine will chide
If 'tis not filled by Rosabelle.'

O'er Roslin all that dreary night
A wondrous blaze was seen to gleam;
'Twas broader than the watch-fire light,
And redder than the bright moonbeam.

It glared on Roslin's castled rock,
It ruddied all the copse-wood glen;
'Twas seen from Dryden's groves of oak,
And seen from cavern'd Hawthornden.

Seem'd all on fire that chapel proud,
Where Roslin's chiefs uncoffined lie,
Each Baron, for a sable shroud
Sheath'd in his iron panoply.

Seem'd all on fire within, around,
Deep sacristy and altar's pale;
Shone every pillar foliage-bound,
And glimmer'd all the dead men's mail.

Blazed battlement and pinnet high,
Blazed every rose-carved buttress fair
So still they blaze when fate is nigh
The Lordly line of high St.Clair.

There are twenty of Roslin's barons bold
Lie buried within that proud chapelle;
Each one the holy vault doth hold
But the sea holds lovely Rosabelle.

And each St.Clair was buried there
With candle, with book, and with knell;
But the sea-caves rung, and the wild winds sung
The dirge of lovely Rosabelle.

But in *Proud Maisie*, a poem worthy to stand beside the best of the traditional poetry Scott loved so well and collected so carefully, the elements (to quote Coleridge again) have been 'recreated' and the poem is 'vital'.

Proud Maisie is in the wood,
Walking so early;
Sweet Robin sits on the bush
Singing so rarely.

'Tell me, thou bonny bird,
When shall I marry me?'
'When six braw gentlemen
Kirkward shall carry ye.'

'Who makes the bridal bed,
Birdie, say truly?'
'The grey-headed sexton
That delves the grave duly.'

'The glow-worm o'er grave and stone
Shall light thee steady;
The owl from the steeple sing
Welcome, proud lady.'

In 1812 Byron (1788–1834) published the first two cantos of *Childe Harold's Pilgrimage* and during the next four years six tales in verse with such exotic titles as *The Giaour* and *The Bride of Abydos*. The new poet became instantly famous, and Scott turned to writing novels, publishing *Waverley* in 1814. Byron, not without some relish, enacted, in his early life the part of the romantic, outcast, rebel poet, and became a symbolic figure throughout Europe. He despised the Lake poets, as Wordsworth, Southey and Coleridge had come to be called; they could do, he said, with 'a course in the passions, beginning with a little simple adultery and compounding it as they went along', and he thought them political turncoats. He affected an attitude of aristocratic disdain towards his own writings, and would have us regard them as the idle scribblings of a milord with nothing better to do. In 1818 he finished *Childe Harold* and the following year began *Don Juan*, the rambling colloquial satire he was never to complete. His other important satire, *A Vision of Judgement* was written in 1822. Of his voluminous works, which include several blank verse dramas, we select two samples. The first is a piece of romantic rhetoric from the fourth canto of *Childe Harold*. The Childe is contemplating the ruins of Rome.

CVI

Then let the winds howl on! their harmony
Shall henceforth be my music, and the night
The sound shall temper with the owlets' cry,

As I now hear them, in the fading light
Dim o'er the bird of darkness' native site,
Answering each other on the Palatine,
With their large eyes, all glistening gray and bright,
And sailing pinions.—Upon such a shrine
What are our petty griefs?—let me not number mine.

CVII

Cypress and ivy, weed and wallflower grown
Matted and massed together, hillocks heap'd
On what were chambers, arch crush'd, columns strown
In fragments, choked up vaults, and frescos steep'd
In subterranean damps, where the owl peep'd
Deeming it midnight:—Temples, baths, or halls?
Pronounce who can; for all that Learning reap'd
From her research hath been, that these are walls—
Behold the Imperial Mount! 'tis thus the mighty falls.

CXX

Alas! our young affections run to waste,
Or water but the desert; whence arise
But weeds of dark luxuriance, tares of haste,
Rank at the core, though tempting to the eyes,
Flowers whose wild odours breathe but agonies,
And trees whose gums are poisons; such the plants
Which spring beneath her steps as Passion flies
O'er the world's wilderness and vainly pants
For some celestial fruit forbidden to our wants.

CXXII

Of its own beauty is the mind diseased,
And fevers into false creations:—where,
Where are the forms the sculptor's soul hath seized?
In him alone. Can nature show so fair?
Where are the charms and virtues which we dare
Conceive in boyhood and pursue as men,
The unreached Paradise of our despair,
Which o'er-informs the pencil and the pen,
And overpowers the page where it would bloom again?

CXXIV

We wither from our youth, we gasp away—
Sick—sick; unfound the boon, unslaked the thirst,
Though to the last, in verge of our decay,

Some phantom lures, such as we sought at first—
But all too late,—so are we doubly curst.
Love, fame, ambition, avarice—'tis the same,
Each idle, and all ill, and none the worst—
For all are meteors with a different name,
And Death the sable smoke where vanishes the flame.

CXXVI

Our life is a false nature: 'tis not in
The harmony of things,—this hard decree,
This ineradicable taint of sin,
This boundless upas, this all-blasting tree,
Whose root is earth, whose leaves and branches be
The skies which rain their plagues on men like dew—
Disease, death, bondage—all the woes we see,
And worse, the woes we see not—which throb through
The immedicable soul, with heart-aches ever new.

Byron's posturings are perhaps not very interesting today, but the
verse has energy and feeling; he has adapted the Spenserian stanza
to his own voice. The reader will note that I have not quoted consecutive stanzas, and if he looks up the original will find, I think, that
this does not much harm the poem, and to say this is to make a
damaging comment on its quality. Nevertheless, the last two cantos
of *Childe Harold* are worth reading, and we must remember that Byron
tried to do something about the woes he saw. The voyage to Misso-
longhi was not an empty gesture or a pose.

The romantic mode, though it offered a means of dramatizing his
personal problems, would not contain his wit, his intelligence, his
intense political convictions. Neo-classic satire, which he admired so
much, could not be recreated, as his attempts at this form show. He
invented, and this is where his genius lies, a kind of burlesque verse
whose manner and rhythms and tone, unromantic, and deliberately
unliterary, enabled him to speak freely, in a mature voice purged of
self-pity. Here is his own account of the matter, from Canto IV,
stanzas 3 and 4 and Canto XV, stanza 19.

As boy, I thought myself a clever fellow,
    And wished that others held the same opinion;
They took it up when my days grew more mellow,
    And other minds acknowledge my dominion:
Now my sere fancy 'falls into the yellow
    Leaf', and Imagination droops her pinion,
And the sad truth which hovers o'er my desk
Turns what was once romantic to burlesque.

And if I laugh at any mortal thing,
　　'Tis that I may not weep; and if I weep,
'Tis that our nature cannot always bring
　　Itself to apathy, for we must steep
Our hearts first in the depths of Lethe's spring,
　　Ere what we least wish to behold will sleep:
Thetis baptized her mortal son in Styx;
A modern mother would on Lethe fix.

I perch upon an humbler promontory,
　　Amidst life's infinite variety:
With no great care for what is nicknamed glory,
　　But speculating as I cast my eye
On what may suit or may not suit my story,
　　And never straining hard to versify,
I rattle on exactly as I'd talk
With anybody in a ride or walk.

In the following stanzas his hero arrives within sight of London and the reader may compare them with Wordsworth's famous sonnet on *Westminster Bridge*.

　　　　　. . . Juan now was borne
Just as the day began to wane and darken,
　　O'er the high hill, which looks with pride or scorn
Towards the great city.—Ye who have a spark in
　　Your veins of Cockney spirit, smile or mourn
According as you take things well or ill:
Bold Britons, we are now on Shooter's Hill!

The sun went down, the smoke rose up, as from
　　A half-unquenched volcano, o'er a space
Which well beseem'd the 'Devil's drawing-room'
　　As some have qualified that wondrous place:
But Juan felt, though not approaching *home*,
　　As one who, though he were not of the race,
Rever'd the soil, of those true sons the mother,
Who butcher'd half the earth, and bullied t'other.

Lastly, here is a longer passage from the third canto. Juan has been shipwrecked, rescued, and revived by the fair Haidée, daughter of a pirate, who

　　　　　was the mildest manner'd man
　　That ever scuttled ship or cut a throat,
With such true breeding of a gentleman,
　　You never could divine his real thought;
No courtier could, and scarcely woman can

> Gird more deceit within a petticoat;
> Pity he loved adventurous life's variety,
> He was so great a loss to good society. . . .

Haidée thinks he is dead; the period of mourning is over, and the household is feasting:

> they were diverted by their suite
> Dwarfs, dancing-girls, black eunuchs, and a poet,
> Which made their new establishment complete. . . .

We quote the passage in which the poet sings about his native Greece. It shows the range of feeling, the adroitness and wit that Byron deployed in this poem. The poet stands for writers like Southey, whom Byron believed to have reneged on the principles of their youth, and to have settled for a comfortable life supporting established power; he also has some of the characteristics of Childe Harold—Byron is mocking his own youthful attitudinizing; and he is partly a true romantic poet since inspiration sometimes seizes him, in spite of himself:

> But he had genius,—when a turncoat has it.
> The 'Vates irritabilis' takes care
> That without notice few full moons shall pass it. . . .

The 'full moons' are no doubt a reminiscence of Shakespeare's famous collocation of 'the lunatic, the lover and the poet'. The song he sings is noble and resounding, informed with Byron's love of Greece and hatred of tyranny, and dramatically fitted to the poet's situation and the progress of the narrative. After its theatrical climax (the poet is a skilled performer, and so is Byron) we drop back again into the tone of mockery. It is this management of tone that gives the poem its complexity, and enables Byron to say or imply several things at once, and achieve something of the richness of the best Augustan satire.

> Their poet, a sad trimmer, but no less
>   In company a very pleasant fellow,
> Had been the favourite of full many a mess
>   Of men, and made them speeches when half mellow;
> And though his meaning they could rarely guess,
>   Yet still they deign'd to hiccup or to bellow
> The glorious meed of popular applause,
> Of which the first ne'er knows the second cause.
>
> But now being lifted into high society,
>   And having pick'd up several odds and ends
> Of free thoughts in his travels, for variety,
>   He deem'd being in a lone isle, among friends,

That without any danger of a riot, he
  Might for long lying make himself amends;
And singing as he sung in his warm youth,
Agree to a short armistice with truth.

He had travell'd amongst the Arabs, Turks, and Franks,
  And knew the self-loves of the different nations;
And having lived with people of all ranks,
  Had something ready upon most occasions—
Which got him a few presents and some thanks.
  He varied with some skill his adulations;
To 'do at Rome as Romans do' a piece
Of conduct was which he observed in Greece.

Thus usually, when he was asked to sing,
  He gave the different nations something national;
'Twas all the same to him—'God save the king',
  Or 'Ça ira', according to the fashion all:
His muse made increment of anything,
  From the high lyric down to the low rational:
If Pindar sang horse-races, what should hinder
Himself from being as pliable as Pindar?

In France for instance, he would write a chanson;
  In England a six-canto quarto tale;
In Spain he'd make a ballad or romance on
  The last war—much the same in Portugal;
In Germany, the Pegasus he'd prance on
  Would be old Goethe's—(see what says De Staël);
In Italy he'd ape the 'Trecentisti',
In Greece, he'd sing some sort of hymn like this t'ye:

I

The isles of Greece, the isles of Greece!
  Where burning Sappho loved and sung,
Where grew the arts of war and peace,
  Where Delos rose, and Phoebus sprung!
Eternal summer gilds them yet,
But all, except their sun, is set.

2

The Scian and the Teian muse,
  The hero's harp, the lover's lute,
Have found the fame your shores refuse:

Their place of birth alone is mute
To sounds which echo further west
Than your sires 'Islands of the Blest'.

3

The mountains look on Marathon—
   And Marathon looks on the sea;
And musing there an hour alone,
   I dreamed that Greece might still be free;
For standing on the Persian's grave,
I could not deem myself a slave.

4

A King sate on the rocky brow
   Which looks o'er sea-born Salamis;
And ships, by thousands, lay below,
   And men in nations;—all were his!
He counted them at break of day—
And when the sun set where were they?

5

And where are they? and where art thou,
   My country? On thy voiceless shore
The heroic lay is tuneless now—
   The heroic bosom beats no more!
And must thy lyre, so long divine,
Degenerate into hands like mine?

6

'Tis something, in the dearth of fame,
   Though link'd among a fettered race,
To feel at least a patriot's shame,
   Even as I sing, suffuse my face;
For what is left the poet here?
For Greeks a blush—for Greece a tear.

7

Must *we* but weep o'er days more blest?
   Must *we* but blush?—Our Fathers bled.
Earth! render back from out thy breast
   A remnant of our Spartan dead!
Of the three hundred grant but three,
To make a new Thermopylae!

8

What, silent still? and silent all?
   Ah! no;—the voices of the dead
Sound like a distant torrent's fall,
   And answer, 'Let one living head,
But one arise,—we come, we come!'
'Tis but the living who are dumb.

9

In vain—in vain: strike other chords;
   Fill high the cup with Samian wine!
Leave battles to the Turkish hordes,
   And shed the blood of Scio's vine!
Hark! rising to the ignoble call—
How answers each bold Bacchanal!

10

You have the Pyrrhic dance as yet;
   Where is the Pyrrhic phalanx gone?
Of two such lessons, why forget
   The nobler and the manlier one?
You have the letters Cadmus gave
Think ye he meant them for a slave?

11

Fill high the bowl with Samian wine!
   We will not think of themes like these!
It made Anacreon's song divine:
   He served—but served Polycrates—
A tyrant; but our masters then
Were still, at least, our countrymen.

12

The tyrant of the Chersonese
   Was freedom's best and bravest friend;
That tyrant was Miltiades!
   Oh! that the present hour would lend
Another despot of the kind!
Such chains as his were sure to bind.

13

Fill high the bowl with Samian wine!
   On Suli's rock, and Parga's shore,

Exists the remnant of a line
  Such as the Doric mothers bore;
And there, perhaps, some seed is sown,
The Heracleidan blood might own.

14

Trust not for freedom to the Franks—
  They have a king who buys and sells;
In native swords, and native ranks,
  The only hope of courage dwells:
But Turkish force, and Latin fraud
Would break your shield, however broad.

15

Fill high the bowl with Samian wine!
  Our virgins dance beneath the shade—
I see their glorious black eyes shine;
  But gazing on each glowing maid
My own the burning tear drop laves,
To think such breasts must suckle slaves.

16

Place me on Sunium's marbled steep,
  Where nothing, save the waves and I,
May hear our mutual murmurs sweep;
  There, swan-like, let me sing and die:
A land of slaves shall ne'er be mine!
Dash down yon cup of Samian wine!

Thus sung, or would, or could, or should have sung,
  The modern Greek, in tolerable verse;
If not like Orpheus quite, when Greece was young,
  Yet in these times he might have done much worse:
His strain display'd some feeling—right or wrong;
  And feeling, in a poet, is the source
Of other's feeling; but they are such liars,
And take all colours—like the hands of dyers.

But words are things, and a small drop of ink,
  Falling like dew, upon a thought, produces
That which makes thousands, perhaps millions, think;
  'Tis strange, the shortest letter which man uses
Instead of speech, may form a lasting link
  Of ages; to what straits old Time reduces
Frail man, when paper—even a rag like this,
Survives himself, his tomb, and all that's his!

And when his bones are dust, his grave a blank,
  His station, generation, even his nation,
Become a thing, or nothing, save to rank,
  In chronological commemoration.
Some dull MS. oblivion long has sank,
  Or graven stone found in a barrack's station
In digging the foundations of a closet,
May turn his name up, as a rare deposit. . . .

That part of the verse of Shelley (1792–1822) which retains most vitality is concerned with his private feelings. Typical are these lines from *Stanzas Written in Dejection Near Naples.*

I see the Deep's untrampled floor
  With green and purple seaweeds strown;
I see the waves upon the shore,
  Like light dissolved in star-showers thrown:
  I sit upon the sands alone;
The lightning of the noontide ocean
  Is flashing round me, and a tone
Arises from its measured motion—
How sweet! did any heart now share in my emotion.

Shelley is fascinated by the world under the sea, but his ocean is not Marvell's metaphysical one, where 'each kind/Can straight its own resemblance find'; it is untrampled, mysterious and solitary. By this time nature's beauties untainted by man's misery are a commonplace in verse. The brilliant evanescence of the light dissolved in star showers is characteristic Shelley—he loved all effects of light and air and cloud; equally characteristic is the vagueness of the word 'tone', which carries little meaning and appears merely to be brought in for the rhyme. Typical also the pity for his solitude, the complaint that none can share his feelings. Here indeed is the 'heart that lives along/Housed in a dream, at distance from the Kind!' Wordsworth bade that heart farewell: Shelley indulged it.

Next is another poem which can stand as a typical expression of the feeling of isolation, of solitude, of the impossibility of communication which affected so many romantic artists. Its title, too, is significant: *A Dream of the Unknown*:

I dream'd that as I wander'd by the way
  Bare Winter suddenly was changed to Spring,
And gentle odours led my steps astray,
  Mix'd with the sound of waters murmuring

Along a shelving bank of turf, which lay
   Under a copse, and hardly dared to fling
Its green arms round the bosom of the stream,
But kiss'd it and then fled, as thou might'st in a dream.

There grew pied wind-flowers and violets,
   Daisies, those pearl'd Arcturi of the earth,
The constellated flower that never sets;
   Faint oxlips; tender blue-bells, at whose birth
The sod scarce heaved; and that tall flower that wets—
   Like a child, half in tenderness and mirth—
Its mother's face with heaven's collected tears,
When the low wind, its playmate's voice, it hears.

And in the warm hedge grew lush eglantine,
   Green cow-bind and the moonlight-coloured may,
And cherry blossoms, and white cups, whose wine
   Was the bright dew yet drain'd not by the day;
And wild roses, and ivy serpentine
   With its dark buds and leaves, wandering astray;
And flowers azure, black, and streak'd with gold,
Fairer than any waken'd eyes behold.

And nearer to the river's trembling edge
   There grew broad flag-flowers, purple prank with white,
And starry river buds among the sedge,
   And floating water-lilies, broad and bright,
Which lit the oak that overhung the hedge
   With moonlight beams of their own watery light;
And bulrushes, and reeds of such deep green
As soothed the dazzled eye with sober sheen.

Methought that of these visionary flowers
   I made a nosegay, bound in such a way
That the same hues, which in their natural bowers
   Were mingled or opposed, the like array
Kept these imprison'd children of the Hours
   Within my hand,—and then, elate and gay,
I hasten'd to the spot whence I had come,
That I might there present it—O! to Whom?

    The erotic imagery of the opening lines, about the bank of turf and
the stream's bosom, and the mysterious thou, is very characteristic of
Shelley. The reader must not think what real banks and streams are
like, or he will, to adapt a line from the poet, say this imagery is so

vague the sense gets muddled picturing it; the only thing to do is to submit to the dream-flux. The beautiful flower passage owes much to Spenser, Shakespeare and Milton, but the sinuous flowing movement of the verse is Shelley's own. So, too, is the awkward parenthesis 'wets—like a child . . . its mother's face'. The last stanza continues the dream action, and there is a return to the speed and energy of the opening lines; we realize that the poem is an allegory. The world of imagination is more beautiful than the world of reality (the flowers in the dream are 'fairer than any waken'd eyes behold'); the poet can make a nosegay of the flowers, a pattern, a poem, a work of art, exhibiting the order and beauty of his vision ('the same hues' . . . 'the like array'), but when he has done so no one wants it. The last lines, with their extraordinary feeling of lightness and eagerness in 'elate and gay/I hastened' declining to the dull rhyme 'come . . . Whom', the shock of finding nobody there, the way the dream turns to nightmare, seem to me extremely moving. Shelley has dramatized and generalized his plight and achieved a poignancy and power he rarely commands. Next, the well-known *Ode on the West Wind*.

1

O, wild West Wind, thou breath of Autumn's being,
　　Thou, from whose unseen presence the leaves dead
Are driven, like ghosts from an enchanter fleeing.

Yellow and black, and pale, and hectic red,
　　Pestilence-stricken multitudes: O, thou
Who chariotest to their dark wintry bed

The wingèd seeds, where they lie cold and low,
　　Each like a corpse within its grave, until
Thine azure sister of the spring shall blow

Her clarion o'er the dreaming earth, and fill
　　(Driving sweet buds like flocks to feed in air)
With living hues and odours plain and hill:

Wild Spirit, which art moving everywhere;
Destroyer and preserver; hear, oh, hear!

2

Thou on whose stream, 'mid the steep sky's commotion,
　　Loose clouds like earth's decaying leaves are shed,
Shook from the tangled boughs of Heaven and Ocean,

Angels of rain and lightning: there are spread
  On the blue surface of thine aery surge,
Like the bright hair uplifted from the head

Of some fierce Maenad, even from the dim verge
  Of the horizon to the zenith's height,
The locks of the approaching storm. Thou dirge

Of the dying year, to which this closing night
  Will be the dome of a vast sepulchre,
Vaulted with all thy congregated might

Of vapours, from whose solid atmosphere
Black rain, and fire, and hail, will burst: oh, hear!

3

Thou who didst waken from his summer dreams
  The blue Mediterranean, where he lay
Lull'd by the coil of his crystalline streams,

Beside a pumice isle in Baiae's bay,
  And saw in sleep old palaces and towers
Quivering within the wave's intenser day,

All overgrown with azure moss and flowers,
  So sweet, the sense faints picturing them! Thou
For whose path the Atlantic's level powers

Cleave themselves into chasms, while far below
  The sea-blooms and the oozy woods which wear
The sapless foliage of the ocean, know

Thy voice, and suddenly grow grey with fear,
And tremble and despoil themselves: oh hear!

4

If I were a dead leaf thou mightest bear;
  If I were a swift cloud to fly with thee;
A wave to pant beneath thy power, and share

The impulse of thy strength, only less free
  Than thou, O uncontrollable! if even
I were as in my boyhood, and could be

The comrade of thy wanderings over Heaven,
  As then, when to outstrip thy skyey speed
Scarce seemed a vision, I would ne'er have striven

As thus with thee in prayer in my sore need.
  Oh, lift me as a wave, a leaf, a cloud;
I fall upon the thorns of life! I bleed!

A heavy weight of hours has chained and bowed
One too like thee: tameless, and swift, and proud.

5

Make me thy lyre, even as the forest is:
  What if my leaves are falling like its own!
The tumult of thy might harmonies

Will take from both a deep, autumnal tone,
  Sweet though in sadness. Be thou, Spirit fierce
My spirit! Be thou me, impetuous one!

Drive my dead thoughts over the universe,
  Like withered leaves to quicken a new birth!
And, by the incantation of this verse,

Scatter, as from an unextinguished hearth
  Ashes and sparks, my words among mankind!
Be through my lips to unawakened earth

The trumpet of a prophecy! O Wind
If Winter comes, can Spring be far behind?

'The incantation of this verse'—the phrase is the best description of the poem. The three stanzas of invocation seem to drive resistlessly on with the movement of the 'rushing mighty wind' they call upon, and the way to read the poem is to submit to this movement, for the poem's rhythm is in itself an image of the poem's meaning. Indeed when you read Shelley it is best not to stop and think, but let the verse carry you away. Otherwise you stumble over such ugly lines (few of Shelley's poems are without them) as

Beside a pumice isle in Baiae's bay

and are, perhaps, put off by the characteristically Shelleyan ecstasy of

So sweet, the sense faints picturing them

In *The Defence of Poetry* when he is speaking of 'the bucolic writers, who found patronage under the lettered tyrants of Sicily and Egypt', he says, 'Their poetry is intensely melodious; like the tuberose it overcomes and sickens the spirit with excess of sweetness'. This remark applies to many passages of his own work; but a fairer comment, from the same source, might be: 'the language of poets has ever affected a certain uniform harmonious recurrence of sound, without which it were not poetry, and which is scarcely less indispensable to the communication of its influence than the words themselves. . . .'

We are made to feel the irresistible speed of the wind by the way the sense units overrun the lines, and fight, as it were, against the strictly-rhymed sonnet form of each stanza:

>   . . . the leaves dead
> Are driven . . .
> Thine azure sister of the Spring shall blow
> Her Clarion . . .

and especially the sentence: 'there are spread . . . the locks of the approaching storm'.

The image about the clouds, leaves and boughs means that the clouds are water vapour, drawn up to Heaven from Ocean, and also that in a great storm 'the sea, mounting to the welkin's cheek' seems to mingle with the sky. It parallels the picture of the dead leaves at the beginning of the first stanza, but it is difficult to see how Heaven and the Ocean make a forest. Shelley speaks somewhere of Lucretius liming 'the swift wings of his spirit with the dregs of the sensible world'; and to him this is a cause for regret; yet however, 'ethereal', 'aerial' the swift spirit's 'evanescent visitations of thoughts and feelings' may be, they must be expressed in images from 'this sensible world', and their expression will not be clear or forceful if the images are muddled. Writing of this sort makes us apply to Shelley himself the words of Asia to Panthea in *Prometheus Unbound*:

> Thou speakest, but thy words
> Are as the air; I feel them not . . . .

The locks of the approaching storm and the dome vaulted with vapours are far more effective than the tangled boughs.

After the invocation comes, in stanzas four and five, the prayer. If the poet were part of nature, if he were a child, still, in imagination, at one with natural forces, this prayer would not be needed. Shelley wrote of the dead Keats 'he is made one with nature', and here he prays to be made part of the mighty strength thundering around him. He invites our pity and our admiration; we may feel such tribute unnecessary, an act of supererogation, since the poet is paying it already, and so fervently, to himself.

The last stanza is much stronger. Here the poet sees himself as
prophet, as 'unacknowledged legislator' of future change and revolution. We may note, but if we are to read the poem sympathetically we
must not worry about, the fact that in stanza one the leaves are pestilence
stricken, and it is the winged seeds that hold the promise of the future;
that it is difficult to see how his thoughts can be 'dead', if they are to
bring life, though we may agree that seeds may well grow better in
leaf mould. Next, the poet is an 'unextinguished hearth'—or, perhaps
it is not the poet, but the poetic imagination in general, that is meant,
for we are reminded of this famous passage from the *Defence*: 'the
mind in creation is as a fading coal, which some invisible influence,
like an inconstant wind, awakens to transitory brightness'; The
thoughts, clothed in words, are now ashes and sparks. We can see the
point of the sparks, they may ignite great conflagrations; minute, they
hold the sacred fire: but what is the point of the ashes? Does this mean
that some of the words are alive, and others dead? Or are we to take
it that the ashes are there because this is a picture of the 'sensible world'
—a real wind would blow ashes as well as sparks—and the poet has not
integrated the details of his image with his meaning, has not made a
sufficiently 'careful observation of the inspired moment'? It might be
worth the reader's while to compare this passage with an ashes and
fire image organized by a poet for whom the 'sensible world' was not
'dregs':

> In me thou seest the glowing of such fire,
> That on the ashes of his youth doth lie,
> As the death-bed whereon it must expire,
> Consum'd with that which it was nourished by.

Shelley's poem ends in hope and aspiration, noble and vague.

We know that Shelley was a revolutionary—at least that he ardently
desired and earnestly recommended social change; that he attacked the
monarchy and the church; that he wished to resolve, to harmonize,
what, in a fine phrase, he termed 'the dissonance of arms and superstition', and that he believed 'the inventive and creative faculty' would
further the changes he hoped for. All this is admirably put in the
quotation from the *Defence* at the beginning of this chapter, but it
doesn't get into the best of his verse. There is a sense of wholeness in
Donne, in Dryden, in Pope and Johnson which is absent in Shelley.
The point can be briefly made if we consider this sonnet *England in
1819*, and compare it with Wordsworth's on Napoleon:

> An old, mad, blind, despised, and dying king,—
> Princes, the dregs of their dull race, who flow

Through public scorn,—mud from a muddy spring,—
Rulers, who neither see, nor feel, nor know,
But leech-like to their fainting country cling,
Till they drop, blind in blood, without a blow,—
A people starved and stabbed in the untilled field,
An army, which liberticide and prey
Makes as a two-edged sword to all who wield,—
Golden and sanguine laws which tempt and slay;
Religion Christless, Godless—a book sealed;
A Senate,—Time's worst statute unrepealed,—
Are graves, from which a glorious Phantom may
Burst, to illumine our tempestuous day.

The attack is searing, violent and solidly expressed, though if we compare it with the lines from Johnson's *Vanity of Human Wishes* we may think it somewhat shrill and hysterical. But the poem ends in bathos: we can't believe in the phantom, even with a capital P, and nothing could be feebler than 'may/Burst...' We might apply to this part of Shelley's work—it includes such poems as *The Masque of Anarchy* and *Song to the Men of England*—his own words, applied to those poets who 'have frequently affected a moral aim,' that 'the effect of their poetry is diminished in exact proportion to the degree to which they compel us to advert to this purpose.' He further says 'a poet ... would do ill to embody his own conception of right and wrong, which are usually those of his place and time, in his poetical creations, which participate in neither'.

Yet the Wordsworth sonnet 'participates' in its author's 'place, and time', and embodies its author's conceptions of right and wrong, and we can scarcely think that Wordsworth 'did ill' to write it. To claim that 'poetical creations' must not participate in the author's place and time is to claim that most verse since Milton is not poetry, and this indeed is what most nineteenth-century readers believed. Wordsworth, as we have noted, inherited the discursive tradition of the Augustan age, and *The Prelude* is an all-embracing poem. Now the novel becomes all-embracing, and poetry more and more limited. No Victorian poems have the scope or importance of *Bleak House*, *Little Dorrit*, or *Middlemarch*.

Here are two passages from Shelley's verse drama *Prometheus Unbound*. In the preface to this work he says: 'it is a mistake to suppose that I dedicate my poetical compositions solely to the direct enforcement of reform ... Didactic poetry is my abhorrence'. He continues: 'My purpose has ... been simply to familiarize the highly refined imagination of the more select classes of poetical readers with beautiful

idealisms of moral excellence'. Note 'highly refined' and 'select':
Shelley knows he is addressing a minority within a minority. Prometheus in the play is one of these 'beautiful idealisms' who symbolizes
humanity's desire for justice and freedom. Zeus, his tormentor, stands
for tyranny, so that Shelley is 'idealizing' his 'passion for reforming
the world', but the poem is not didactic.

The two passages quoted are from speeches by Prometheus; the
first is the opening of the play, the second comes from his address to
Asia and Ione after he has been freed by Hercules.

> Monarch of Gods and Daemons, and all Spirits
> But One, who throng these bright and rolling worlds
> Which Thou and I alone of living things
> Behold with sleepless eyes! regard this Earth
> Made multitudinous with thy slaves, whom thou
> Requitest for knee-worship, prayer, and praise,
> And toil, and hecatombs of broken hearts,
> With fear and self-contempt and barren hope.
> Whilst me, who am thy foe, eyeless in hate,
> Hast thou made reign and triumph, to thy scorn,
> O'er mine own misery and thy vain revenge.
> Three thousand years of sleep-unsheltered hours,
> And moments aye divided by keen pangs,
> Till they seemed years, torture and solitude,
> Scorn and despair,—these are mine empire.
> More glorious far than that which thou surveyest
> From thine unenvied throne, O, Mighty God!
> Almighty, had I deigned to share the shame
> Of thine ill tyranny, and hung not here
> Nailed to this wall of eagle-baffling mountain,
> Black, wintry, dead, unmeasured; without herb,
> Insect, or beast, or shape or sound of life.
> Ah me! alas, pain, pain ever, for ever. . . .
>
> And yet to me welcome is day and night,
> Whether one breaks the hoar frost of the morn,
> Or starry, dim, and slow, the other climbs
> The leaden-coloured east; for then they lead
> The wingless, crawling hours, one among whom
> As some dark Priest hales the reluctant victim—
> Shall drag thee, cruel King, to kiss the blood
> From these pale feet, which then might trample thee
> If they disdained not such a prostrate slave.
> Disdain! Ah no! I pity thee. . . .

> Asia thou light of life,
> Shadow of beauty unbeheld: and ye,
> Fair sister nymphs, who made long years of pain
> Sweet to remember, thro' your love and care:
> Henceforth we will not part. There is a cave,
> All overgrown with trailing odorous plants,
> Which curtain out the day with leaves and flowers,
> And paved with veinèd emerald, and a fountain
> Leaps in the midst with an awakening sound.
> From its curved roof the mountain's frozen tears
> Like snow, or silver, or long diamond spires,
> Hang downward, raining forth a doubtful light:
> And there is heard the ever-moving air,
> Whispering without from tree to tree, and birds,
> And bees; and all around are mossy seats,
> And the rough walls are clothed with long soft grass;
> A simple dwelling, which shall be our own;
> Where we will sit and talk of time and change,
> As the world ebbs and flows, ourselves unchanged.
> What can hide man from mutability?
> And if ye sigh, then I will smile; and thou
> Ione, shalt chaunt fragments of sea-music,
> Until I weep, when ye shall smile away
> The tears she brought, which yet were sweet to shed.
> We will entangle buds and flowers and beams
> Which twinkle on the fountain's brim, and make
> Strange combinations out of common things,
> Like human babes in their brief innocence;
> And we will search, with looks and words of love,
> For hidden thoughts, each lovelier than the last,
> Our unexhausted spirits; and like lutes
> Touched by the skill of the enamoured wind,
> Weave harmonies divine, yet ever new
> From difference sweet where discord cannot be. . . .

The first passage—obviously indebted to the description of Satan, whom Shelley believed to be the hero of *Paradise Lost*,—has neither the sonority of Milton nor the vitality of Shakespeare. We agree about the state of humanity, and approve the nobility of Prometheus, without feeling ourselves deeply involved. The language is either self-consciously literary (eagle-baffling mountain) or purveys a kind of thin hysteria—

> Ah me! alas, pain, pain ever, for ever. . . .

Shelley, we feel, is attempting something he is ill-equipped to do. In the second passage, however, as soon as the necessary 'dramatic'

bit of dialogue is over (note in passing that Asia is both a light and a
shadow, a characteristically Shelleyan muddle of imagery) he launches,
with the words 'There is a cave . . .' into a description of an ecstatic
dream world far more poetically convincing than his evocation of
'Prometheus' passion and misery. The description can be derived from
Spenser (mutability) from Shakespeare (I know a bank . . .) from
Comus, from a whole tradition which made poetry out of worlds of
faery and enchantment. Stock romantic images abound—for example
the Aeolian harp (lutes touched by the wind), favourite symbol of
poetic inspiration, and the innocent child.

During the late eighteenth century, and the Regency there was a
renewed interest in Elizabethan literature, especially in Spenser, the
more romantic parts of Shakespeare, the early Milton and the lyrists. We
have already noticed this influence in Blake. Here is a song by Shelley
which has affinities with the Elizabethan lyric in its simplicity and
elegant melody, and yet is obviously romantic in its imagery and the
way in which the images are put nakedly down, and left 'to vibrate
in the memory' with little rhetorical structure to maintain them.
It seems to me one of the most successful of Shelley's short poems.

> A widow bird sate mourning for her love
> Upon a wintry bough;
> The frozen wind crept on above,
> The freezing wind below.
> There was no leaf upon the forest bare,
> No flower upon the ground,
> And little motion in the air
> Except the mill-wheel's sound.

John Keats was born in 1795 and died of tuberculosis in 1821. This
quotation from a letter by Gerard Manley Hopkins suggests a useful
approach to his work.

'. . . Keats died very young and we have only the work of his first
youth. Now if we compare that with Shakespeare's early work . . .
such as *Venus and Adonis* and *Lucrece*, it is, as far as the work of two
very original minds ever can be, greatly like in its virtues and its
vices; more like, I do think, than that of any writer you could quote
after the Elizabethan age . . . . He was young; his genius intense in
its quality; his feeling for beauty, for perfection intense; he had found
his right way in his Odes; he would find his way right at last to the
true functions of his mind. And he was at a great disadvantage in
point of education compared with Shakespeare. Their classical attain-
ments may have been much of a muchness, but Shakespeare had the
school of his age. It was the Renaissance; the ancient Classics were

H

deeply and enthusiastically studied and influenced directly or indirectly all, and the new learning had entered into a fleeting but brilliant combination with the medieval tradition. All then used the same form and keepings. But in Keats's time, and worst in England, there was no one school; but experiment, division, and uncertainty.'

Endymion, a Poetic Romance was begun in 1817, published the following year, and badly cut up by the *Quarterly Review*. In 1820, when Keats was dying, Shelley wrote a letter to the editor protesting against the 'contemptuous phraseology' in which the poem had been dismissed, admitting that it was a poem 'considerably defective', but pleading that it showed the 'promise of ultimate excellence'. He refers the editor to a number of passages which seem to him proof that the poem 'deserved milder usage'. Here is one of them:

> He saw far in the concave green of the sea
> An old man sitting calm and peacefully.
> Upon a weeded rock this old man sat,
> And his white hair was awful, and a mat
> Of weeds were cold beneath his cold thin feet;
> And, ample as the largest winding-sheet,
> A cloak of blue wrapped up his aged bones,
> O'erwrought with symbols by the deepest groans
> Of ambitious magic: every ocean form
> Was woven in with black distinctness; storm,
> And calm, and whispering, and hideous roar,
> Quicksand, and whirlpool, and deserted shore,
> Were emblem'd in the woof; with every shape
> That skims, or dives, or sleeps, 'twixt cape and cape.
> The gulphing whale was like a dot in the spell,
> Yet look upon it, and 'twould size and swell
> To its huge self; and the minutest fish
> Would pass the very hardest gazer's wish,
> And show his little eye's anatomy.
> Then there was pictured the regality
> Of Neptune; and the sea nymphs round his state,
> In beauteous vassalage, look up and wait.
> Beside this old man lay a pearly wand,
> And in his lap a book, the which he conn'd
> So stedfastly, that the new denizen
> Had time to keep him in amazed ken
> To mark these shadowings, and stand in awe.

First, note the freedom of the couplets; not only are they run on, but pauses occur anywhere in the line—for example the semi-colon which divides the last foot in

> Was woven in with black distinctness; storm,
> And calm, . . .

A year before Hunt had boasted that he had seen, owing to his influence, 'all the reigning poets . . . break up their heroic couplets into
freer modulations', and Keats was here following Hunt. Later he
'felt the weight of too much liberty' and, when he was writing *Lamia*,
turned for a model to Dryden. As we read we must remember that
'awful' meant 'awe-inspiring' and overlook the bathos which the
modern vogue-word usage gives the lines about the old man's hair.
His figure owes something to 'Camus reverend sire' in *Lycidas*, with his
'mantle hoary and his bonnet sedge/Inwroght with figures dim'. What
is interesting, and what, perhaps impressed Shelley is the solidity of
much of the detail, the attempt at translating sensations into words. The
weeds and the rock and the cold and the old man are all felt. Remember
what Keats said about the sparrow pecking in the gravel: 'I am that
sparrow.' So, he *is* this old man. We may ignore the grammatical
error; we may find the 'cold thin feet' faintly absurd, but the solidity
of the description remains. The 'deepest groans/Of ambitious magic'
is a piece of metrical cluminess, and, like the winding sheet, a
piece of not very successful Gothic horror. The 'black distinctness'
is more evidence of Keat's desire for exactness and precision and he
certainly makes us see this old man far more clearly than we see the
phantoms of Shelley. The sounds of the sea are well done; 'emblem'd
in the woof' is an unfortunate piece of fine writing, but the verbs,
'skim,' 'dive,' 'sleep' give vitality to the figures. Note the curious but
effective sub-Shakespearian use of 'size' for 'grow bigger' and the tiny
fishes 'little eye's anatomy'. Neptune and the sea nymphs are stock
properties; the line

> And in his lap a book, the which he conn'd

is pastiche of Spenser; denizen/ken is a forced and clumsy rhyme—the
whole end of the passage peters out. Yet there is a new tune, a new
talent here. The reviewer was right when he found the poem muddled
and tasteless, but Shelley was also right to see in it 'a very remarkable
production for a man of Keats' age'. The poet himself may well have
the last word; in his preface he says this: 'The imagination of a boy is
healthy, and the mature imagination of a man is healthy; but there is a
space of life in between, in which the soul is in a ferment, the character
undecided, the way of life uncertain, the ambition thick-sighted:
thence proceeds mawkishness. . . .'
Such capacity for self-criticism, for detached intelligent self-analysis

is one of Keats' most marked characteristics, and it is apparent in this
sonnet, *On Sitting Down to Read King Lear Once Again*:

> O golden-tongued Romance, with serene lute!
> 　Fair plumed Syren, Queen of far-away!
> 　Leave melodising on this wintry day,
> Shut up thine olden pages, and be mute:
> Adieu! for, once again, the fierce dispute
> 　Betwixt damnation and impassion'd clay
> 　Must I burn through; once more humbly assay
> The bitter-sweet of this Shakespearian fruit:
> Chief Poet! and ye clouds of Albion,
> 　Begetters of our deep eternal theme!
> When through the old oak Forest I am gone,
> 　Let me not wander in a barren dream,
> But, when I am consumed in the fire,
> Give me new Phoenix wings to fly at my desire.

Keats has devoted himself to 'golden-tongued romance', but he realizes
that such poetry is not the greatest. He therefore turns to Shakespeare,
from the melodies of the 'Queen of far-away' to the 'fierce dispute' of
King Lear, from romanticism to a kind of literature which he feels to
be more complex, more serious. To hold that Shakespeare is the greatest of English poets is an opinion common and conventional: to realize
the difference in kind between Romantic poetry and his poetry is rarer.

The opening of the sonnet is clumsy: 'serene lute' is an unhappy
accentuation, and in 'fair plumed Syren', 'leave melodising', 'olden
pages' we recognize the kind of easy lushness of Hunt and his followers,
unkindly termed by the *Quarterly Review* 'the Cockney school of
poetry'. The phrases might be supposed to have their point, since they
are typical of the kind of thing Keats was rejecting, but if irony is
intended it finds no echo in the rhythm; and the general effect is coy
and saccharine. The next lines are pointed and vigorous, harsh and
tragic. Note especially the verb 'burn': the experience of reading *Lear*
is at once grim and purifying; it is (humbly) to be approached in a
spirit of humility, but also (consider the connotations of the verb
'assay') with critical intelligence. The sestet invokes the spirit of Shakespeare, and Albion calls up the ancient England of the play and is a
kind of timeless name, fitting the clouds and the eternal theme, which
Keats believes—the pronoun 'our' implies this—he shares with the dead
bard.

> 'When through the old oak Forest I am gone'

is a haunting line. It could mean 'when I have read the play', that is, when I have accompanied Lear and Gloucester on their journeys'. But it also recalls the wandering knights of Spenser, endlessly questing, and therefore may stand for the country of romance, of dream, which the poet now finds sterile and from which he wants to escape. The fire resumes the image of 'burn through', and leads on to the Phoenix, symbol of the poet, unique and eternal. 'To fly at my desire' implies that till now his work has been derivative, written, so to speak, at other people's desire. Now he prays for power to write as he alone can.

We quote next from *The Eve of St. Agnes*, a romantic tale in Spenserian stanzas, set in the faery world of medieval romance and legend, favourite themes of the period, a genre that Coleridge and especially Scott had made popular. It concerns a pair of lovers who elope on a stormy night from a castle full of the lady's unpleasant relations. Here the first four verses:

> St. Agnes' Eve—Ah, bitter chill it was!
> The owl, for all his feathers, was a-cold;
> The hare limp'd trembling through the frozen grass,
> And silent was the flock in woolly fold:
> Numb were the Beadsman's fingers, while he told
> His rosary, and while his frosted breath,
> Like pious incense from a censer old,
> Seem'd taking flight for heaven, without a death,
> Past the sweet Virgin's picture, while his prayer he saith.

> His prayer he saith, this patient, holy man;
> Then takes his lamp, and riseth from his knees,
> And back returneth, meagre, barefoot, wan,
> Along the chapel aisle by slow degrees:
> The sculptur'd dead, on each side, seem to freeze,
> Emprison'd in black, purgatorial rails:
> Knights, ladies, praying in dumb orat'ries,
> He passeth by; and his weak spirit fails
> To think how they may ache in icy hoods and mails.

> Northward he turneth through a little door,
> And scarce three steps, ere Music's golden tongue
> Flatter'd to tears this aged man and poor;
> But no—already had his deathbell rung:
> The joys of all his life were said and sung:
> His was harsh penance on St. Agnes' Eve:
> Another way he went, and soon among
> Rough ashes sat he for his soul's reprieve
> And all night kept awake, for sinners sake to grieve.

That ancient Beadsman heard the prelude soft;
And so it chanc'd, for many a door was wide,
From hurry to and fro. Soon, up aloft,
The silver, snarling trumpets 'gan to chide:
The level chambers, ready with their pride,
Were glowing to receive a thousand guests:
The carved angels, ever eager-eyed,
Star'd, where upon their heads the cornice rests,
With hair blown back, and wings put cross-wise on their breasts.

and here is the poem's conclusion:

She hurried at his words, beset with fears,
For there were sleeping dragons all around,
At glaring watch, perhaps, with ready spears—
Down the wide stairs a darkling way they found.—
In all the house was heard no human sound.
A chain-droop'd lamp was flickering by each door;
The arras, rich with horseman, hawk, and hound,
Flutter'd in the beseiging wind's uproar;
And the long carpets rose along the gusty floor.

They glide, like phantoms, into the wide hall;
Like phantoms, to the iron porch, they glide;
Where lay the Porter, in uneasy sprawl,
With a huge empty flagon by his side:
The wakeful bloodhound rose, and shook his hide,
But his sagacious eye an inmate owns:
By one, and one, the bolts full easy slide:—
The chains lie silent on the footworn stones;—
The key turns, and the door upon his hinges groans.

And they are gone: aye, ages long ago
These lovers fled away into the storm
That night the Baron dreamt of many a woe
And all his warrior-guests with shade and form
Of witch, and demon, and large coffin-worm,
Were long be-nightmar'd. Angela the old
Died palsy-twitch'd, with meagre face deform;
The Beadsman, after thousand aves told,
For aye unsought for slept among his ashes cold.

The Gothic chapel, the Beadsman, the carved angels, the arras, the
Baron—these are all stock properties, for we are in the world of ''Tis
the middle of the night by the castle clock', of *Marmion*, *Rosabelle*,
Ivanhoe and *Quentin Durward*. Such historical romance has many
descendants in the nineteenth century, and much of it is bloodless.

Keats' peculiar sensibility gives his poem life. The puffed owl, the trembling hare, the Beadsman's numb fingers and his frozen breath all make us feel the cold. Note too, the action, the movement. The hare limps, the Beadsman tells his rosary, his breath moves upwards, and the verse moves too, with slow fluent grace, through to the end of the stanza, whose culminating alexandrine draws our eyes after the thin cloud.

In the second stanza we are made to feel the old man's laboured movements; we have to pause, as he pauses:

> Then takes his lamp, and riseth from his knees,

and the regular plod of the metre

> And back returneth, meagre, barefoot, wan ...

echoes his slow steps. The detail about the sculptured dead is not mere scenery: the old man's fancy brings them in to reinforce the feelings of cold and death. In stanza three the music (we hear it when the door opens) brings in life and youth. Note the effect of the verb 'flatter'd'— the pleasure is agreeable but deceiving—and the pathos of the old man's tears. His is the winter 'of pale misfeature' contrasting dramatically with the gaiety of the feast and the secret joy of the lovers, symbolized by the eager-eyed angels; again the picturesque details are not mere ornaments, they are working in the poem. The epithet 'snarling' and the verb 'chide' show us Keats translating his sensations into words. Wordsworth saw: Keats tasted, touched, heard and felt as well. 'O', he said, 'for a life of sensation rather than thought!' and in his verse he tries to embody all his sensations, which is what makes his best pieces so convincing. The arras, as we have said, is a stock property, but the carpets rising along the floor, as if the besieging wind had breached the castle's defences, is a truly Keatsian detail, and so is the bloodhound 'shaking his hide'.

The last stanza firmly places the poem in the realm of faery, of romance—'aye, ages long ago'. The witches, demons and coffin-worms are the gothic appanages of the period; evil and age are evoked as contrast to the lovers' happiness.

What makes this poem more successful than either *Lamia* or *Isabella* is its lack of pretension. Keats is writing the kind of story that Scott's profuse talent had made so popular, a romantic tale set in a glamorous (we owe this word to Scott) past. Like much of his work it is in part a technical exercise—here, in the manipulation of the Spenserian stanza. The reader may compare his verses with those of Spenser himself, and with Byron's. Keats achieves a tune of his own, and the poem is everywhere touched with his genius for realizing, making concrete, his sensations.

His greatest poems are, by common consent, the four *Odes*, on the *Nightingale*, *Autumn*, the *Grecian Urn* and *Melancholy*. In them he expresses, and harmonizes the themes of beauty and death, the immortality of art, the relentless passing of time, the fears that he 'may cease to be ... before high-piled books in charctery/Hold like rich garners the full ripen'd grain'. We must always remember that Keats knew all about tuberculosis; he had had a medical training, had nursed his brother Tom who died of the disease, and recognized his own symptoms. 'That' he said, looking at his pillow after a haemorrhage, 'is arterial blood'. All the more striking therefore is the poise and balance of these poems, their lucid architecture. Their mellifluous beauty, and the richness of their imagery have made them popular, and an important influence on the poets of the Victorian age. What has been less generally recognized is their intelligence.

Here is the *Ode to Autumn*.

I

Season of mists and mellow fruitfulness,
    Close bosom-friend of the maturing sun;
Conspiring with him how to load and bless
    With fruit the vines that round the thatch-eaves run;
To bend with apples the moss'd cottage-trees,
    And fill all fruit with ripeness to the core;
      To swell the gourd, and plump the hazel shells
    With a sweet kernel; to set budding more,
And still more, later flowers for the bees,
Until they think warm days will never cease,
    For summer has o'er-brimm'd their clammy cells.

II

Who hath not seen thee oft amid thy store?
    Sometimes whoever seeks abroad may find
Thee sitting careless on a granary floor,
    Thy hair soft-lifted by the winnowing wind;
Or on a half-reap'd furrow sound asleep,
    Drows'd with the fume of poppies, while thy hook
      Spares the next swath and all its twined flowers:
And sometimes like a gleaner thou dost keep
    Steady thy laden head across a brook;
Or by a cider-press with patient look
    Thou watchest the last oozings hours by hours.

III

Where are the songs of Spring? Ay, where are they?
 Think not of them, thou hast thy music too,—
While barred clouds bloom the soft-dying day,
 And touch the stubble-plains with rosy hue;
Then in a wailful choir the small gnats mourn
 Among the river sallows, borne aloft
  Or sinking as the light wind lives or dies;
And full-grown lambs loud bleat from hilly bourn;
 Hedge-crickets sing; and now with treble soft
 The red-breast whistles from a garden-croft;
  And gathering swallows twitter in the skies.

Autumn brings the fruition of the year, and its death. This, though sad, is inevitable, and a necessary part of the cycle of life. Its music is not a funeral march, but part of life, a harmony 'nor harsh nor grating though of ample power/To chasten and subdue'. A rich and calm resignation imposes the acceptance of nature's, of life's rhythm.

In much of Keats' verse there is a sense of strain. He said a poet should 'load every rift with ore', and sometimes you can feel him doing it, as in this passage from *Lamia*:

Of wealthy lustre was the banquet room,
 Fill'd with pervading brilliance and perfume:
Before each lucid panel fuming stood
A censer fed with myrrh and spiced wood,
Each by a sacred tripod held aloft,
Whose slender feet wide-swerv'd upon the soft
Wool-woofed carpets; fifty wreaths of smoke
From fifty censers their light voyage took
To the high roof, still mimicked as they rose
Along the mirrored walls by twin clouds odorous.
Twelve sphered tables, by silk seats insphered.
High as the level of a man's breast rear'd
On libbard's paws, upheld the heavy gold
Of cups and goblets, and the store thrice told
Of Ceres' horn and, in huge vessels, wine
Come from the gloomy tun with merry shine. . . .

But in the *Ode* he spreads Autumn's riches in effortless profusion. Note how much of the work is done by verbs: run, load, bless, bend, fill, set budding; how 'bosom-friend' and 'conspiring' contrive to suggest a mysterious magic intimacy, a power creating life and wealth everywhere. We can compare the use of 'plump' as a verb with the use of 'size' in the passage quoted from Endymion. 'Maturing' and 'ripeness' work together, and lead to the hint of sadness, of mutability, in the bees thinking warm days will never cease, and yet, of course, they will. Ripeness is a moment of perfection, which must, in the nature of things, pass; a climax after which there can only be a decline: yet this ripeness, this perfection, sustains life.

In the second verse Autumn is personified, but this is no frigidly conventional neo-classic literary device. Autumn is not described; the god, or goddesses (at once mysterious and homely) share in or contemplate the season's tasks. The modern reader must remind himself that threshing with flails, reaping with scythes and sickles, gleaners, and handworked cider-presses were all common country sights; Keats is not being fanciful or picturesque, but realistic. The figure of the gleaner is active; we feel the weight and balance of her burden—see how the sense moves adroitly across from one line to the next, as she crosses the plank bridge. The other three figures are in a kind of timeless repose, careless, drows'd, patient, 'as if warm days would never cease'. The reaper recalls death, but even his sickle is suspended and nature's bounty, the corn, remains ungathered; nature's beauty, the flowers, remains undestroyed. We are lulled into a kind of trance.

The repeated question at the beginning of the next verse calls us back into the world of time. In Autumn is no bird song, but we are not to regret this because autumn has a music of its own, which is sad but not despairing because autumn is in the harmony of things. The day, like the year, is dying, but softly; it is 'bloomed' by the rosy light reflected from the clouds which also tinges the bare dead stubble fields. 'Bloom' as a verb is a Keatsian coinage, which unites the associations of spring, when flowers blossom, with the bloom on autumn fruits, and renders Keats' feeling for what Hopkins would call the 'inscape' of this special sunset light effect. Compare a MS. draft of this line:

> While a gold cloud gilds the soft-dying day . . .

and you will see with what ore this rift came to be loaded. The verse rises and falls mournfully with the cloud of gnats, but the lambs bleat loud. They may no longer 'bound as to the tabor's sound' and they are protesting because they have been separated from the ewes, but they will live on; they symbolize life's continuity, like the robin who whistles cheerfully through the winter and the migrating swallows who will return from the 'warm south', as Keats, alas, did not.

John Clare was born in 1793, the son of a farm labourer. His verse is simple, vigorous, and direct, and, at its best, singularly uninfluenced by literary fashion. We quote from *The Shepherd's Calendar*, published in 1827, in the text edited by Robinson and Summerfield.

The first passage is from *August*.

The fields now claim them where a motley crew
Of old and young their daily tasks pursue
The barleys beard is grey and wheat is brown
And wakens toil betimes to leave the town
The reapers leave their beds before the sun
And gleaners follow when home toils are done
To pick the littered ear the reaper leaves
And glean in open field among the sheaves
The ruddy child nursed in the lap of care
In toils rude ways to do its little share
Beside its mother poddles o'er the land
Sun burnt and stooping with a weary hand
Picking its tiny glean of corn or wheat
While crackling stubbles wound its legs and feet
Full glad it often is to sit awhile
Upon a smooth green baulk to ease its toil
And feign would spend an idle hour to play
With insects strangers to the moiling day
Creeping about each rush and grassy stem
And often wishes it was one of them
In weariness of heart that it might lye
Hid in the grass from the days burning eye
That raises tender blisters on his skin
Thro hole or opening that have lost a pin
Free from the crackling stubs to toil and glean
And smiles to think how happy it had been
Whilst his expecting mother stoopes to tye
Her handful up and waiting his supply
Misses the resting younker from her side
And shouts of rods and morts of threats beside
Pointing to the grey willows while she tells
His fears shall fetch one if he still rebells
Picturing harsh truths in its unpracticed eye
How they who idle in the harvest lye
Shall well deserving in the winter pine
Or hunt the hedges with the birds and swine
In vain he wishes that the rushes height
Were tall as trees to hide him from her sight
Leaving his pleasant seat he sighs and rubs
His legs and shows scratched wounds from piercing stubs
To make excuse for play but she disdains
His little wounds and smiles when he complains
And as he stoops adown in trouble sore
She sees his grief and bids him sob no more
And bye and bye on the next sabbath day
She'll give him well earned pence as well as play. . . .

This is written by a man who knows from experience what work in the harvest field is like, who really formed part of that 'humble and rustic life' with which Wordsworth proposed to deal. It is salutary, sometimes, when we read the romantics on rural life, to remember what one famous peasant farmer thought of his lot. Wordsworth spoke of him 'in glory and in joy/Following his plough along the mountain side': Burns himself described his life as 'the moil of a galley-slave, coupled with the solitude of a hermit'. Clare is the voice of this life, and he would be valuable on that account alone; but he has a far more than documentary worth. The countryside that bred him spoke a language a poet could use, and was informed by a culture that could nourish him. In his day it was dying, and in our last quotation, he laments its passing. The lines come from *June*, and describe sheep-shearing and the feast that followed. This is the world Shakespeare knew.

> The shepherds idle hours are over now
> Nor longer leaves him neath the hedgrow bough
> Or shadow pillowd banks and lolling stile
> Wilds looses now their summer friends awhile
> Shrill whistles barking dogs and chiding scold
> Drive bleating sheep each morn from fallow fold
> To wash pits where the willow shadows lean
> Dashing them in their fold stained coats to clean
> Then turnd on sunning sward to dry agen
> They drive them homeward to the clipping pen
> In hurdles pent where elm or sycamore
> Shut out the sun—or in some threshing floor
> There they wi scraps of songs and laugh and tale
> Lighten their annual toils while merry ale
> Goes round and gladdens old mens hearts to praise
> The threadbare customs of old farmers days
> Who while the sturting sheep wi trembling fears
> Lies neath the snipping of his harmless sheers
> Recalls full many a thing by bards unsung
> And pride forgot—that reigned when he was young. . . .
>
> Tho fashions haughty frown hath thrown aside
> Half the old forms simplicity supplyd
> Yet there are some prides winter deigns to spare
> Left like green ivy when the trees are bare
> And now when sheering of the flocks are done
> Some ancient customs mixed wi harmless fun
> Crowns the swains merry toiles—the timid maid
> Pleasd to be praisd and yet of praise affraid
> Seeks her best flowers not those of woods and fields

But such as every farmers garden yield
Fine cabbage roses painted like her face
And shining pansys trimmed in golden lace
And tall tuft larkheels feathrd thick wi flowers
And woodbines climbing oer the door in bowers
And London tufts of many a mottld hue
And pale pink pea and monkshood darkly blue
And white and purple jiliflowers that stay
Lingering in blossom summer half away. . . .

But the old beachen bowl that once supplyd
Its feast of frumity is thrown aside
And the old freedom that was living then
When masters made them merry with their men
Whose coat was like his neighbours russet brown
And whose rude speech was vulgar as his clown
Who in the same horn drank the rest among
And joined the chorus while a labourer sung
All this is past—and soon may pass away
The time torn remnant of the holiday
As proud distinction makes a wider space
Between the genteel and the vulgar race
Then must they fade as pride oer custom showers
Its blighting mildew on her feeble flowers

6

THE VICTORIANS

Nineteenth-century verse derived from the Romantics, and the changes
of taste gradually brought about by the poetry and criticism of the
writers discussed in the last chapter became in this period an orthodoxy.
It took longer for this to happen than is generally realized, but by the
forties most traces of Augustan taste had faded, and romantic influences
were everywhere to be seen. The feeling of excitement at being in a
revolutionary situation had gone; satire died with Byron, social
criticism was largely relegated to prose, and the discursive verse of the
period is of little interest today. It would be a crude but not altogether
inaccurate generalization to say that poetry in this age was in full flight
from the results of the industrial revolution.

We begin with Tennyson (1809–1892) whose life spans our period,
and who was the most widely read and most respected poet of his day.

He was an accomplished technician; he attempted to express and to comment on the spirit of his age (he succeeded Wordsworth in the laureateship in 1850) but his bulkier works are lifeless. The following quotations illustrate his lyric, elegiac, 'private' verse—that part of his poetry which retains most interest for us. First, two stanzas from the *Lotos Eaters* and their *Choric Song*, published in his *Poems* 1833. The weary mariners arrive first at the island of the Lotos, and then celebrate the calm forgetfulness of the world and sorrow that the magic fruit brings them.

> The charmed sunset linger'd low adown
> In the red West: thro' mountain clefts the dale
> Was seen far inland, and the yellow down
> Bordered with palm, and many a winding vale
> And meadow, set with slender galingale;
> A land where all things always seem'd the same!
> And round about the keel with faces pale,
> Dark faces pale against that rosy flame,
> The mild-eyed melancholy Lotos-eaters came.
>
> Branches they bore of that enchanted stem,
> Laden with flower and fruit, whereof they gave
> To each, but whoso did receive of them,
> And taste, to him the gushing of the wave
> Far far away did seem to mourn and rave
> On alien shores; and if his fellow spake,
> His voice was thin, as voices from the grave;
> And deep-asleep he seem'd, yet all awake,
> And music in his ears his beating heart did make. . . .
>
>
> Lo! in the middle of the wood,
> The folded leaf is woo'd from out the bud
> With winds upon the branch, and there,
> Grows green and broad, and takes no care,
> Sun-steep'd at noon, and in the moon
> Nightly dew-fed; and turning yellow
> Falls, and floats adown the air.
> Lo! sweeten'd with the summer light,
> The full-juiced apple, waxing over-mellow,
> Drops in a silent autumn night.
> All its allotted length of days,
> The flower ripens in its place,
> Ripens and fades, and falls, and hath no toil,
> Fast-rooted in the fruitful soil.

Hateful is the dark-blue sky,
Vaulted o'er the dark-blue sea.
Death is the end of life; ah, why
Should life all labour be?
Let us alone. Time driveth onward fast,
And in a little while our lips are dumb.
Let us alone. What is it that will last?
All things are taken from us, and become
Portions and parcels of the dreadful Past.
Let us alone. What pleasure can we have
To war with evil? Is there any peace
In ever climbing up the climbing wave?
All things have rest, and ripen towards the grave
In silence; ripen, fall and cease:
Give us long rest or death, dark death, or dreamful ease.

How sweet it were hearing the downward stream,
With half-shut eyes ever to seem
Falling asleep in a half dream!
To dream and dream, like yonder amber light,
Which will not leave the myrrh-bush on the height;
To hear each other's whispered speech;
Eating the Lotos day by day,
To watch the crisping ripples on the beach,
And tender curving lines of creamy spray;
To lend our hearts and spirits wholly
To the influence of mild-minded melancholy;
To muse and brood and live again in memory,
With those old faces of our infancy
Heap'd over with a mound of grass,
Two handfuls of white dust, shut in an urn of brass!

The skill in this verse, published when Tennyson was twenty-four, is immense, and the poet never surpassed it. Spenser's influence is strong, especially in the first two stanzas; indeed such lines as

>   ... whereof they gave
> To each, but whoso did receive of them,
> And taste, to him the gushing of the wave
> Far far away did seem. ...

are in effect a pastiche. We note the archaisms—whereof, whoso, adown, and the constant use of 'did'. There are debts to Shelley, for the dream landscape, and to Keats for the more solid detail—the 'full-juiced apple'—though we have only to turn back to the *Ode to Autumn* to see how comparatively commonplace the *Lotos Eaters* is. Yet there

is no doubt that it has a new, a personal tune. The swooning melancholic rhythms are, it is true, dramatically appropriate to the theme of
the poem; but it is equally true that these rhythms, this lush melancholy
is the characteristic Tennysonian voice, representing the longing of the
age of steam and progress, travelling for ever down the 'ringing grooves
of change' for a land 'where all things always seem'd the same.'

Our next quotation is from a kind of domestic eclogue *The Gardener's
Daughter*, published in 1842. The speaker is an artist. He is being taken
to see the beautiful Rose, the gardener's daughter, who will inspire him
to paint as never before, and who in due course will make him most
happy by faltering 'I am thine'.

> Not wholly in the busy world, nor quite
> Beyond it, blooms the garden that I love.
> News from the humming city comes to it
> In sound of funeral or of marriage bells;
> And, sitting muffled in dark leaves, you hear
> The windy clanging of the minster clock;
> Although between it and the garden lies
> A league of grass, wash'd by a slow broad stream,
> That, stirr'd with languid pulses of the oar,
> Waves all its lazy lilies, and creeps on,
> Barge laden, to three arches of a bridge
> Crown'd with the minster-towers.
>   The fields between
> Are dewy fresh, brows'd by deep-udder'd kine,
> And all about the large lime feathers low,
> The lime a summer home of murmurous wings. . . .
>
> And sure this orbit of the memory folds
> For ever in itself the day we went
> To see her. All the land in flowery squares
> Beneath a broad and equal-blowing wind,
> Smelt of the coming summer, as one large cloud
> Drew downward: but all else of Heaven was pure
> Up to the Sun, and May from verge to verge,
> And May with me from head to heel. And now,
> As tho' 'twere yesterday, as tho' it were
> The hour just flown, that morn with all its sound,
> (For those old Mays had thrice the life of these,)
> Rings in mine ears. The steer forgot to graze,
> And, where the hedge-row cuts the pathway, stood,
> Leaning his horns into the neighbour field
> And lowing to his fellows. From the woods
> Came voices of the well-contented doves.
> The lark could scarce get out his notes for joy,

But shook his song together as he near'd
His happy home, the ground. To left and right,
The cuckoo told his name to all the hills;
The mellow ouzel fluted in the elm;
The redcap whistled; and the nightingale
Sang loud, as tho' he were the bird of day.

This is an accomplished domestication of the picturesque elements in romantic nature poetry. The verse has a kind of creamy smoothness, a luxurious cosiness, from which all harshness has been carefully excluded. Thought, vision, feeling, move with languid richness on a flood of carefully manipulated vowel sounds; almost the whole of the Tennysonian tune, the essence of Tennysonian verse can be felt in the one line

The mellow ouzel fluted in the elm.

In Memoriam, the long meditative elegy on his friend Arthur Hallam, records Tennyson's doubts, his struggles to find a faith. It is a serious poem, but not a very interesting one. Here is a characteristic section.

LIII

Oh yet we trust that somehow good
  Will be the final goal of ill,
  To pangs of nature, sins of will,
Defects of doubt, and taints of blood;

That nothing walks with aimless feet;
  That not one life shall be destroy'd,
  Or cast as rubbish to the void,
When God hath made the pile complete;

That not a worm is cloven in vain;
  That not a moth with vain desire
  Is shrivel'd in a fruitless fire,
Or but subserves another's gain.

Behold, we know not anything;
  I can but trust that good shall fall
  At last—far off—at last, to all,
And every winter change to spring.

So runs my dream; but what am I?
  An infant crying in the night:
  An infant crying for the light:
And with no language but a cry.

The poetic dialect which Tennyson made for himself out of those elements of romantic writing which appealed to his temperament is too limited, too denatured, to encompass anything more complicated than the poetry of dream, of pathos, of luxurious despair. He had the misfortune to write in an age when verse was being relegated to the drawing-room table. Its finest minds were expressing themselves in prose.

Of the work of Robert Browning (1812–1889), we need consider only one aspect. He attempted, notably in the volumes entitled *Men and Women*, 1855, and *Dramatis Personae*, 1864, to use in his verse the rhythms of spoken language and to convey character by means of the dramatic monologue; but these rhythms are rarely convincing. The 'speech' is too often a jerky jumble of archaisms, distorted syntax and romantic clichés. We quote one well-known short piece, *My Last Duchess*. An Italian renaissance duke is showing the portrait of his late wife to the emissary who is arranging his next marriage.

> That's my last duchess painted on the wall,
> Looking as if she were alive. I call
> That piece a wonder, now: Fra Pandolf's hands
> Worked busily a day, and there she stands.
> Will't please you sit and look at her? I said
> 'Fra Pandolf' by design, for never read
> Strangers like you that pictured countenance,
> The depth and passion of its earnest glance,
> But to myself they turned (since none puts by
> The curtain I have drawn for you, but I)
> And seemed as they would ask me, if they durst,
> How such a glance came there; so, not the first
> Are you to turn and ask me thus. Sir, 'twas not
> Her husband's presence only, called that spot
> Of joy into the Duchess' cheek; perhaps
> Fra Pandolf chanced to say 'Her mantle laps
> 'Over my lady's wrist too much', or 'Paint
> 'Must never hope to reproduce the faint
> 'Half-flush that dies along her throat:' such stuff
> Was courtesy, she thought, and cause enough
> For calling up that spot of joy. She had
> A heart—how shall I say?—too soon made glad
> Too easily impressed; she liked whate'er
> She looked on, and her looks went everywhere.
> Sir, 'twas all one! My favour at her breast,
> The dropping of the daylight in the West,

The bough of cherries some officious fool
Broke in the orchard for her, the white mule
She rode with round the terrace—all and each
Would draw from her alike the approving speech,
Or blush, at least. She thanked men,—good! but thanked
Somehow—I know not how—as if she ranked
My gift of a nine-hundred-years-old name
With anybody's gift. Who'd stoop to blame
This sort of trifling? Even had you skill
In speech—(which I have not)—to make your will
Quite clear to such an one, and say, 'Just this
'Or that in you disgusts me; here you miss,
'Or there exceed the mark'—and if she let
Herself be lessoned so, nor plainly set
Her wits to yours, forsooth, and made excuse,
—E'en then would be some stooping; and I choose
Never to stoop. Oh sir, she smiled, no doubt,
Whene'er I passed her; but who passed without
Much the same smile? This grew; I gave commands;
Then all smiles stopped together. There she stands
As if alive. Will't please you rise? We'll meet
The company below, then. I repeat,
The Count your master's known munificence
Is ample warrant that no just pretence
Of mine for dowry will be disallowed;
Though his fair daughter's self, as I avowed
At starting, is my object. Nay, we'll go
Together down sir. Notice Neptune, though,
Taming a sea-horse, thought a rarity,
Which Claus of Innsbruck cast in bronze for me!

The poem has a roughness of surface which gives it at least the appearance of vigour. It is ingeniously arranged to make the reader work out for himself the implications of the story; the duke's pride, his treatment of his wife as one of his possessions, his jealousy, his cruelty, her death of a broken heart and his proposing to add another unfortunate young woman to his collection. But the effort (not by any standards a very great one) we put into solving the puzzle only reveals a conventionally ironical anecdote, and is in no way related to the effort we have to put in when we read, say, *Good Friday, Riding Westward*. Donne invites us, we might say forces us, to share his struggles; Browning asks us to admire his prestidigitation. But he did at any rate try to bring dramatic rhythms back into verse, and readers who feel I have undervalued this poem will find much in his work to attract them.

Both Tennyson and Browning discussed the intellectual and religious problems of their day, and, in particular, the disputes between religion and science—how hard it was to fit into the scheme of orthodox dogma the new knowledge that geology, the theory of evolution, the application of historical scholarship to divinely inspired sacred texts was forcing on their attention. We are concerned with the sort of verse they wrote on topics like these. Here are two short samples—the opening lines of Tennyson's *The Two Voices*, and Browning's *Easter Day*.

> A still small voice spake unto me,
> 'Thou art so full of misery,
> Were it not better not to be?'
>
> Then to the still small voice I said
> 'Let me not cast in endless shade
> What is so wonderfully made.'
>
> To which the voice did urge reply;
> 'Today I saw the dragon-fly
> Come from the wells where he did lie.
>
> 'An inner impulse rent the veil
> Of his old husk: from head to tail
> Came out clear plates of sapphire mail.
>
> 'He dried his wings: like gauze they grew:
> Thro' crofts and pastures wet with dew
> A living flash of light he flew.'
>
> I said, 'When first the world began,
> Young Nature thro' five cycles ran,
> And in the sixth she moulded man.
>
> 'She gave him mind, the lordliest
> Proportion, and, above the rest,
> Dominion in the head and breast.'
>
> Thereto the silent voice replied;
> 'Self-blinded are you by your pride:
> Look up thro' night: the world is wide.
>
> 'This truth within thy mind rehearse,
> That in a boundless universe
> Is boundless better, boundless worse. . . .'

How very hard it is to be
A Christian! Hard for you and me,
Not the mere task of making real
That duty up to its ideal,
Effecting thus complete and whole,
A purpose of the human soul—
For that is always hard to do;
But hard, I mean, for me and you
To realise it, more or less,
With even the moderate success
Which commonly repays our strife
To carry out the aims of life.
'This aim is greater,' you will say,
'And so more arduous every way.'
But the importance of their fruits
Still proves to man, in all pursuits,
Proportional encouragement.
'Then what if it be God's intent
'That labour to this one result
'Should seem unduly difficult?'
Ah, that's a question in the dark—
And the sole thing that I remark
Upon the difficulty, this;
We do not see it where it is,
At the beginning of the race:
As we proceed, it shifts its place
And where we looked for crowns to fall,
We find the tug's to come,—that's all. . . .

The reader is invited to turn back to Donne, Herbert and Marvell and compare their verses with these. The poverty of Victorian poetic language is at once apparent. We do not doubt these poets' sincerity or earnestness, but neither can command, on themes of this sort, that vitality of rhythm and imagery which will make a poem impose itself on our imagination. Their ideas such as they are, gain nothing from being put into verse; we feel, indeed, a kind of awkwardness about the whole performance, and must conclude that the metaphysical range is beyond the Victorian poet, whose successes are limited to lotus eating and dreams.

Tennyson's lapses of taste and his occasional vulgarity were in part at least the result of the lack of critical standards, of what Hopkins called 'forms and keepings'. Matthew Arnold (1822–1888) struggled to civilize his age, to make it less provincial, more enlightened, more humane; and to persuade it to find in 'culture', in poetry, in the arts, standards and values which were no longer, he believed, to be found in any contemporary religious or civil establishment. All this critical, polemical part of his work is in prose. What he thought of the age of progress he lived in may be gathered from this passage from *Friendship's Garland*:

'Your middle-class man thinks it the highest pitch of development and civilisation when his letters are carried twelve times a day from Islington to Camberwell, and from Camberwell to Islington, and if railway-trains run to and fro between them every quarter of an hour. He thinks it is nothing that the trains only carry him from an illiberal dismal life at Islington to an illiberal dismal life at Camberwell; and the letters only tell him that such is the life there'.

Pope berated the dunces in verse, but in Arnold's day, satire was not a poetic possibility. Indeed, both Pope and Dryden, whose poetry, he said, was 'conceived in their wits', not in their 'souls', were, for him 'classics of our prose'.

What he thought criticism could do to improve the sad state of affairs in Islington and Camberwell is illustrated by these quotations from the essay *On the Function of Criticism at the Present Time*.

'Its business is . . . simply to know the best that is known and thought in the world, and by in its turn making this known, to create a current of true and fresh ideas. Its business is to do this with inflexible honesty. . . .'

Later he speaks of criticism's

'best spiritual work; which is to keep man from a self-satisfaction which is retarding and vulgarising, to lead him towards perfection, by making his mind dwell upon what is excellent in itself, and the absolute beauty and fitness of things.'

The principles on which he believed his verse must be written he explained in the Preface to the volume of *Poems* published in 1853.

'. . . in the sincere endeavour to learn and practise, amid the bewildering confusion of our times, what is sound and true in poetical art, I seemed to myself to find the only sure guidance, the only solid footing, among the ancients. They, at any rate, knew what they wanted in Art, and we do not.

This sounds like a reaction against romanticism; against 'the English poetry of the first quarter of this century,' which 'with plenty of energy, plenty of creative force, did not know enough'. But Arnold's verse is romantic in tone and feeling. It is elegant and tasteful, at its best very beautiful in a literary, derivative way. Our first quotation is the conclusion from *Sohrab and Rustum*, an heroic tale in blank verse.

But the majestic River floated on,
Out of the mist and hum of that low land,
Into the frosty starlight, and there mov'd,

Rejoicing, through the hush'd Chorasmian waste,
Under the solitary moon: he flow'd
Right for the Polar Star, past Orgunjè,
Brimming, and bright, and large: then sands begin
To hem his watery march, and dam his streams,
And split his currents; that for many a league
The shorn and parcell'd Oxus strains along
Through beds of sand and matted rushy isles—
Oxus, forgetting the bright speed he had
In his high mountain cradle in Pamere,
A foil'd circuitous wanderer:—till at last
The long'd-for dash of waves is heard, and wide
His luminous home of waters opens, bright
And tranquil, from whose floor the new-bath'd stars
Emerge, and shine upon the Aral Sea.

The lines owe much to the formal pictorial similes in *Paradise Lost*; we recognize Miltonic cadences

> ... there mov'd,
> Rejoicing, through the hush'd Chorasmian waste ...

and the Miltonic use of sonorous proper names; at the same time they are suffused with romantic feeling for nature, and are given their unity and strange hypnotic power by the fact that the river symbolizes (though this is never made explicit) the life of man, his bright youth, his futile struggles with society (the poet is himself the foiled circuitous wanderer), his longing for the peace of death.

The Scholar Gipsy is based on the story of 'an Oxford scholar poor' who 'forsook his friends/and went to learn the Gipsy lore', mysterious wisdom, which, when learned, he would 'to the world impart/But it needs heaven-sent moments for this skill'. Arnold, who is a scholar school-inspector, makes of him a potent symbol.

These stanzas evoke the Oxfordshire landscape:

Here, where the reaper was at work of late,
In this high field's dark corner, where he leaves
His coat, his basket, and his earthen cruse,
And in the sun all morning binds the sheaves,
Then here, at noon, comes back his stores to use;
Here will I sit and wait,
While to my ear from uplands far away
The bleating of the folded flocks is borne,
With distant cries of reapers in the corn—
All the live murmur of a summer's day.

Screen'd is this nook o'er the high, half-reap'd field
And here till sun-down, Shepherd, will I be.
   Through the thick corn the scarlet poppies peep,
And round green roots and yellowing stalks I see
   Pale blue convulvulus in tendrils creep:
     And air-swept lindens yield
Their scent, and rustle down their perfum'd showers
   Of bloom on the bent grass where I am laid,
   And bower me from the August sun with shade;
   And the eye travels down to Oxford's towers. . . .

In the next passage Arnold compares himself and his contemporaries with the Scholar Gipsy. 'Thou', he says, 'possessest an immortal lot'. . . . Because thou hadst—what we, alas, have not':

For early didst thou leave the world, with powers
   Fresh, undiverted to the world without,
     Firm to their mark, not spent on other things;
   Free from the sick fatigue, the languid doubt,
     Which much to have tried, in much been baffled, brings
       O Life unlike to ours!
   Who fluctuate idly without term or scope,
     Of whom each strives, nor knows for what he strives,
     And each half lives a hundred different lives;
     Who wait like thee, but not, like thee, in hope.

Thou waitest for the spark from Heaven: and we,
   Vague half-believers of our casual creeds,
     Who never deeply felt, nor clearly will'd,
   Whose insight never has borne fruit in deeds,
     Whose weak resolves never have been fulfill'd;
       For whom each year we see
   Breeds new beginnings, disappointments new;
     Who hesitate and falter life away,
     And lose tomorrow the ground won to-day—
     Ah, do not we, Wanderer, await it too? . . .

O born in days when wits were fresh and clear,
   And life ran gaily as the sparkling Thames;
     Before this strange disease of modern life,
With its sick hurry, its divided aims,
   Its heads o'ertax'd, its palsied hearts, was rife—
       Fly hence, our contact fear!
Still fly, plunge deeper in the bowering wood!
   Averse, as Dido did with gesture stern
   From her false friend's approach in Hades turn,
     Wave us away, and keep thy solitude.

Still nursing the unconquerable hope,
  Still clutching the inviolable shade,
    With a free onward impulse brushing through,
By night, the silver'd branches of the glade—
    Far on the forest skirts, where none pursue,
      On some mild pastoral slope
    Emerge, and resting on the moonlit pales,
    Freshen thy flowers, as in former years,
    With dew, or listen with enchanted ears,
      From the dark dingles, to the nightingales. . . .

As we noted in Tennyson, the pictures are more interesting than the thinking, the nostalgia more potent than the analysis: but Arnold is clear. The expository, or rhetorical bits of the poem, the lines, for example, beginning 'Thou waitest for the spark from Heaven to fall', have the virtues of his excellent prose—all of them, except, of course, irony. This is the verse of an intelligent, talented man of taste, soaked in the tradition of English poetry that runs from Spenser and Milton to the Romantics. He avoids the Tennysonian excesses of sentiment, and the grotesquery of Browning; he is never vulgar. 'If', he said, 'we cannot attain the mastery of the great artists—let us, at least, have so much respect for our Art as to prefer it to ourselves—let us transmit to (our successors) the practice of Poetry, with its boundaries and wholesome regulative laws . . .' Not a revolutionary programme, but not an ignoble one. We end with *Dover Beach*, a poem which analyses the predicament of the mid-nineteenth century, as Arnold saw it, with tragic clarity. In it there is unity of thought and feeling; the beautifully worked out movement of the sea is not a piece of dream decoration, but an integral part of the meaning. Arnold's taste, learning and skill are here perfectly fused with his theme. This is his individual voice, that still speaks directly to us with 'inflexible honesty'.

    The sea is calm tonight,
    The tide is full, the moon lies fair
    Upon the Straits;—on the French coast, the light
    Gleams, and is gone; the cliffs of England stand,
    Glimmering and vast, out in the tranquil bay.
    Come to the window, sweet is the night air!
    Only, from the long line of spray
    Where the ebb meets the moon-blanch'd sand,
    Listen! you hear the grating roar
    Of pebbles which the waves suck back, and fling,
    At their return, up the high strand,
    Begin, and cease, and then again begin,

With tremulous cadence slow, and bring
The eternal note of sadness in.

   Sophocles long ago
Heard it on the Aegean, and it brought
Into his mind the turbid ebb and flow
Of human misery; we
Find also in the sound a thought,
Hearing it by this distant northern sea.

The sea of faith
Was once, too, at the full, and round earth's shore
Lay like the folds of a bright girdle furl'd;
But now I only hear
Its melancholy, long, withdrawing roar,
Retreating to the breath
Of the night-wind down the vast edges drear
And naked shingles of the world.

Ah, love, let us be true
To one another! for the world, which seems
To lie before us like a land of dreams,
So various, so beautiful, so new,
Hath really neither joy, nor love, nor light,
Nor certitude, nor peace, nor help for pain;
And we are here as on a darkling plain
Swept with confused alarms of struggle and flight,
Where ignorant armies clash by night.

It is convenient to consider Dante Gabriel Rossetti and William Morris together, since they share the label 'Pre-Raphaelite'. The term was first applied to a group of painters which included Holman Hunt and Millais, whose object was to restore to art the precise and loving attention to the details of natural life which they found in early Renaissance pictures, but which they believed the post-Raphael schools of 'history painting' had lost. The group soon broke up, and the label has, as far as literature is concerned, little critical-descriptive value. A taste for medieval themes, a mannered archaic diction, a curious kind of false simplicity and a hatred of nineteenth-century industrialism are the main ingredients which these poets share.

Many of Tennyson's poems have medieval settings and both he and Morris wrote about Sir Galahad. It might help the reader to taste the Pre-Raphaelite flavour if he compares the two poems. First, Tennyson:

My good blade carves the casques of men,
  My tough lance thrusteth sure,
My strength is as the strength of ten,
  Because my heart is pure.
The shattering trumpet shrilleth high,
  The hard brands shiver on the steel,
The splinter'd spear-shafts crack and fly,
  The horse and rider reel:
They reel, they roll in clanging lists,
  And when the tide of combat stands,
Perfume and flowers fall in showers,
  That lightly rain from ladies' hands.

How sweet are looks that ladies bend
  On whom their favours fall!
For them I battle to the end,
  To save from shame and thrall:
But all my heart is drawn above,
  My knees are bowed in crypt and shrine:
I never felt the kiss of love,
  Nor maiden's hand in mine.
More bounteous aspects on me beam,
  Me mightier transports move and thrill;
So keep I fair thro' faith and prayer
  A virgin heart in work and will.

Now Morris:

              . . . a drowsiness
    Came on me, so that I fell half asleep,
      As I sat there not moving: less and less

  I saw the melted snow that hung in beads
    Upon my steel-shoes; less and less I saw
  Between the tiles the bunches of small weeds:
    Heartless and stupid, with no touch of awe

  Upon me, half-shut eyes upon the ground,
    I thought: O Galahad! the days go by,
  Stop and cast up now that which you have found,
    For sorely you have wrought and painfully.

  Night after night, your horse treads down alone
    The sere damp fern, night after night you sit
  Holding the bridle like a man of stone,
    Dismal, unfriended: what thing comes of it?

Tennyson's thumping coarse resounding rhythms have been replaced
by sounds more tenuous and more tentative, as the verse follows the
knight's self-questioning. Morris really tries to imagine what it was
like to be Sir Galahad, and more, what it was like to deal out and to
suffer violence. Hopkins's phrase for Tennyson's medievalizing poems—
'charades from the middle ages'—fits his Sir Galahad perfectly, and no
more words need be wasted on so trite a performance. What is characteristically Pre-Raphaelite about the Morris verses is the detail—the
beads of melted snow, the bunches of weeds between the tiles, the
sere damp fern; the self-conscious simplicity—'I fell half asleep/As I
sat there not moving', and the archaic turns of phrase: 'cast up now
that which you have found', 'So sorely you have wrought', 'what thing
comes of it?'

Tennyson is vague, literary and sentimental:

> How sweet are looks that ladies bend
> On whom their favours fall! ...

> I never felt the Kiss of love,
> Nor maiden's hand in mine ...

He evades the issue. Morris produces this:

> Yea, what if Father Launcelot ride out,
>   Can he not think of Guinevere's arms, round
> Warm and lithe, about his neck, and shout
>   Till all the place grow joyful with the sound?

This is at any rate an attempt to put down the truth. Yet when we recall
that at about this period Dickens was writing *Bleak House* and *Hard
Times* we cannot help feeling that Victorian verse of this sort is marginal.

Rossetti's best known poem is *The Blessed Damosel*, and it exhibits his
peculiar blend of eroticism and religiosity. The lady leans out 'from
the gold bar of heaven'; she looks forward to the day when she can
welcome her lover, when she 'will ask of Christ the Lord/Thus much
for him and me:—/Only to live as once on earth/With Love ...' Here
is a sample stanza:

> Herseemed she had been scarce a day
>   One of God's choristers;
> The wonder was not yet quite gone
>   From that still look of hers;
> Albeit, to them she had left, her day
>   Had counted as ten years. ...

The tricks of style we noted in the verse of Morris are to be seen here too—the archaisms 'herseemed', 'albeit': the mannered simplicity: 'The wonder was not yet quite gone/From that still look of hers'. Pater, whose tastes and opinions were so influential in the latter years of the century said of this poem: 'One of the peculiarities of *The Blessed Damosel* was a definiteness of sensible imagery, which seemed almost grotesque to some ... as naively detailed as in the pictures of those early painters contemporary with Dante' and this will give us some idea of the effect this kind of verse had on the cultivated reader of that time. Yet when we read in the last stanza that the lady 'cast her arms along/The golden barriers/And laid her face between her hands' we wonder how Pater came by his 'definiteness of sensible imagery'.

These stanzas, from *Love's Nocturn*, melodious, hypnotic, deliberately remote from reality, are a further sample of what 'the poetic' was, at this period, considered to be:

> Vaporous, unaccountable,
>   Dreamland lies forlorn of light,
> Hollow like a breathing shell.
>   Ah! that from all dreams I might
>   Choose one dream and guide its flight!
>   I know well
>   What her sleep should tell tonight.
>
> There the dreams are multitudes:
>   Some whose buoyance waits not sleep,
> Deep within the August woods;
>   Some that hum while rest may steep
>   Weary labour laid a-heap;
>   Interludes,
>   Some, of grievous moods that weep.
>
> Poets' fancies all are there:
>   There the elf-girls flood with wings
> Valleys full of plaintive air;
>   There breathe perfumes; there in rings
>   Whirl the foam-bewildered springs;
>   Siren there
>   Winds her dizzy hair and sings ...

Rossetti's most considered work is to be found in his sonnet sequence *The House of Life*, from which we quote No. XLIV *The Sun's Shame*.

> Beholding youth and hope in mockery caught
> From life; and mocking pulses that remain
> When the soul's death of bodily death is fain;

> Honour unknown, and honour known unsought;
> And penury's sedulous self-torturing thought
>   On gold, whose master therewith buys his bane;
>   And longed-for woman longing all in vain
> For lonely man with love's desire distraught;
> And wealth, and strength and power and pleasantness,
>   Given unto bodies of whose souls men say,
>   None poor and weak, slavish and foul, as they:—
> Beholding these things, I behold no less
> The blushing morn and blushing eve confess
>   The shame that loads the intolerable day.

The reader should compare this sonnet with Shakespeare's No. 66, 'Tir'd with all these for restful death I cry . . .' of which it is an (unconscious?) paraphrase, and with the sonnets of Hopkins.

From 1868 to 1870 Morris published a collection of tales in verse, significantly enough entitled *The Earthly Paradise*. From it we may quote these verses which explain what sort of poetry it is, and why it was written. First from the *Apology* which introduces the book:

> Of Heaven or Hell I have no power to sing,
> I cannot ease the burden of your fears,
> Or make quick-coming death a little thing
> Or bring again the pleasure of past years,
> Nor for my words shall ye forget your tears,
> Or hope again for aught that I can say,
> The idle singer of an empty day. . . .
>
> Dreamer of dreams, born out of my time,
> Why should I strive to set the crooked straight?
> Let it suffice me that my murmuring rhyme
> Beats with light wings against the ivory gate,
> Telling a tale not too importunate
> To those who in the sleepy region stay,
> The idle singer of an empty day. . . .
>
> So with this Earthly Paradise it is,
> If ye will read aright and pardon me,
> Who strive to build a shadowy isle of bliss
> Midmost the beating of the steely sea,
> Where tossed about all hearts of men must be;
> Whose ravening monsters mighty men shall slay,
> Not the poor singer of an empty day.

Now the opening lines of the *Prologue* to the stories:

> Forget six counties overhung with smoke,
> Forget the snorting steam and piston stroke,
> Forget the spreading of the hideous town;

Think rather of the pack-horse on the down,
And dream of London, small, and white, and clean,
The clear Thames bordered by its gardens green;
Think, that below bridge the green lapping waves
Smite some few keels that bear Levantine staves,
Cut from the yew wood on the burnt-up hill
And pointed jars that Greek hands toiled to fill,
And treasured scanty spice from some far sea,
Florence gold cloth, and Ypres napery,
And cloth of Bruges, and hogsheads of Guienne;
While nigh the thronged wharf Geoffrey Chaucer's pen
Moves over bills of lading—mid such times
Shall dwell the hollow puppets of my rhymes.

A nameless city in a distant sea,
White as the changing walls of faërie,
Thronged with much people clad in ancient guise
I now am fain to set before your eyes. . . .

Morris is an honest and unpretentious writer; but poetry became more and more for him a relaxation, literally an escape from his serious life, which he devoted with immense talent, energy and generosity to the fight for a juster and more beautiful society. He *was* one of the 'mighty men' who tried to slay the 'ravening monsters' but his weapon in this battle was prose and the craft of his hands, not poetry.

In 1866 Swinburne (1837–1909) published the first series of his *Poems and Ballads*, a 'revel of rhymes', 'songs of dead seasons that wander/On wings of articulate words'. Many of his young contemporaries found his rhythms intoxicating. Here are some samples. The first is from *A Ballad of Death*.

By night there stood over against my bed
Queen Venus with a hood striped gold and black,
Both sides drawn fully back
From brows wherein the sad blood failed of red,
And temples drained of purple and full of death.
Her curled hair had the wave of sea-water
And the sea's gold in it.
Her eyes were as a dove's that sickeneth.
Strewn dust of gold she had shed over her,
And purple and amber on her feet.

Here is the end of the *Hymn to Proserpine*:

O daughter of earth, of my mother, her crown and blossom of birth,
I am also, I also, thy brother; I go as I came unto earth.

In the night where thine eyes are as moons are in heaven, the night where
thou art,
Where the silence is more than all tunes, and where sleep overflows from
the heart,
Where the poppies are sweet as the rose in our world, and the red rose
is white,
And the wind falls faint as it blows with the fume of the flowers of the
night,
And the murmur of spirits that sleep in the shadow of Gods from afar
Grows dim in thine ears and deep as the deep dim soul of a star,
In the sweet low light of thy face, under heavens untrod by the sun,
Let my soul with their souls find place, and forget what is done and undone.
Thou art more than the Gods who number the days of our temporal
breath; ·
For these give labour and slumber; but thou, Proserpina, death.
Therefore now at thy feet I abide for a season in silence. I know
I shall die as my fathers died, and sleep as they sleep; even so.
For the glass of the years is brittle wherein we gaze for a span;
A little soul for a little bears up this corpse which is man.
So long I endure, no longer; and laugh not again, neither weep.
For there is no God found stronger than death; and death is a sleep.

Last a stanza from *Ave Atque Vale*, his elegy on Baudelaire.

For always thee the fervid languid glories
    Allured of heavier suns in mightier skies;
    Thine ears knew all the wandering watery sighs
Where the sea sobs round Lesbian promontories,
    The barren kiss of piteous wave to wave
    That knows not where is that Leucadian grave
Which hides too deep the supreme head of song.
    Ah, salt and sterile as her kisses were,
    The wild sea winds her and the green gulfs bear
Hither and thither, and vex and work her wrong,
    Blind gods that cannot spare.

Such verse is to be intoned or chanted, but not to be thought about.
In the sixties Swinburne's themes seemed shocking, his iconoclasm and
his revolutionary fervour exhilarating; they are so no longer. There
can be few poets who so little repay rereading. The first quotation is
full of the stylistic tricks we have associated with Pre-Raphaelitism;
the second exhibits the poet's favourite triple metre, and shows him
sacrificing, as he so often does, sense to sound. There is no doubt
that the elegy on Baudelaire is deeply felt, though the stanza we
quote is full of reminiscences, of *Othello* (I know not where is that
Promethean fire . . .), of *Lycidas* (That sunk so low that sacred head of

thine), of Tennyson. Swinburne read with worshipful enthusiasm the poems of Hugo, Gautier and Baudelaire, whom he appears to have believed to be poets of equal and similar merit. The reader has only to turn to *Les Fleurs du Mal* and read, say, *La Cygne* or *Les Petites Vieilles* to see how little he understood his master. The vulgar Hugo wrote to Baudelaire: 'Vous nous avez donné un nouveau frisson', and Swinburne would have agreed, for a delicious shudder was what he aimed at producing. If he gives you goose-pimples (the Housman syndrome) well and good. If he doesn't there is, as Chaucer puts it, 'namoore to say'.

Gerard Manley Hopkins (1844–1889) was a great innovator, a profound technician, a forger of new rhythms. Scattered through his letters and journals there are many detailed and learned discussions of prosody and metrics; but what we want to grasp is the general principle which underlies all the detail, the accent-markings and the technical terms, and this principle is really very simple. English is a heavily stressed language, and English verse is built on stresses. Most English verse since Spenser has been constructed so that each stressed syllable is always accompanied by a uniform number of unstressed ones, so that in practice the basic units are ti pom, pom ti, ti ti pom, or pom ti ti. Many skilful variations are admitted into this scheme, but to Hopkins it seemed deadening and cramping, and he substituted for it a method he called 'sprung rhythm', which he describes thus in the preface to his poems:

> 'Sprung Rhythm, as used in this book, is measured by feet of from one to four syllables, regularly, and for particular effects any number of weak or slack syllables may be used. It has one stress, which falls on the only syllable if there is only one, or, if there are more, then scanning . . . on the first . . .'

He says, further, that 'it is the rhythm of common speech and of written prose, when rhythm is perceived in them' and that 'it has in fact ceased to be used since the Elizabethan age. . . .'

In a letter to Bridges in 1877 he wrote in reply to his friend's criticism of *The Wreck of the Deutschland*:

> 'Why do I employ sprung rhythm at all? Because it is the nearest to the rhythm of prose, that is the native and natural rhythm of speech, the least forced the most rhetorical and emphatic of all possible rhythms, combining, as it seems to me, opposite and, one wd. have thought, incompatible excellences, markedness of rhythm—that is rhythm's self—and naturalness of expression—for why, if it is forcible in prose to say "lashed: rod", am

I

I obliged to weaken this in verse, which ought to be stronger, not weaker, into "lashed birch-rod" or something?

My verse is less to be read than heard, as I have told you before; it is oratorical, that is the rhythm is so.'

There follows in the same letter a passage which shows the poet's intense conviction of the rightness of his methods and his sense of his own isolation, for if Bridges, a poet himself, could not understand, who could?

'I cannot think of altering anything. Why shd. I? I do not write for the public. You are my public and I hope to convert you.

You say you wd. not for any money read my poem again. Nevertheless I beg you will. Besides money, you know, there is love. . . .'

In his attitude to language he was also original. What he did not like about his contemporaries, the sort of thing he was reacting against, may be gathered from this passage. He has been saying that he avoids inversions 'because they weaken and because they destroy the earnestness or inearnestness of the utterance . . . they must not seem to be due to the verse: that is what is so enfeebling. . . .'

He continues:

'So also I cut myself off from the use of *ere, o'er, wellnigh, what time, say not*, (for *do not say*), because, though dignified, they neither belong to nor ever cd. arise from, or be the elevation of, ordinary modern speech. For it seems to me that the poetical language of an age shd. be the current language heightened, to any degree heightened and unlike itself, but not (I mean normally: passing freaks and graces are another thing) an obsolete one. This is Shakespeare's and Milton's practice and the want of it will be fatal to Tennyson's Idylls and plays, to Swinburne, and perhaps to Morris.'

That was written in 1879 but as early as 1864 he said 'a horrible thing has happened to me. I have begun to *doubt* Tennyson. . . .'

The reader will find archaic and obsolete words in Hopkins, some of them no doubt 'passing freaks and graces', but most used for their strength, their muscularity, and because they help to convey what he calls 'inscape' and 'instress'. Some idea of what he means by these concepts—of cardinal importance in understanding his poetry—can be seen in the following quotations, which may serve to illustrate not only what we are to understand by 'inscape' but also his admirable prose. The letters and journals are full of intelligence, feeling and wit; they are worth reading for their own sake and are an invaluable guide to his mind and art.

'All the world is full of inscape and chance left free to act falls into an order as well as purpose: looking out of my window I caught it in the random clods and broken heaps of snow made by the cast of a broom. The same of a path trenched by footsteps in ankledeep snow across the fields leading to Hodder wood through which we went to see the river. The sun was bright, the broken brambles and all boughs and banks limed and cloyed with white, the brook down the clough pulling its way by drops and by bubbles in turn under a shell of ice. . . . The ashtree growing in the corner of the garden was felled. It was lopped first: I heard the sound and looking out and seeing it maimed there came at that moment a great pang and I wished to die and not to see the inscapes of the world destroyed any more. . . .'

Journal 1873

'Poetry is speech framed for contemplation of the mind by the way of hearing or speech framed to be heard for its own sake even over and above its interest of meaning. Some matter and meaning is essential to it but only as an element necessary to support and employ the shape which is contemplated for its own sake. (Poetry is in fact speech only employed to carry the inscape of speech for the inscape's sake—and therefore the inscape must be dwelt on. Now if this can be done without repeating it *once* of the inscape will be enough for art and beauty and poetry but then at least the inscape must be understood as so standing by itself that it could be copied and repeated. If not/ repetition, *oftening, over and overing, aftering* of the inscape must take place in order to detach it into the mind and in this light poetry is speech which alters and oftens its inscape, speech couched in a repeating figure and verse is sound having a repeating figure.)

Journal *c.* 1873–1874

'No doubt my poetry errs on the side of oddness. I hope in time to have a more balanced and Miltonic style. But as air, melody is what strikes me most of all in music and design in painting, so design, pattern or what I am in the habit of calling 'inscape' is what I above all aim at in poetry. Now it is the virtue of design, pattern, or inscape to be distinctive and it is the vice of distinctiveness to become queer. This vice I cannot have escaped. . . .'

Letter to Bridges 1879

'. . . what I call *inscape*, that is species or individually-distinctive beauty of style. . . .'

Letter to Coventry Patmore 1886

Here is a poem, written in 1866 when he was twenty-two, which escaped the 'slaughter of the innocents' as he called the burning of his early work.

The Habit of Perfection

Elected Silence, sing to me
And beat upon my whorlèd ear,
Pipe me to pastures still and be
The music that I care to hear.

Shape nothing, lips; be lovely-dumb:
It is the shut, the curfew sent
From there where all surrenders come
Which only makes you eloquent.

Be shellèd, eyes, with double dark
And find the uncreated light:
This ruck and reel which you remark
Coils, keeps, and teases simple sight.

Palate, the hutch of tasty lust,
Desire not to be rinsed with wine:
The can must be so sweet, the crust
So fresh that come in fasts divine!

Nostrils, your careless breath that spend
Upon the stir and keep of pride,
What relish shall the censers send
Along the sanctuary side!

O feel-of-primrose hands, O feet
That want the yield of plushy sward,
But you shall walk the golden street
And you unhouse and house the Lord.

And, poverty, be thou the bride
And now the marriage feast begun,
And lily-coloured clothes provide
Your spouse not laboured-at nor spun.

The first thing to note about this poem is that it shows a complete
mastery of form: If his later work is 'queer', it is not because he couldn't
handle conventional rhythms, but because, to convey his vision, he had
to create new ones. The tunes of Tennyson and of the Pre-Raphaelites
are audible:

> ... the curfew sent
> From there where all surrenders come ...

and

> What relish shall the censers send
> Along the sanctuary side! ...

With the last two lines we can compare, from Tennyson's *Galahad*,

> Pure gleams the snowy altar cloth,
>   The silver vessels sparkle clean,
> The shrill bell rings, the censer swings,
>   And solemn chants resound between. . . .

Similarly, the last six lines recall the Pre-Raphaelite manner. But when we make the comparison, acknowledge the indebtedness—it is no more than we should expect in a young poet—we are aware of an extraordinary difference. We may feel a little dubious about 'relish': indeed there is a touch of hothouse lusciousness in Hopkins's poem; yet we feel at once that it is 'about' something. Here is a poet trying to interpret, to convey, to impose upon us, the whole of his feelings, sensations, thoughts, of his inner self and its relationship to the theme of the poem. We have only to listen to Hopkins' lines, and then to Tennyson's, to see how thin and conventional the latter's are. Not since Keats has there been a poet capable of conveying with such immediacy his sensual apprehension of the 'goings on of the universe'; and to do this he calls on the whole range of the language. For the purpose of poetry there is for him no part of the vocabulary of English that he calls common or unclean. The pastures, the whorled ear, lovely-dumb, we recognize as current literary procedure; but the hutch, rinsed, can, plushy, are not the sort of words Victorians expected to find in poetry. We see, too, a characteristic boldness in the manipulation of linguistic forms. 'Shut' is used as a noun; the elliptical compound adjective 'feel-of-primrose' is, in terms of contemporary taste, startling. For the 'ruck and reel' which 'coils keeps and teases' the nearest parallels are Shakespearian (cabin'd, cribb'd, confin'd, bound in); Shakespearian, too, is the doublet 'stir and keep' of pride. In the contrast between this rough harsh energy, and the lyric melody of 'pipe me to pastures still', the drama of the poet's choice between the secular world of the sense and the divine world of his vocation is embodied. Fifteen years later Hopkins was writing like this:

Inversnaid

> This darksome burn, horseback brown,
> His rollrock highroad, roaring down,
> In coop and in comb the fleece of his foam
> Flutes and low to the lake falls home.
>
> A windpuff-bonnet of fáwn-fróth
> Turns and twindles over the broth

Of a pool so pitchblack, féll-frówing,
It rounds and rounds Despair to drowning.

Degged with dew, dappled with dew
Are the groins of the brase that the brook treads through,
Wiry heathpacks, flitches of fern,
And the beadbonny ash that sits over the burn.

What would the world be, once bereft
Of wet and of wildness? Let them be left,
O let them be left, wildness and wet;
Long live the weeds and the wilderness yet.

I quote this poem because its theme is clearly related to the Romantic-Victorian tradition of 'nature poetry'—'I come from haunts of coot and hern'. A scene, a landscape, is evoked; the wild, 'unspoilt', untouched by human hand, is celebrated, its value proclaimed: every post-Wordsorthian bosom returns an echo to

Long live the weeds and the wilderness. . . .

Yet it is unlike the usual run of Victorian verse. This poem expresses a common but not a conventional experience; it is, to use the poet's favourite term, full of inscape, 'the sweet especial rural scene'.

The burn is brown because its waters are in flood and tinged with peat. Darksome is formed like gladsome: a coinage, but the poet is using a standard suffix. Why horseback? Most horses are brown, and this odd adjectival usage together with the rhythm of the line helps to evoke the galloping swaying movement of the rounded brown waves of water. 'Rollrock' conveys the burn's power, 'coop' the constriction of the water in pools and eddies, 'comb' the way in which it flows between stones and boulders which stick up like teeth and divide the fleece of foam, and also perhaps it points a resemblance to little ridges of foam like cocks' combs. Flutes *is* an oddity, but it sounds right, is associated with frills, and makes the right dramatic contrast to 'low to the lake falls home' which with its extra length (we have to stress both 'falls' and 'Home') and long vowels images the calm final glide into peaceful waters. If we think of the number of words beginning with fl which give the sense of sudden movement—flash, fling, flap, flounce, fluke and so on, we can explain our feeling of rightness. Compare Pope:

Flaunts and goes down an unregarded thing . . .

Hopkins puts stress-marks on fáwn-fróth and féll-frówning to remind the reader (he knew from experience with his correspondents that this was necessary) that each line is carried by four stresses. A windpuff-bonnet is a hatshaped clump of foam so light it might be blown away by the wind. 'Twindles' seems to twist and dwindle; 'broth' pictures the dark boiling thickness of the flood waters—Brown Windsor, perhaps. Hopkins writes 'pitchblack' without the hyphen because we are to feel the two elements as one—and we have only to think for a moment of the structure of this common adjective to see that when he coins rollrock, windpuff, beadbonny he is using a device quite normal in English. 'Fell' means ruthless and destructive, and these lines say that the hypnotic swirling circular motion of the water in the pool might draw the desperate to suicide but in fact draws the poet's despair to drowning—it is destroyed by his delight in the prospect of the burn. 'Degged' is a dialect word for sprinkled; 'dappled' unites dabbled with piedness, and the rocks on the surface of the curving braes are associated with the groins which support vaults. 'Treads' is a strange word to use of water but 'treads through' images the stream's resistless march, reinforced by the heavy alliteration and echoed in the drum-beat rhythm of this line, with its extra stressed syllable, giving a kind of bass 'pom, pom' at the end. 'Wiry' and 'flitches' (meaning ragged bunches) carry on the feeling of unkempt strength in the landscape, relieved by the pretty rowan ash comfortably 'sitting' by the brook side.

The last stanza is a clear, pure, touching appeal. To take away wildness would bereave the world. 'Long live' habitually acclaims the king, the established and reputable institutions of society. The poet uses it to hail what is outside society because of its specialness, its inscape, whose value consists in what makes it itself, unique, different from everything else in the universe. The poem is not Wordsworthian—Hopkins is a devout Catholic; it is not a tract on the therapeutic virtues of the unspoilt countryside. We might get nearer its essence if we think of the Psalmist (though the poem is not on that scale): 'The Heavens declare the glory of God, and the firmament showeth his handiwork'; or of Hopkins' own lines in his poem *Spring*

> What is all this juice and all this joy?
> A strain of the earth's sweet being in the beginning
> In Eden garden.

The sonnet, *Ribblesdale*, is about man dominating nature, destroying inscape, so that we cannot guess 'the beauty been', but the poem contains no easy condemnations. Hopkins wrote many sonnets, and brought new life to the form, for its balance of statement and comment, conflict and resolution, suited many of his themes, and its strictness excited his technical interests.

RIBBLESDALE

Earth, sweet Earth, sweet landscape, with leavès throng
And louchèd low grass, heaven that dost appeal
To, with no tongue to plead, no heart to feel;
That canst but only be, but dost that long—
Thou canst but be, but that thou well dost; strong
Thy plea with him who dealt, nay does now deal
Thy lovely dale down thus and thus bids reel
Thy river, and o'er gives all to rack or wrong.

And what is Earth's eye, tongue, or heart else, where
Else, but in dear and dogged man?—Ah, the heir
To his own selfbent so bound, so tied to his turn,
To thriftless reave both our rich round world bare
And none reck of world after, this bids wear
Earth brows of such care, care and dear concern.

The sweet landscape can only be, can only exist, but it has existed for
long, it endures, it exists well. The words could not be simpler: Earth
is well—'He saw that it was good'. Of 'throng' the poet says: 'I mean
it as an adjective as we use it here in Lancashire', and 'louched' he says
is 'a coinage of mine and is to mean much the same as slouched,
slouching'. The earth appeals to heaven through the fact of its existence,
by merely being, for, unlike man, it has no emotions and no language.
It is interesting to see how Hopkins makes us feel intensely towards
this sweet existence without such conventional devices as personification, without the pathetic fallacy. Theological disciplines are behind
all this: the categories of creation are distinguished, and to the MS.
there is prefixed a quotation from St. Paul: 'For the earnest expectation
of the creation waiteth for the revealing of the sons of God. For the
creation was subject to vanity, not of its own will, but by reason of
him who subjected it'. Hopkins was not a 'vain half-believer in a casual
creed'; he has a solid scaffolding to work from. The dumb creation's
being appeals to man as well as to heaven, but man is deaf, intent on
destroying, 'dealing down', the valley; he acted thus in the past and is
still so acting.

Yet earth's eye, tongue and heart are in man and nowhere else, in
man who is dogged—obstinately determined in his course of action—
but still dear. (It is a priest speaking.) He is the heir to earth's beauty,
but he is so enslaved by his own desires, so bound to his turn of mind,
that he plunders the world which is ours—it belongs to the poet and
those who share his feelings as well as to the makers of industrial

Lancashire—and no one cares what the world will be like when he has finished with it. This it is which makes earth seem so sad.

If we read the sonnet aloud—and Hopkins as we have seen, always insisted that his verse was meant to be heard—the odd syntax, so characteristic of this poet, seems to fall into place, and such constructions as 'heaven that dost appeal to' come easily to the ear and hence to the mind. There is an intricate interplay of the long 'e' sound, throughout the octet: sweet, leaves, appeal, plead, feel, be, deal, reel; and 'appeal' coming at the end of the line and being, to use the poet's own term, 'rove over' to its preposition, makes of the phrase, as we say it, a kind of gesture, as if we first saw the upflung arms and then understood their meaning. Most of the 'queerness' in Hopkins' best verse is the result of his straining to shape some run of feeling; and, after all, he had precedents enough in English poetry, though not in the sort of poetry his contemporaries most admired:

> Yet, good faith, Leontes,
> I love thee not a jar o' the clock behind
> What lady she her lord. . . .

We accept 'strong thy plea with him who dealt. . . .' and 'heaven that dost appeal to . . .' is no more difficult. Hopkins is working, as always, with the grain of the language.

The poem contains eleven disyllables—all the other words are monosyllables—and this is one of the reasons for its great strength. The varied word-order forces on our attention the weight and meaning of each in itself simple word, and alliteration and repetition hammer that meaning home. Note especially the whole down-moving image of destruction in the last three lines of the octet. There are indeed 'excellencies higher than clearness at a first reading'.

As a further example of such excellencies which Hopkins took so much trouble to explain to his correspondents, let us take his poem on Henry Purcell.

Henry Purcell

The poet wishes well to the divine genius of Purcell and praises him that, whereas other musicians have given utterance to the moods of man's mind, he has beyond that, uttered in notes the very make and species of man as created both in him and in all men generally.

> Have fair fallen, O fair, fair have fallen, so dear
> To me, so arch-especial a spirit as heaves in Henry Purcell,
> An age is now since passed, since parted; with the reversal
> Of the outward sentence low lays him, listed to a heresy here.

Not mood in him nor meaning, proud fire or sacred fear,
Or love, or pity, or all that sweet notes not his might nursle:
It is the forgèd feature finds me; it is the rehearsal
Of own, of abrúpt sélf there so thrusts on, so throngs the ear.

Let him oh! with his air of angels then lift me, lay me! only I'll
Have an eye to the sakes of him, quaint moonmarks, to his pelted
                                                    plumage under
Wings: so some great stormfowl, whenever he has walked his while.

The thunder-purple seabeach, plumèd purple-of-thunder,
If a wuthering of his palmy snow-pinions scatter a colossal smile
Off him, but meaning motion fans fresh our wits with wonder.

Hopkins is the best commentator on his own work. Here are some of the things he has to say about this poem.

'The sonnet on Purcell means this: 1–4 Purcell is not damned for being a Protestant, because I love his genius. 5–8 And that not so much for gifts he shares, even though it shd. be in higher measure, with other musicians as for his own individuality. 9–14 So that while he is aiming only at impressing me his hearer with the meaning in hand I am looking out meanwhile for his specific, his individual markings and mottlings, "the sakes of him". It is as when a bird thinking only of soaring spreads its wings: a beholder may happen then to have his attention drawn by the act to the plumage displayed. In particular, the first lines mean: May Purcell, O may he have died a good death and that soul which I love so much and which breathes and stirs so unmistakeably in his works have parted from the body and passed away, centuries since though I frame the wish, in peace with God! so that the heavy condemnation under which he outwardly or nominally lay for being out of the true Church may in consequence of his good intentions have been reserved. "Low lays him" is merely "lays him low" that is/strikes him heavily, weights upon him. . . . "Listed" . . . is! "enlisted". "Sakes" is hazardous: about that point I was more bent on saying my say than on being understood in it. . . . I meant "fair fall" to mean *fair (fortune be) fall*. . . .'

and again:

'The sestet of the Purcell sonnet is not so clearly worked out as I could wish. The thought is that as the sea-bird opening his wings with a whiff of wind in your face means the whir of the motion, but also unaware gives you a whiff of knowledge about his plumage, the markings of which stamps his species, that he does not mean, so Purcell, seemingly intent only on the thought or feeling he is to express or call out, incidentally lets you remark the individualising marks of his own genius.

'*Sake* is a word I find it convenient to use. . . . It is the *sake* of "for the sake of", *forsake, namesake, keepsake,* I mean by it the being a thing by virtue of which especially it has this being abroad ... as for a voice and echo clearness ... for a man genius, great achievements, amiability and so on. In this case it is ... distinctive quality of genius'.

Some readers may feel uneasy about the archaic 'nursle' meaning to foster; and think it sticks awkwardly out, and wonder why the poet should deliberately have chosen, in a sonnet, to rhyme to Purcell. Many more will be shocked at Hopkins thinking Purcell may be damned for being a heretic; but both the tight-rope rhyming and the theology are part of the 'sakes' of the poet, and I cannot think they spoil what he called 'one of my very best pieces'. What he here says of Purcell, 'the abrupt self there so thrusts on, so throngs the ear' well fits his own verse. It is fascinating to hear the romantic Swinburnian pulse (which he could command as well as anyone when he needed it)

Not mood in him nor meaning, proud fire or sacred fear

turn 'abruptly' to the dramatic force of

It is the forgèd feature finds me; ...

How apt and exact is the simple 'finds'! So often what is striking in Hopkins is not the oddness, but the ordinariness of his diction. There is an enormous amplitude about the stormfowl 'walking his while the thunder-purple seabeach, plumèd purple-of-thunder', a great image of the creative power of the music. Has anyone better described the experience art gives us than to say it 'fans fresh our wits with wonder'? In 1885 Hopkins wrote, in a letter to Alexander Baillie:

'The melancholy I have all my life been subject to has become of late years not indeed more intense in its fits but rather more distributed, constant, and crippling. One the lightest but a very inconvenient form of it, is daily anxiety about work to be done, which makes me break off or never finish all that lies outside that work ... when I am at the worst, though my judgment is never affected, my state is much like madness. I see no ground for thinking I ever get over it or ever succeed in doing anything that is not forced on me to do of any consequence.'

This melancholy is expressed in the so-called 'terrible' sonnets, in which the poet strives to reconcile his dark conviction of spiritual sterility with his faith. The sonnet we conclude with was written in 1889, the year of the poet's death. It is preceded by a quotation from Jeremiah, XII, i: 'Righteous art thou, O Lord, when I plead with thee: yet let me talk with thee of thy judgements: Wherefore doth the way of the wicked prosper?'

> Thou art indeed just, Lord, if I contend
> With thee; but, sir, so what I plead is just.
> Why do sinners' ways prosper? and why must
> Disappointment all I endeavour end?
>   Wert thou my enemy, O thou my friend,
> How wouldst thou worse, I wonder, than thou dost
> Defeat, thwart me? Oh, the sots and thralls of lust
> Do in spare hours more thrive than I that spend,
> Sir, life upon thy cause. See, banks and brakes
> Now, leavèd how thick! lacèd they are again
> With fretty chervil, look, and fresh wind shakes
> Them; birds build—but not I build; no, but strain,
> Times eunuch, and not breed one work that wakes.
> Mine, O thou Lord of life, send my roots rain.

The poem is a prayer. The two quatrains paraphrase, expand and dramatize the prophet's lament; the tercets evoke the bountiful life of nature's spring, and contrast it with the poet's sterility. The metaphor of roots and rain in the last line unites poet with nature: he, too, is one of God's creatures who needs mercy as the plants need rain.

Hopkins said of the sonnet form: 'if one does not know nor avail oneself of the opportunities which it affords it is a pedantic encumbrance and not an advantage.' He also said that because of differences in language 'The English sonnet is ... in comparison with the Italian short, light, tripping and trifling'. Therefore 'the best sonnets show various devices successfully employed to make up for the short-comings'. One such device we have already noted in *Ribblesdale* is the use of monosyllables, apparent also in this poem, which must, as he wrote to Bridges, 'be read *adagio molto* and with great stress'. The parenthetic invocations, Lord, Sir, O thou my friend, slow up our reading and we have to pause after the questions, to which there is no answer. The lines are full of d's, th's and t's which the rhythm and meaning force us to enunciate; one cannot say 'art indeed just' quickly, and the effort and stress of pronunciation images the strife of the poet's prayer, of 'the war within' made all the more personal and poignant by his addressing God as 'sir'. Alliteration and internal rhyming add to the sense of heaviness and struggle:

> How wouldst thou worse, I wonder, than thou dost
> Defeat, thwart me?

'Strain' is indeed the key word of the poem. Strain bursts the bonds of form: it forces the run-over lines, as in 'if I contend/With thee', and 'Why must/Disappointment all I endeavour end'. The first quatrain is self-contained, but the second treads over into the first line of the sestet: 'Do in spare hours more thrive than I that spend/Sir, life upon thy cause'. Changes in normal word order and ellipses insist that we attend slowly to the meaning as in 'birds build—but not I build'. We feel an acute and agonizing awareness of time passing, conveyed by the way the word 'life' is emphasized. There is a dramatic antithesis between 'spare hours' and 'life'; a contrast between the brutal dull-vowelled 'sots and thralls of lust' and 'thrive' 'I' and 'life'. The word seems to surge out of the line because between the verb 'spend' and its object is interpolated the vocative 'Sir' which interrupts with an imploring cry what we expect to be a run-on line. The leaves, the 'laced fretty chervil' (cow-parsley) the fresh wind and the building birds evoke with condensed and touching power the inscape of spring, whence we plunge to the abrupt and horrifying 'Time's eunuch'. In poems like this Hopkins raises the 'romantic agony' to the level of tragedy.

7

THE TWENTIETH CENTURY

Thomas Hardy (1840–1928) published his first collection of verse, *Wessex Poems*, in 1898, and it was followed, at regular intervals, by six others. The complete poems make a bulky volume, and span a period extending from the sixties of the last century to the twenties of the present one. Hardy was not an innovator; he adapted forms ready to his hand. His writing was often clumsy, his themes repetitive, his ironies and satires of circumstance too pat, his home-made pessimism provincial, his gloom unrelieved, his taste uncertain. These are the stock objections to his work, and they do not lack foundation. Yet the reader who plods through the collected poems, who *reads* the poet as he expected to be read, depressed though he may become at the high illegitimacy rate in Wessex, and the way things always turn out wrong, will be in the end rewarded. He will come across many very good poems. Hardy always tried to be strictly honest, and to tell the truth, and to say exactly what he meant. Consider for example, this poem:

A MAN
(In memory of H. of M.)

In Casterbridge there stood a noble pile,
Wrought with pilaster, bay, and balustrade

In tactful times when shrewd Eliza swayed.—
   On burgher, squire, and clown
It smiled the long street down for near a mile.

But evil days beset that domicile;
The stately beauties of its roof and wall
Passed into sordid hands. Condemned to fall
   Were cornice, quoin, and cove,
And all that art had wove in antique style.

Among the hired dismantlers entered there
One till this moment of his task untold.
When charged therewith he gazed, and answered bold:
   'Be needy I or no,
I will not help lay low a house so fair!

Hunger is hard. But since the terms be such—
No wage, or labour stained with the disgrace
Of wrecking what our age cannot replace
   To save its tasteless soul—
I'll do without your dole. Life is not much!'

Dismissed with sneers he packed his tools and went,
And wandered workless; for it seemed unwise
To close with one who dared to criticise
   And carp on points of taste:
Rude men should work where placed, and be content.

Years whiled. He aged, sank, sickened; and was not:
And it was said, 'A man intractable
And curst is gone.' None sighed to hear his knell,
   None sought his churchyard-place;
His name, his rugged face, were soon forgot.

The stones of that fair hall lie far and wide,
And but a few recall its ancient mould;
Yet when I pass the spot I long to hold
   As truth what fancy saith:
'His protest lives where deathless things abide!'

There is a kind of calm, plain objectivity about this piece. Here, the
poet seems to be saying, is exactly what happened. Hardy accepts and
exploits traditional rhythms, and has constructed an ingeniously
wrought and rhymed stanza, a kind of verbal equivalent of the highly
wrought building whose destruction the poem laments. He seems to

be content with stock phrases—noble pile, stately beauties, fair hall, ancient mould. He is sometimes clumsy: 'domicile' is used, surely, just for the rhyme. Some of the diction is archaic: 'clown', 'wove' for 'woven', 'curst'. The poem might be likened to a piece of furniture or a façade, or a tombstone, fashioned by a provincial craftsman familiar with old pattern books but unable to compass the polish and sophistication of the metropolitan professional. It would be easy to adduce, from the *Collected Poems*, examples of ugly phrasing, clumsy rhythms and bathos ('where the worms waggle under the grass'); easy, but irrelevant, because in the good poems they don't matter, and in the best poems they don't exist. (The poet himself has warned us not 'to scrutinize the tool-marks, and be blind to the building'.) *A Man* stands solid, and says exactly what Hardy would have it say. Poet and workman share a technical interest in the building, for Hardy was trained as an architect, and worked for some time as a church restorer, and they both know the quality of 'cornice, quoin and cove' in a way the layman cannot. The building is conjured up partly by these technical details, partly by the agreeably ironic placing of

> In tactful times when shrewd Eliza swayed

(the wit is refreshingly different from the usual solemn Victorian glamour) and especially by the phrase 'It smiled the long street down'. The verb does more work than many lines of conventional descriptive writing.

The second stanza introduces the theme—familiar enough to us—of beauty destroyed by the 'sordid hands' of the developer. Hardy rarely succeeded in writing believable dialogue of serious intent, as may be seen from his novels, and we don't imagine that any workman really would say 'Be needy I or no'; yet the speech convinces, because it is carried by the rhythmic weight of the stanza, and because the words have a dramatically appropriate gnarled brevity. 'What our age cannot replace/to save its tasteless soul' has the force of the poet's own feelings behind it. 'Dole' is an unfortunate word: it does not mean 'wages' and seems forced by the need of a rhyme. The pettiness and timidity of provincial society punishes the worker, and his tragedy is summed up in one potent line:

> Years whiled. He aged, sank, sickened; and was not: . . .

The use of 'whiled' as a verb, another piece of Hardyesque roughage, here seems to be completely successful; there is in it something of the feeling of Hopkins for the nature of English. The conclusion illustrates what one means when one speaks of Hardy's peculiar honesty. The orotund last line is the conventional, the expected, Victorian conclusion to an anecdote such as this, and is in its phrasing and rhythm a kind of parody of the appropriate sentiment a sympathetic reader in search of comfort should feel. But Hardy does not believe in it, and he implies as much; but he does not produce a crude contradiction and he does not sneer: his response is more tender and more subtle. 'I long to hold as truth what fancy saith . . .' The longing is there; but the regrettable truth—his truth—must be told.

He was not always grim. Here are his church-restorer's reflections on *The Levelled Churchyard*:

THE LEVELLED CHURCHYARD

'O Passenger, pray list and catch
    Our sighs and piteous groans,
Half stifled in this jumbled patch
    Of wrenched memorial stones!

'We late-lamented, resting here,
    Are mixed to human jam,
And each to each exclaims in fear,
    "I know not which I am!"

'The wicked people have annexed
    The verses on the good;
A roaring drunkard sports the text
    Teetotal Tommy should!

'Where we are huddled none can trace,
    And if our names remain,
They pave some path or porch or place
    Where we have never lain!

'Here's not a modest maiden elf
    But dreads the final Trumpet
Lest half of her should rise herself,
    And half some sturdy strumpet!

'From restorations of Thy fane
    From smoothings of Thy sward,
From zealous Churchmen's pick and plane
    Deliver us O Lord! Amen!'

And here is his satirical note on a doting young mother:

THE NEW TOY

> She cannot leave it alone,
>   The new toy;
> She pats it, smooths it, rights it, to show it's her own,
> As the other train-passengers muse on its temper and tone
>   Till she draws from it cries of annoy:—
> She feigns to appear as if thinking it nothing so rare
>   Or worthy of pride, to achieve
> This wonder a child, though with reason the rest of them there
>   May so be inclined to believe.

One of the reasons for Hardy's continuing influence is, I think, that he uses verse to say whatever he is thinking or feeling at the moment. All sorts of topics, public or private anecdotes, narratives, grave or trivial, are dealt with. He needs no great theme, no bardic pose, no singing robes; and this suits contemporary taste.

Here is one tiny, beautifully formed lyric on the theme of past and present. The last two lines mean that we did not at the time realize the blessings of that day, *le vert paradis* of childhood, for we were thinking of other things, other places, other people, of ambitions, of the future. The grown man can place the moment in time, in relation to his mature experience, and truly value it.

THE SELF UNSEEING

> Here is the ancient floor,
> Footworn and hollowed and thin,
> Here was the former door
> Where the dead feet walked in.
>
> She sat here in her chair,
> Smiling into the fire;
> He who played stood there,
> Bowing it higher and higher.
>
> Childlike, I danced in a dream;
> Blessings emblazoned that day;
> Everything glowed with a gleam;
> Yet we were looking away!

At Castle Botrel also enshrines a memory.

> As I drive to the junction of lane and highway,
>   And the drizzle bedrenches the waggonette,

I look behind at the fading byway,
   And see on its slope, now glistening wet,
     Distinctly yet

Myself and a girlish form benighted
   In dry March weather. We climb the road
Beside a chaise. We had just alighted
   To ease the sturdy pony's load
     When he sighed and slowed.

What we did as we climbed, and what we talked of,
   Matters not much, nor to what it led,—
Something that life will not be balked of
   Without rude reason till hope is dead,
     And feeling fled.

It filled but a minute. But was there ever
   A time of such quality, since or before,
In that hill's story? To one mind never,
   Though it has been climbed, foot-swift, foot-sore,
     By thousands more.

Primaeval rocks form the road's steep border,
   And much have they faced there, first and last,
Of the transitory in Earth's long order;
   But what they record in colour and cast
     Is—that we two passed.

And to me, though Time's unflinching rigour,
   In mindless rote, has ruled from sight
The substance now, one phantom figure
   Remains on the slope, as when that night
     Saw us alight.

I look and see it there, shrinking, shrinking,
   I look back at it amid the rain
For the very last time; for my sand is sinking,
   And I shall traverse old love's domain
     Never again.

The voice quietly speaks through the formal stanza pattern, with its double rhymes and dying fall. Here, as always in the best of Hardy's verse, we are not jostled or perturbed by harshness or straining. The swaying rhythm carries and strengthens the sober pedestrian description and narrative:

We climb the road
Beside a chaise. We had just alighted
To ease the sturdy pony's load . . .

accommodates the quickening feeling of

It filled but a minute. But was there ever
A time of such quality, since or before,
In that hill's story?

and reinforces the strain of

Though it has been climbed, foot-swift, foot-sore . . .

The next stanza expresses the contrast—a Hardyean theme so
favourite that it often becomes a cliché—between the permanent unfeel-
ing earth and the brief lives that crawl upon its surface. Here there is a
noble pathos. Time and the universe are, as always in Hardy, 'mindless',
their revolutions a 'rote', a mechanical repetition; man is powerless to
affect the world, yet his love, transitory as life though it may be, has a
value that transcends the mechanism, and produces within itself a
'time' of 'quality'.

Hardy continues the tradition of English nature poetry. The next
poem has something of Clare about it, his directness and lack of
sentimentality.

AN UNKINDLY MAY

A Shepherd stands by a gate in a white smock-frock:
He holds the gate ajar, intently counting his flock.
The sour spring wind is blurting boisterous-wise,
And bears on it dirty clouds across the skies;
Plantation timbers creak like rusty cranes,
And pigeons and rooks, dishevelled by late rains,
Are like gaunt vultures, sodden and unkempt,
And song-birds do not end what they attempt:
The buds have tried to open, but quite failing,
Have pinched themselves together in their quailing.
The sun frowns whitely in eye-trying flaps
Through passing cloud-holes, mimicking audible taps.
'Nature, you're not commendable today!'
I think. 'Better tomorrow!' she seems to say.
That shepherd still stands in that white smock-frock
Unnoting all things save the counting his flock.

The lines about the 'sun's eye-trying flaps' 'Mimicking audible taps', harsh and clumsy, are strikingly exact. We see between 'frowns' and 'whitely', the suddenness of the transition from dark to light, a suddenness conveyed too by 'flaps', as its brevity is by the taps: 'eye-trying' gives us a kind of climax of discomfort, and the whole poem is a tiny example of Hardy's honesty. The tone of the mood is placed, its scale precisely indicated by the rueful 'Nature you're not commendable today'; the scene is framed between two glimpses of the indifferent, preoccupied shepherd, too busy to be concerned about the weather. He has work to do, and no time to indulge in 'sensibility'.

Hardy has always been accused of teaching a 'pessimistic philosophy'; but he denied having a consistent 'view' and described his poems as a 'series of fugitive impressions which I have never tried to co-ordinate'. In the *Apology* prefixed to *Late Lyrics and Earlier*, and dated 1922, he speaks of '"attempts to explain or excuse the presence of evil and the incongruity of penalising the irresponsible'; of the 'exploration of reality ... with an eye to the best consummation possible: briefly, evolutionary meliorism'. He hopes that 'whether the human and kindred animal races survive till the exhaustion or destruction of the globe, or whether these races perish and are succeeded by others before that conclusion comes, pain to all upon it, tongued or dumb, shall be kept down to a minimum by loving-kindness, operating through scientific knowledge, and actuated by the modicum of free will conjecturally possessed by organic life when the mighty necessitating forces—unconscious or other—that have "the balancing of the clouds", happen to be in equilibrium, which may or may not be often.' His thoughts 'run uncomfortably on the precarious prospects of English verse at the present day ... And a forward conjecture scarcely permits the hope of a better time, unless men's tendencies should change. So indeed of all art, literature, and "high thinking" nowadays. Whether owing to the barbarising of taste in the younger minds by the dark madness of the late war, the unabashed cultivation of selfishness in all classes, the plethoric growth of knowledge simultaneously with the stunting of wisdom "a degrading thirst after outrageous stimulation" (to quote Wordsworth again) or from any other cause, we seem threatened with a new Dark Age.' The parallel with some of the ideas in Wordsworth's Preface is striking; its truth or relevance must be left to the reader's own taste and experience.

We end with three poems. The first, a sonnet from his last volume, *Winter Words*, is a reflection on 'these disordered years of a prematurely afflicted century,' and in it we see that Hardy still retained the nineteenth-century confidence to make, as Wordsworth did, or Hopkins in *Tom's Garland*, a public statement.

WE ARE GETTING TO THE END

We are getting to the end of visioning
The impossible within this universe,
Such as that better whiles may follow worse,
And that our race may mend by reasoning.
We know that even as larks in cages sing
Unthoughtful of deliverance from the curse
That holds them lifelong in a latticed hearse,
We ply spasmodically our pleasuring.
And that when nations set them to lay waste
Their neighbours' heritage by foot and horse,
And hack their pleasant plains in festering seams,
They may again,—not warely, or from taste,
But tickled mad by some demonic force.—
Yes. We are getting to the end of dreams!

Of the next two poems the first, published in 1922, is dated 1867; the
second, from *Winter Words* was written in 1926.

A YOUNG MAN'S EXHORTATION

Call off your eyes from care
By some determined deftness; put forth joys
Dear as excess without the core that cloys,
And charm life's lourings fair.

Exalt and crown the hour
That girdles us, and fill it full with glee,
Blind glee, excelling ought could ever be
Were heedfulness in power.

Send up such touching strains
That limitless recruits from Fancy's pack
Shall rush upon your tongue, and tender back
All that your soul contains.

For what do we know best?
That a fresh love-leaf crumpled soon will dry,
And that men moment after moment die,
Of all scope dispossest.

If I have seen one thing
It is the passing preciousness of dreams;
That aspects are within us; and who seems
Most kingly is the King.

HE NEVER EXPECTED MUCH
OR
A CONSIDERATION ON MY EIGHTY-SIXTH BIRTHDAY

Well, World, you have kept faith with me,
    Kept faith with me;
Upon the whole you have proved to be
    Much as you said you were.
Since as a child I used to lie
Upon the leaze and watch the sky,
Never, I own, expected I
    That life would all be fair.

'Twas then you said, and since have said,
    Times since have said,
In that mysterious voice you shed
    From clouds and hills around:
'Many have loved me desperately,
Many with smooth serenity,
While some have shown contempt of me
    Till they dropped underground.

'I do not promise overmuch,
    Child; overmuch;
Just neutral tinted haps and such',
    Wise warning for your credit's sake.
Which I for one failed not to take,
And hence could stem such strain and ache
    As each year might assign.

Verse written at the turn of the century perpetuates minor romantic and Victorian modes, and an example, elegantly elegiac, is *The Shropshire Lad* by A. E. Housman (1859–1936) published in 1896, and followed, in 1922 by *Last Poems*. For all its accomplishment, his verse is limited in scope, tending to monotony. But it may well stand for what poetry before the first world war was considered to be.

Here is No. XXXIX from *The Shropshire Lad* containing the familiar Housman mixture of nature, nostalgia and self-pity, neatly and melodically deployed.

'Tis time, I think, by Wenlock town
    The golden bloom should blow;
The hawthorn sprinkled up and down
    Should charge the land with snow.

Spring will not wait the loiterer's time
  Who keeps so long away;
So others wear the broom and climb
  The hedgerows heaped with may.

O tarnish late on Wenlock Edge,
  Gold that I never see;
Lie long, high snowdrifts in the hedge
  That will not shower on me.

And here is No. LXI

The vane on Hughley steeple
  Veers bright, a far-known sign,
And there lie Hughley people,
  And there lie friends of mine;
Tall in their midst the tower
  Divides the shade and sun,
And the clock strikes the hour
  And tells the time to none.

To south the headstones cluster,
  The sunny mounds lie thick;
The dead are more in muster
  At Hughley than the quick.
North, for a soon-told number,
  Chill graves the sexton delves,
And steeple-shadowed slumber
  The slayers of themselves.

To north, to south, lie parted,
  With Hughley tower above,
The kind, the single-hearted,
  The lads I used to love.
And, south or north, 'tis only
  A choice of friends one knows,
And I shall ne'er be lonely
  Asleep with these or those.

The reader might compare this poem with one of Hardy's using a
similar tune. It is called *The Farm-Woman's Winter*.

I

If seasons all were summers,
And leaves would never fall,
And hopping casement-comers

Were foodless not at all,
And fragile folk might be here
That white winds bid depart;
Then one I used to see here
Would warm my wasted heart!

II

One frail, who, bravely tilling
Long hours in gripping gusts,
Was mastered by their chilling,
And now his ploughshare rusts.
So savage winter catches
The breath of limber things,
And what I love he snatches,
And what I love not, brings.

Both poems, we may say, are about death; both poems are simple; both consist of plain statements we can easily grasp and both depend for much of their effect on incantation; but the rhythm of Hardy's verse is stronger and more compelling. The 'if' clauses lead us through the first stanza to the climactic 'Then . . .' and there is here a kind of dramatic unity, for the 'ifs' are all impossibilities: leaves do fall, birds starve in winter, the swallow does migrate; so, death is inevitable; and this individual death, so poignant to the speaker, is felt as part of the changeless impersonal universal rhythm, is related to the whole of human experience. The sentiments in Housman lie log-like side by side, and some of them are nonsense. It is not, for example, true to say that the clock tells the time to none. One gathers that suicides are buried to the north of the church. Is this so? Or does he mean that the sunny side has filled up first? Are the graves here really chillier than anywhere else? And why should the number be soon told? Because it is easy to count the rest of the population? But is the whole village going to die out? I shall welcome death, the poet is saying, so that I can lie in the churchyard among my friends, who are all dead too; and the ones I am fondest of, he seems to imply, are the suicides. We concur, in comfortable nostalgic gloom, responding to the picturesque-village ingredients; but inspection reveals only banality. The poem's structure dissolves.

The strength of Hardy's poem remains. It is interesting to see how all the imagery comes from the life of the imagined speaker. We can know her feeding the birds, watching the seasons, gazing at the rusting ploughshare. 'Limber things' unites the birds and all young hopeful life, beautiful and fragile: 'bravely tilling' sums up a life's struggle with the soil. One is reminded of the stoic resignation of Johnson. Death is a fact, but life must be endured.

Rudyard Kipling (1865–1936), journalist, short-story writer, novelist, was the most widely read poet of the early years of the century. Of his crude minatory drum-beats, which echoed round the Empire, this sample should suffice. It is the *Dedication* to the *Barrack-Room Ballads*.

> Beyond the path of the outmost sun through utter darkness hurled—
> Farther than ever comet flared or vagrant star-dust swirled—
> Live such as fought and sailed and ruled and loved and made our world.
> They are purged of pride because they died; they know the worth of their bays;
> They sit at wine with the Maidens Nine and the Gods of the Elder Days—
> It is their will to serve or be still as fitteth Our Father's praise.
> 'Tis theirs to sweep through the ringing deep where Azrael's outposts are,
> Or buffet a path through the Pit's red wrath when God goes out to war,
> Or hang with the reckless Seraphim on the rein of a red-maned star.
> They take their mirth in the joy of the Earth—they dare not grieve for her pain.
> They know of toil and the end of toil; they know God's Law is plain;
> So they whistle the Devil to make them sport who know that Sin is vain.
> And oft-time cometh our wise Lord God, master of every trade,
> And tells them tales of his daily toil, of Edens newly made,
> And they rise to their feet as He passes by, gentlemen unafraid.
> To those who are cleansed of base Desire, Sorrow and Lust and Shame—
> Gods for they knew the hearts of men, men for they stooped to Fame—
> Borne on the breath that men call Death, my brother's spirit came.
> He scarce had need to doff his pride or slough the dross of earth—
> E'en as he trod that day to God so walked he from his birth,
> In simpleness and gentleness and honour and clean mirth.
> So cup to lip in fellowship they gave him welcome high
> And made him place at the banquet board—The Strong Men ranged thereby,
> Who had done his work and held his peace and had no fear to die.
> Beyond the loom of the last lone star, through open darkness hurled,
> Further than rebel comet dared or hiving star-swarm swirled,
> Sits he with those that praise our God for that they served His world.

It was Mr. Eliot's opinion that Kipling's verse had some affinity with that of Dryden.

In this poem, by Walter de la Mare (1873–1956) we hear 'the horns of elf-land', the last strains of the romantic faery tradition. Like all his best verse, it has a melting charm, a skilfully modulated tune.

ARABIA

Far are the shades of Arabia,
    Where the Princes ride at noon,
'Mid the verdurous vales and thickets,
    Under the ghost of the moon;
And so dark is that vaulted purple,
    Flowers in the forest rise
And toss into blossom 'gainst the phantom stars
    Pale in the noonday skies.

Sweet is the music of Arabia
    In my heart, when out of dreams
I still in the thin clear mirk of dawn
    Descry her gliding streams;
Hear her strange lutes on the green banks
    Ring loud with the grief and delight
Of the dim-silked dark-haired Musicians
    In the brooding silence of night.

They haunt me—her lutes and her forests;
    No beauty on earth I see
But shadowed with that dream recalls
    Her loveliness to me:
Still eyes look coldly upon me
    Cold voices whisper and say—
'He is crazed with the spell of far Arabia,
    They have stolen his wits away.'

Of the poets who were killed in the 1914–18 war, two of the most interesting are Edward Thomas and Wilfred Owen, in whose work we may detect a movement away from the clichés and stale rhythms of the period.

Thomas (1878–1918) earned his living as a literary journalist. In 1914 he became friends with the American poet, Robert Frost, then living in England, who encouraged him, arguing that poetry should and could be made from the rhythms and vocabulary of common speech; and between this date and his death Thomas put into verse his intense love of the English countryside and its life. The horror of war, his constitutional melancholy, and the knowledge that what he so dearly loved was passing, that his poems were elegies for a dying culture, united to give his best work a profound intensity.

First a poem called *The Owl*.

Downhill I came, hungry, and yet not starved;
Cold, yet had heat within me that was proof
Against the North wind; tired, yet so that rest
Had seemed the sweetest thing under a roof.

Then at the inn I had food, fire, and rest,
Knowing how hungry, cold and tired was I.
All of the night was quite barred out except
An owl's cry, a most melancholy cry

Shaken out long and clear upon the hill,
No merry note, nor cause of merriment,
But one telling me plain what I escaped
And others could not, that night, as in I went.

And salted was my food, and my repose,
Salted and sobered, too, by the bird's voice
Speaking for all who lay under the stars,
Soldiers and poor, unable to rejoice.

One of Thomas' greatest pleasures was walking, and the opening of the poem communicates the pleasure of the end of a day's walk—the last lap downhill, tired, hungry and cold, but safe in the knowledge that food and comfort await at the inn, where 'all of the night was quite barred out'. The poet's 'heart luxuriates' in this situation; his enjoyment comes from his consciousness of, from 'knowing', the contrast between the room at the inn and the night. Then comes the owl's cry, and the way the second stanza runs on to the third echoes the length of the bird's note. The verb used for the cry, 'shaken out', is surprising, but apt; we hear the note tremble. The immediate literary associations with 'When icicles hang by the wall' are contradicted by 'No merry note, nor cause of merriment', and this brings in the contrast between the poet who has escaped privation, and others who are not so fortunate. 'Salted', another surprising verb, implies seasoning—food without salt is insipid, so the poet's enjoyment of the inn is heightened by the contrast with the cold world outside. But tears are salt, and his mood is sobered by a sudden serious sympathy with all who cannot escape what he has escaped, what, indeed, he has never really been in danger of, those for whom hunger and fatigue and cold are not pleasurable enhancements of a long country walk, but the normal concomitants of existence, what Hardy called 'earth's ingrained conditions'. The piece says more about war than many poems dealing directly with the subject.

The next poem *Gone, Gone Again* is a spare, disciplined lyric, expressing Thomas' melancholy, and showing his characteristic simplicity and clarity of diction, marked by a muted rhythm that follows the flow of the feeling.

> Gone, gone again
> May, June July,
> And August gone,
> Again gone by.
>
> Not memorable
> Save that I saw them go,
> As past the empty quays
> The rivers flow.
>
> And now again,
> In the harvest rain,
> The Blenheim oranges
> Fall grubby from the trees
>
> As when I was young—
> And when the lost one was here—
> And when the war began
> To turn young men to dung.
>
> Look at the old house
> Outmoded, dignified
> Dark and untenanted,
> With grass growing instead
>
> Of the footsteps of life
> The friendliness, the strife;
> In its beds have lain
> Youth, love, age, and pain:
>
> I am something like that:
> Only I am not dead,
> Still breathing and interested
> In the house that is not dark:—
>
> I am something like that:
> Not one pane to reflect the sun,
> For the schoolboys to throw at—
> They have broken every one.

Last, *The Path*, a piece of blank verse, which the reader can compare with earlier passages, to see how Thomas moulds a traditional form to suit his needs. The minute observation, the loving description of natural appearances, we have met before: the mysterious symbolic ending of the path, the rejection of the legendary and the fancied, are the poet's own.

> Running along a bank, a parapet
> That saves from the precipitous wood below
> The level road, there is a path. It serves
> Children for looking down the long smooth steep
> Between the legs of beech and yew, to where
> A fallen tree checks the sight: while men and women
> Content themselves with the road and what they see
> Over the bank, and what the children tell.
> The path, winding like silver, trickles on,
> Bordered and even invaded by thinnest moss
> That tries to cover roots and crumbling chalk
> With gold, olive, and emerald, but in vain.
> The children wear it. They have flattened the bank
> On top, and silvered it between the moss
> With the current of their feet, year after year.
> But the road is houseless, and leads not to school.
> To see a child is rare there, and the eye
> Has but the road, the wood that overhangs
> And underyawns it, and the path that looks
> As if it led on to some legendary
> Or fancied place where men have wished to go
> And stay; till, sudden, it ends where the wood ends.

The quietness, the small scale, of Thomas' work should not conceal from us the fact that he is a serious, original poet, who found a tune to fit his feelings, a tune not to be heard in his predecessors. From this point of view the contrast between his work and Housman's is striking.

Wilfred Owen was born in 1893, enlisted in 1915 and was killed in action on November 4th, 1918. He had from his youth regarded poetry as his vocation; his whole serious interests were concentrated on acquiring the technique, the craft, of verse. In 1915 he wrote: '*To be able* to write as *I know how to*, study is necessary: a period of study, then of intercourse with kindred spirits, then of isolation. My heart is ready, but my brain unprepared, and my hand untrained'. His early work is Keatsian, romantic, derivative. He felt his solitude keenly: 'I am alone among unseen voices'. The experience of war brought him sudden maturity.

'Owen' writes Edmund Blunden in the memoir prefixed to his edition of the poems, 'was preparing himself to the last moment in experience, observation, and composition for a volume of poems, to strike at the conscience of England in regard to the continuance of the war . . .' Part of the preface to this volume is as follows:

> 'This book is not about heroes. English poetry is not yet fit to speak of them.
>
> Nor is it about deeds, or lands, nor anything about glory, honour, might, majesty, dominion, or power, except War.
>
> Above all I am not concerned with Poetry.
> My subject is War, and the pity of War.
> The poetry is in the pity.'

This poem *Futility* shows us something of Owen's temper and technique.

> Move him into the sun—
> Gently its touch awoke him once,
> At home, whispering of fields unsown.
> Always it woke him, even in France,
> Until this morning and this snow.
> If anything might rouse him now
> The kind old sun will know.
>
> Think how it wakes the seeds,—
> Woke, once, the clays of a cold star.
> Are limbs, so dear-achieved, are sides,
> Full-nerved—still warm—too hard to stir?
> Was it for this clay grew tall?
> —O what made fatuous sunbeams toil
> To break earth's sleep at all?

The mingling of half-rhymes with whole ones enhances the poem's quiet despair. From the 'fields unsown' we gather that the dead soldier was a farmer, a man who lived by the sun, and whose natural habits persisted 'even in France'. The next stanza relates the sun, the source of life, to the whole of evolution, and leads us to the unanswerable question 'Was it for this the clay grew tall?' in which the word 'clay' unites the Darwinian scientific picture with the creation of Adam in Genesis. Owen achieves in work like this, an extraordinary detachment; the poem is tragic, not topical; it is truly a poem of pity, not of propaganda.

It may seem cold-blooded to discuss Owen's technique, but, as we have seen, it was a subject he was himself deeply interested in, and we are thinking of him as a poet, not as one of war's innumerable sacrifices; as a poet who was trying to come to terms with himself and his age. Here is a sonnet *Hospital Barge at Cérisy*, in which we can see the new manner and the old in the same poem.

Budging the sluggard ripples of the Somme
A barge round old Cérisy slowly slewed.
Softly her engines down the current screwed
And chuckled in her, with contented hum.
Till fairy tinklings struck their crooning dumb,
And waters rumpling at the stern subdued.
The lock-gate took her bulging amplitude.
Gently into the gurgling lock she swum.

One reading by that sunset raised his eyes
To watch her lessening westward quietly:
Till, as she neared the bend, her funnel screamed.
And that long lamentation made him wise
How into Avalon in agony
Kings passed in the dark barge which Merlin dreamed.

The barge 'budges' the ripples as she 'slews' round, her engines 'screwing' and 'chuckling'. Owen attempts to reproduce the noise, the bulk, the effort of the clumsy craft. But the water running into the lock, audible as the barge stops, is called 'fairy tinklings', a feeble phrase, further enfeebled by the mechanical ticking over of the plodding iambics. It is true that the irony of the poem consists in the contrast between the peaceful scene, the drably useful barge, and its load of wounded men, an irony pointed by the 'scream' of the funnel which disturbs the reading poet and leads to the deliberately 'beautiful' and reminiscent Tennysonian conclusion. I take it that the poet's 'wise' may either imply that the wounded soldiers are heroes as noble as King Arthur and his knights, or that the wars of romance were in truth as sordid as modern ones. The new vocabulary is fitted into a perfectly conventional framework, whose rhythm is constricted by the sonnet form, in which there are few cadences we have not heard many times before. In *Miners* or *Futility* the rhythm is living, and an inextricable part of the sense, as it is here:

THE SEND-OFF

Down the close, darkening lanes they sang their way
To the siding shed,
And lined the train with faces grimly gay.

Their breasts were stuck all white with wreath and spray
As men's are, dead.
Dull porters watched them, and a casual tramp
Stood staring hard,

Sorry to miss them from the upland camp.
Then, unmoved, signals nodded and a lamp
Winked to the guard.
So secretly, like wrongs hushed-up, they went.
They were not ours:
We never heard to which front these were sent.

Nor there if they yet mock what women meant
Who gave them flowers.

Shall they return to beatings of great bells
In wild train-loads?
A few, a few, too few for drum and yells,
May creep back, silent, to village wells
Up half-known roads.

At about this time D. H. Lawrence (1885–1930) began writing
poetry, first using traditional forms and then free verse. 'Do not ask'
he wrote of it, 'for the qualities of the unfading timeless gems'; and
again: 'I think ... that my rhythms fit my mood pretty well. I have
always tried to get an emotion out in its own course, without altering
it. ... Often I don't bring it off, sometimes I do. ...' He said that
Edward Marsh liked Flecker's *Golden Journey to Samarkand* (which 'only
took place on paper') because 'it fits your habituated ear ... Well, I
don't write for your ear. This is the constant war, I reckon, between
new expression and the habituated, mechanical transmitters and
receivers of the human constitution'. This last remark is one that all
readers of modern poetry, or, indeed, of any poetry unfamiliar to them
should always keep in mind. Here are three poems, which may be
judged in the light of Lawrence's remarks.

SORROW

Why does the thin grey strand
Floating up from the forgotten
Cigarette between my fingers,
Why does it trouble me?

Ah, you will understand;
When I carried my mother downstairs,
A few times only, at the beginning
Of her soft-foot malady,

I should find, for a reprimand
To my gaiety, a few long grey hairs
On the breast of my coat; and one by one
I watched them float up the dark chimney.

The poem has a delicate, unobtrusive rhyme scheme. The first line of each stanza rhymes fully, and so do the second lines of the second and third. The last line of each is lightly rhymed. How should we scan it? Such a question is irrelevant. Here, again, is Lawrence himself. 'I think I read my poetry more by length than by stress—as a matter of movements in space than footsteps hitting the earth. . . .' 'I hate an on-foot method of reading . . . it is the hidden emotional pattern that makes the poetry, not the obvious form. . . .'

HUMMING-BIRD

I can imagine, in some otherworld
Primeval-dumb, far back
In that most awful stillness, that only gasped and hummed,
Humming-birds raced down the avenues.

Before anything had a soul,
While life was a heave of Matter, half inanimate,
This little bit chipped off in brilliance
And went whizzing through the slow, vast, succulent stems.

I believe there were no flowers then,
In the world where the humming-bird flashed ahead of creation.
I believe he pierced the slow vegetable veins with his long beak.
Probably he was big
As mosses, and little lizards, they say, were once big.
Probably he was a jabbing, terrifying monster.
We look at him through the wrong end of the long telescope of
Time,
Luckily for us.

MYSTIC

They call all experience of the senses *mystic*, when the experience
is considered.
So an apple becomes *mystic* when I taste in it
the summer and the snows, the wild welter of earth
and the insistence of the sun.
All of which things I can surely taste in a good apple.
Though some apples taste preponderantly of water, wet and sour,
and some of too much sun, brackish sweet
like lagoon-water, that has been too much sunned.
If I say I taste these things in an apple, I am called *mystic*, which
means a liar.

K

> The only way to eat an apple is to hog it down like a pig
> and taste nothing
> that is real.
> But if I eat an apple, I like to eat it with all my senses awake.
> Hogging it down like a pig I call the feeding of corpses.

The dangers of such writing are vagueness and flaccidity: its virtue, freedom from the echoes of the past which at this period dominated so much English verse.

T. S. Eliot (1888–1965) published his first volume of verse, *Prufrock and Other Observations* in 1917. Encouraged and tutored by his fellow countryman and fellow exile, Ezra Pound, then well launched on his long career of literary pedagogy and experiment (he was later to 'bring Yeats up to date'), Eliot quickly achieved an important, and later a commanding, position in metropolitan literary society. His first public impact was made by *Poems 1919–1925* containing the *Waste Land*, which horrified the academic and delighted the young.

In one of the collection of essays published in honour of the poet's seventieth birthday, Harold Nicholson wrote: 'He tuned my ear to new rhythms'. He thus tuned all our ears. What were these new rhythms?

To call poems 'Observations', as Eliot does in the title of his first volume, implies a certain coolness and detachment on the part of the poet, an unromantic, possibly a satirical intention. Here to begin with, is one of the smallest of these pieces. It is called *The Readers of the Boston Evening Transcript*.

> The readers of *The Boston Evening Transcript*
> Sway in the wind like a field of ripe corn.
> When evening quickens faintly in the street,
> Wakening the appetites of life in some
> And to others bringing the *Boston Evening Transcript*,
> I mount the steps and ring the bell, turning
> Wearily, as one would turn to nod good-bye to Rochefoucauld,
> If the street were time and he at the end of the street,
> And I say, 'Cousin Harriet, here is the *Boston Evening Transcript*.'

This is obviously different from anything we have read yet, and is a poem which is still capable of arousing, in many readers, feelings of discomfort. 'It is not,' they say, 'poetry'. There is nothing odd about the metre of the first line, which is blank verse with a weak or feminine ending: compare 'The slings and arrows of outrageous fortune'. But a mild shock is administered by the appearance of the prosaic evening newspaper, in a poem apparently serious, for the next line, with its romantic nature image, is immediately recognizable as 'poetry'. This line has ten syllables and five stresses, so arranged as to echo the swaying of the corn. (Remember what happens to ripe corn: 'there is a reaper whose name is death'.) To oppose banal and poetic elements, to create tension between them, to force the reader's mind to admit disparate feelings, is part of Eliot's poetic technique. The next two lines are strictly metrical. We respond, as the romantics have taught us to do, to the evening coming to life—though this is no 'Evening of Extraordinary Splendour and Beauty'. It quickens but faintly, and in the street, too. (For this sort of contrast between the romantic, the literary, the stock response to nature, and the harsh urban reality compare the first line of Baudelaire's *Crépuscule du Soir*:

Voici le soir charmant, ami du criminel. . . .)

As we would expect, or at least hope, nature wakens appetites of life; but only in some—in the poet, no doubt, and his sympathetic reader: to others it brings the newspaper, which is now, we see, becoming a symbol of urban futility, of modern civilization. Humanity is divided into two groups: the spiritually quick and the spiritually dead. The poet, the observer, is also urban man, returning home, enmeshed in the 'same blank bald routine', and he bears, though he does not read, the symbolic journal. Here the movement of the verse changes, and we are no longer conscious of the five beats in a line. The wearied gesture spans two lines, bringing the adverb heavily and emphatically at the start of the second, and then the long perspective of the street turns into a perspective of time, a surrealist, nightmare effect. At the end stands La Rochefoucauld, symbol of world-weariness and cynicism, a man who, as Eliot said of Machiavelli, 'blew the gaff on human nature'. (He may also stand for aristocratic culture.) The poet is on familiar terms with the duke, since he nods to him, and the sympathetic reader is supposed to know him too, since this is the sort of thing 'one' would do. He also establishes the poet as a writer in the European tradition—they are both in the same street, and *Les Maximes* are observations. It is interesting to hear how the rhythm, after the regular plod of 'I mount the steps and ring the bell', changes with 'turning wearily', and seems to embody the drawn-out languid gesture. The penultimate line has five hard stresses, spaced, at the beginning and end, in triplets, stretching out the length of the time-street. The deliberately bathetic last line has six stresses. Cousin Harriet we feel, is one of the readers, not one of the quickened. I read this line with six stresses, but I cannot help feeling that it needs a Boston voice to do it justice. Indeed, the poem was recognized in Harvard as expressing standard college attitudes to the citizens of Boston; behind it there appears to be a family joke to which Eliot has given a kind of universality.

This tiny, and if you will, insignificant poem, extends the range of verse. It admits wit; it expects the reader to be alert and awake to nuances of rhythm and expression; it plays off the cadences of tradition against the rhythms of speech and the tone of the speaking voice; it makes potent symbolic use of ordinary everyday objects.

Perhaps the poet is not so ironic about himself as he is about the swayers in the wind. Perhaps he breathes a small degree of self-approval which, by implication, he invites the reader (who also knows, or pretends he knows, who La Rochefoucauld is and what he stands for) to share. There is a hint of coldness towards those who are not among the elect. But the new rhythm is audible, a fresh disciplined tune is at the service of a new freedom, and this is what is important.

Here is the longest of the observations in this volume, the title poem, *The Love Song of J. Alfred Prufrock*. Eliot's dramatic monologues are said to owe something to Browning's. It is true that Pound's earlier work in this mode exhibits Browningesque quirks and rhythms, but in Eliot there is no trace of the characteristic sound of the older poet.

> Let us go then, you and I,
> When the evening is spread out against the sky
> Like a patient etherised upon a table;
> Let us go, through certain half-deserted streets,
> The muttering retreats
> Of restless nights in one-night cheap hotels
> And sawdust restaurants with oyster shells:
> Streets that follow like a tedious argument
> Of insidious intent
> To lead you to an overwhelming question. . . .
> Oh, do not ask, 'What is it?'
> Let us go and make our visit.
>
> In the room the women come and go
> Talking of Michelangelo.
>
> The yellow fog that rubs its back upon the window-panes,
> The yellow smoke that rubs its muzzle on the window-panes
> Licked its tongue into the corners of the evening,
> Lingered upon the pools that stand in drains,
> Let fall upon its back the soot that falls from chimneys,
> Slipped by the terrace, made a sudden leap,
> And seeing that it was a soft October night,
> Curled once about the house, and fell asleep.

And indeed there will be time
For the yellow smoke that slides along the street
Rubbing its back upon the window panes;
There will be time, there will be time
To prepare a face to meet the faces that you meet;
There will be time to murder and create,
And time for all the works and days of hands
That lift and drop a question on your plate;
Time for you and time for me,
And time yet for a hundred indecisions,
And for a hundred visions and revisions,
Before the taking of a toast and tea.

In the room the women come and go
Talking of Michelangelo.

And indeed there will be time
To wonder, 'Do I dare?' and, 'Do I dare?'
Time to turn back and descend the stair,
With a bald spot in the middle of my hair—
(They will say: 'How his hair is growing thin!')
My morning coat, my collar mounting firmly to the chin,

My necktie rich and modest, but asserted by a simple pin—
(They will say: 'But how his arms and legs are thin!')
Do I dare
Disturb the universe?
In a minute there is time
For decisions and revisions which a minute will reverse.

For I have known them all already, known them all—
Have known the evenings, mornings, afternoons,
I have measured out my life with coffee spoons;
I know the voices dying with a dying fall
Beneath the music from a farther room.
     So how should I presume?

And I have known the eyes already, known them all—
The eyes that fix you in a formulated phrase,
And when I am formulated, sprawling on a pin,
When I am pinned and wriggling on the wall,
Then how should I begin
To spit out all the butt-ends of my days and ways?
     And how should I presume?

And I have known the arms already, known them all—
Arms that are braceleted and white and bare,
(But in the lamplight, downed with light brown hair!)
Is it perfume from a dress
That makes me so digress?
Arms that lie along a table, or wrap about a shawl.
   And should I then presume?
   And how should I begin?

      .   .   .   .   .

Shall I say, I have gone at dusk through narrow streets
And watched the smoke that rises from the pipes
Of lonely men in shirt-sleeves, leaning out of windows? . . .

I should have been a pair of ragged claws
Scuttling across the floors of silent seas.

      .   .   .   .   .

And the afternoon, the evening, sleeps so peacefully!
Smoothed by long fingers,
Asleep . . . tired . . . or it malingers,
Stretched on the floor, here beside you and me.
Should I, after tea and cakes and ices,
Have the strength to force the moment to its crisis?
But though I have wept and fasted, wept and prayed,
Though I have seen my head (grown slightly bald) brought in upon
                                     a platter,
I am no prophet—and here's no great matter;
I have seen the moment of my greatness flicker
And I have seen the eternal Footman hold my coat and snicker,
And in short, I was afraid.

And would it have been worth it, after all,
After the cups, the marmalade, the tea,
Among the porcelain, among some talk of you and me,
Would it have been worth while,
To have bitten off the matter with a smile,
To have squeezed the universe into a ball
To roll it toward some overwhelming question,
To say: 'I am Lazarus, come from the dead,
Come back to tell you all, I shall tell you all'—
If one, settling a pillow by her head,
Should say: 'That is not what I meant at all.
That is not it, at all.'

And would it have been worth it, after all,
Would it have been worth while,

After the sunsets and the dooryards and the sprinkled streets,
After the novels, after the teacups, after the skirts that trail along
the floor—
And this, and so much more?—
It is impossible to say just what I mean!
But as if a magic lantern threw the nerves in patterns on a screen:
Would it have been worth while
If one, settling a pillow or throwing off a shawl,
And turning towards the window, should say:
'That is not it at all,
That is not what I meant, at all.'

. . . . . .

No! I am not Prince Hamlet, nor was meant to be;
Am an attendant lord, one that will do
To swell a progress, start a scene or two,
Advise the prince; no doubt, an easy tool,
Deferential, glad to be of use,
Politic, cautious, and meticulous;
Full of high sentence, but a bit obtuse;
At times, indeed, almost ridiculous—
Almost, at times, the Fool.

I grow old. . . . I grow old. . . .
I shall wear the bottoms of my trousers rolled.

Shall I part my hair behind? Do I dare to eat a peach?
I shall wear white flannel trousers, and walk upon the beach.
I have heard the mermaids singing, each to each.

I do not think that they will sing to me.

I have seen them riding seaward on the waves,
Combing the white hair of the waves blown back
When the wind blows the water white and black.

We have lingered in the chambers of the sea
By sea-girls wreathed with seaweed red and brown
Till human voices wake us, and we drown.

Few poets can have started forth so fully armed in so complete a steel
of technique as Eliot. The virtuosity of this piece is dazzling.

The rhythm of the opening is unanalysable in standard terms.
Certainly we must not 'scan' the first line as 'falling' or trochaic metre:
Lét us/gó then/yoú and/I. Rather we should feel two beats, on 'go',
and 'I'. The next line has three, on the first syllable of 'evening', on 'out',
and on 'sky'. The word-group 'where the evening' is a rhythmical
equivalent of 'let us go then'. On this scheme we would divide the

line: When the evening/is spread out a/gainst the sky. The 'read' effect, emphasizing 'spread out' nearly equally, and feeling a sub-stress on the second syllable of 'against', imposes itself on this scheme. In the next line there are again three main stresses, on 'patient' 'etherised' and 'table'; and because 'Like a patient' is the metrical equivalent of 'when the evening', 'etherised' is a sort of inversion, and hits us with the horrid hospital simile. (Note how the romantic evening is deflated, as in the *The Boston Evening Transcript* poem. Spread out—like a banner? No. Far from it.) The next line sounds more like what we are used to, and five beats are audible; but so are three, on 'go', 'half' and 'streets'. The rhythm is ambiguous, like J. Alfred's love. The next line carries two beats, and the following couplet is metrically orthodox, each line having ten syllables and five stresses, an orthodoxy which, while reassuring the ear, points the sordid unorthodoxly unpoetic content. In the next line I feel three main beats, on 'fóllow', 'tédious' and 'árgument'. 'Streets that fóllow' equals 'like a patient', and 'tedious argument' makes a pattern like 'patient etherised'. Back to two beats, and then a regular eleven syllable five stressed line. (What is the meaning of this pointless existence? The maze of city streets symbolizes Prufrock's puzzlement.) The final exasperated double rhymed couplet should be stressed:

> Óh, dó not ásk, 'What ís it?
> Lét us gó and máke our vísit.

This 'Let us go' should not sound like the first one.

I will not pursue the tedious argument, which is a crude attempt to show, first *why* the poem sounds different, and second, that Eliot is a master of original, calculated and subtle effects. This is not the sprung rhythm of Hopkins, nor Lawrence's free verse ('a bird with broad wings, lapsing and flying through the air'); it is a new tune, and strictly deliberated.

The trite couplet about the women stands for the party J. Alfred is on his way to, and the sort of elegant and futile milieu he moves in. (I feel there is more of Henry James than of Browning behind this poem.)

We are expected to do without elaborate transitions. The structure of the poem (its narrative element is negligible) consists in its pattern of images, related and contrasted. We are intended to follow the movements of a mind as it turns in spasms of feeling from one topic to the next, and formal rhetoric is abjured in the interests of truth to mental reality. Of course the poem has a structure, but it is not that of Satan's speeches, or of Pope's story about Sir Balaam.

The fog, like the streets, is both real and symbolic: it is a great yellow cat. Eliot does not say so; he makes the fog do cat-like things, and verbs carry us softly and inexorably along. We can note again how when the poet produces a 'correctly' sonorous line:

> Lingered upon the pools that stand in drains

he deflates it. The 'drains' are deliberately anticlimactic. The first three lines of this passage have three main stresses; the fifth carries five and then we have two regular ten syllabled rhymed lines separated by an alexandrine, so it is thereby stiffened towards the end by familiar rhythms.

Prufrock meditates on time: time for the fog, for the processes of nature; time for the mechanisms of social life, time for murder and creation. We are led by this beyond Prufrock himself to think of the time span of history since the Fall; and the classical 'works and days', and Michelangelo's Sistine Chapel ceiling both help us onwards. But everything ends in bathos. The plate, the toast, the tea stand for Prufrock's sterile life: he moves from the sordid to the silly. He can't make up his mind. Even if he had a vision, he would revise it. Time includes Prufrock; it includes everything—the whole universe, whose course he cannot contemplate modifying by any action of his, however insignificant.

The rhythm hammers harder in the next section. Three, then four consecutive rhymes, the repetition of 'Do I dare?', the imagined comments of the ladies, create a kind of comic hysteria beneath which there are heard faintly the drum-beats of fate. One of the units of rhythm which give the passage its characteristic flavour can be heard in its pure state in the four-stressed last line:

> For decísions and revísion which a mínute will revérse . . .

It is basically a heavy stress followed by three unstressed syllables. This group occurs frequently: 'fírmly to the chín', 'wónder do I dáre', 'mínute there is tíme'. These are the rhythms of popular music, of the *café concert*, strongly evident in the lilting opening of the next section, in which Prufrock, weighed down by a sense of his own insignificance, lyrically laments his life, misspent among trivialities. The movement of the verse adroitly follows the changing movements of his mind. The sad satiety of the first two lines is set to a jaunty tune, leads to the bitter 'I have measured out my life with coffee spoons', is followed by the exquisite cadence of the dying voices, and finishes with the overwhelming question. A detail is added to our knowledge of Prufrock's life—he goes to musical soirées where some of the audience talk through the music—and to the contents of his mind—he quotes *Twelfth Night*—and we, too, can turn wearily to nod to Duke Orsino. (Does it matter very much if we don't notice him?)

Then comes a more unpleasant thought. This society is intelligent; its members are witty, and make epigrams about each other: in a word, they observe. Mr. Eliot, as we have noted, does the same. Indeed, we are reading 'the formulated phrase' extended to a poem, and as we read we too observe, and what we see is precisely those wrigglings that Prufrock dreads exhibiting. His tormentors don't put their specimens in the killing bottle before adding them to their collections—that would spoil the fun. To one who has been, or who may be, treated so, change, conversion, is impossible. The language in this stanza is dramatically vigorous, especially the climactic 'To spit out all the butt-ends of my days and ways'.

The third stanza is sentimental. The ladies (to one of whom, we gather, our hero may be on his way to propose) with their white arms, their beauty, their shawls, their perfume, have enchanted him. Enchanted, but not blinded, for he, too is an 'eye', and the light brown hair is an original Prufrockian observation. Not all these arms are as white as their owners would have him believe.

Alain Fournier, writing about Laforgue, spoke of 'des vers, des bribes de phrases, qui étaient l'expression parfaite et poignante de quelque chose. . . .'—and this seems to me an excellent description of the effect of the next three lines. Prufrock is a man of sensibility; but what does he feel about? He embodies in this touching inadequate image (unlikely, he knows, to impress the owners of the eyes and the arms) what his creator called, in the fourth *Prelude*

> The notion of some infinitely gentle
> Infinitely suffering thing. . . .

For Prufrock, in his society, this is the only kind of positive statement possible. The first line, 'Shall I say . . .' is an alexandrine; as you read, mark the slightest of caesuras after 'gone'. The next is the regular blank verse plus trivial content we have noticed before, and the third falls into two halves, with two stresses in each, tied by the alliteration of 'leaning' and 'lonely', the line Eliot was to develop later in his plays.

The ragged claws bring in time again, and evolution. (The hair on those white arms may be relevant here.) Was it for this Prufrock grew tall? Better some humble primitive form of life, than humanity.

The afternoon, like the fog, is a sort of cat, which is stroked and sleeps on the floor, and like much else in the poem it is ambiguous—asleep, tired, or it malingers, only pretending fatigue. Then follows a splendid burst of rhetoric. The burlesque-sounding double rhyme, ices, crisis, enforces the comic tone, and also implies that, in this ambiance, nothing serious is possible. Prufrock proclaims his sufferings, indeed his martyrdom, but deflates the outburst by the wryly ironic parenthesis about his baldness. He is a John the Baptist, a harbinger, with nothing to announce, and can only await death who appears, appropriately enough in this setting, as the eternal Footman.

He has seen himself as St. John, and now he sees himself as Lazarus. To the theme of time are added the themes of redemption and immortality; and this stanza and the next turn on the difficulties of communication: 'It is impossible to say just what I mean.' Prufrock's difficulties were also his author's, whose efforts to 'purify the language of the tribe' were unremitting and lifelong. Images crowd: in appearance the random contents of a random mind, yet each related to the pattern of the poem. He dare not put his question, not so much through fear of a refusal, but because no one will understand him.

Now Prufrock resigns himself to his fate. He is doomed to be a minor character, at best Polonius, at worst the fool. The first line in this paragraph has, I think, five stresses, on 'No', 'not', 'Hamlet', 'nor' and 'meant'. There are two extra weak syllables, a kind of double feminine ending, making the line tail off and echo the speaker's indecision and despair. Then the verse tightens to regularity as he pictures his part in the drama of life. The rhythms here imitate those of late Shakespearian and Jacobean blank verse, and Eliot catches the movement exactly, its force, and easy enjambement—'one that will do/To start a progress . . .' The rhyme binds all together. 'Fool', the sad climax, is prepared for five lines before, where the sardonically emphatic 'tool' is left, as it were, hanging, while the busy, ludicrous, 'use', meticulous', 'obtuse', 'ridiculous' tick by, so the ear triumphantly accepts a final resolution in the last word of the passage.

The despairing Prufrock accepts his fate—'I grow old . . .' and decides to dress the part. Vanity remains. A new parting may conceal for a time the bald patch now only visible to those who, giggling, descend the stairs behind him. He doubts his digestion (peaches are associated with ladies, and eating fruit with the tree of knowledge, and therefore with asking questions) and he resolves to live beside the seaside. ('I'll purge and live cleanly as a gentleman should.') The beach brings in the mermaids, symbols of Prufrock's romantic youth, and of his poetic vision. He needs, and his creator needs, besides sawdust restaurants and toast and tea and sprinkled streets, something more potent. Walking on the beach he faces the sea, the source of life and symbol of death—it has already been in his mind. The reiterated perfect tense—'I have heard' 'I have seen' . . . emphasizes that this experience is irrevocably in the past. The mermaids, though beautiful—and Eliot shows in this passage that he can produce romantic incantation with the best—are ambiguous creatures: they enchant, but they destroy. We can only live under their spell by denying life (remember the Lotos eaters). Human voices have awakened Prufrock, and he is drowning in air; he can speak neither with mermaid nor with human, and whether he can survive is not clear. But we think so. The drowning is his final pathetic piece of self-pity.

One reason for the feeling of exhilaration which, in my experience, this poem never fails to generate, is its virtuosity. It is, apart from other claims on our attention, a triumphant exhibition of skill. There has, surely, been nothing so expertly agile since Pope.

Eliot wrote a number of poems in rhymed quatrains, several of them about a character called Sweeney, whom we may take to be *l'homme moyen sensuel*. Strictness of form, brevity, wit, qualities which at the same time permit reference to larger issues, make the point of these poems. The technical model is Gautier, and the difference in intention and tone between Eliot and his model may be seen if we compare

> Carmen est maigre. Un trait de bistre
> Cerne son œil de gitana. . . .

with

> Grishkin is nice: her Russian eye
> Is underlined for emphasis. . . .

Gautier intends his *femme fatale* to be taken seriously: not so Eliot.

Here is *Sweeney Erect*. The grim anecdote is introduced by a superb romantic evocation of the deserted Ariadne, as she might be painted in the high renaissance manner. We are invited to fill our minds with the heroic, with Theseus and Ariadne, Ulysses and Nausicaa, and the monster Polypheme, and then sink them suddenly to the sordid Sweeny *ménage*.

SWEENEY ERECT

> *And the trees about me,*
> *Let them be dry and leafless; let the rocks*
> *Groan with continual surges; and behind me*
> *Make all a desolation. Look, look, wenches!*

> Paint me a cavernous waste shore
> Cast in the unstilled Cyclades,
> Paint me the bold anfractuous rocks
> Faced by the snarled and yelping seas.

Display me Aeolus above
   Reviewing the insurgent gales
Which tangle Ariadne's hair
   And swell with haste the perjured sails.

Morning stirs the feet and hands
   (Nausicaa and Polypheme).
Gesture of orang-outang
   Rises from the sheets in steam.

This withered root of knots of hair
   Slitted below and gashed with eyes,
The oval O cropped out with teeth:
   The sickle motion from the thighs

Jackknifes upward at the knees
   Then straightens out from heel to hip
Pushing the framework of the bed
   And clawing at the pillow slip.

Sweeney addressed full length to shave
   Broadbottomed, pink from nape to base,
Knows the female temperament
   And wipes the suds around his face.

(The lengthened shadow of a man
   Is history, said Emerson
Who had not seen the silhouette
   Of Sweeney straddled in the sun.)

Tests the razor on his leg
   Waiting until the shriek subsides.
The epileptic on the bed
   Curves backward, clutching at her sides.

The ladies of the corridor
   Find themselves involved, disgraced,
Call witness to their principles
   And deprecate the lack of taste

Observing that hysteria
   Might easily be misunderstood;
Mrs. Turner intimates
   It does the house no sort of good.

> But Doris, towelled from the bath,
> Enters padding on broad feet,
> Bringing sal volatile
> And a glass of brandy neat.

The reader who has listened with care to *Prufrock* will be able to hear and respond to the changes of melody, of tone and of language which Eliot manipulates within his quatrains, and which form a main element in his poem's structure, moving from

> Paint me the bold anfractuous rocks
> Faced by the snarled and yelping seas.

where we are invited to enjoy the sonorous rhetorical flourish to

> Mrs. Turner intimates
> It does the house no sort of good.

which brings us back to the sordid present.

The stanza about Emerson and Sweeney is a hint of Eliot's decisive rejection of what is usually, and vaguely, known as the liberal tradition, a rejection which began at Harvard and became more marked with time. There is more than a tinge of inhumanity in this brilliant piece. We remember that it is written by the man who, inveighing in the name of eeclesiastical authority against 'the inner voice' wrote:

> 'The possessors of the inner voice ride ten in a compartment to a football match in Swansea, listening to the inner voice which breathes the eternal message of vanity, fear, and lust.'

The *Waste Land* is too long and too important a poem to be dealt with here in detail, and it hardly admits of quotation, so closely are the sections welded together. One of the difficulties of discussing modern poetry lies here. It is possible to talk about bits of the *Moral Essays* or the *Prelude* because these works are discursive, and move from topic to topic. So, one can see that the authors of *Macflecknoe* and *Tirocinium*, though separated by a hundred years, are working in the same tradition. But now there is no tradition, and each important work tends to be a law unto itself. We quote the last two paragraphs of the first section, *The Burial of the Dead*, and the whole of the fourth, *Death by Water*. Remember, as you read, the poet's own description in *The Use of Poetry*, of the 'auditory imagination'. It is, he says, 'the feeling for syllable and rhythm, penetrating far below the conscious levels of thought and feeling, invigorating every word. It . . . fuses the old and obliterated and the trite, the current and the new and surprising, the most ancient and the most civilized mentality'.

Madame Sosostris, famous clairvoyante,
Had a bad cold, nevertheless
Is known to be the wisest woman in Europe,
With a wicked pack of cards. Here, said she
Is your card, the drowned Phoenician Sailor,
(Those are pearls that were his eyes. Look!)
Here is Belladonna, the Lady of the Rocks,
The lady of situations.
Here is the man with three staves, and here the Wheel,
And here is the one-eyed merchant, and this card,
Which is blank, is something he carries on his back.
Which I am forbidden to see. I do not find
The Hanged Man. Fear death by water.
I see crowds of people, walking round in a ring.
Thank you. If you see dear Mrs. Equitone,
Tell her I bring the horoscope myself:
One must be so careful these days.

Unreal City,
Under the brown fog of a winter dawn,
A crowd flowed over London Bridge, so many,
I had not thought death had undone so many.
Sighs, short and infrequent were exhaled,
And each man fixed his eyes before his feet.
Flowed up the hill and down King William Street,
To where Saint Mary Woolnoth kept the hours
With a dead sound on the final stroke of nine.
There I saw one I knew, and stopped him, crying; 'Stetson'!
'You who were with me in the shipes at Mylae!
'That corpse you planted last year in your garden,
'Has it begun to sprout? Will it bloom this year?
'Or has the sudden frost disturbed its bed?
'Oh keep the Dog far hence, that's friend to men,
'Or with his nails he'll dig it up again!
'You! hypocrite lecteur!—mon semblable—mon frère!'

The cards, from the Tarot pack used in fortune-telling, stand for fate, and also for the futility of a society which, lacking religion, relapses into superstition. Beneath the luxury of the city lies barbarism. The whole passage presages doom, and its very vagueness both comments ironically on the studied ambiguities of fortune tellers, and intensifies the horror. The incident is brilliantly realized in itself, and also leads us to look beyond it to the theme of the whole poem—the Waste Land. The crowds of people walking round in a ring are at exercise in the 'shades of the prison house'. The passage is written in a very free blank verse, that follows the rhythms and intonations of the speaking voice. Madam Sosostris' client quotes *The Tempest* to himself (there is something of Prufrock in him) in conscious defensive irony, but his irony doesn't protect him: 'Look!' he says, in fascinated horror. And the slick detached professionalism of the fortune-teller comes through. She does not allow a bad cold to interfere with her pursuit of profit; the laconic 'Thank you' acknowledges her fee, and she briskly deals with the next business on her mind. She will bring the horoscope herself because she fears prosecution. The verse leads us to hear all the overtones of feeling present in this scene, to construct the characters; and this dramatic quality is one of the remarkable things about this poem. Its images are actions.

So in the next section. The crowd flow to work like so many automata, their tramping feet echoed by the repeated 'many' and by the regularity of the couplet

> And each man fixed his eyes before his feet.
> Flowed up the hill and down King William Street . . .

whose rhyme seems to emphasize the inescapable monotony of their existence. Their numbers appal the poet, and he sees them as an army of the dead, and the city whose presence he so powerfully evokes as 'unreal'. Note how the 'private' image, about the church clock ('a phenomenon which I have often noticed') reinforces the theme of death. And then the poet hails a friend, whose name has American associations. He is accused of crime; there follows a quotation from the dirge in the *White Devil*, and the last line of the prefatory poem in *Les Fleurs du Mal*. Any reader who lets the images work on him must feel the power and horror of these lines, whether or not he can make out precisely what is going on. They exemplify one type of the 'obscurity' so often complained of in 'modern' poetry. The allusion to the ships at Mylae makes the poet and Stetson and the crowd represent human-ity, and the moment on London Bridge extend back into all of human history. Respectable suburban season-ticket holders cultivate their gardens. Stetson has planted a corpse in his. Death and violence are everywhere. The mad Cornelia in Webster's play calls for 'the robin redbreast and the wren' to cover with leaves and flowers 'the friendless bodies of unburied men'; and ends

> But keep the wolf far hence, that's foe to man,
> For with his nails he'll dig them up again.

Eliot turns the wolf into a dog, and foe into friend. What are we to make of this? That the dog is man's friend is a sentiment with which the plodders over London Bridge might be expected to concur. Are we to conclude that the dog is superior to man? Again, the plodders might agree. Or is this just another 'twist of the knife'? Should we worry about all this, or allow it to 'penetrate' (if it will) 'below the conscious levels of thought and feeling'? The force of the last line is clear. The reader, who is one with the plodders and with Stetson, is hypocritical—his virtue, his civilization is a pretence. But the poet is so too, and he hails the reader as his brother. As Flamineo says, when he has heard Cornelia's song:

> I have a strange thing in me, to the which
> I cannot give a name, without it be
> Compassion.

Next, section IV of the poem, entitled *Death By Water*.

> Phlebas the Phoenician, a fortnight dead
> Forgot the cry of gulls, and the deep sea swell
> And the profit and loss.
>   A current under sea
> Picked his bones in whispers. As he rose and fell
> He passed the stages of his age and youth
> Entering the whirlpool.
>   Gentile or Jew
> O you who turn the wheel and look to windward,
> Remember Phlebas, who was once handsome and tall as you.

This is an epitaph, and has the brevity, dignity and pathos suited to 'lapidary inscriptions'. The rhythm of the lines seems to follow the movement of the sea, and to convey its mystery, silence and sinister power. We are not aware of any standard metrical pattern, and yet to call this verse 'free' would seem to be a misnomer. It does not, for example, sound at all like Lawrence's. Its structure is based on balanced phrases, tied together by alliteration and rhyme, stiffened by two lines, the fifth and the seventh, of blank verse, and concluded with a line of six stresses and two pauses (I think one must feel a pause, however, slight, after 'once' as well as at the comma). Each section of the poem starts in mid-line; a four-square pattern would destroy its symbolic fluidity. The first two and half lines tell us Phlebas is dead. He forgets the beauty of the sea, and its menace, and he forgets his merchandise. The prosaic 'profit and loss' makes us apprehend him as a real person, and establishes him as a merchant, and therefore related to other figures in the poem, and to the city. Each half of the first line has two, each half of the second three stresses, and the concluding phrase of the section, two. The next sentence seems, as the drowned man drifts, and his life runs backwards, to enact his silent dissolution, in rhythms which show the influence of Jacobean verse. The sixth line balances two pairs of stresses. In the last section 'Gentile or Jew' involves us all in Phlebas' fate; turning the wheel and looking to windward (to ward off future danger) symbolizes man's struggle in life, a struggle in which beauty and strength are of no avail.

Miss Helen Gardiner, in her book *The Art of T. S. Eliot*, says that *Ash Wednesday* is 'the most obscure (of Eliot's poems) . . . the most at the mercy of the temperament and beliefs of the individual reader'. In so far as 'we receive but what we give' this must be true of all poetry, all art; yet the form of a work imposes a pattern on our responses, though it is not always easy to give a rational account of the process. Language, as we have seen, and as Eliot often complained, is an impure medium, but, as Sweeny remarked, in reply to a misunderstanding, 'I gotta use words when I talk to you.' What we can say is that in *Ash Wednesday*, as in much of the work that followed it, incantatory rhythm plays a larger part, and that the symbols are obscurer and vaguer—at least they appear so to the reader. They may be precise enough for the poet, and they are certainly potent. Of the beauty and accomplishment of this work there can be no doubt. The poem we quote is the second of the series.

> Lady, three white leopards sat under a juniper tree
> In the cool of the day, having fed to satiety
> On my legs my heart my liver and that which had been contained
> In the hollow round of my skull. And God said
> Shall these bones live? shall these
> Bones live? And that which had been contained
> In the bones (which were already dry) said chirping:
> Because of the goodness of this Lady
> And because of her loveliness, and because
> She honours the Virgin in meditation,
> We shine with brightness. And I who am here dissembled
> Proffer my deeds to oblivion, and my love
> To the posterity of the desert and the fruit of the gourd.
> It is this which recovers
> My guts the strings of my eyes and the indigestible portions
> Which the leopards reject. The Lady is withdrawn
> In a white gown, to contemplation, in a white gown.
> Let the whiteness of bones atone to forgetfulness.
> There is no life in them. As I am forgotten
> And would be forgotten, so would I forget
> Thus devoted, concentrated in purpose. And God said
> Prophesy to the wind, to the wind only for only

The wind will listen. And the bones sang chirping
With the burden of the grasshopper, saying

Lady of silences
Calm and distressed
Torn and most whole
Rose of memory
Rose of forgetfulness
Exhausted and life-giving
Worried reposeful
The single Rose
Is now the Garden
Where all loves end
Terminate torment
Of love unsatisfied
The greater torment
Of love satisfied
End of the endless
Journey to no end
Conclusion of all that
Is inconclusible
Speech without word and
Word of no speech
Grace to the Mother
For the Garden
Where all love ends.

Under a juniper-tree the bones sang, scattered and shining,
We are glad to be scattered, we did little good to each other,
Under a tree in the cool of the day, with the blessing of sand,
Forgetting themselves and each other, united
In the quiet of the desert. This is the land which ye
Shall divide by lot. And neither division nor unity
Matters. This is the land. We have our inheritance.

The complex *Four Quartets* form one poem, which the author wished 'to be judged as a single work'. In 1933, in a lecture at New-haven, he spoke of 'poetry so transparent that we should not see the poetry, but that which we are meant to see through the poetry . . .', and suggested that it might be possible 'to get *beyond poetry*, as Beethoven, in his later works, strove to get beyond music'. The reference to Beethoven gives us a clue to the reason for the title, and to Eliot's feelings about the relation of these poems to his other work.

In this passage paradox, conceit and rhythm remind us of the seventeenth century, of those metaphysical poets whose work Eliot found so nourishing at the beginning of his poetic career. The element

of pastiche, which we have seen used elsewhere for comic ends, is here
a serious tribute to the great devotional poets, his forerunners. Whether
this poem will stand the comparison is something the reader must
decide for himself.

IV

The wounded surgeon plies his steel
That questions the distempered part;
Beneath the bleeding hands we feel
The sharp compassion of the healer's art
Resolving the enigma of the fever chart.

Our only health is the disease
If we obey the dying nurse
Whose constant care is not to please
But to remind of our, and Adam's curse,
And that, to be restored. our sickness must grow worse.

The whole earth is our hospital
Endowed by the ruined millionaire,
Wherein, if we do well, we shall
Die of the absolute paternal care
That will not leave us, but prevents us everywhere.

The chill ascends from feet to knees,
The fever sings in mental wires.
If to be warmed, then I must freeze
And quake in frigid purgatorial fires
Of which the flame is roses and the smoke is briars.

The dripping blood our only drink,
The bloody flesh our only food:
In spite of which we like to think
That we are sound, substantial flesh and blood—
Again, in spite of that, we call this Friday good.

In the Quartets as a whole we can trace, raised to tragic intensity, or
muted to meditative resignation, the themes of time, of solitude, of the
worthlessness of human effort which echo in Prufrock. But the overwhelming question has now, of course, been answered.

W. B. Yeats (1865–1939) was a prolific poet, and his later work is,
from one point of view, a kind of commentary on his life and times,
loaded with allusions to Irish personalities and the private symbolism
of his visions, which are stumbling blocks to many readers, to whom

he appears esoteric and obscure. This is a mistaken view. The first thing to grasp about Yeats is that he is a public poet, a rare thing in this age: he may be the last of his kind. He worked, and worked hard and devotedly, within his society. He had friends who supported, enemies who detested him; he had causes into which he could wholeheartedly throw himself, values he could defend and propagate in the hope that they might purify and ennoble the life of his fellow men. 'He wanted', he wrote in his diary in 1909, 'to oppose the new ill-breeding of Ireland which may in a few years destroy all that has given Ireland a distinguished name in the world'. And Ireland was a small enough community for a man to make a mark in. Yeats saw two sources of strength—the aristocracy, symbolized by Lady Gregory's Coole Park, and the peasantry, still nourished by a living folk-culture and a living speech. About these aspects of Irish life he was sometimes silly, snobbish and sentimental. There can be few readers who share his weakness for 'hard riding country gentlemen'. (When Brendan Behan was asked for a definition of an Anglo-Irishman he replied: 'A Protestant on a horse'.) Yet an innate scepticism, a tough intelligence, a fanatical devotion to his craft (if ever poet 'learned his trade' Yeats did) enabled him to produce works which override personal weakness, and to forge out of the local and temporal struggles of a tiny rejected and provincial community a noble rhetoric which must command universal attention and assent—

> Whatever flames upon the night
> Man's own resinous heart has fed.

He began to write like this:

> Among those feasting men Cuchulain dwelt
> And his young sweetheart close beside him knelt
> Stared on the mournful wonder of his eyes,
> Even as Spring upon the ancient skies,
> And pondered on the glory of his days;
> And all around the harp-string told his praise,
> And Conchubar, the Red Branch king of kings,
> With his own fingers touched the brazen strings. . . .

'That meditative man, John Synge' had a word for this aspect of the Celtic Twilight: he called it 'Cuchulainoid'. The poem comes from a volume called 'The Rose' published in 1893. In 1905 we find Yeats writing to Arthur Symons: 'the error of late periods like this is to believe that some things are inherently poetical, and pull them on to the scene at every moment. It is just these seeming inherent poetical things that wear out.' He was thinking here of the drama, but this attitude to language was soon to influence all his work. We might compare Lawrence: 'Skilled verse is dead in fifty years'.

From the title poem of *In the Seven Woods* (1902) come these lines:

> I have forgot awhile
> Tara uprooted, and new commonness
> Upon the throne and crying about the streets
> And hanging its paper flowers from post to post. . . .

The image of the paper flowers, and the freer rhythms, the collocation of myth and contemporary comment, all look forward to the later work; they are not 'inherently poetical'. But we have only to turn the page to find this:

> 'Your well-beloved's hair has threads of grey,
> And little shadows come about her eyes. . . .'

which is pure William Morris Pre-Raphaelite.

The new style begins to be evident in *Responsibilities* (1914). Here is the conclusion of *To a Shade*, a poem about Parnell, a piece of noble rhetoric:

> Go unquiet wanderer,
> And gather the Glasnevin coverlet
> About your head till the dust stops your ear,
> The time for you to taste of that salt breath
> And listen at the corners has not come:
> You had enough of sorrow before death—
> Away, away! You are safer in the tomb.

The image of the shade revisiting Dublin and listening at corners to hear if his name, his reputation, the memory of his work for Ireland, are part of the common speech, the common tradition of men, is vividly real; the more so for its contrast with the resounding 'taste of that salt breath'. The poem is both a tribute to the dead hero and a bare ironic comment on the nation that forgets him.

There is at the end of this volume a short poem called *A Coat* in which the poet records his new attitude to his craft:

> I made my song a coat
> Covered with embroideries
> Out of old mythologies
> From heel to throat;
> But the fools caught it,
> Wore it in the world's eyes
> As though they'd wrought it.
> Song, let them take it,
> For there's more enterprise
> In walking naked.

And here, also from *Responsibilities*, another comment on government
and society. The contrast between fumbling man and elegant animal,
between the fog of reason and the clear beam of instinct is common
in post-romantic poetry. ('I think I could turn and live with animals
...') Yeats' toughness, wit and elegance stamp these lines with originality; the poem moves as beautifully and economically as the squirrel.
It does not express the generalized or second-hand feelings of an
outsider, one who laments calamity read in a newspaper, but the ire and
exasperation of a participant in the struggle.

AN APPOINTMENT

Being out of heart with government
I took a broken root to fling
Where the proud, wayward squirrel went,
Taking delight that he could spring;
And he, with that low whinnying sound
That is like laughter, sprang again
And so to the other tree at a bound.
Nor the tame will, nor timid brain,
Nor heavy knitting of the brow
Bred that fierce tooth and cleanly limb
And threw him up to laugh on the bough;
No government appointed him.

From the next volume, *The Wild Swans at Coole*, we take this lyric,
a warning to all commentators. The reader can reflect on the change
that has come over the author of the inescapable and unquotable *Lake
Isle of Innisfree*.

THE SCHOLARS

Bald heads forgetful of their sins,
Old, learned, respectable bald heads
Edit and annotate the lines
That young men, tossing on their beds,
Rhymed out in love's despair
To flatter beauty's ignorant ear.

All shuffle there; all cough in ink;
All wear the carpet with their shoes;
All think what other people think;
All know the man their neighbour knows.
Lord, what would they say
Did their Catullus walk that way?

In the same volume there is this epigram:

The Balloon of the Mind

Hands, do what you're bid:
Bring the balloon of the mind
That bellies and drags in the wind
Into its narrow shed.

And here are lines from *The Tower* which reflect the conscious deliberate effort of will and intelligence that went into Yeats' ordering of his
experience.

> I pace upon the battlements and stare
> On the foundations of a house, or where
> Tree, like a sooty finger, starts from the earth;
> And send imagination forth
> Under the day's declining beam, and call
> Images and memories
> From ruin or from ancient trees,
> For I would ask a question of them all. . . .

'I have', he wrote, 'no speech but symbol, the pagan speech I made/
Amid the dreams of youth'. In some poems the symbolism remains
largely private, or needs a lot of 'coughing in ink' to elucidate. In
others—the poem about the squirrel for example—it comes out of the
common stock. The reader might ponder the image of the tree, in the
lines just quoted. Yeats omits definite or indefinite article, giving
the word the effect of a proper name, and hence of something special or
significant; the ordinary has become strange. The tree is dark against
the twilight sky: 'sooty' carries associations of intense blackness, and
of the fires, perhaps, of hell. The tree 'starts', because it is perceived
with a sudden intensity, and 'finger' makes it a gesture, admonitory or
sinister, from another world. Oh, do not ask, 'What is it'? Allow the
feelings it arouses to resound in the mind, and see that the poet is
'sending' his imagination to 'call' others (these are commanding verbs)
and that the meaning of the poem lies in the way he organizes them
in that particular structure. We might adapt Lawrence's well-known
dictum about the teller and the tale and say: 'Never trust the symbol,
trust the poem'.

This dialogue, the seventh section of *Vacillation*, from *The Winding
Stair*, 1933, seems relevant:

> THE SOUL   Seek out reality, leave things that seem.
> THE HEART   What, be singer born and lack a theme?

THE SOUL   Isaiah's coal, what more can man desire?

THE HEART   Struck dumb in the simplicity of fire!

THE SOUL   Look on that fire, salvation walks within.

THE HEART   What theme had Homer but original sin?

I have chosen poems which I think to be among Yeats' major work to illustrate something of his power and his range, but no brief account can hope to do him justice. First, *Sailing to Byzantium* from *The Tower*, 1928.

I

That is no country for old men. The young
In one another's arms, birds in the trees
—Those dying generations—at their song,
The salmon-falls, the mackerel-crowded seas,
Fish, flesh, or fowl, commend all summer long
Whatever is begotten, born, and dies.
Caught in that sensual music all neglect
Monuments of unaging intellect.

II

An aged man is but a paltry thing,
A tattered coat upon a stick, unless
Soul clap its hands and sing, and louder sing
For every tatter in its mortal dress,
Nor is there singing school but studying
Monuments of its own magnificence;
And therefore have I sailed the seas and come
To the holy city of Byzantium.

III

O sages standing in God's holy fire
As in the gold mosaic of a wall,
Come from the holy fire, perne in a gyre,
And be the singing-masters of my soul.
Consume my heart away; sick with desire
And fastened to a dying animal
It knows not what it is; and gather me
Into the artifice of eternity.

IV

> Once out of nature I shall never take
> My bodily form from any natural thing,
> But such a form as Grecian goldsmiths make
> Of hammered gold and gold enamelling
> To keep a drowsy Emperor awake;
> Or set upon a golden bough to sing
> To lords and ladies of Byzantium
> Of what is past, or passing, or to come.

One of the themes of Yeats' later work is old age,

> This caricature,
> Decrepit age, that has been tied to me
> As to a dog's tail. . . .

The opening stanza of this poem celebrates, and turns away from, the fertile, abundant natural world, the cycle of begetting, birth and death; in opposition to the pulsating rhythms of nature are placed the 'monuments of unaging intellect'. Monuments are static, unchanging, a defence against time: they proclaim. Fish, flesh, fowl, trees are born, mature and die: they are. The feeling of the stanza does not condemn life. Age regrets the 'sensual' the temporal, the active; but the 'sensual' is 'music', and in the beautiful phrase 'commend all summer long/ Whatever is begotten, born and dies' the poet pays tribute to that music. In a way one can say that he turns regretfully to the monuments neglected by the young because there is nothing else he can do. As he writes in *The Tower*, the poem that follows this one,

> It seems that I must bid the Muse go pack,
> Choose Plato and Plotinus for a friend
> Until imagination, ear and eye,
> Can be content with argument and deal
> In abstract things; or be derided by
> A sort of battered kettle at the heel.

Yet these monuments can, and I think they do, also stand for the works of art it is the poet's vocation to create; and the subject of the monuments is whatever is begotten born and dies. There is a kind of triumph somewhere.

The body decays, and the man begins to resemble a scarecrow, but the soul sings the louder. It is interesting to put beside the image of the tattered dress, and the soul clapping its hands and singing, this couplet from a poem by Waller:

> The soul's dark cottage, battered and decayed,
> Lets in new light through chinks that time has made. . . .

Here we see the metaphysical conceit being tidied up by the neo-classic desire for order; this is the rational working out of an analogy. The realistic detail of the 'chinks' harks back to the 'quainter' aspects of minor metaphysical writing, but the clear syntax, the personification of Time, the neat fitting of syntactical unit to metrical pattern, the calm, assured 'polite' tone look forward to the Augustan mode. And for Waller, the light comes from outside: it is knowledge of God that shines through the crevices. He appeals to an orthodoxy. Yeats' image works in a quite different way. The key is in the soul clapping its hands and singing, rejoicing in its own energy, its power to create 'monuments of its own magnificence'. We may recall how the poet, in another mood, wrote—I quote again from *The Tower*—

> And I declare my faith:
> I mock Plotinus thought
> And cry in Plato's teeth,
> Death and life were not
> Till man made up the whole,
> Made lock, stock and barrel
> Out of his bitter soul. . . .

There is no way for the poet to 'learn his trade', no 'singing school' but the monuments of art, of which the formal hieratic mosaics of Byzantium, where artist and priest are one, are a symbol.

In the next stanza the poet invokes the wisdom of the past. To 'perne' is to wind as on a spool; the 'gyres' are the great cyclical patterns in which Yeats believed history to move, and the 'sages' are probably remembered from mosaics in Ravenna—images from the visual arts abound in Yeats' poetry—so the 'obscure' allusion to the poet's 'private' world-view means that he asks the masters of the past to aid him in his present task, an idea no more difficult of apprehension than the customary invocation of the Muse. The 'dying animal' repeats with an increased and shocking intensity the theme of the opening lines of the first two stanzas. The 'holy fire' in which the sages stand will burn and purge away the temporal and lead the poet into 'the artifice of eternity'. 'Artifice' is the key word here. What is eternal is what has been constructed by the artist, because his constructions conquer, as far as such conquest is possible, the depredations of time, of that nature which the poet's body is subject to. We can see now that the poem has, in part, a traditional theme:

> Not marble, nor the gilded monuments
> Of princes shall outlive this powerful rhyme. . . .

Yeats's own note on the last stanza is this:

> 'I have read somewhere that in the Emperor's palace at Byzantium was a tree made of gold and silver, and artificial birds that sang'.

The casual 'somewhere' should warn us not to fuss about the real historical Byzantium. The anecdote caught (the cliché is exact) Yeats's fancy, and he uses it here to symbolize his art. Note how the repetition of 'gold', the precious and incorruptible metal, reinforces the theme, and how the rhythm and structure of the lines

> But such a form as Grecian goldsmiths make
> Of hammered gold and gold enamelling. . . .

echo, even at this late stage of the poet's progress, his Pre-Raphaelite masters: indeed, the whole stanza is an exquisite example of his command of romantic melody. The last line summarizes the themes of his work—his treatment of Celtic legend, his comments on contemporary society and his vision of the movement of time and history.

Byzantium is the title of the next poem, which comes from *The Winding Stair* published in 1933. In it Yeats imagines himself within the symbolic city towards which, in the last poem, he was sailing. But we shall not be able to come to terms with this superb, difficult and greater work if we mechanically apply to it an interpretation of the Byzantine symbol adduced from the earlier poem. Yeats' symbols change their significance. Common meanings, associations, themes, they may have, but in any poem these are part of a whole and their range of reference is controlled by the structure of the poem itself. As we have already quoted

> I have no speech but symbol, the pagan speech I made
> Amid the dreams of youth

Yes. But content, tone, intention are important elements in speech modifying our apprehension of the words or symbols used in it. In one of his comments on contemporary society Yeats wrote that 'Unity of being' has as its enemy 'abstraction, meaning by abstraction not the distinction, but the isolation of occupation or class or faculty'. Abstraction in this sense is equally inimical to the 'unity of being' of poems. We can usefully 'distinguish' symbol, image, rhythm and so on, but we must not 'isolate' them.

BYZANTIUM

The unpurged images of day recede;
The Emperor's drunken soldiery are abed;

Night resonance recedes, night-walker's song
After great cathedral gong;
A starlit or a moonlit dome disdains
All that man is,
All mere complexities,
The fury and the mire of human veins.

Before me floats an image, man or shade,
Shade more than man, more image than a shade;
For Hades bobbin bound in mummy-cloth
May unwind the winding path;
A mouth that has no moisture and no breath
Breathless mouths may summon;
I hail the superhuman:
I call it death-in-life and life-in-death.

Miracle, bird or golden handiwork,
More miracle than bird or handiwork,
Planted on the star-lit golden bough,
Can like the cocks of Hades crow,
Or, by the moon embittered, scorn aloud
In glory of changeless metal
Common bird or petal
And all complexities of mire or blood.

At midnight on the Emperor's pavement flit
Flames that no faggot feeds, nor steel has lit,
Nor storm disturbs, flames begotten of flame,
Where blood-begotten spirits come
And all complexities of fury leave,
Dying into a dance,
An agony of trance,
An agony of flame that cannot singe a sleeve.

Astraddle on the dolphin's mire and blood,
Spirit after spirit! The smithies break the flood,
The golden smithies of the Emperor!
Marbles of the dancing floor
Break bitter furies of complexity,
Those images that yet
Fresh images beget,
That dolphin-torn, that gong-tormented sea.

Any reader of Yeats should ponder the superbly modulated first line
of this poem. Of its five stresses, three come together on the second,
third and fourth syllables; the last two are regularly spaced. Such an

arrangement—it is a common device in this metre—gives a calm, solid, conclusive feeling to the second half of the line. Here it serves to bring out the force of 'recedes'. We have in any case to isolate this word, if we give, as we should, full emphasis to the important 'day': the change of tongue position from pronouncing a—y, and then rolling the initial 'r' controls this; and so does the fact that 'recede' is the predicate, and the whole of the rest of the line the subject, of the sentence. These facts, and the long vowels following the short huddled consonant-obstructed vowels in 'images of' make the line open out and die away, and seem to recede into a remote distance. The images of day, of waking natural life are unpurged; the images of poetry, we are to infer, are purged, and the poem is an 'artifice', a 'something to perfection brought'. The conscious intellect, the will, is active here, but we must also remember that Yeats, and with him all poets who have claimed 'inspiration' believed the purgation to be also effected by unconscious powers:

> A passion driven exultant man sings out
> Sentences that he never thought . . .

The lines that follow evoke a real city. The drunken soldiery and the night-walkers are silenced by the great cathedral gong, the curfew that ends day and ushers in night, symbol, like the dome of the sky, or the dome of St. Sophia (both I think are present) of an order, 'the artifice of eternity', greater than man, to whose complexities, fury and mire it makes a noble, geometrical and simple contrast.

The beginning of the next stanza illustrates Yeats' detachment from, his conscious manipulation of, his images and symbols. We may be reminded of Blake's couplet:

> With my inward eye 'tis an old man grey,
> With my outward a thistle across my way.

and of Yeats' own note on *The Dolls* in *Responsibilities*:

> 'After I had made the poem, I looked up one day into the blue of the sky, and suddenly imagined, as if lost in the blue of the sky, stiff figures in procession. I remembered that they were the habitual image suggested by blue sky, and looking for a second fable called them "The Magi" . . .'

The strip of cloth that binds the mummy is a clue, like Ariadne's thread, that may lead to the truth. Breathless mouths (they correspond to the sages in the earlier poem) speak wisdom unavailable to those involved in the mire and fury. The last line alludes to that most famous of romantic supernatural poems, *The Ancient Mariner*. He is saved from the 'nightmare Life-in-Death' by the 'spring of love' that 'gushed' in his heart as he blesses 'unaware' (this is not a conscious movement) the water snakes. Yeats 'hails the superhuman' because the dead are in life (they speak to him) and, paradoxically, are in one sense more living, in the artifice of eternity, than those who are still struggling in the complexities of nature.

The next stanza returns to the image of the bird, repeating the structure of the lines about the image, the man and the shade, focusing our attention on the word 'miracle' as the previous lines focus on 'image'. The dome disdains, the bird scorns, the mere complexities of human life, the products of nature. The third central image is the dance, which makes a comprehensible, beautiful and meaningful pattern out of the raw material of human movement. I take it that no one can read

> Flames that no faggot feeds, nor steel has lit
> Nor storm disturbs. . . .

without surrendering to the poet's enchantment, for the poem is, among other things, a kind of spell. The flames begotten of flames represent a further purging of the blood-begotten spirit: the flame in its purity has no fury—it cannot singe a sleeve. The pavement, the faggot, the steel, the storm, the sleeve are all concrete images that help to make the strange vision credible, to 'compel our imagination'. The spirits ride to the palace on dolphins, creatures closely associated in myth with human beings; and they may stand, made of mire and blood, for the body, part of nature, and it is the soul's desire as it is the poet's, to be 'out of nature.' So the soul passes through life—life as a sea, a flood, is a common enough image—within the complexity of the body. 'The smithies break the flood'. Here we see Yeats' symbolism at its most condensed; yet we are to note that this condensation comes at the end of the poem, when the previous symbols have set up a structure of response. The smith is an artificer (he makes the golden bird), he creates a work of art that defies the fury of the flood. The lines

> Those images that yet
> Fresh images beget

remind us of the poet making the poem. Such glimpses of the smith at his anvil are common in Yeats' later verse, giving it an extra dimension of distance and irony. We have spirits begotten of blood, flames begotten of flame, and now images begotten of images. The poem is constructed of images, which proliferate; but the poet, the artificer, the smith, selects and orders them. He concludes with the sea, the flood that the Emperor's smithies break, and this sea is torn by the wakes of the dolphins, symbolizing here the beauty that mire and blood can be moulded into by nature, for we associate dolphins with grace, happiness and sympathy. ('No dolphin ever was so gay/Upon a tropic sea'); and the sea is tormented by the gong, symbol of rule and order, of the Emperor's command, which in the first verse sounds the curfew after which night resonance recedes.

Within the poem there exists a tension, which increases in the last stanza, between the dome and the fury, the changeless metal and the complexities, the smithies and the flood, the disorder and violence of life and the timeless constructions of the artist, and this tension is what the poem is about. It could not exist were the poem a simple ascetic withdrawal from, or condemnation of life. The poet can't do without the dolphin.

Among School Children comes from Yeats' previous volume, *The Tower*, 1928. He was now famous, respected and a Senator of the Irish Free State who took his duties seriously, and who thought that senators should be like 'coral insects with some design in our heads of the ultimate island'. This poem is about his thoughts as he pays an official visit of inspection to a school.

AMONG SCHOOL CHILDREN

I

I walk through the long schoolroom questioning;
A kind old nun in a white hood replies;
The children learn to cipher and to sing,
To study reading-books and histories,
To cut and sew, be neat in everything
In the best modern way—the children's eyes
In momentary wonder stare upon
A sixty-year-old smiling public man.

II

I dream of a Ledæan body, bent
Above a sinking fire, a tale that she
Told of a harsh reproof, or trivial event
That changed some childish day to tragedy—
Told, and it seemd that our two natures blent
Into a sphere from youthful sympathy,
Or else, to alter Plato's parable,
Into the yolk, and white of the one shell.

III

And thinking of that fit of grief or rage
I look upon one child or t'other there
And wonder if she stood so at that age—
For even daughters of the swan can share
Something of every paddler's heritage—
And had that colour upon cheek or hair,
And thereupon my heart is driven wild:
She stands before me as a living child.

IV

Her present image floats into the mind—
Did Quattrocento finger fashion it
Hollow of cheek as though it drank the wind
And took a mess of shadows for its meat?
And I though never of Ledæan kind
Had pretty plumage once—enough of that,
Better to smile on all that smile, and show
There is a comfortable kind of old scarecrow.

V

What youthful mother, a shape upon her lap
Honey of generation had betrayed,
And that must sleep, shriek, struggle to escape
As recollection or the drug decide,
Would think her son, did she but see that shape
With sixty or more winters on its head,
A compensation for the pang of his birth,
Or the uncertainty of his setting forth?

VI

Plato thought nature but a spume that plays
Upon a ghostly paradigm of things;
Solider Aristotle played the taws
Upon the bottom of a king of kings;
World-famous golden-thighed Pythagoras
Fingered upon a fiddle-stick or strings
What a star sang and careless Muses heard:
Old clothes upon old sticks to scare a bird.

VII

Both nuns and mothers worship images,
But those the candles light are not as those

That animate a mother's reveries,
But keep a marble or a bronze repose.
And yet they too break hearts—O Presences
That passion, piety or affection knows,
And that all heavenly glory symbolise—
O self-born mockers of man's enterprise;

VIII

Labour is blossoming or dancing where
The body is not bruised to pleasure soul,
Nor beauty born out of its own despair,
Nor blear-eyed wisdom out of midnight oil.
O chestnut-tree, great-rooted blossomer,
Are you the leaf, the blossom or the bole?
O body swayed to music, O brightening glance,
How can we know the dancer from the dance?

The first stanza quietly rehearses the facts and sets the scene in which
the ensuing meditation takes place. It appears that we are not to take
'In the best modern way' as irony, but as grave approval. Yeats knows
the wonder in the children's eyes is only 'momentary'. The 'smiling
public man', though he may have some tiny 'coral insect' influence on
the conditions of their education, can have no living relationship with
them.

And immediately we plunge into the mind behind the smiling public
face—'I dream of a Ledæan body. . . .' Leda was wooed by Jupiter in
the shape of a swan, a myth which fascinated Yeats. Here it means no
more, I think, than a body beautiful enough to catch an immortal eye.
The stanza recreates a childhood memory of a moment when, listening
to a tale of grief, he felt at one with the teller, experienced for a moment
'unity of being'. He looks back at the real children before him and
wonders if 'she' looked like that at her age. 'She' is Maud Gonne, but
it is not necessary to know this in order to understand the poem, for
it is clear that the poet is recalling a lost love, and that is all we need
to know. Yeats was inclined to classify humanity into swans and paddlers, and his love was, of course, one of the swans, who may nevertheless as a child have resembled the paddlers before him. The association
brings him keen anguish.

He then thinks of her grown up. She had the kind of beauty seen,
say, in the pictures of Botticelli. The hollow cheek and the wind lead
on to his bitter feelings about her sterile (as they seemed to him)
political activities—the mess of shadows. (Elsewhere he says she became
'an old bellows full of angry wind'.) He himself had once some claim

to a kind of physical distinction, but he turns away from futile regrets to do his public duty, to 'smile on all that smile'; he is, he knows, a scarecrow, 'a tattered coat upon a stick', but he won't frighten the children.

He moves from memories of private sorrow to thinking about the common progress from youth to age. He explains in a note that he has taken the phrase 'honey of generation' from Porphyry's *Cave of the Nymphs*, a work not readily accessible to the general reader. But without referring to the poet's esoteric sources we can make out that the child is born because of the sweetness of the act of love; and that the soul of the child, which has no say in the matter, is betrayed by this act to leave eternity and enter the world. It is not new to hear the child's cries as cries of protest ('we do waul and cry/That we are come to this great stage of fools'); recollection of the eternal decides the cries: the drug of human existence decides the sleep.

Next the powers of three classical sages are evoked, only to be dismissed, for they are scarecrows too. The lines about Plato refer to his belief that what we call reality is only a shadow of eternal and ideal truth. The king of kings is Alexander the Great, whose tutor, legend says, Aristotle once was. Pythagoras believed the secret of the universe to lie in numerical relationships, like those between harmonics—hence the fiddle stick and the strings. Note that Yeats is here treating ironically beliefs that have played a great part in some of his work; and that he himself, in his coral-insect school-inspector role, has some remote connection with 'solider Aristotle'.

The next line joins mothers and nuns, life in the world, and life withdrawn from it, together: both worship images; the one a living child, the other a statue. Both sorts of image break hearts, because devotion to an ideal may be as difficult and disappointing as devotion to a living person. Now comes, disturbing the regular stanza pattern, the great apostrophe that ends the poem, and harmonizes all its themes. Passion (the poet's), piety (the nun's), affection (the mother's) make those who feel such emotions aware of presences—powers greater than themselves: the mother and child, the statues of saints and madonnas are symbols of heavenly glory. But they are self born—man creates them 'lock stock and barrel', and they are so much greater, finer, more beautiful than anything he can achieve in practice, that they mock his enterprise. What he manages to do always falls short of what he can imagine. Yeats addresses these Presences (the coral insect view of the ultimate island) and proposes an ideal beyond them all. He propounds a paradox: 'Labour is blossoming and dancing'. Labour recalls the curse of Adam, blossoming lost Eden, and the dance is a favourite

symbol for the perfection of human activity. Labour cannot be made
to blossom and dance by the practice of a religion based on asceticism;
this line recalls the nun at the beginning of the poem. Nor can the
work of the artist, creating beauty out of his own despair, achieve this.
The despair alludes to the lines about the poet's unhappy love, and
beyond that to the whole human condition. Blear-eyed wisdom refers
to the sages. Philosophy, made by the labours of the intellect alone, is
not clear-sighted. Only 'unity of being' can achieve the ideal perfection.
The chestnut-tree is such a unity; so is the dancer.

It would be relevant, I think, to quote here part of Yeats' long note on
the group of poems in *Responsibilities* which deal with public controversies.

> 'These controversies, political, literary, and artistic, have showed that
> neither religion nor politics can of itself create minds with enough recepti-
> vity to become wise, or just and generous enough to make a nation. Other
> cities have been as stupid . . . but Dublin is the capital of a nation, and an
> ancient race has nowhere else to look for an education. Goethe in *Wilhelm
> Meister* describes a saintly and naturally gracious woman, who, getting
> into a quarrel over some trumpery detail of religious observance, grows—
> she and all her little religious community—angry and vindictive. In Ireland
> I am constantly reminded of that fable in the futility of all discipline that is
> not of the whole being. Religious Ireland—and the pious Protestants of
> my childhood were signal examples—thinks of divine things as a round of
> duties separate from life and not as an element that may be discovered in
> all circumstance and emotion, while political Ireland sees the good citizen
> but as a man who holds a certain opinion and not as a man of good will.
> Against all this we have but a few educated men and the remnants of an
> old traditional culture among the poor. Both were stronger forty years
> ago, before the rise of our new middle class which made its first public
> display during the nine years of Parnellite split, showing how base at
> moments of excitement are minds without culture.'

'The futility of all discipline that is not of the whole being' is surely
the theme of *Among School Children*.

At Ballylee was the tower which Yeats restored and lived in when
he married. He had this inscription carved on a stone there:

> I, the poet William Yeats,
> With old mill boards and sea-green slates,
> And smithy work from the Gort forge,
> Restored this tower for my wife George;
> And may these characters remain
> When all is ruin once again.

Coole Park was the great house where Lady Gregory lived and where

she entertained, encouraged and aided the writers and poets of the Irish
movement.

COOLE PARK AND BALLYLEE 1931

Under my window-ledge the waters race,
Otters below and moor-hens on the top,
Run for a mile undimmed in Heaven's face
Then darkening through 'dark' Raftery's 'cellar' drop,
Run underground, rise in a rocky place
In Coole demesne, and there to finish up
Spread to a lake and drop into a hole.
What's water but the generated soul?

Upon the border of that lake's a wood
Now all dry sticks under a wintry sun,
And in a copse of beeches there I stood,
For Nature's pulled her tragic buskin on
And all the rant's a mirror of my mood:
At sudden thunder of the mounting swan
I turned about and looked where branches break
The glittering reaches of the flooded lake.

Another emblem there! That stormy white
But seems a concentration of the sky;
And, like the soul, it sails into the sight
And in the morning's gone, no man knows why;
And is so lovely that it sets to right
What knowledge or its lack had set awry
So arrogantly pure, a child might think
It can be murdered with a spot of ink.

Sound of a stick upon the floor, a sound
From somebody that toils from chair to chair;
Beloved books that famous hands have bound,
Old marble heads, old pictures everywhere;
Great rooms where travelled men or children found
Content or joy; a last inheritor
Where none has reigned that lacked a name and fame
Or out of folly into folly came.

A spot whereon the founders lived and died
Seemed once more dear than life; ancestral trees,
Or gardens rich in memory glorified
Marriages, alliances and families,
And every bride's ambition satisfied.

Where fashion or mere fantasy decrees
We shift about—all that great glory spent—
Like some poor Arab tribesman and his tent.

We were the last romantics—chose for theme
Traditional sanctity and loveliness;
Whatever's written in what poets name
The book of the people; whatever most can bless
The mind of man or elevate a rhyme;
But all is changed, that high horse riderless,
Though mounted in that saddle Homer rode
Where the swan drifts upon a darkening flood.

In this poem the symbols spring from the 'naked' and vivid evocation of the landscape the poet is contemplating, and we are drawn into the mood, complex, nostalgic, ironic, in which the poet watches the trees the sunset and the waters. We are aware of the life of the waters, mysterious and hidden in the otters, simple and gay in the moor-hens. 'Dark' Raftery was a blind bard and ballad singer and the hole in the limestone the river drops through is traditionally known as his 'cellar'. He stands for one of the poles of Irish culture—the traditional; Coole demesne for the other—the aristocratic. Water which runs for a time 'undimmed in Heaven's eye' and then vanishes is like the soul in this world of generation, the world of 'whatever is begotten lives and dies'.

It is winter, the death of the year, the tragic time, and the sunset is theatrically appropriate. Notice that it is not described. The allusive, literary 'tragic buskin', the ironic 'rant'—nature is out-Heroding Herod—place the poet's detachment. He is serious, but at the same time mockingly aware of the scene he plays. The diction of this stanza 'mirrors' his mood, as it moves between the flat statement of 'Under my window-ledge the waters race,' the plain colloquialism of the 'dry sticks', 'drop into', 'finish up', the romantic 'undimmed in Heaven's face' and the personification of Nature as the Tragic Muse.

We follow the poet's movement—he is dramatically in the poem— as the swan mounts powerfully skyward. Note how everything seems to be acting, in both senses of the word, how the branches 'break' the shining waters; how we follow the poet's mind in 'another emblem there'. He invites us, as he so often does, to experience the pictorial symbolic nature of his thought. To say that the swan 'is like' or 'represents' the soul is to offer a sapless paraphrase. Knowledge which is the fruit of reason is for Yeats inadequate, falsifying, 'old clothes upon old sticks'. It 'sets things awry', and so does ignorance. The beauty of the swan, or rather the poet's imaginative apprehension of that beauty, sets them to rights. We see in these lines the traditional romantic claim for the primacy of the creative imagination. Note the aptness of the swan's 'arrogance'. It fits the real bird and helps to keep the real scene alive in our minds, and fits, too the certainty of the soul's apprehension of truth; and as the child might believe a single spot of ink could kill the swan (it is extraordinary how powerful is the shock of 'murder' and 'ink', how the whiteness of the swan is intensified) so perhaps the ink of the reasoner may kill the imagination of the poet, and (should we add?) the ink of the commentator the poem.

The next two stanzas are a noble and graceful tribute to Lady Gregory, and a celebration of that ancestral tradition which Yeats believed supported the artist, and whose inevitable collapse leaves him solitary. Without a coherent scheme of values 'rich in memory', modern man is a nomad; and the uncomfortable fidgety 'shift' seems to rob his wanderings of all aim and dignity.

In the last stanza the poet places himself and his companions in the gyre of time

We were the last romantics. . . .

and rehearses their themes, the holiness of ancient beliefs, the beauty of legend, ballad lore. Like Milton, he aspires to 'build the lofty rhyme'. Now as he says elsewhere, this is an 'unfashionable gyre'. Homer, emblem of the traditional bard, could mount Pegasus, but now the sacred horse has no one on his back. The sun has set, Nature's 'rant' has died away; the poet's meditation ends in a vision of the solitary soul adrift in chaos.

From the *Last Poems*, 1936–1939 comes *The Circus Animals' Desertion*.

I

I sought a theme and sought for it in vain,
I sought it daily for six weeks or so.
Maybe at last, being but a broken man,
I must be satisfied with my heart, although
Winter and summer till old age began
My circus animals were all on show,
Those stilted boys, that burnished chariot,
Lion and woman and the Lord knows what.

II

What can I but enumerate old themes?
First that sea-rider Oisin led by the nose
Through three enchanted islands, allegorical dreams,
Vain gaiety, vain battle, vain repose,

Themes of the embittered heart, or so it seems,
That might adorn old songs or courtly shows;
But what cared I that set him on to ride,
I, starved for the bosom of his faery bride?

And then a counter-truth filled out its play,
The Countess Cathleen was the name I gave it;
She, pity-crazed, had given her soul away,
But masterful Heaven had intervened to save it.
I thought my dear must her own soul destroy,
So did fanaticism and hate enslave it,
And this brought forth a dream and soon enough
This dream itself had all my thought and love.

And when the Fool and Blind Man stole the bread
Cuchulain fought the ungovernable sea;
Heart-mysteries there, and yet when all is said
It was the dream itself enchanted me:
Character isolated by a deed
To engross the present and dominate memory.
Players and painted stage took all my love,
And not those things that they were emblems of.

III

Those masterful images because complete
Grew in pure mind, but out of what began?
A mound of refuse or the sweepings of the street,
Old kettles, old bottles, and a broken can,
Old iron, old bones, old rags, that raving slut
Who keeps the till. Now that my ladder's gone
I must lie down where all the ladders start,
In the foul rag-and-bone shop of the heart.

To read Yeats is to be all the time reminded of what he called 'the spiritual intellect's great work'.

'Nor can there be work so great,' he wrote elsewhere, 'As that which cleans man's dirty slate.' We see him, in this poem, turning that keen ironic 'spiritual intellect' upon his own life and work. Drifting on the darkening flood, through old age towards death, he speaks directly to the reader, dominating him by his rhetoric, involving him in the process of writing the poem. In old age he can find no 'theme', no emblem of tradition, no structure of belief, no symbol of eternal process; he can no longer mount 'that high horse', and is reduced to his 'heart', to himself as he is when all the masks are put away. Contemptuously he dismisses the symbolic figures that in the past have filled out his verse: they are circus animals, trained to perform at the crack of the ring-master's whip.

He passes in review, in the next stanza, the phases of his work and points their inner meaning, their relation to his life. He moves from the reworking of the Cuchulain legend, 'that might adorn old songs or courtly shows', to the counter-truth of the political struggle. (The Countess Cathleen symbolizes Ireland.) In all this, he repeats, 'it is the dream,' the imagination, 'the artifice of eternity' which he loves and which enchants him; and so it is with the symbolism of his plays. Here the 'spiritual intellect' produces a flash of insight into the very nature of drama:

> Character isolated by a deed
> To engross the present and dominate memory.

In the final stanza he thinks better of his 'images'. They are 'masterful' because they are 'complete'; because the poem creates them as we read, so that at the end of it they are whole and living. It is so that the 'dolphin-torn, gong-tormented sea', the chestnut tree and the dancer, and the swan adrift upon the darkening flood are masterful. These images are 'grown in pure mind' as he 'sends imagination forth'. The sordid refuse in which they begin seems to stand for the 'fury and the mire of human veins' (if you will, for the Freudian unconscious), but also for the broken world in which he 'shifts about'; the 'raving slut' may be the 'lust and rage' which 'dance attendance on his old age'; she may also be what Cathleen na Houlihan has now become.

His ladder, his masterful imagery, he says is gone. The poem ought to be despairing, but it is not. Every line is informed with the poet's familiar strength and will. The voice is as powerful, the accent as incisive as ever. He can do without the ladder, and we feel that, histrionic to the last, he knows it.

Yeats has been condemned for posing, for assuming masks, for acting, for being rhetorical. All this, it is true, is in his verse. But what matter? The actor moves us, the rhetoric persuades, the gestures are meaningful.

Here are the second and last sections of *Under Ben Bulben*, the poem he placed at the end of his work.

> Many times man lives and dies
> Between his two eternities,
> That of race and that of soul,
> And ancient Ireland knew it all.
> Whether man die in his bed
> Or the rifle knocks him dead,
> A brief parting from those dear
> Is the worst he has to fear.

Though grave-diggers' toil is long
Sharp their spades, their muscles strong,
They but thrust their buried men
Back in the human mind again. . . .

Under bare Ben Bulben's head
In Drumcliff churchyard Yeats is laid,
An ancestor was rector there
Long years ago, a church stands near,
By the road an ancient cross.
No marble, no conventional phrase;
On limestone quarried near the spot
By his command these words are cut:
  Cast a cold eye
  On life, on death.
  Horseman, pass by!

INDEX

321